A DICTIONARY OF GREEK AND LATIN LEGAL TERMS IN RABBINIC LITERATURE

by

DANIEL SPERBER

BAR-ILAN UNIVERSITY
INSTITUTE FOR LEXICOGRAPHY

Directors
M.H. GOSHEN–GOTTSTEIN M.Z. KADDARI

Associate Director
J.C. GREENFIELD

DICTIONARIES OF TALMUD, MIDRASH AND TARGUM

I

A DICTIONARY
OF
GREEK AND LATIN LEGAL TERMS

IN RABBINIC LITERATURE

by
DANIEL SPERBER

BAR-ILAN UNIVERSITY PRESS
1984

The publication of this volume was made possible
throught the generosity of the
Milan Rovan Chair for Talmudic Studies

ISBN 965-226-050-9

Typesetting — "Ram-Ot Ltd."
Plates by Kefir
Printed at Ahva Press
Jerusalem, 1984

To the memory of
Prof. Saul Lieberman (1898-1983),
who was to have
written the foreward
to this volume

CONTENTS

SIGNS, ETC

◇	in LW2 under different form.
*	not in Gk lexica
[*]	in Gk lexica with different meaning
(64)	nos. in brackets after entry heading refer to pagination in LW2; absence indicates the word is not in LW2 (except perhaps in incidental ref)
( )	in main heading, alternative form
[ ]	(1) in main heading: postulated form based either on Ms. evidence, or conjecture, (2) throughout: editorial insertion.
< >	editorial deletion
°	form not attested, but posited by extant forms
→, ←	indicates direction of language borrowing
↑	see above
↓	see below
//	parallel (and derivative) texts
▽	variant readings
<, >	represents, and indicates direction of interchange between one vowel or consonant and another
=	equal or equivalent to, the same as
~	represents part of word identical to preceding form
...	indicates an omitted part of a quotation

ABBREVIATIONS

abbr	abbreviation
AC	Aruch Completum, ed. A. Kohut, Vienna 1878–92
ACAdd	Additions at end of vol. 8 of AC (with separate pagination)
ACSup	Additamenta ad Librum Aruch Completum, ed. S. Krauss, Vienna 1937
Aggur	Samuel b. Jacob Jama, Aggur, ed. S. Buber, apud Jubelschrift zum Siebzigsten Geburtstage des Prof. Dr. H. Graetz, Breslau 1888
AHW	W. von Soden, Akkadischer Handwörterbuch, Wiesbaden 1965–
AJP	American Journal of Philology
Akkad	Akkadian
Annuaire	Annuaire d'Institut de Philologie et d'Histoire Orientales et Slaves
Ar	Aruch
Aram	Aramaic
Arm	Armenian
ARN	Avot de-R. Nathan, ed. S. Schechter, Vienna 1887
ArndtGingrich	W. F. Arndt and F. W. Ginrich, A Greek-English Lexicon of the New Testament and Other Early Christian Literature, Chicago 1957
AZ	Avoda Zara
B	Bavli (Babylonian Talmud)
BacherAgTan	W. Bacher, Die Agada der Tannaiten, Strassburg 1884–1903
BacherMeliẓa	Likkutim min Sefer ha-Meliẓa, ed. W. Bacher, Budapest 1900 (appendix to Bacher, HebPers)

BacherTanJer	Aus dem Wörterbuch Tanḥum Jeruschalmi's ..., (Jahresbericht des Landes-Rabbinerschule in Budapest 26, 1902/03), Budapest 1903
BarBahlul	Bar Bahlûl, Lexicon Syriacum, ed. R. Duval, Paris 1890–1901
BatMid	Batei Midrashot[2], ed. S. A. Wertheimer, Jerusalem 1952
BB	Bava Batra
Bech	Bechorot
Ber	Berachot
Berger	A. Berger, Encyclopedic Dictionary of Roman Law (Transactions of the American Philosophical Society, NS 43/2, 1953), Philadelphia 1953, 1968[2]
BHM	Beit ha-Midrash, ed. A. Jellinek,[1] Leipzig 1853–Vienna 1878, second ed., Jerusalem 1938
bibl bibliogr	bibliography
BK	Bava Kama
BM	Bava Meẓia
BNJ	Byzantinisch Neugriechische Jahrbücher
Brand	Y. Brand, Klei Haḥeres Besifrut Hatalmud (Ceramics in Talmudic Literature), Jerusalem 1953
Brockelm[2]	C. Brockelmann, Lexicon Syriacum[2] Halis Saxonum 1928
BrüllJahrb	Jahrbücher für Jüdische Geschichte und Literatur, ed. N. Brüll
Brüll Redensarten	A. Brüll, Fremdsprachliche Redensarten, Leipzig 1869
BrüllTrachten	A. Brüll, Trachten der Juden, Frankfurt aM, 1883
Bruns-Sachau	K. G. Bruns and E. Sachau, Syrisch-Römisches Rechtsbuch aus dem Fünften Jahrhundert, Leipzig 1880
Buxtorf	J. Buxtorf, Lexicon Chaldaicum, Talmudicum et Rabbinicum ..., Basiliae 1640
Byz	Byzantine
BZ	Byzantinische Zeitschrift
CAD	Chicago Assyrian Dictionary
CantR	Canticles Rabba
CantZ	Canticles Zuta, apud Midrash Zuta, ed. S. Buber, Berlin 1894 = Agadath Shir Hashirim, ed. S. Schechter, Cambridge 1896
CGL	Corpus Glossariorum Latinorum, ed. G. Goetz, Leipzig 1923–51
Chajes	H. P. Chajes, Beiträge zur Nordsemitischen Onomatologie, Vienna 1901
Chron	Chronicles

CII	Corpus Inscriptionum Iudaicarum, ed. J.-P. Frey[2], Rome 1936 (1975), 1952
CIS	Corpus Inscriptionum Semiticarum
CookGloss	S. A. Cook, A Glossary of the Aramaic Inscriptions, Cambridge 1898
corr	correct (verb), corrupt
corr acc	correct accordingly
Czerný	Czerný, Coptic Etymological Dictionary, Cambridge 1976
Dalman	G. Dalman, Neuhebräisches Handwörterbuch zu Targum, Talmud und Midrash[2], Göttingen
Dan	Daniel
DeissmannLAE	Deismann, Light from the Ancient East, London 1927
DeLaraID	David Cohen De Lara, Ir David, Amsterdam 1638
De LaraKK	David Cohen De Lara, Sefer Keter Kehuna, Hamburg 1668
DER	Derech Ereẓ Rabba, ed. Vilna, and ed. Higger in Massechtot Erech Ereẓ (The Treatises Derek Ereẓ), New York 1935
deriv	derivation, derivative
Deut	Deuteronomy
DeutR	Deuteronomy Rabba, Standard ed., and ed. Lieberman[2], Jerusalem 1964
DEZ	Derech Ereẓ Zuta, ed. Vilna, and ed. Higger,in Massechtot Derech Ereẓ (The treatises Derek Ereẓ), New York 1935; edDSperber, Jerusalem 1982[2]
Dict	Dictionary
DISO	C.-F. Jean and J. Hoftijzer, Dictionnaire des Inscriptions Semitiques de l'Ouest, Leiden 1965
Ducange	Glossarium ad Scriptorum Mediae et infimae Graecitatis, Lugdunum 1688, reprint Graz 1958
DurhamVocMen	D. B. Durham, The Vocabulary of Menander considered in its relation to the Koine, Princeton 1913, reprint Amsterdam 1969
Eccles	Ecclesiastes
EcclesR	Ecclesiastes Rabba
ed	edited, editor, edition

edd	editions
edprinc	editio princeps = first edition
EdDiocl	Diokletians Preisedikt, ed. S. Lauffer, Berlin 1971
emend	emending, emendation
Epiph	Epiphanius
EpsteinAmoraim	J. N. Epstein, Mavo le-Sifrut ha-Amoraim, Jerusalem 1962
EpsteinGK	Der gaonäische Kommentar zur Mischnaordnung Tehoroth, ed. J. N. Epstein, Berlin 1921, 1924
EpsteinGKE	Der gaonäische Kommentar zur Ordnung Tehoroth . . . Eine kritische Einleitung . . ., Berlin 1915
EpsteinMavo	J. N. Epstein, Mavo le-Nusaḥ ha-Mishna, Jerusalem 1948
EpsteinTannaim	J. N. Epstein, Mavo le-Sifrut ha-Tannaim, Jerusalem 1957
Er	Eruvim
ER	Seder Eliahu Rabba, ed. M. Friedman², Jerusalem 1960
Est	Esther
EstR	Esther Rabba
euph	euphemism, euphemistic
Ex	Exodus
ExR	Exodus Rabba
EZ	Seder Eliahu Zuta, ed. M. Friedman², Jerusalem 1960
Ezek	Ezekiel
Fauna	I. Löw, Fauna und Mineralien der Juden, Hildesheim 1969
fem	feminine
Fest, Festschr	Festchrift
Flora	I. Löw, Die Flora der Juden, Vienna and Leipzig 1924—34
form	formation
Fraenkel	S. Fraenkel, Die aramäische Fremdwörter im Arabischen, Leiden 1886 (reprint Hildesheim 1962)
fragm	fragment(s), fragmentary
FrgmTrg	Das Fragmententhargum, ed. M. Ginsburger, Berlin 1899
FrgTrgKlein	The Fragment-Targum of the Pentateuch According to the Extant Sources, ed. Michael L. Klein, vol. 1, Rome 1920 (Analecta Biblica 76). (V = Ms Vat. Ebr. 440; P = MsParis,Bibliothèque Nationale Hebr 110)
Fürst	J. Fürst, Glossarium Graeco-Hebraeum, Strasbourg 1890
Gaon	Gaonic
GaonHark	A. A. Harkavy, Zichron le-Rishonim ve-Gam la-Aḥarohim 1/4 Berlin 1887, (usually called: Teshuvot ha-Geonim-Harkavy)

GasterMaasiyot	M. Gaster, The Exempla of the Rabbis, London-Leipzig 1924, (Heb. sect. Sefer ha-Maasiyot)
GasterST	M. Gaster, Studies and Texts, 1–3, London 1925–28
gen	genitive
Gen	Genesis
GenR	Genesis Rabba, standard ed., and ed. J. Theodor and Ch. Albeck[2], Jerusalem 1965, and see M. Sokoloff, The Geniza fragments of Bereshit Rabba, Jerusalem 1982
Gignac	Francis Thomas Gignac, A Grammar of the Greek Papyri of the Roman and Byzantine Period 1, Phonology, Milano 1975 (Testi e Documenti per lo Studio dell 'Antichita' LV)
GinzbergLegends	L. Ginzberg, Legends of the Jews 1–8, Philadelphia 1909–38
Git	Gittin
GH	S. Lieberman, Greek and Hellenism in Jewish Palestine[2], Jerusalem 1962, (Hebrew: Yevanim ve-Yavnut be-Ereẓ Yisrael)
Gk	Greek
GrünhutLikkutim	L. Grünhut, Sefer ha-Likkutim, 1–6, Jerusalem 1892–94
GS	L. Ginzburg, Ginze Schechter (= Genizah Studies) 1, New York, 1928
Ḥag	Ḥagiga
Heb	Hebrew
HechR	Hechalot Rabbati
Hesych	Hesychius, ed. Albertus, Lugdunum Batavum 1746, ed. H. Latte, Copenhagen 1963–66
HoffmannFestschr	Festschrift zum siebzigsten Geburtstage David Hoffmann's ed. S. Eppenstein, M. Hildesheimer, J. Wohlgemuth, Berlin 1914
HoffmannJahrb	Jahrbuch d. jüdische literarische Gesellschaft, ed. D. Hoffmann
HorowitzPAC	I. S. Horowitz, Palestine and the Adjacent Countries, Vienna 1923 (Heb)
Hos	Hoseah
Ḥul	Ḥulin
IGLS	Inscriptions grecques et latines de la Syrie d. L. Jalabert et R. Mouterde, Paris 1929–
IJMS	Israel Journal of Medical Science
Is	Isaiah
JA	Journal Asiatique

Jastrow	M. A. Jastrow, A Dictionary of the Targumim, the Talmud Babli and Yerushalmi and the Midrashic Literature, London, New York 1903
JNES	Journal of Near Eastern Studies
Jos	Joshua
Joüon	P. Joüon, "Mots grecs de l'araméen d'Onkelos ou de l'hébreu de la Michna qui se trouve aussi dans les Évangiles", Recherches de science religieuse 22, 1932, 463–69
JQR	Jewish Quarterly Review (New Series)
JQROS	Jewish Quarterly Review, Old Series
JSS	Journal of Semitic Studies
Juster,LesJuifs	J. Juster, Les Juifs dans l'Empire Romain, Paris 1914
JZ	Judische Zeitschrift
Kadm	S. Krauss, Kadmoniyot ha-Talmud, 1, Berlin–Vienna, no date: 2. Tel-Aviv 1929, 1945
Katzenelsohn	I. L. Katzenelsohn, Ha-Talmud ve-Choḥmat ha-Refu'ah, Berlin 1928, (Talmud und Medizin)
Kaufman	S. A. Kaufman, The Akkadian Influences on Aramaic, Chicago 1974
Ket	Ketubot
Kil	Kilaim
KleinYishuv	S. Klein, Sefer ha-Yishuv 1, Jerusalem 1939
KraussMT5/1	S. Krauss, Monumenta Talmudica 5/1, Griecher und Römer, Vienna & Leipzig 1914 (reprint Darmstadt 1972)
KraussPR	S. Krauss, Paras ve-Romi ba-Talmud u-ba-Midrashim, Jerusalem 1948
KraussSynAlt	S. Krauss, Synagogale Altertümer, Berlin-Vienna 1922
Krengel	J. Krengel, Das hausgerät in der Misnah, Frankfurt a.M., 1899
KutscherGA	E. Y. Kutscher, Studies in Galilean Aramaic, Ramat-Gan 1976
l	line
LagardeGA	P. A. de Lagarde, Gesammelte Abhandlung, Leipzig 1868
LagardeSem	P. A. de Lagarde, Semitica, Göttingen 1878–79
Lam	Lamentations
LamentR	Lamentations Rabba, standard ed., and ed. Buber, Vilna 1899
Lampe	G. W. H. Lampe, A Patristic Greek Lexicon, Oxford 1972
Lat	Latin

LevR	Leviticus Rabba, standard ed., and ed. M. Margulies, Jerusalem 1953–60
Levy	J. Levy, Neuhebräische und chaldäische Wörterbuch über die Talmudim und Midrasch, Leipzig 1876–89
LevyTrgWb	J. Levy, Chaldäisches Wörterbuch über die Targumim[3], Leipzig 1881
LewySemFremdw	M. Lewy, Die semitischen Fremdwörter im griechischen, Berlin 1895
LidzbardskiHb	Lidzbarski, Handbuch der nordsemitischen Epigraphik, Weimar 1898
lit	literature
LSJ[9]	H. G. Liddell, R. Scott, H. S. Jones, A Greek-English Lexicon[9], Oxford 1961
LSJSuppl	Greek English Lexicon, A Supplement, ed. E. A. Barber, Oxford 1968
LT	Midrash Lekaḥ Tov, by R. Tuvia ben Eliezer (XI cent., Balkans). Edd.: Gen, Ex (called Pesikta Zutreta) ed. Buber, Vilna 1880; Ruth, ed. Bamberger, Leipzig 1887; Lament, ed. Greenup, London 1908; Cant, ed. Greenup, London 1909; Eccles, ed. Feinberg, Berlin 1904; fragm as indicated
LW	S. Krauss, griechische und lateinische Lehnwörter im Talmud, Midrasch und Targum, Berlin 1898, 1899, (reprinted Hildesheim 1964)
M	Mishna
Mach	Yalkut ha-Machiri. Edd.: Isaiah, ed. Schapira, Berlin 1893; Prov, ed. Grünhut, Jerusalem 1902, and ed. Badahb, Jerusalem 1927; Minor Prophets, ed. Greenup, London 1909, 1913, and (on Hos) JQR 15, 1924–25, 141–212; Psalms, ed. Buber, Berditchev 1900
MaigneD'Arnis	W.-H. Maigne D'Arnis, Lexicon Manuale ad Scriptores Mediae et Infirmae Latinitatis . . . published by J.P. Migne, Paris 1890
MAMA	Monumenta Asiae Minoris Antiqua
MannBible1	J. Mann, The Bible as Read and Preached in the Old Synagogue 1, Cincinnati, 1940, (second ed. New York 1971)
MannBible2	J. Mann & I. Sonne, The Bible as Read and Preached in the Old Synagogue 2, Cincinnati 1966
Mand	Mandaic

MandDict	E. S. Drower and R. Macuch, A Mandaic Dictionary, Oxford 1963
marg	marginal note, marginalia
masc	masculine
Mason	H. J. Mason, Greek Terms for Roman Institutions – A Lexicon and Analysis (American Studies in Papyrology, vol. 13), Toronto 1974
Mayser	E. Mayser, Grammatik der griechischen Papyri aus der Ptolemäerzeit 1^2, 1, Berlin 1970
Mech	Mechilta de R. Ishmael, ed. H. S. Horowitz and I. A. Rabin[2], Jerusalem 1960
MechRashbi	Mechilta de Rashbi (= R. Simon bar Yoḥai), ed. J. N. Epstein and E. Z. Melamed, Jerusalem 1965
Meg	Megila
Men	Menaḥot
metaph	metaphor, metaphoric
metath	metathesis
MG	Midrash ha-Gaddol. Edd.: Gen, ed. Magulies, Jerusalem 1947, (ed. Schechter, Cambridge 1902); Ex, ed. Margulies, Jerusalem 1956; Lev, ed. E. N. Rabinowitz, New York 1932, and ed. A. Steinzaltz, Jerusalem 1975; Num, ed. Z. M. Rabinowitz, Jerusalem 1967; Deut, ed. S. Fisch, Jerusalem 1972
MGWJ	Monatsschrift der Geschichte d. Wissenschaft des Judenthums
Mid	Midrash
MidPs	Midrash Psalms, ed. Buber, Vilna 1891
MidTan	Midrash Tannaim, ed. D. Hoffmann, Berlin 1909
MillerMizMaarav	J. Müller (Miller), Teshuvot Geonei Mizraḥ u-Maarav–Responsen der Lehrer des Ostens und Westens, Berlin 1888
MishnatR.Eliezer	Mishnat R. Eliezer, ed. H. Enelow, New York 1933
MK	Moed Katan
MM	J. H. Moulton and G. Milligan, The Vocabulary of the Greek Testament, London 1952
MnHm	Menorat Ha-Maor, by Israel ibn Al-Nakawa, ed. H. G. Enelow, New York 1929–32
MT	Massoretic Text
Mussaf	Benjamin Mussafia, apud Aruch (AC pass)
MV	Maḥzor Vitri, ed. S. Horowitz, Berlin 1899–1907
MZS	Magyar-Zsidó Szemle

Naz	Nazir
Ned	Nedarim
Neh	Nehemiah
NöldekePersSt2	Th. Nöldeke, Griechische und aramäische Fremdwörter in Persischen, (Persische Studien 2), Sitzenberichte der Berlin Akademie, Ph.Hist. Klass 126, 1892
Num	Numbers
NumR	Numbers Rabba
OhG	Oẓar ha-Geonim, ed. B. (M.) Lewin, Haifa and Jerusalem 1928–43 (Berachot-mid Bava Meẓia), Sanhedrin, ed. H. Z. Taubes, Jerusalem 1966
OLD	Oxford Latin Dictionary, Oxford 1968–1982
OLZ	Orient Literatur Zeitung
OM	Oẓar Midrashim, ed. J. D. Eisenstein, New York 1915
PAAJR	Proceedings of the American Academy of Jewish Research
Palm	Palmyrene
Perles	J. Perles, Zur rabbinischen Sprach- und Sagenkunde, Breslau 1873
PerlesBeiträge	J. Perles, Beiträge zur rabbinischen Sprach- und Alterthumskunde, Breslau 1893, (first appeared in MGWJ 37)
PerlesES	J. Perles, Etymologische Studien, Breslau 1871, (first appeared in MGWJ 1870)
Pes	Pesaḥim
Pflanz	I. Löw, Aramaische Pflanzennamen, Leipzig 1881
PG	Patrologia Graeca, ed. Migne
pl	plural
PL	Patrologia Latina, ed. Migne
PnS	R. Payne Smith, Thesaurus Syriacus, Oxford 1879–1900
PnSSupple	J. P. Margoliouth, Supplement to Thesaurus Syriacus of R. Payne Smith, S. T. P., Oxford 1927
PR	Pesikta Rabbati, ed. M. Friedmann, Vienna 1880
PRE	Pirkei de-R. Eliezer, ed.Luria, Warsaw 1852, ed. Higger, Ḥorev 8–10, 1944–48
Preisigke	F. Preisigke, Wörterbuch der griechischen Papyruskunden, Berlin 1925–31
PRK	Pesikta de Rav Kahana Edd.: ed. Buber Lyck 1868, ed. B. Mandelbaum, New York 1962. The page

	numbers refer first to the Buber ed., and then to the Mandelbaum ed. The text is usually cited according to Mandelbaum's reading
Ps	Psalms
Psaltes	S. B. Psaltes, Grammatik der byzantinischen Chroniken, 1913, (reprinted Gottingen 1974)
R.	Rabbi, Rav
R	Rabba (e.g., ExR = Exodus Rabba, etc)
Rabb	Rabbinic
RabbinowitzVL	R. Rabbinowicz, Variae Lectiones in Mischnam et in Talmud Babylonicum (Dikdukei Soferim), Munich 1867–84
RabinovitzGM	Z. M. Rabinovitz, Ginzé Midrash, Tel-Aviv 1976
RAO	Recueil d'archéologie orientale, ed. Clermont-Ganneau
Ratner	B. Ratner, Ahawath Zion We-Jeruscholaim, Vilna 1901–13, reprinted Jerusalem 1967
RavPoalim	R. Avraham of Vilna, Sefer Rav Poalim, ed. S. M. Chones, Warsaw 1894
ref	reference(s), referring to
RH	Rosh ha-Shana
ReinachMélanges	Th. Reinach, "Un Contrat du mariage du temps de Basile le Bulgaratone", Mélanges offerts à M. G. Schlumberger, Paris 1924, 1, pp. 118–32
Rivmaẓ	R. Isaac, b. R. Malki-Ẓedek of Simponte (Siponte), ed. M. Sachs, Jerusalem 1975
RosenthalPiyyutim	A. Rosenthal, Ha-Piyyutim ha-Aramiim le Shavuot, M.A. thesis, Hebrew University 1966 (unpublished)
SachsBeiträge	M. Sachs, Beitraege zur Sprach- und Alterthumsforschung, Berlin 1852, 1854
Sanh	Sanhedrin
Schall	A. Schall, Studien über griechische Fremdwörter im Syrischen, Darmstadt 1960
SchatterVerGr	Schlatter, Verkanntes griechische,(Beiträge zur Förderung christl. Theologie 414)
SchönhakMashbir	J. Schönhak, Sefer ha-Mashbir (= Aruch ha-Ḥadash), Warsaw 1858
SchönhakMiluim	J. Schönhak, Hamiluim oder Masbir Hachadasz, Warsaw 1869
Schulthess	F. Schulthess, Lexicon Syropalaestinum, Berlin 1903

SchwabVocabulaire	Moise Schwab, Vocabulaire de l'angélologie d'après les manuscrits hébreux de la Bibliothèque Nationale, Paris 1879
SCI	Scripta Classica Israelitica
sect	section
Sem	Semitic
Shab	Shabbat
Shev	Sheviit
Shevu	Shevuot
Sif	Sifre. Edd.: Num, ed. H. S. Horovitz, Leipzig 1917; Deut. ed. L. Finkelstein, Berlin 1939, (reprinted New York 1969)
sing	singular
Skr	Sanskrit
Soph	E. A. Sophocles, Greek Lexicon of the Roman and Byzantine Period, Cambridge Mass. and Leipzig 1914
Souter	A. Souter, A Glossary of Later Latin, Oxford 1964
SperberRP	D. Sperber, Roman Palestine 200–400; Money and Princes, Ramat-Gan 1974
StarrJews	J. Starr, The Jews in the Byzantine Empire (Texte und Forschung zur byzantinisch-neugriechische Philologie, vol. xxx), Athens 1939
STov	Midrash Sechel Tov, ed. Buber, Berlin 1900
SY	L. Ginzberg, Seridei ha-Yerushalmi, New York 1909
Syr	Syriac
T	Tosefta. Edd: Zuckermandel, Halberstadt 1881; ed. Lieberman, Zeraim, New York 1955, Moed, New York 1962, Nashim, New York, 1967, 1973. When two page numbers are given, the first refers to Lieberman's ed., the second to Zuckermandel's. When one, it is to Zuckermandel
TA	S. Krauss, Talmudische Archäologie, Leipzig 1910–12
Taan	Taanit
Tanḥ	Midrash Tanḥuma, Vilna 1833
TanhB	Midrash Tanḥuma, ed. S. Buber, Vilna 1885
Tanbenschlag[2]	R. Taubenschlag, The Law of Greco-Roman Egypt in the Light of the Papyri[2], Warsaw 1955
term	termination
THG	Tshuvot ha-Geonim. When no further specification refers to A. A. Harkavy, Teshuvot ha-Geonim (= Zichron le-Rishonim Ve-Gam le-Aḥaronim 1/4, etc.), Berlin 1887

TK	S. Lieberman, Tosefta ki-fshuṭah, New York 1955–73
TR	S. Lieberman(n), Tosefth Rishonim, 2, Jerusalem 1938, 3–4, Jerusalem 1939
transcr	transcription
transf	transferred (meaning)
Trg	Targum
Trg2	Targum Sheni (to Esther)
TrgGins	M. Ginsburger, Thargum Jonathan ben Usiël zum Pentateuch . . . Berlin 1903
TrgJ	Targum (Pseudo-) Jonathan
TrgO	Targum Onkelos
TrgSperber	A. Sperber, The Bible in Aramaic 4a, Leiden 1968, (on Chron, Ruth, Cant, Lament, Eccles, Est)
TrgY	Targum Yerushalmi
v	verse
Ve-Hizhir	Mar Ḥefeẓ Alluf, Sefer Ve-Hizhir, ed. Freimann, Warsaw 1873
W	West
WZKM	Wiener Zeitschrift für die Kunde des Morgenländer
Y	Yerushalmi. Ms Leiden Cod. Scal. 3, facsimile ed. Kedem, Jerusalem, 1971; ed. princ. Venice 1523(?), and standard edd.
Yalk	Yalkut Shimoni. Edd.: ed. princ. Salonica 1527; ed. Hyman, Lehrer & Shiloni (called ed. Shiloni) Jerusalem 1973 in progress. The first number is of the standard ed., and the second (in Gen. and Ex.) is the Shiloni ed.
Yelamd	Yelamdenu
Yev	Yevamot
Z	Zuta
ZA	Zeitschrift für Assyriologie
Zav	Zavin
ZATW	Zeitschrift für die alttestamentliche Wissenschaft
ZDMG	Zeitschrift der deutschen morgenländische Gesellschaft
Zech	Zechariah
Ziegler	I. Ziegler, Die Königsgleichnisse des Midrasch beleuchtet durch die römische Kaiserzeit, Breslau 1903
Zimmern	H. Zimmern, Akkadische Fremdwörter als Beweis für babylonischen Kultureinfluss[2]. Leipzig 1917

INTRODUCTION

Choice of Words

This dictionary serves a dual purpose: on the one hand it presents to the scholar a specialized reference work on a clearly defined topic, Greek and Latin legal terms in Rabbinic literature. And at the same time it serves as a kind of pilot project for a larger dictionary (of lesser detail) which will encompass all Greek and Latin loanwords in Rabbinic literature, thus correcting, augmenting and indeed superceding the magnificent pioneer work of Samuel Krauss, *Griechische und Lateinische Lehnwörter im Talmud, Midrasch und Targum,* published in Berlin 1899 (and reprinted in Hildesheim 1964).[1] This latter project is a long-term one – there are well over three thousand Greek and Latin loanwords in Rabbinic literature, whereas this dictionary encompasses less than two hundred words – and in the interim stage it was thought worthwhile to produce a series of small specialized dictionaries dealing with specific topics. This work constitutes the first in this series, and deals as stated above with legal terminology.

The policy decision as to what to include and what not to include under the category of legal terminology is not completely clear-cut, especially in the peripheral cases. Thus while the *hegemon* and the *stratiotes* may appear in legal texts as fulfilling judicial functions, it was considered that they belonged primarily in the category of administrative and/or military terminology. And, on the other hand, one might well argue that the names of instruments of interrogation and torture, such as the *camus, burdillus* and the *flagellum,* are not strictly legal terms. However, they were included because they help clarify points of legal procedure. Furthermore, loanwords in Rabbinic literature which appear to originate in a language other than Greek or Latin have not been included.[2]

Chronological Range

The terms included in this work are mainly from Rabbinic literature. Chronologically they belong to a period from the first five or six centuries of the common era. And although some Rabbinic tets may editorially postdate this period (e.g., Exodus, Numbers and Deuteronomy Rabba), the material they contain generally belongs to the Roman and early Byzantine period.

In some cases, however, we have included material that is possibly of the later Byzantine period (or even after that), because of its specific legal intyerest. Thus, legal terms in the *Sefer ha-Maasim* literature, such as *kindynon,* or in Gaonic sources, such as *zemion,* or in early contracts, such as *akolythos,* have been included. On the other hand, very late words, even though they may be of incidental interest, have not been included.[3]

We have not attempted to date the words in this dictionary. This may be done, to a certain extent, from the texts referred to in the entry, Tannaitic, Amoraic or otherwise.

Sources

The sources drawn upon are, as indicated above, primarily Rabbinic, covering the whole range of Tannaitic and Amoraic halachic and Midrashic literature. In addition some "sub-Rabbinic" literature was included, such as the *Sefer ha-Maasim* material, some early legal documents (see above "Chronological Range") and some Byzantine *piyyutim* (see e.g., *apologos*). Furthermore, a good deal of mediaeval Bible commentaries and halachic discourses were examined, both for the valuable readings of earlier Talmudic and Midrashic sources, as well as for citations of Aggadic passages, otherwise unknown to us, (e.g., Maḥzor Vitry, Ramban, Baḥya, etc.).

We have not given any dates to the sources. For this the reader is referred to the Hebrew Language Academy's (problematic) Sefer ha-Mekorot (Jerusalem 1963), published for the Historical Dictionary of the Hebrew Language.

Organization of Material

The organization of the material presents a number of problems, to which there exists no single solution. For example, similar or closely related words may be grouped together under one main heading, with separate sub-headings and full alphabetic cross-references, or they may appear each in its own alphabetic position, with full cross-reference to related material. Under the heading "similar words" we may distinguish a number of different categories, such as: the same word in a different spelling, one word with derivative forms, etc. Each category may, in theory, be treated differently.

Our own solution to this complex of problems is not one hundred percent consistent, but, I venture to suggest, makes good lexicographic sense. As a rule, when the same word appears in different *spellings,* they all appear under one main heading (e.g., ארכי, ערכי, under ארכי). This is also true of variant forms of the same word (e.g., כסוריא, אכסוריא, under אכסוריא), even when the variant form is very different (e.g., קילוילוסין under קילווסים). In such cases the word appears either in the earlier position in the alphabet, or under its most commonly found form.

Directly derivative forms, which appear to have the same meaning as the original word, when their derivation occurred within Rabbinic parlance, are given under their primary form (e.g., אוניתא under אוני, אפוכיתא under אפוכי). However, when the derivative has a new meaning, it is listed separately (e.g., אפיטרופיא, אפיטרופסות). Similarly, when closely related terms appear as separate entries in Greek (or Latin) lexica, (e.g., סיקה פנטיון, סקיפנטים), or if the Rabbinic forms, close though they be, derive from different Greek forms (e.g., גמיקון, גממסות), they have been given separate headings.

As to the organization of the material within the entries, see below our detailed discussion in "Guidelines etc."

Signs, etc.

A number of signs have been used to facilitate use of this work. However, some significant phenomena have not been allotted *sigla*.

Thus, no special sign has been given to words which do not appear in LW2 (except as an incidental mention). For this fact becomes evident from the absence of any bracketed number in the main heading, which refers to the pagination in LW2 (see below "Guidelines" 1.6).

More complex is the issue of *hapax legomena*. We have not given a special *siglum* indicating this important item of data, firstly, because it usually becomes manifestly evident from the references. Thus, if only one text is referred to as attesting to the existence of the word in Rabbinic literature, it is presumably a *hapax*. Secondly, if the word appears in primary and derivative texts (e.g., the Talmud and the Talmud as cited in the Yalkut Shimoni), the word is also a hapax. However, in some cases, it is not altogether clear what is a parallel source and what is a derivative one (e.g., early Midrashim vis-à-vis Midrash ha-Gaddol in certain cases), and in such an instance it is difficult to determine exactly whether or not the word is a hapax. (See above "Sources").

These Loanwords in other Languages

It will be seen that usually at the end of the entry references are made to the appearance of the word as a loanword in other languages (Syriac, Armenian, Arabic, etc.). Below, in "Guidelines", we have discussed the problematic nature of these references. Here we will limit ourselves to remarking that this comparative material raises a whole series of questions to one who wishes further to delve into it. Thus, a Greek loanword in Syriac may have reached Syriac directly or via Aramaic. Latin loanwords in Rabbinic literature usually came via the medium of Greek. In Arabic, the word may have come directly or via Syriac . . . and so forth.

It is beyond the scope of a dictionary of this nature to give answers to all these questions.

Abbreviations

Since a great many sources are referred to in this work, and it is tiresome for the reader to have constantly to refer to the list of abbreviations in order to understand the references, we have tried to design the abbreviations to be easily interpreted. Thus, while *Yel* may be short, it is not so readily identifiable as *Yelamd,* which, to anyone acquainted with Rabbinic sources will automatically be read as *Yelamdenu.* If we have thereby added somewhat to the bulk of the volume, we have done so out of concern for the reader's convenience.

As to references to classical, epigraphic, patristic and papyrological sources, here we have used the standard abbreviations as found in the major reference works, Liddell and Scott, Lampe, etc. There is no absolute consistency between these publications and, as a consequence, there is a certain degree of inconsistency within this volume. Hence, the Oxyrrhynchus papyri may sometimes appear as PO and sometimes as POxy. I beg the reader's forbearance therefor.

Use of manuscript sources

There has been no *systematic* recourse to manuscript sources in the preparation of this work. However, in the case of difficult and problematic readings in texts for which there are no critical editions, or where the critical edition has not taken into account a manuscript of major importance, (such as MsVatican 60 of Genesis Rabba which was not used in the Theodor-Albeck edition), we have consulted facsimile or microfilm copies of the main manuscripts.

Methodological Problems

These have been treated extensively in a lengthy discussion by the author in Bar-Ilan 14–15, 1977, pp. 6–60, and ibid. 16–17, 1977, pp. 9–30, and need not be repeated here. Any reader interested in this field is referred thereto, and will find full bibliographic references there.

Fields for further research

It is hoped that the material contained in this work will pave the way to detailed studies in a number of fields, philological, historical and cultural. Questions such as: Why did these Greek words become loanwords and not others? How much legal Greek in Jewish Palestine?[4] What are the socio-historical and cultural implications of this material? and many others, will, I trust be taken up by those qualified to deal with them, helping further to illumine a fascinating period of Roman Jewish history.

Acknowledgements

My introduction to this field of studies came firstly from the writings of Prof. Saul Lieberman, undoubtedly the greatest living authority in this (and so many other) field(s). Later on, I had the privilege of meeting him, and even spending a full year in his close proximity, at the Institute for Advanced Studies of the Hebrew University. Through such and subsequent contact I gained enormous benefits, more than can ever be acknowledged in mere page references.

At an early stage in my "etymological activities" I had the good fortune to come into contact with the late Prof. E. Y. Kutscher, he who left his stamp upon a whole generation of students of Rabbinic lexicography. It was he who introduced me to the disciplines of the field, and turned me from dilettante dabblings to a critical control of the material. It is with great pleasure that I acknowledge my debt of gratitude to this great scholar, and to a unique pedagogic personality. I only hope I am fulfilling some of his expectations.

I am also fortunate in that I have had among my circle of colleagues at Bar-Ilan University a number of outstanding philologists working on various aspects of Rabbinic lexicography. Among them I sadly recall the late Dr. M. Moreshet, who barely completed correcting the proofs of his book "A Lexicon of New Verbs in Tannaitic Hebrew" (Hebrew), when he suddenly passed away. (The book was published in 1980 by Bar-Ilan University Press.)

Prof. M. Sokoloff, who is currently working, in a most systematic manner, on a dictionary of Galilean Aramaic, has been a constant source of help and information.

A number of scholars working on critical editions of Rabbinic texts have showed great generosity with their material: Dr. Y. Tabory – Esther Rabba, Mr. P. Mandel – Lamentations Rabba, Dr. Marc G. Hirschman – Ecclesiastes Rabba and others.

I have had occasional help from a number of people on a variety of occasions, and to all of them my heartfelt thanks.

Historically this work emerged slowly and unevenly, first out of a long string of articles containing etymological notes[5], which led on to my annotating my copy of LW2 for personal convenience. The material grew copious, my collecting became more systematic, and the annotations no longer fitted in the margins of my LW. The outcome was a large card-index, containing many strata of notations often with conflicting data.

The transition from writing articles on etymologies[5] and updating cards to producing a Dictionary was by no means easy. The task of forcing me to give understandable shape to a great body of disorderly and illdigested lexical data fell upon Prof. M. Goshen-Gottstein, director of Bar-Ilan University's Institute for Lexicography. With great patience and generosity of time he guided me through the various drafts that this work underwent, until it attained some measure of acceptable form. My extreme thanks to him for his help and encouragement, and for his perspicacity in prodding me to think things through to the end.

It is with particular pleasure that I express mydebt of gratitude to Prof. Joseph Méléze-Modrzejewski, of Paris. I met him at Bar-Ilan University some years ago, at an international Congress for classicists, and had the opportunity briefly to outline to him the nature of this project. Somewhat hesitantly I then inquired whether he would be interested in looking it over. Much to my delight he assented enthusiastically. I sent him copies of an earlier draft, and was rewarded with his comments, corrections and additional bibliographic references to juristic material. His vast erudition and bibliographic knowledge is proverbial, and I was able to enhance my work with his contributions, which saved me from errors, gave further clarification on a number of points, and enriched my references to relevant comparative material. His comments (in French) with which he honoured me have been incorporated in the text (in English translation) with full acknowledgements.

However, ultimately this work is a one-man-job. Hence, all aberrations, mistakes and howlers are my own responsibility alone.

My thanks to Mrs. Miriam Drori, who directs our University Press, for undertaking this difficult challenge, and seeing it through to a successful completion. And likewise to the workers of "Ram Ot", and most specifically to the master-typesetter Mr. Charles E. Vos, and the director Mr. G. Hartman, for the handling of this complex piece of typesetting.

In any of my works I can never express sufficiently my debt of gratitude to my parents: to my father, from who I have learned so much, both in understanding Rabbinic sources, and in a critical approach to them, and to my mother for her constant love and never-failing encouragement.

As I draw near the completion of this work – and this stage of the larger project – I think back on the long path I have travelled. I began my annotating with one child; now she is ten and there are six more. Some are old enough to ask in puzzlement, "What are those cards you are always scribbling on?" Others are so young that their only pleasure is in chewing up my cards, if they're given the chance. Many cards are stained with babies' droolings, while others bear testimony to more advanced child-activity, in the form of stick-figures drawn (usually) on the back. Withall, in their own way they have encouraged me in my work, despite their healthy scepticism as to its value. Indeed, it is only when I tell them I'm playing that they appreciate and endorse my activities.

Finally, it is my wife who has had to bear the brunt of my tedium and to her go my ultimate thanks.

Jerusalem, May 1981

NOTES

On this work see my detailed discussion in Bar-Ilan 14–15, 1977, pp. 9 et seq. Needless to say we have not included words which we do not believe derive from Greek or Latin. Thus, we have not included רטושק, which we understand to be Semitic, and unrelated to Latin *restitutum*, (contra Tur-Sinai, Ha-Lashon ve-ha-Sefer 3, Jerusalem, 1955, p. 270). The following are some additional remarks on a selection of words not in this dictionary. I have not included בניגני (160) in BAZ 24a (▽ בנוגני), which Jastrow i 17a suggested to be *benignae,* mitigating circumstances, since Prof Lieberman assures me that the word is not Gk. (Reject, Guggenheimer, Leshonenu 36, 1972, 118–19: *lignum,* writing tablet, meaning unattested; AC 5, 349a, PerlesES 35: Pers: *namak,* rejected by Geiger, ACSup 75ab; Levy 3, 401b, Arab etym, rejected by Fleischer ibid 718a; SchönhakMil 44b sv ננגי: *nuncio* (?). See also THGAssaf 1942, 158: בספר חשבונם, but no etym. The issue is complicated by ניגמי in TrgEst 2, 7:1, Sperber 190, LevyTrgWb 2, 90b, which may be related. However, see ACSup 75b adfin. Reject further my suggestion in my Greek and Latin in the Mishna, Talmud and Midrashic Literature, Jerusalem 1982, Eng sect 44: *νίγλα* = *τρόπαια,* Pers, Hesych.) Most recently the late Prof ESRosenthal published (posthumously) an article in Irano-Judaica, edSShaked, Jerusalem 1982, entitled "*For the Talmudic Dictionary* – Talmudica Iranica" (Heb). There (44–45, 92–95) he again discussed this word in great detail and demonstrated most convincingly that the correct reading should be נביגני (or perhaps we have a metath), from Pehl *nibēg* (+ pl term), here meaning "records", (cf DNMackenzie, A Concise Pehlevi Dictionary, 1971, 59sv, etc). As such it corresponds exactly with פנקסותיהן in the // in EstR 3:3 (1.6), from *πίναξ* = *codex* (+ fem pl term).

So too עיטרא (or איטרא) in BBM 38b and BBB 29b (in both cases with *alephs* in MsM, and so too in BacherMeliẓa 29_{18}), which AC 6, 190a linked to *ἑταιρεία, ~ία,* was rightly rejected in ACSup 309b. See further Jastrow 1068b, relating it to עיטור (ibid), and Levy 3, 637b–638a, to Arabic. The meaning is some kind of document of partnership (rather than Jastrow's "deed of separation"), and *ἑταιρεία,* though an attractive suggestion, is clearly incorrect. The word is surely Semitic in origin, perhaps neo-Babylonian, as DBWeisberg, HUCA 39, 1968, 71, 74–75. (My thanks to Dr. S. Shilo for calling my attention to this term and Weisberg's article.)

Likewise פולסא,(426), found in Babylonian sources, BBM 47a, 85b, BBK 19b, BYoma 77a, BḤag 15a (KallaRabbati 2.9, edHigger 202_{39}), is not *pulsus* (Krauss, Buxt 1748), or *πάλος* (Buxtibid?), or *πάλσις* (AC 6, 354a), but Semitic of unclear origin (Krauss, Dvir 1, 1923, 106), perhaps related to Syr: בלצוציתא (Brockelm[2], 77b), meaning "sparks", (Ginzberg, Legends 6, 150 n269 [?], and cf., most recently DBoyarin, Tarbiẓ 50, 1981, 171 n25). Incidentally, Prof IGruenwald, Jerusalem, informs me that this phrase, whips or scourges of fire, appears in the Gnostic Nag Hammadi texts, The Book of Thomas the Contender (CG 2, 7, 142_{42}–143_{2}).

So too קולא (LW 3, 503) has nothing to do with *κλοίος*, but is probably "good Semitic" (Löw ibid, suggesting relationship with קלע, apparently accepted by Brockelm[2] 652a, see ACSup 352a). (See further Levy 4, 260a; Jastrow 1327b, and reject.) See below sv קילה.

I have not included אסטליסטיקין in ExR 43. 4, which Krauss (LW2, 87b) identified as *σχολαστικός*, and in PR113, 138 (following SachsBeiträge 2, 180–81) explained to be lawyers. (Cf Krauss, REJ 78, 1924, 149–55, 89, 1930, 394.) For Prof Lieberman (private communication 1981) prefers the reading in MsOxf 147. 1: איסטיליקון, which he explains as *ἀστυδίκης* = *praetor urbanus* (otherwise called *ἀστυνόμος*). They were of higher rank then the local *shilton* ruler in that text, which explains why they sat (on the *cathedra*) and appeared to be standing. See on them, Mommsen, Römisches Staatsrecht[3]; Leipzig 1887–88, 1/1, 193 et seq.

Similarly I have not included אספלטייה, which Jastrow 53a explained as *ἰσοπολιτεία* (already in Brüll, Jahrb 5, 1883, 120), "civic rights granted to strangers", and which Löw (apud LW2, 37a sv איספטיא) claimed was "the nicest identification in the whole of Jastrow's work and undoubtedly correct" (rejecting Krauss' *ὁσπιτάλιον*, following Levy 1, 128a; Fürst 66a; AC 1, 187a; Mann, Bible 1, Heb 102_{19} n53; Schorr, He-Ḥaluẓ 13, 1899, 114, on Aggur 29), since LiebermanGH 46–48 (basing himself on BacherMeliẓa 48_{139}) has proved that the correct identification is *σπατάλη*, idleness (*σπαταλῶν*), etc.

I have not been persuaded by Krauss (SynAlt 334, Kadm 1/2, 428, PR 113 n36) that בסילקי (LW2, 161b) is the place of a judicial tribunal or that it has any intrinsically judicial character. I see it as no more than a basilica, a public building with colonnades, serving a variety of functions.

סמס, in YShek 5. 2, 48d 28, has not been included. Krauss (following Levy 3, 547b) (LW 2, 398b) suggested an adjectival form from *ζημίωσις*. This was rejected by Löw (adloc and in index 662b),who preferred the reading cited by Brüll (Jahrb 7, 1885, 61): מסמם, suggesting a Sem root: סמם, to poisen. (Brüll's reading has no real authority.) So too rejected by Zuntz, JSS1, 1956, 132, arguing that *ζημίωσις* is attested only once, in Arist (Pol 1300b 22), with a different meaning. However, Rosén, JSS 8, 1963, 61–62, demonstrates that its meaning is "a sort of general type of *iniuria*", and that in NTGk the meaning of *ζημι~* is merely "damaging, causing injury," which notion fits admirably our context. However, he notes that the phonetic representation of the word סמס remains troubling (ibid 61; cf LW 1, 119?). We would therefore suggest that we have here an adjectival form formed out of *σαμία* (= *ζημία*), LSJ[9] 755b. The initial *samech* is the result of the widespread *ζ* > *σ* interchange; see Gignac 1, 123, for examples. סמס would therefore be something like **σαμ<ι>ος* (?) = *ζημιώδης*, harmful. (AC 6, 75b: semus, which does not seem to bear the meaning Kohut attributed to it, see Souter 373a; ACSup 296b, citing JNEpstein, JQR NS12, 1922, 332–33, to cure, nurse – which meaning is problematic; Jastrow 1002b and 808b sv מסמס II seeks a Sem root but is not convincing; for similar approach see Dalman [2]294a who emends, without textual basis: מסמס, from Sem root מסס.) We should further take account of the ▽ in edSchreiber-Sopher 58: סמי, from Sem סמם to poison, though I suspect this is a copyist's "correction". Whatever the correct etym be, the word seems to have no (even residual) legal connotation, despite the original (?) legal meaning of *ζημιόω*, and has therefore been excluded.

פורפוריא in MidPs 9. 13, 89 is not *πάπυρος* (Buberibid n92),a kind of legal record, but simply *πορφύρα*, the purple toga of royalty (as in LW2, 436a). Cf partial parallels. So too, פניאס (465), in NumR 11. 5, TanḥNumNaso 10, B18 n89, is not *ποινή*, *poena*,

Levy 4, 65a, and AC6, 371a (nor is it to be corrected: ליפס = *λοιπάς*, cf LW2, 316b; nor *ἄφενος*, Fürst 173a; nor: פיגאס, *φυγάς*, LLöw, Ha-Shaḥar 1, 60; nor *persiones*, LWibid; and cf Jastrow 1189a). The meaning and etymology remain unclear to me, but it is probably some kind of tax term, and not a legal one.

I have also not included קטיזמי (525) (YBK 4. 6, 5a4) in this dictionary. For though Krauss (following Schorr, He-Ḥaluẓ 11, 1880, 64) identified this word with **καταζημία* (and Jastrow 1349 with *κτίσμα*), ILevy (comment ad loc, Jerusalem reprint 1970, 146) and Lieberman, Tarbiẓ 20, 1949, 115, have shown the correct etymology to be *κοττισμός* = *κυβεία* (see CGL 2, 354_{14}: *κοττισμός aler*), "dice-playing."

קטנטין (LW2, 526a) in MidPs 54. 2, 289 // YalkPs 771 and MachPs 54. 4, 289: קטנתן, was explained by Krauss (following PerlesBeiträge 20 = MGWJ 1892, 114, and Zeigler 114) as *κτάντης*, murderer. However, this was rejected by Zuntz (JSS 1. 1956, 134), who pointed out that the word *κτάντης* was hazarded by Dosiades (IV CE) as an artificial formation (Ara 10), and never used again. Krauss himself rejected this identification later (PR 140 n86). Other suggestions are not much better (Brüll, Jahrb 8, 1887, 71, emending: קטפטין = *καταπάτητης*, AC 7, 83b: *κατανθείς*), and the most convincing identification is that of Lieberman (JQR 35, 1944, 35), emending to קטנרין = *κεντηνάριος* = *centenarius*.

Another interesting case in point is רפוסא in ExR 37. 2, which Krauss (LW2, 579a; cf Levy 4, 463a; AC 7, 294a etc) explained as *Rufus* = *Rufilus* (= *Rufulus*), some kind of military tribune, or alternatively as: פ[רפוס]יטא = *praepositus* (and cf Jastrow 1489b: פריטור, *praetor!*), rightly rejected by Löw (LW 2, index 683a). Two Mss of ExR (Paris 187/15 and Sassoon 920/1) read ריפוסא, while two more very fine Mss (Oxf 147. 1 and 2353) have דיפוסא, suggesting that we emend to דיפנסור, *defensor*. The context in the passage, relating the term to Ex 18:19, "And Moses sat to *judge* the people, suggested to me the *defensor* [*civitatis*], a legal functionary. However, chronological problems – the text appears to be of the III cent while the position of *defensor civitatis* was first instituted around the middle of the IV cent (Berger 428a; Rees, JJP 6, 1952, 73; Jones LRE 3, 224 n31; idem, The Greek City 331–32) – and others made this identification untenable. I approached my colleage, Prof Ranon Katzoff, a noted juristic papyrologist, and he convinced me (in a joint paper shortly to be published) that the *defensor* in this passage functioned in an administrative, and not judicial capacity, one involved in appointment to public office. Likewise, הפינסור read: דיפינסור = *defensor*, in TanḥDeutShoftim 10, is some kind of tax official. (See Krauss, LW 2, 449b; idem PR 225; LiebermanGH 115 n30; idem Tarbiẓ 27, 1958, 57 n2, etc. Reject Krauss, ibid: *νεωκόρος;* Levy 4, 65b, and Fürst 174a: *φανηφόρος;* AC 6, 371a: *σύγκελλος;* Löw, ad loc: *censor;* Schwab, apud Lieberman, Tarbiẓ 43, 1931, 37 n7: *pensor*. Löw, ad loc, cited Brüll, Centralanzeiger 35: *defensor* = *decurio*, which he rejected.) Hence, although the *defensor* is normally equated with the *ἔκδικος*, and the *ἔκδικος*, clearly a legal personage, has been included in this dictionary (↓ אגדיקוס), the *defensor* himself will not be found here.

2 To give but two examples:

מגלב (1) whip (2) lashes of a whip: *μαγγλάβ<ιον>*.

(1) GenR 40 (41) 2, 389_6 = 52.13, 554_3 (Cf //Tanḥ GenLech 5, Bibid 8.66). LevR

27.6, 635_4 //NumR 10.1, CantR 5.16, MGGen 45.3, 762_{22}, YelamdNum 23:7, apud Ar (ACl, 2316), GrünhutLikkutim 4, 66a. (Not in PRK 76b, 155_4, TanḥLevEmor 10, Bibid 13, 92, YalkMich 554.) TrgProv 26:3, LevR 15. 4, 327.

(2) GenR 81.1, 1002_8 //YalkGen 140, 715_{62}, ibid Job 904, TanḥExBe-Shalaḥ 8, 57, Ve-Hizhir 1.38. (Cf ↓ בורדיילין): TanḥExBo 1 //Ar (AC5, 76a) citing YelamdEx 10.21, ExR 14.1.

Sachs Beiträge 1, 114–16; Levy 3, 16a; Fleischer apud LevyTrgWb 2, 567a, from Egypt-Arab root; ACSup246ab; Krauss, Dvir 1, 1923, 94; idem TA 2, 96; Lieberman, JQR NS 35, 1944, 16 n101; S. Zeitlin, Josephus on Jesus, 1931, 36, 102; idem, JQR NS 20, 1929–30, 16; Eisler, ibid 21, 1930–31, 37–38; Zeitlin, ibid 401, on the Slavonic *maglawijen*. See further, Noeldeke, ZDMG 54, 1900, 161–62. (Contra Sophocles 7266, explaining as *manus clavus;* Psaltes 59, 185: *manusclavis.*)

The Gk derives from the Sem, see LevySemFremdw 111. The Rabbinic מגלב seems also to derive directly from the Aram, rather than from ByzGk *μαγκλαβίον*. DuCange 946–49. See most recently the detailed discussion of ESRosenthal, Irano-Judaica, Jerusalem 1982, 121–23 n4–45, who reaches much the same conclusion.

Syr: מגלבא, Brockelm[2] 117a.

Arm: *manklav*, Brockelmann, ZDMG 46, 1893, 36; Thumb, BZ9, 1900, 407.

מרגנין scourges: *μάραγν<α>* (+ pl term).

Trg 1 Kings 12: 11, 14 //Trg 2 Chron 10.11, 14 (transl: בעקרבים).

LevyTrgWb 2, 66b; AC5, 2416; Jastrow 836a. (Reject Krauss' identification of מורנית with this word, in LW2, 329b, Löw ad loc).

Cf. Krauss, Dvir 1, 1923, 102.

Syr: מרגנא, PnS 2214.

Mand: *margna*, MandDict 252b–253a.

However, the etymology of this word is from Pehlevi *mārgan*, stick for killing snakes (MandDict 252b, and cf. Brockelm², 4026, citing Noeldeke, Mandäische Grammatik, Halle 1875, xxx, and Hübschmann, KZ 36, 175.)

The Targumic word presumably derives directly from the Pehlevi, rather than via Gk.

3 To give a further two examples:

אישטיפנומטא, nuptials: *στεφανώματα*. Responsa of Isaiah di Trani (Bari XIIcent.), edWertheimer no 37 col 173 (Ms.Cantab. sect. 27, 62a). See Lieberman, TK 5, 1182; Schechter, JQR 4, 1892, 99 n1, citing Robertson Smith. (Contra SAssaf, Be-Oholei Yaakov, 1963, 106 n40, explaining: *εἰστεφανώματα*, festival of crowning with garlands.) Cf Sophocles 1010a.

קארטופילוס, notary: *χαρτοφύλαξ*. Belleli, JQR 17, 1905, 166, from Corfu Ms of Maḥzor Romania. Cf DuCange 1736–39.

4 See, for example, Lieberman in article in JQR NS, 35, 1944, pp. 1–57, entitled "Roman Legal Institutions in Early Rabbinics and in the Acta Martyrum," idem, in Biblical and Other Studies, ed. A. Altmann, Cambridge Mass. 1963, pp. 123–41, essay entitled "How Much Greek in Jewish Palestine," etc. Further bibliography may be found in my study in Bar-Ilan, 14–15, 1977. See further KraussPR 101–42.

Another interesting problem is why certain words entered Rabbinic parlance with only

some meanings, and not others. A case in point is טרמנטן (278): *tormentum* |to which add: MGEx 14. 13, 264_{22}; MechRashbi $55_{2\ 3}$; MidTan 122; MGDeut 20. 20, 456; SifDeut 204, 240_{2}; and cf SY 213_{11}, vocalized: טַרְמַנְטַן|, which appears only in its military meaning, "a general term for catapults, ballistas and other machines for discharging missiles in war" (OLD 1950a, sv tormentum 2), while its other meaning (or one of its others) no less important and no less frequent in Latin sources, "torture (as an instrument of judicial inquiry or punishment)" (ibid 3, and cf Berger 738—39), is never found in Rabbinic sources. (See Krauss' observation in Dvir 1, 1923, 99.) |On *tormentum* see further LW2, 333b sv מטרניא, SifDeut 204, 240_{2}: מטרנייאות ▽ מטרסאות, Yalk, which Jastrow 527a and 770a explained as: טורמנטאות, *tormenta* (and already earlier Buber, Yeshurun 3, 101, SchönhakMiluim 37b sv מטרן, and later DZHoffmann, MT 122 n5.) Accepted by Löw (LWad loc) and Krauss (PR 280 n25). (Contra Brüll, Jahrb 1, 1874, 177: *metatores;* PerlesES 21: *materies,* followed by Fürst 139b, Levy 3, 94b, and AC 5, 125b; Schorr, He-Ḥaluẓ 11, 1880, 58: *ἀμυντήρια.*)|
A somewhat similar case is that of קופלא רגיא (LW2, 517b) in YelamdShemini, apud Ar (AC 7, 165a), explained by Brüll (Jahrb 8, 1887, 71, and followed by Krauss, LW ibid) as *κουφολογία* = empty talk (Hesych, edLatte 2, 522_{76}: *κουφολογία φλυαρία*), but now convincingly proved by HJacobson (IllClassStud 5, 1981, 59) to be *καλοπραγία*. For though *καλοπραγία* is known to us only from the schol adApollRhod 3. 68, where it means "justice, righteousness", here it means suitable for heroic, noble acts; (cf counterpart *καλοπραγία*).
A very knotty problem is the extent and nature of bilingualism in Rabbinic Palestine. See GAllon's sharply polemic review of Lieberman's Greek in Jewish Palestine (New York 1942), in his Meḥkarim be-Toldot Yisrael 2, 1958, 248—77 (first appeared in Kirjath Sepher 20, 1943, 76—95). Compare the recent review study of MSilva in Biblica 61, 1980, pp. 198—219 (with bibl).
A very problematic issue, which remains to be assessed critically, is my treatment of dialectology. For it will be noted that there is a tendency in this work, perhaps even over-zealous, to try to explain "aberrant" variants by reference to equivalences found in Egyptian papyri, epigraphic testimonies, or other (relevant) sources for Greek dialectic forms. Have natural errors of scribal transmission, or the slips of a tired copyist working by candlelight in XIV cent Germany to a crippling deadline, been "explained" by reference to phonological phenomena known from areas adjacent to Roman Palestine and of a roughly contemporary period? Or have we truly uncovered a wealth of new information on Greek dialect embedded in mediaeval manuscripts of Rabbinic literature? I leave this to the judgement of the scholarly reader. (Cf e g ESRosenthal, apud Irano-Judaica, Jerusalem 1982, Heb sect 93 n11.)
Finally an issue I have not dealt with in this context is that of *loan-translations* of legal terms. See, eg, ASRosenthal's comment in his article in YuvalShay, edBKurzweil, Ramat-Gan 1958, 300 n76, that the Heb terms (הלכה) חתך, קטע, פסק correspond exactly with the Byz juristic terminology: *κρίνεσθάι τε καὶ τέμνεσθαι,* or *τὰς δίκας τέμνειν* (Corp Iur Nov 67. 13, and Cod 3.1.12), though he does not discuss whether these are parallels or borrowings, and if the latter in which direction.

5 See now my Essays on Greek and Latin in the Mishna, Talmud and Midrashic Literature, Jerusalem 1982 (Hebrew and English).

GUIDELINES TO THE USE OF THIS DICTIONARY

1. *MAIN ENTRIES*

1.1. *Which forms make the main entry?*

With rare exceptions (marked with a siglum ^{0}) only forms attested in printed editions and Mss. are given in the main entry.

1.2. *Multiple forms*

Where singular and plural forms are known, the singular is given. As a rule, where many alternative forms are attested, the fullest one is given, unless it is very rare, in which case the commoner one is given (e.g., קולר, rather than קולרין).

1.3. *Square brackets*

Where the attested form is patently corrupt, the emended reading (based on manuscript material or on the author's conjectures) is given in square brackets.

1.4. *Alternative terminations*

Where there are attestations of alternative terminations, ~יא is preferred to ~יה, ~ין to ~ים.

1.5. *Round brackets*

In certain cases alternative forms are cited immediately following the main entry in round brackets.

1.6. *References to LW2*

The bracketed number after the main entry refers to the pagination in Krauss "Lehnwörter" vol. 2, (LW2). Where such a number does not appear, it may be assumed that the word does not appear in LW2.

1.7. *Meanings*

Where a word has several meanings, they are given numbered, usually, but not always, in order from the more primary to the more derivative meaning, or first the commonest, and then the rarer one. Even when only one meaning is of legal significance, the others (and the references etc.) are given, to indicate the full semantic range of the word. It should be noted that the meanings given are based on their appearance in Rabbinic contexts, and are not necessarily equivalent to their generally attested meaning in Greek and Latin sources. Where, however, the Rabbinic context does not clarify sufficiently the precise meaning, we have tended to translate the word by one of its suitable Greek or Latin usages.

1.8. *Greek and Latin etymologies*

The Greek or Latin equivalents, or etymological sources, are given in a form demonstrating their morphological relationship to the Rabbinic form. Thus *~ι<ο>ν* corresponds to the Rabbinic ~ין, and it is assumed that some such form, *~ιν*, existed in the Greek milieu from which the Rabbinic loanword derived. (See Class. Phil. 43, 1948, 243–60.)

1.9. *Relationship between Greek and Latin etymologies*

In all cases the Greek precedes the Latin. However, if the Greek is a loanword from the Latin, this is indicated by a directional arrow, thus: Greek ← Latin. And where the reverse is the case, the arrow points from the Greek to the Latin, thus: Greek → Latin.

1.10. *Multiple Greek forms*

On occasions two Greek forms appear under one entry, this where the Mss. material is so involved that to disentangle it would not add to the reader's convenience.

2. *THE SOURCES*

2.1 *Order of references*

Sources are grouped in accordance with the meanings given in the main entry, and given in the order of the meanings. Their internal order is usually roughly chronological. Thus Tannaitic sources (Mishna, Tosefta, Mechilta, Sifra, Sifre) are usually followed by the Palestinian and Babylonian Talmud, the earlier Midrashim (Genesis and Leviticus Rabba etc.),and then by the later ones (Exodus, Numbers and Deuternonomy Rabba etc.). Still later material, i.e., the Yalkutim, Pirke de-Rabbi Eliezer, and the Targumic material (which is always difficult to date), follows after that. Where, however, a close relationship exists between chronologically disparate sources, they are brought together, as, for example, when the Talmuds explain a Mishnaic text.

2.2. *Choice of texts chosen and references*

Where the word is rare, or a hapax legomenon, an attempt has been made to cite all (printed) texts in which it is known to occur. Where the word is more common, a selection of texts characterizing the usages or morphological forms is given. In the latter case no attempt has been made to give a full concordance to the whole of Rabbinic literature.

2.3. *Partial citation of texts*

As a rule, enough of the source has been cited to give a context sufficient to clarify the meaning of the word. Where parts of the text have been omitted, this is indicated by dots, thus: ...

2.4. *Editions used*

The texts are cited from critical editions where they exist, or from standard editions.

2.5. *Translations*

The texts are given in the original Rabbinic Hebrew or Aramaic, and then in English translation. The translation tends to be literal rather than literary. Note, the terms gentile, idolator, *kuti,* etc., are used indiscriminately in printed Rabbinic texts, and this for reasons of censorship. We have translated according to the reading in the standard editions.

2.6. *Vocalizations in texts*
The texts cited are not vocalized. Only when a manuscript has an interesting vocalization of the entry under discussion is vocalization given.

2.7. *Cross-references within the sources*
When there appears in the text a word which is discussed elsewhere in this dictionary, the reader is referred to it by arrows above ↑ or below ↓.

2.8. *Variant readings*
As to variant readings (▽), usually only significant ones are recorded, and the reader will find an analysis of them in the subsequent discussion. Only occasionally are manuscript sources cited. Details of manuscripts can usually be found in the introductions to the critical editions.

2.9. *Parallels etc*
In the matter of parallels (//), we have not distinguished between true parallels (e.g., similar texts occurring within the Talmuds, or in the Palestinian Talmud and Genesis Rabba, etc.), and derivative texts (e g, the Talmuds or Genesis Rabba as cited in Yalkut Shimoni and Yalkut Machiri, etc). In certain cases this distinction cannot readily be clarified, (i.e., texts found in Midrash ha-Gaddol, which have been partially re-edited and do not exactly correspond to their "sources", and which may be derived from, and be attestation to, an early parallel source, like the Midrash Tannaim). Those intimately acquainted with Rabbinic literature may make such distinctions for themselves. But such close literary analysis of each text was not deemed to be within the scope of this lexicographic project.

3. *DISCUSSION*

3.1. *Topics discussed*
This part of the entry admits to being of wide variety of treatments and topics. Subjects touched upon may be legal, historical, philological, text-critical, exegetical, etc.

3.2. *Rejected attestations*
Attestations of the entry cited in earlier lexica, but rejected by us are discussed. The reason for their rejection is given, and a heading under which they should come (possibly in another dictionary) is usually suggested.

3.3. *Dialectology*
Special attention is paid to morphological and dialectical phenomena (found especially in the variant readings) and their relationship to Greek dialectology as attested in epigraphic and papyrological sources. (Cf above note 4.)

4. *BIBLIOGRPAHY*

4.1. *Source of our etymology*
The main (earliest, most authoritative, etc.) bibliographic source for our

etymological identification is normally referred to, except when the case is so clear that all lexica have it without differences of opinion. This is generally the *first* bibliographic reference listed.

4.2. *Dissenting etymological opinions*
Where there are numerous and dissenting etymological opinions, the *first* bibliographic item(s) listed is the authority for our identification (as above 4.1.). Other views, which we have rejected, follow, usually preceded by the word "Contra", and comments and discussions on these views are interspersed within the bibliography.

4.3. *Other subjects referred to in the bibliography*
Specific discussions of texts or subjects related to the sources are also referred to. Related material from non-Rabbinic literature is also cited, as are discussions on the forms of the Greek and Latin words, in their different periods and dialectic forms. Occurrence of our word in the New Testament, Patristic, Byzantine and Mediaeval Greek literature is indicated by reference to the standard works (Arndt Gingrich, MM, Lampe, DuCange, etc.).

4.4. *Dependence on other bibliographic works*
Where major reference works give bibliographies (as is the case with Arndt Gingrich, Berger, etc.), we do not repeat their bibliographies.

5. *THE LOANWORD IN OTHER LANGUAGES*

5.1. *Significance of references to other languages*
When the word under discussion appears as a loanword in other languages, the (main) form and (basic) references are given: Syriac from Payne Smith's Thesaurus (and occasionally Brockelmann[2]), Palmyrene etc., from Cook, Lidzbarski, DISO etc. Occassionally Armenian and Arabic is also cited.

Here it should be noted that the precise nature of the loanword in those other languages has not been closely examined. Thus the word may appear in Syriac with a meaning quite different to the Rabbinic one. Furthermore, the authenticity and antiquity of the word in those other languages has not been determined. It may be no more than a lexical entry that was never in actual current usage, (as seems to be the case with many "Bar Bahlulian" words). Thus the significance of these references is often questionable and problematic. This whole field was beyond the scope of this work and the competence of its author. Nonetheless, the data was considered of sufficient interest to be offered to the scholarly reader.

6. *CROSSREFERENCES*

6.1. At the end of each entry all words of related interest (form, meaning, etc.) within this dictionary have crossreferences, with an arrow directing the reader above ↑ or below ↓. The crossreferences direct the reader to other main entries, but may be intended to refer him to incidental discussions within those entries.

7. *SECONDARY HEADINGS*

7.1. *Variant forms*

Attested forms, not appearing under the main heading are given in secondary headings and crossreferences to the main heading. However, it should be noted that the only variant forms given secondary headings are those found in printed books readily available to the reader. Additional forms attested in manuscripts may be listed among the variant readings (▽), but will not be given a secondary heading.

7.2. *Secondary forms*

Often a single entry contains a primary form, which constitutes the main entry, and a (number of) secondary entry (-ies). So, for example, a verb is listed under its root-form (e.g., קטרג) but a variety of its forms are cited (e.g., מקטרגין). In such a case, the secondary forms will appear in secondary headings and crossreferenced to the main heading.

א

אבלגין ↓ **אילוגין**

אגבאסטט exactor: *ἐγβιαστής* (= *ἐκβιαστής*)

GenR 12. 10, 108_4, according to Ar (ACI, 21a): במדינה ממונה אגבאסטט, in the city the exactor is responsible... ▽ **אגבטוס, אגבס סתום, אגאבאסטט, אגבבסטוס**. Printed ed: **אגוסטוס**. // MachPs 68. 7, 1. 327: **אבגסטוס** YalkPs 794: **אנגיטוס**.

Lieberman, Tarbiẓ 36, 1967, 401. (Contra ACI, 21a and 25b sv **אגוסטלא**, and DeLaraKK 3a, who also had a ms reading **אגבא סטט**, both explaining as **אגוסטוס** on basis of printed ed reading.) The meaning *exactor* is not altogether suitable to the full context of the text, and it may therefore be that this is a slightly corrupt ▽ of ↓ **אגבה בסטט**: *ἐγβιβαστής*.
On the other hand, it should be noted that both Aquila and Theodotion render **שֹׁטֵר** in Prov 6:7 with this word. See further Lampe 425b, Sophocles 431b.
For *ἐκ* > *ἐγ* see J&LRobert, REG 86, 1973, 74, and Gignac 1, 59, 174, and cf ↓ **אגדיקוס**.

Cf ↓ **אגבה בסטט**

אגבה בסטט apparitor, one who executes a sentence: *ἐγβιβαστής* (= *ἐκβιβαστής*)

GenR 12. 10, 108_4: אגבה בסטט במדינה ממונה על ביה (↓ **ביא**) שלה, the apparitor of the city is responsible for redressing injustice in (the city). Read as one word: **אגבהבסטט**. ▽ **אגבבסטוס, אגבא בסטט**.

Lieberman,Tarbiẓ 36, 1967, 401. (Contra LW2, 9a sv **אגוסטוס**; cf Theodor, GenR ad loc, and Löw apud LW2, 595b sv **אגוסטוס**.)
See CGL 3, 519_{23}: ekbibastes *efficax*.
Aquila renders **שטרים** in Deut 16:18 with this word, (LXX *γραμματεῖς*).

See note in JRieder & NTurner, Index to Aquila, Leiden 1966 (Supple to Vet Test 12) 76, who prefer ~βιασ~ (↑ אגבאסטס) in view of meaning in MT.
Cf Lampe 424b sv ἐκβιβαστής 3, Sophocles 431b, DuCange 360: *viator, apparitor*, officer whose duty it was to summon persons before the magistrate; LydMag 3. 11. 12, CodIust 3. 2. 4.
For ἐκ > ἐγ see J&LRobert, REG 86, 1973, 74, and Gignac 1, 59, 174, and cf ↓ **אגדיקוס.**

Cf. ↑ **אגבאסטס**

אגדיקוס (8) public prosecutor, or advocate: *ἔγδικος* (= *ἔκδικος*)

GenR 12. 10, 108_4: אגדיקוס במדינה ממונה על ביה (↓) שלה, The public prosecutor in a city is responsible for redressing its injustice. ▽ אגריקוס, אנדיקוס. // YalkPs 794: אגריסוק, corr: אגדיקוס (metath); Ar (ACI, 30a): אגדיקוס; MachPs 68. 7, 1. 327: אנדיקוס (corrected by the ed אגוסטוס!), corr: אגדיקוס.
CantR 7. 9: דוכסין ואגדיקין והאגמונין (ref to Dan 32: 3: וכל שלטני מדינתא, "all the rulers of the provinces"), *duces*, public prosecutors and rulers.

The reading: אגריקוס in GenR and // is perhaps the result of scribal "emendation" by association with *agric* ~ *ἄγροικος*, countrydweller, responsible for *βίος*, sustenance of the city?
For ἐκ > ἐγ see J&LRobert, REG 86, 1973, 74_{39}, and cf ↑ **אגבאסטס, אגבה בסטס**. See further Mayser I/1[2], 201-02; Gignac 1, 59, 174: *ἐγδίκου* inPMerton 104. 11 (early Rom), PO 261 = MChron 346. 14 (55 CE), etc.
On κ > γ in general, LW1, 108. On pl form ין~, see LW1, 178, and cf ibid 218.
Note that אגדיקוס שבמדינה translates *defensor civitatis*, which in turn corresponds to *ἔκδικος*. See Mason 42a; Berger 428a; Jones, The Greek City, Oxford 1940, 151.
CGL 3, 276_{23}: *ἔκδικος uindex;* ibid480a: *defensor ἔκδικος*.
Wartski, Leshon ha-Midrashim 191.

Syr: אגדיקוס, PnS 23, Bruns-Sachau 14_8, 24_{15}, Bar Bahlul 23.

אגדיקין ↑ אגדיקוס

◇**אגוריאות** (9) judicial assembly: *ἀγορά* (+ pl term)

BGit 88b (line 22): היה ר׳ טרפון אומר: כל מקום שאתה מוצא אגוריאות של עובדי כוכבים, אע״פ שדיניהם דיני ישראל, אי אתה רשאי להיזקק להם, R. Tarfon used to say: Everywhere you find judicial assemblies of idolators,even though their laws are in accordance with the laws of Israel, you may not use them. ▽ MsMunich: ערכאי׳ של גוים (cf ↓ **ארכי**). // TanḥExMishpatim 6: **אגוריאות** (sic edprinc); Sheiltot2, ed. Mirsky1, 23_{12} ▽ **אוגריות**; Machls 17, 12_{40}: **אנגריאות**, read: **אגוריאות**. (// in MGEx 21. 1, 459_{21}: **אורכיות**, cf ↓ **ארכי**.)

This specialized meaning of *ἀγορά* is noted in MM6a: *forum*, in sense of judicial assembly (citing

Wilcken, Archiv 3, 366ff, and referring to OGIS 517n7, and BGU III, 888, 4). Cf Mason 19a: *ἀγορά δικῶν;* ArndtGingrich 12ab. אנגריאות influenced by אנגריא: *ἀγγαρεία* (LW2, 63b).
Syr: אגורא, PnS 25.
Cf ↓ ארכי

אגדיקוס ↑ אגריקוס, אגריסיק

אילוגין ↓ אולוגלגין, אולוגין, אולוגים, אוגלוגוס, אוגולין

אומולוגייא (20) receipt for money collected (proving the payment and cancellation of a debt): *ὁμολογία*

YKet 9. 11, 33c5-6: אין שם אומולוגייה? ולית רב אומולוגייא? אית רב אומולוגייא, כהן דמר: אבד כרטיסן (↓ קרטיס) עבד חורן, And was there no receipt? Perhaps Rav is of the opinion that one is not required to write a receipt. [No.] Rav does require a receipt, in accordance with the opinion of him who says, if one's promissory note is lost, write a duplicate [for him]. (Ie it is theoretically possible for a creditor to be in possession of more than one promissory note for the same debt. Hence, when the debtor pays up, he must keep a receipt to prove the debt has been cancelled. Then, even should the creditor appear at some later time with a document purporting to show that the "debtor" owes him money, the debtor will be able to produce the receipt and prove he has paid up his debt – Thus Pnei Moshe.)
YMK 3. 3, 82a37: אימולוגים (sic MsL and edprinc), receipts, (transl the Mishna's שוברים, receipts).

See Ratner to YMK 107, citing reading of R Hananel to BMK 18b: אומי לוגיאוס. (Corr his ref to YalkJob 920 [sic], for which see ↓ **אילוגין**. So also corr Levy 1, 40b sv אומולוגין in accordance with Fürst 44b–45a, where אמלוגין in PR 44, 183a should be read אנולוגין, cf ↓ **אילוגין**.).
On YKet ibid see ZWRabinovitz, Sha'are Torath Eretz Israel, Jerusalem 5700 (1940), 394 for his emendations.
Prof JModrzejewski informs me that the sense of receipt for *ὁμολογία* is attested in Egyptian papyri, and that the verb *ὁμολογεῖν* is the technical term for receipt (*ὁμολογῶ ἀπέχειν, ὁμολογῶ ἐσχηκέναι,* etc). He refers to HvonSoden, Untersuchungen zur Homologie in den griechischen Papyri Aegyptens bis Diokletian, Köln-Wien 1973, especially 40 sq: "Quittungshomologien"; HARupprecht, Studien zur Quittung im Recht der graeco-ägyptischen Papyri, München 1971, pass. This *homologia* is, from a diplomatic point of view, a *cheirographon* in *subjective style* (*ὁμολογῶ ἐσχηκέναι,* like *ὁμολογῶ πεπρακέναι,* etc, for *ἔσχον, πέπρακα,* etc). See HJWolf, Das Recht der griech Papyri Aegyptens in der Zeit der Ptolemäer und des Prinzipats, 2, München 1978, 106 sq. Finally, see BCohen, Jewish and Roman Law, New York 1966, 336n320. (On the Gk *ὁμολογία* see ABSchwarz, JJP 13, 1961, 177-242.)

Syr: אומליגיא. PnS 69, (citing only BB. See BB66$_{12}$, 183$_{23}$: אמולוגיא, 187$_{6}$: אמלגיא)
Palm: אמלגיא, DISO 17.

אונה, אונו, אונות ↓ אוני

אוני (~נו, ~נה, ~ניתא) (21) (1) sale (2) deed of sale: *ὠνή*

(1) YPes 4. 9, 31b49: מיסתיוסים (↓) כאוני, Lease is like a sale.

(2) GenR 2. 2, $15_{4\ 5\ 8}$: למלך שקנה לו ב׳ עבדים, שניהם באוני אחד ובטימי (↓) אחד, Like a king who purchased two slaves, both on one deed and for one price. (Or perhaps: in one purchase = *ὠνή*.) // GenRabbati 36_{21}; YalkGen 4, $12_{76\ 78}$ 13_{81}.
TAZ 3. 16, 464_{26}: המוכר עבדו לגוים ... כתב לו אונו, הרי זה גט שחרורו, He who sold his slave to gentiles, ... if he wrote him a deed of sale, this constitutes his document of manumission. // BKid 6b: כתב עליו אונו, He wrote a deed for him; BGit 85b.
GenR 79. 7, $949_{1\ 2}$: ומי כותב את האוני? ... ומי מעיד על האוני?, Who writes the deed of sale? ... And who witnesses the deed of sale? ▽ האונו, האוניא, האונה etc. // YalkGen 133, 681_{43}, 682_{44}.
GenR 96, 1201_{2}: היכן הוא דייתיקי (↓) שלהן, והאוני שלהן?, When is their will, and their deed of sale? // TanḥGenVa-Yeḥi 8 (in B 9, 217 absent); MachProv 25. 2, 53a; YalkGen 157, 833_{5} (but absent ibid Job 906).
YKid 1. 5, 60c42: אונו; ibid 1 45: אוני.
BBB 154b: אונו. YBM 1. 8, 8a 39: אונו.
PR 25, 127a: והיכן הוא האונ׳?, And where is the deed of sale? For // see אפוכי.

Pl forms: ~ות, ~יות.

TanḥBGen Va-Yeshev 13, 184: נעשו עליו שלש אוניות, Three deeds of sale were made on him. // GenR 84. 22, 1028_{4}: YalkGen 143, 730_{29}; STovGen 39. 28, 221: אנאת, read: אוניות.
BBB 52a: אונות.

Additional sing forms: אוניתא, ~ענ (22, 415).

YTaan 4. 8, 69a, 26: והוון משלחין אוניתא, and they would send a deed of sale. // LamR 2. 2, 103: אוניתא ▽ אוניתיה, but edprinc: עניתיה; ibid 4. 18 (not in Buber ed): עינותיה ▽ edprinc: ענותיה; GasterMaasiyot LXXVa, 50_{28}: אוניתא. (LamR ibid: והוה טעין אוסיתיה, read אוניתיה with most LamentR Mss.)
TrgY2Gen 49: 21: ואייתי אוניתא דחקלא, and he brought the field's deed of sale. // FragmTrgKlein (P and V).

See PRK 151a, 336, בפיסין בהוניות ובזמיות, different kinds of taxes. ▽ אוניות, ובארנויות, read: ובארנוניות (LW2, 133a, and 66ab: *ἀννώνα*, *annona*). Perhaps an unrelated tax term, or "contract for farming of taxes" – *ὠνή* (LSJ[9] 2034b sv *ὠνή* II).

See further MidPs 104. 21, 446: אלו האוניות שעושין לישראל (a word-play on אניות, ships, in Ps 104:26). Löw, apud LW 2, 22a, suggests ἀβανία, capitation tax. FPerles, Jewish Stud ... IAbrahams 383: הוניות, Heb from הוניה, oppression, which meaning is applicable to both MidPs and PRK. (See also in Ha-Ẓofeh 10, 1926, 248.) Or perhaps from ὠνή in tax sense. But note // MachPs 104. 75, 2. 149: האומניות?

There are three primary forms attested for this word: (1) אוני: ὠνή, (2) אונו and (3) אונה. אונה: ὠνά Dor, (ὄννα Aeol), frequently found in inscriptions, (eg LSJ[9] 2034b sv ὠνή II 2). As to the (common) form אונו, can this represent an unattested form *ὦνο. Note ὠνοφύλαξ (not ὠνα~ or ὠνη~), meaning keeper of deeds of sale; see LSJSupple 153b, ref BerlSitz, 1936, 368 (Aetolia).
As to the אוניתא, ~ענ form, this is a new Sem fem formation, not an infrequent phenomenon in Rabbinic parlance. Cf אפוכיתא from אפוכי ↓, and טימיתא from טימי ↓.
For the *aleph-'ayin* interchange, see LW 1, 14, and cf ↓ ארכי (— ערכי).
There are two pl forms אוניות and אונות, deriving from the various sing forms אוני and אונו or אונה.
On ὠνή as "deed of sale" Prof Modrzejewski remarks: on the terminology ὠνὴ καὶ πρᾶσις, ὠνή (classical usage), πρᾶσις (late usage), see FPringsheim, The Greek Law of Sale, Weimar 1950, 111sq. On ὠνή as acquisition of ownership ibid179. Cf RRenehan, Glotta 46, 1968, 73.
See BacherTanJer 93.

Cf Syr: הפלא[ו]נא = ἁπλῆ ὠνή, Bruns-Sachau 13_{3}, 31_{13}.

אוני ↑ אוניתא, אוניות

אנקלסיא ↓ אונקליסיא, אונקליטיא

איפטייה ↓ אופטיאה

איפומניטא ↓ אופימשטאטא

ארכי ↓ אורכיות

אורקמסיא oath taken at time of signing treaty: (τα) ὁρκωμόσια

LevR 6. 5, 137_{5}, according to edprinc: א"ר יוחנן: אר' דקמסיות נתנו ביניהן, שאינו כופר בהן והן אינן כופרין בו; read: אורקמסיות with Aggur 34, and MGDeut 9. 16, 179_{7} (▽: אורמסקאות), Said R. Yoḥanan: Oaths were taken by both of them (God and Israel at Sinai), that He would not renounce them, and they would not renounce him.(▽ in printed ed and other MSS read: קופראמסאות; cf ↓ קומפרומיסין).

LiebermanGH 6, Margulies, LevR ad loc, LW2, 510b-511a sv קומפרמיסין, Schorr, He-Ḥaluẓ 13, 1899, 116 (contra Buber, Aggur ibid n250, Fisch MGDeut ad loc). See CGL 3, 277_{7}: ὁρκωμοσία *iuratio*.

דיאתימון ↓ אידייתמין

אילוגין ↓ איזלוגין

אילוגין, אנלגין (33-34, 73) charge, accusation, from *ἐλλογεῖον, elogium,* via Gk forms: **ἐλογι<ο>ν, *ἐνλογι<ο>ν* (~*ειον*)

This term appears in a number of different forms which have here been set out as follows **(1) אילוגין (2) אנלוגין.**

(1) אילוגין

ExR 15. 12: היו יודעין שאני דן דיני נפשות ומחייב. הקריבו לי דורון, שאם תעלו לפני לבימה (↓ **בימה**), שאעבור אילוגין שלכם (לאחר), Know that I deal in capital cases and give sentences of death. Bring me a gift (*doron*), so that if you come up before my seat of judgement (↓ **בימה** *bema* tribunal), I shall pass your charge over to someone else, (or, if we do not read **אחר**: I may dismiss your charge).
Ibid 31. 6: לאחד שהיה אילוגין שלו נקרא לפני הדיין, one whose charge was being read out before the judge.
MidPs 1. 22, 24: קורא אילוגין והן יורדין לגיהנם, He reads the charge, and they descend to Hell. ▽ אלנין, אילגין, corr acc, and see below **אנלגין.**
YalkPs 714: וקורא אילוגין שלָהם, והוא מחזירן שוב לגיהנם, He reads the charge against them, and sends them back to Hell. (Not in // MidPs 31. 3, 238-39, see Buber's note 6 ibid.)
LevR 16. 9, 365_5, according to MsOxf 147: באותה שעה קרא הקב״ה לאילוגין שלו, ואמר: ראו, לא לחנם הכיתי אותו, At that hour the Holy One blessed be He read the charge against him, and said: You see, it is not for nought that I struck (punished) him. ▽ לא נליגון, read: לאנלוגין (cf below), ללגיונותיו (scribal emendation), etc.
TanḥNumShelaḥ 12: הניח המלך האילוגין וחייבו מפיו, The king set aside the charge, and sentenced him by virtue [of the words of] his own mouth. ▽ edprinc: אליגין, edBuber, ibid 22, 69: אילוגין. // MannBible 2, 148: אלוגין; YalkNum 744: אוגולין (sic edprinc), perhaps read: אנגלין (cf below) or איגלין, (with not unusual metathesis, probably through scribal inversion of letter rather then metathesis of a phonological nature); YelamdLev 23:40 and ibid Num 14:12 (GrünhutLikkutim 4, 31a), apud Ar (AC 1, 88ab): **אולוגים** (perhaps reflects Lat ~*ium,* and maybe influenced by *eulogium*) ▽ Ar edVenice: אוגלוגוס, (probably corr from: אנולוגים).

אנלגין (2)

PRK 159b $357_{8\ 10}$: ללסטים (↓ ליסטיס) שהוא נידון לפני הקוסטינר (↓), בתחילה הוא קורא אנלגין שלו ..., It is like unto a *lestes* (brigand) who is being judged before the *quaestionarius;* first he reads the charge .... // MachHos 132. 12, JQR 15, 1924/25, 210, ibid 14. 2, 212: אבלגין; YalkHos 532: אוליגין, corr אנלגין (or in case of YalkHos perhaps: איליגין, see above).

PR 44, 183a: מדת בשר ודם, כותב (אמלוגין) [אילוגין] קשה ומחליפו בממון רב (edprinc: אולגין), The way of flesh and blood is that he levels a serious charge, and commutes it for a large sum ... Read: אנולוגין, אנלגין.

LamR 1. 14, 77: סבורה הייתי שימחול לי על כל עונותי בשעה ששמעתי שאנולוגין שלי נקרע מלמעלה, I thought he would forgive me all my sins, when I heard the charge against me was torn up from the top (sic edprinc). ▽ Buber ed: אונולוגין.

GenR 28. 1, 259_6 apparat: אין הקב״ה פורע מן האומה (אומות, רשעים), עד שהוא קורא לאנאלגין, The Holy One blessed be He does not punish the people (nations, wicked) until He has read the charge [against it (them)]. ▽ אנלגין, אגאליגין, אגליגין, אגליתן, read: אנ(א)ליגין, or ~גון (~תן corr from ~גון); אולוגין read: אנלוגין or אילוגין (cf above). // MGGen 6. 7, 142_{17}: אנלוגין; YalkNum 744: אוגולין (sic edprinc); ibid Job 920: אולוגין; TanḥNumShelaḥ 12, as in Ar (ACI, 88b): אולוגים (perhaps reflects Lat form *~ium*, and maybe influenced by *eulogium*, cf above), read: ~אנ or ~אי; ibid edBuber 22, 69: אליגין, אילוגין.

MidPs 1. 22, 24: קורא איזלוגין והן יורדין לגיהנם, He reads the charge, and they descend to Hell. Read: אינלוגין. ▽ ארגלין, read: אנגלין (metath: אנלגין), אילגין, אלגין, read: אלגין.

The two major forms אילוגין, אנלגין freely interchange. אולוגים in ACI, 88ab is surely to be read: אנלוגים, Lat: *enlogium.*

The strange form אוגלוגוס in Ar edVenice, which we have suggested is probably to be read: אנולוגים, could perhaps be explained as being influenced by *ἐγλογος, account of balance; see LSJSupple 50b sv ἐκλογή 2 and ibid *ἔκλογος (and cf ↑ אגדיקוס on ἐκ > ἐγ).

The strange forms אולוגלגין (Ar, ACI, 88a sv), and אוגלוגלוגין in Ar (ibid) edVenice, citing GenR 28. 1, 259_6 in apparat (see above) are aberrant forms probably to be read: אנלוגלגין, corresponding to: *ἐνλογλ<ο>γι<ο>ν = *ἐνλογι<ο>ν. For a similar example of dittography (or reduplication) see the form אולוליגין (TKelBK 2. 3, 570_{32}) אילולוגין (Aggur 20): ἀναλογεῖον, a reading desk (Buber, Aggur ibid n47, TR 3. 6). Further examples of this phenomenon: לבזביז (LW2, 303a, 608ab), λαβίς according to Krauss (ibid), but more likely λεσβίον (Epstein, GK 47n7; ACSup 242a; Brand 258); פלסלוס (LW2, 462a): φασίολος (but cf Flora 2, 454, and ACSup 327a, Sem). See further LW1, 196-97 (which requires some correction); Mayser 1/1[2], 219-20. And cf ↓ קילווסים, where we discuss the form קילוילוסיו. See also EcclesR 2. 8, edHirschman 121, main reading: פוסיאנין ▽ פסיינין (= φασιανός + pl term, LW2, 469ab); but MsParis 821. 7 has: אפוסיסיאנין.

The forms אולוגין and אבלגין may be influenced by *eulogium* (= εὐλογία), Souter 131a.

For the form אנלגין, cf CGL 2, 84$_{14}$: imputat. ἐνλογεῖ, On unassimilated ν before liquids in papyri see Gignac 1, 169-70, eg: ἐνλογεῖν, BGU 140 = MChr 373. 32 (119 CE), PRyl 243. 11 (II cent CE), etc. See on this Lieberman, JQRNS 35, 1944, 28-29 (followed by Mandelbaum, PRK 357).
See SachsBeiträge 2, 181; Ziegler 109; Levy 1, 64b; Fürst 44b-45a, (and reject Levy 1, 40b sv אומולוגין).
Lieberman (JQR ibid 30) defines the word thus: report of preliminary interrogation conducted by the magistrate, which accompanied the defendent to the proconsul or the legate. Cf Berger 451b; OLD 600c.

אומולוגייא ↑ אימילוגים

איניאומין I have guaranteed: *ἠγγυώμην*

LTGen 31:39, l. 61: איניאומין transl: אנכי אחטנה.

Note that this is a transcription, and not a loanword.
Prof Modrzejewski comments: *ἐγγύη, ἐγγυᾶσθαι* as "surityship," see HWSoest, De civilrechtelijke *ἐγγύη* (garantieovereenkomst) in de griekse papyri uit het Ptolemaeische Tijdvak, Leiden 1963, (cf Modrzejewski, Arch f Pap 26, 1978, 230). Also Taubenschlag 441 sq, 414n8, where he speaks of the *Roman* practise compromising the Gk formulae with *ἐγγυῶμαι*. Here too *iniōmin* was intended and transcribed faithfully.
(Contra Buber ad loc n54, 35, who suggested reading אינגיאלין, from *ἐγγυαλίζω*: put in palm of hand; and Schorr, He-Ḥaluẓ 12, 1887, 79: *ἀνακέομαι*: repair!).
Cf CGL 3, 278$_{54}$: *ἐγγύη uandimonium, fideiussio.*

אפופסים ↓ איספוסין

ספקלטור ↓ איספקלטור, איספקליטור

אסקבטורין, איסקבטיריי (97) scribes of court: **εσκέπτωρ ← exceptor* (+ Aram pl. term)

YKil 9. 4, 32c22: תרין איסקבטיריי דשלמה, Solomon's two court scribes. // MGGen 4. 4, 122$_{19}$ (114) = Gaster, Maasiyot CXXXIX 100$_5$: אסקבטריא, ▽ ריי~, אסקופטריא; Aggur 30: אסקבטור, רין~.

FPerles, SchwarzFest 294-95, followed by Ginzberg, Legends 6,303n99. Cf Brüll, Jahrb 1, 1874, 178: *ἐκσκέπτωρ*. Not to be confused with איסקריטורין (↓) as was in most lexica (Levy 1, 132a, AC 1, 199a, Jastrow 57a, LW2, 97a). (Reject Schorr's suggestion, He-Ḥaluẓ 13, 1889, 115: *σκεπτήριος*; Buber's notes 179-80 in Aggur 30 are very confused and need much correction.) It may also be that

this should be identified with *σκέπτωρ* – *sceptor* (↓ סקיפטורין), which here appears with the prosthetic *aleph* (and some vocalization); see LW 1, 136-50. However, *ἐσ-* for *ἐκ(s)* is attested; eg *ἐσκούβιτος* – *ἐξκ~* (Sophocles 525a).
For specialized meaning of *sceptor*, see ↓ **סקיפטורין**.

Syr: אכסקפטור, (Fraenkel, ZA 17, 1903, 85), PnS 189.
Cf ↓ **סקיפטורין, סקבטרין, איסקיפטורין, איסקריטור**

איסקיפטורין judgement published by reliable jurist (in writing): *sc<r>iptur<a>* (+ pl term)

LevR 21. 3, 478_6: "[אם תקום עלי מלחמה] בזאת אני בוטח" — אמר ר' לוי: באיסקיפטורין שהכתיב משה לזקיני — "וזאת ליהודה", "[Though war should rise against me,] in this will I be confident" (Psalm 27:3) – Said R Levi: In the judgement which Moses dictated to my forefather [will I trust] – "And this is the blessing of Judah ..." (Deut 33:7). ▽ אספקטרין, אספקרין; קוטריס, קטריס (cf ↓ **קרטיס**); סקטנריין, סקווטורים. Latter readings with several variations found in numerous //, eg LevR 21. 2, 407_3; PRK (175a) (= LevR chapter 21, Mandelbaum's note 400_3); MachPs 27. 5, 1. 179, etc.

Lieberman, apud LevR 876. Berger 692b-693a, and note also meaning "single disposition of a last will" (ibid), which may also be suited to our context. Cf AC 6, 117a (and ACSup 302a). On the loss of the R, see Mayser $1/1^2$, 159-60, Gignac 1, 107-08. Not to be confused with **איסקבטיריי** ↑, (as was in lex), nor with אגיסטריין (as was in LW 2, 11a).

Cf ↑ **איסקבטיריי** ↓ **סקבטרין, סקיפטורין**

◇^{0}**איסקריטור** (97) scribe: *scri<p>tor*

YKet 12. 3, 35b26: תרין איסקריטורי (sic edprinc), the two scribes.
AgBer (58) 59, 118: איסקריטורין, scribes.
EcclesR 9. 18: "ושבנה הסופר" סקיוי פטריי (sic edprinc); read: סקריפטר (?) "and Shebna the scribe" (Is 36:3) – [the] *scriptor*.

Buber, AgBer ad loc; Ginzberg, apud ACSup 430a. However, Mussaf (AC 1, 199a), Brüll, Jahrb 1, 1874, 178, Fürst 67b, Löw (apud LW 2, 97a) see this word as *ἀσηκρῆτις* or *σηκρητάριοι*. In the lexica the word has been confused with **איסקבטיריי** ↑ and **סקיפטורין** ↓.
On the loss of the P, see LW 1. 124, where the examples are of the loss of an initial P. (The example of the loss of an intervocal P, ibid 116, הדרוקן, *ὑδρώπικον*, may be dismissed in view of Löw's remarks in LW 2, 222a, suggesting with Jastrow 335a, **ὑδερικόν*.) However, in the papyri we find examples of the loss of P in its clusters /mpt/, /mps/, and before /s/ and /t/. Eg *περιβλέτου* (for *περιβλέπτου*), StudPal iii, 30. 3 (VI cent). See Gignac 1, 64-65.

Cf ↑ **איסקבטיריי**, ↓ **סקיפטורין**.

איסקריטור ↑ **~ין, איסקריטורי**

אפוכי ↓ **איפוכי**

◇ **איפומניטא [איפומני[מ]טא]** (25, 39) (1) minutes of trial read before the sentence (2) the judgement itself: *ὑπομνημάτα*

(1) DeutR 2. 29: הרי איפומניטא שלו נקרין, הרי הוא יוצא ליהרג. הרי איפומניטא שלו נקרין, הרי זה יוצא לישרף; read **איפומני[מ]טא**, Behold the minutes of his trial are read; behold he is led out to be decapitated. Behold the minutes of his trial are read; behold he is led forth to be burnt alive. ▽ edprinc: **איפומנימת**, read: **איפומנימת[א]**; Ar (Ac 1, 219a): **איפומנימא**. // YalkGen 77, 303_{85}, ibidEx 167, 34_{47}: **איפומנימא** ▽ **איפמניטא, איפאנטא, איפאניטא, איפאנעא**, read: **איפומנימ[ט]א**.

(2) ExR 28. 3: אותה שעה בקש הקב״ה ליתן להם את התורה ... משל למלך שבקש לעשות אופימשטאטא חוץ מדעתו של אפרכוס; read **איפומנימאטא**, At that hour the Holy One blessed be He wished to give them the Law (Torah) ... It is like unto a king who wished to pass (lit: make) judgements without the knowledge of the *eparchus*. ▽ MsOxf 147: **אפימנוטא** (gloss above line: **פי׳ הערוך מראות**, ref to AC 1, 218a), MsSassoon 920/1: **אפימנוטא**.

(1) Clearly then are two traditions of the text: (1) **איפומנימא**: *ὑπόμνημα* (sing) and (2) **איפומנימטא**: *ὑπομνήματα* (pl). It would appear that the original reading was **איפומנימטא**, and that this was corrupted to **איפומניטא**, and subsequently emended to the sing **איפומנימא**, since the meaning "minutes" is usually in the pl, *τὰ ὑ.* (LSJ[9] 1889[6], s.v. *ὑπόμνημα* II 3 et seq). Furthermore, the pl use of the verb נקרין, are read, supports the assumption of an original pl form, (see Krauss, MT 5/1, 124 no285 n3).
Lieberman, JQR 35, 1944, 32–33, (citing, inter alia, Bickerman, Aegyptus 13, 1933, 346 et seq). The *ὑπομνήματα* correspond to the *acta* or *gesta*. See also Buxt 186, AC 1, 219a. (Contra Jastrow 58a: *ἐπιτίμια, τά:* sentence.) However, Prof Modrzejewski comments that first and foremost *hypomnemata* corresponds to the Lat *commentarii*, the official journal of an imperial functionary; thus *ἐξ ὑπομνηματισμῶν* of so and so (Egyptian prefect, *strategos* of the *nome*) = *ex commentariis* etc, extracts of the verbal case, a meaning well attested in papyri. See RAColes, Reports of Proceedings in Papyri, Bruxelles 1966.
(2) Lieberman (private communication Dec. 1981), following Jastrow 31b, and AC 1, 219a, argues that, though *ἐπιταγματα* (suggested by SachsBeiträge 1, 170; Levy 1, 44a; Fürst 41a and 69a) may be an attractive suggestion, it may be rejected, since the writing of *ἐπιταγματα* was within the normal jurisdiction of the "king". The writing of the *ὑπομνήματα*, the protocol of the trial, or the judgement itself, on the other hand, was usually carried out by the *ἔπαρχος*, who in the provinces served as a judge. (Contra LW 1, xxviii, ibid 2, 25a: *optimata*; Ziegler 154: *ἀποτίμησις*; ExR edMirkin 19: Syr: **אפומא** + Lat. *status!*)

The ref to Ar in the gloss in ExR MsOxf is, of course, a mistaken identification of our word with *ἐμφώματα (LW 2, 61b), on which see Zuntz, JSS 1, 1956, 139, and cf Syr, Brockelm[2] 26a. See Sperber, Bar-Ilan 16—17, 1979, 71 n36. Note that במגנימין in YRH 1. 3, 57b 28 (according to edprinc) is not to be emended: איפומנימטין, as suggested by Jastrow 176a. Indeed MsL has: בנומין, while SY 147_2 reads: בֵּינוּמִין. See LW 2, 159b, and reject all suggestions. Epstein, Mavo le-Nusaḥ ha-Mishna 722, suggests: *binumerus*, **binumus*, rejected by Lieberman TK 5, 1022—23, who thinks it may be a place-name.

Cf Lampe 1451b sv ὑπόμνημα 2a, Mason 96a, MM 659a sv ὑπόμνησις.
Syr: אופומנימטא, PnS 81, Brocklm[2] 41a; הופמנמטא, הופומנמטא, Bruns-Sachau 14_{11}, 15_{17}, PnS 997.

איפומניטא ↑ איפומנימא

איפופסיס ↓ איפופסין, איפופיס, איפופוסין, איפוסין, איפוסי

איפטייה ↓ איפטיאה

אפוכי ↓ איפוכי

◇ **איפטייה** (39) (1) consulship (2) (regnal) era (3) significant date from which an era is reckoned: [*]ὑπατεία

(1) NumR 1. 1: אבל מי שבא לגדל ישראל מפרסם אי זה מקום, אי זה חדש, אי זו שנה, אי זו אופטיאה לצאתם ממצרים, But he who wishes to enhance the greatness of Israel publicizes which place, which month, which year, which consulship [it is] after their exodus from Egypt. // TanḥNumBa-Midbar 1.
TanḥNumBa-Midbar 5: ... באיזה חדש, בכמה לחדש, באיזה יום, באיזה שבוע, באיזה אפטיא, באיזה מדינה ... הרי הפרכיא ... in which month, on what [date] of the month, on which day, on which week, in which consulship, in which city ... Thus, province (ὑπαρχία) ... // Ibid B5, 6—7: באיזה איפרכיא;NumR 1. 15: הרי נכתבה אופטיאה; YalkNum 684: איפרכיא (sic edprinc, from Tanḥ). Read: איפטיא, or the like, in all sources (?).
Sefer ha-Maasim, edLewin, Tarbiẓ 1/1, 1929, 96: כתב שיצא בלא איפטיאה חמן ואינו מחותם פסול הוא ..., A document which goes forth without a consular [date] and time, and unsigned is invalid.
(2) LevR 36. 3, 843_3 הרי הוא נימנה באיפטייה של מלכים, Behold he is reckoned under the era of the kings. ▽ באיפטיה, באיפטיא, בפיפודיון MsMunich 117 (?); YSanh 17 (10) 1, 27d 20: בפטייה; MachIs 1. 1, 1_{25}: באפטיא. (Cf BSanh 103b—104a.)
PRK 52b—53a, 100_{13} היו מונים איפטייה לפדיון בני ... היו מונים איפטייה ליציאת

מצרים, Reckon the era from the redemption of my son ... Reckon the era from the exodus from Egypt. // PR 15, 66b; YalkEx 190; PRK 211_4.

(3) PRK 52b, $101_{2\ 6}$ למלך שנשא נשים הרבה ולא כתב להן לא גמיקן (↓ גמיקן) ולא איפטייה. כיון שנשא אשה בת טובים ובת גנסין כתב לה גמיקן וכתב לה איפטייה ..., Like a king who married many women, but did not write them either a marriage contract or the era (ie did not make a significant date of these marriages). But when he married a women of noble descent and good family, he wrote her a marriage contract and the era ... ▽ איפאטיא, אפטייה, איפטיה // AgEst 2. 16, 23: איפטיא; YalkEx 190; ibidEst 1053.

Cf SifDeut 26, 38_3: אפו(ו)כי in apparat. ▽ אפטי, which has nothing to do with our word, and should be emended to: אפוכי.

The form in YSanh ibid, פטייה, is characteristic of Galilean Aram, in which initial *alephs* are frequently lost.

See SachsBeiträge 1, 117; KraussPR 69–70; idem MT5, 36–37 no60 n1.

On Sefer ha-Maasim, see Tarbiẓ ibid88.

ὑπατεία, also *ὑπατία* is the office of *ὕπατος*, ie consulate. The meanings of the word in Rabbinic lit seem to be unattested in the classical sources. However, for a similar Byz usage, see DuCange 1634. Cf Lat: *consulatus*.

In (3) perhaps the meaning is "largess", he wrote her a marriage contract and an additional largess. See, for this meaning, Lampe 1435b; Sophocles 1108a sv *ὑπατεία* 2; DuCange ibid.

פיפודיון in LevR 36. 3, 843_3, according to MsMunich 117, should perhaps be read: סינודין: **συνόδιον*, company?

אפופסיס ↓ איפיפורין

אפוכי ↓ איפכי

אכסוריה, כסוריא (45) exile, banishment: *ἐξορία* (sc *ζωή*)

LevR 18. 5, 411_4, 411_1: בשר ודם נותן אכסוריה, והקב"ה נותן אכסוריה — "צו את בני ישראל וישלחו מן המחנה", Man decrees exile, and the Holy One blessed be He decrees exile – "Command the children of Israel that they put out of the camp ..." (Num 5:2). ▽ כסוריא, MsMunich 117, כסיריא Ar (AC 4, 280a) etc. // YalkLev 567: אכסיריא (sic edprinc, where it appears as sect 571).

On כסרא in TrgJob 18: 13 (if this is the right reading, rather than ▽ בסרא); see LW 2, 293b-294a, Levy TrgWb 1,378b, Jastrow 656a. The problem remains, as yet, unresolved. KraussPR 116. The form כסוריא represents aphaeresis of *ἐ*–, see Gignac 1, 319-20, eg: ... *ζουσίαν* (for *ἐξουσίαν*) PAbinn, 63. 15 (350 CE). See further Lampe 500b sv *ἐξόριος* 2, Mason 44a, DuCange 1021. Not to be confused with Lat *exoria*, Maigne D' Arnis 860.

Syr: אכסוריא PnS 185, Brockelm[2] 19a.

Arm: *ark'sor-k'*, (see Hübschmann, ZDMG 46, 1892, 233).

אכסיומא (45) (1) request, petition (2) honour, rank, position: *ἀξίωμα*

(1) MidPs 102. 2, 430: "ה' שמעה תפלתי" — אל תתן אכסיומא שלי בתוכה, אלא תעלה ותעשה פירות, "Hear my prayer, O Lord" (Psalms 102:2) – Do not grant my request within it, but let her rise and bear fruit. (An obscure passage, possibly out of place, see ed n12 ad loc.) // MachPs 102. 6, 2. 126.
MidPs 6. 10, 62: מלך בשר ודם אחרים מקבלין אכסיומא שמושיטין לו, ואני איני מבקש אלא [supply: שתקבל] אכסיומא שלי, לכן נאמר "ה' תפלתי יקח", [In the case of] a king of flesh and blood, others receive the petition presented to him. While I request only [that you receive my] petition. Therefore it is stated, "The Lord will receive my prayer" (Psalms 6:10). ▽ אכסיומיא, MsVat76, בכיומין, ככסיומין, בכסיומין, אנסיומין, אנסיומא. Read: אכסיומא, and אכסיומין (pl). // MachPs 16. 12, 1. 39: אכסיומיא.

(2) GenR 97. 2, 1241_{17}: [נטל] אכסיומה מן המלכות. כד הוה עלל לביתיה, הווה סביה קאים ליה מן קודמוי, בשביל לחלק כבוד למלכות, He rereived a position (of honour) from the imperial authority. When he would come home, his grandfather would stand up before him, to pay respect to the imperial authority.

See KraussPR 116.
On meaning (1), see MM 51a sv *ἀξιόω*; Deissmann, Bible Studies, 1901, 92-93. Since *ἀξιόω* refers to prayer (eg LXX Jer 7:16, 11:14), it relates well to the verse Ps 6:10 in MidPs 6. 10.
As to the form ~יא, in MachPs 6 and MsOxf 76 of MidPs 6, this is probably an example of vowel development; see Gignac 1, 310-11. Other examples may be found in **זיטימיא** in **ζητημια* (for *ζήτημα*), discussed ↓ **זיטמא, מיסתיוסיס** (↓) (for *μίσθωσις*), etc.

Syr: אכסיומא, PnS 186.

אוני ↑ אנאת

אגוריאות ↑ אנגריאות

אנדוכתרי (64) manumission of slave by *manumissio vindicta*: **vindicatori<a>*?

BGit 20a: עבד שיצא בכתב שעל גבי טבלא ופינקס יצא לחרות, אבל לא בכתב שעל גבי כיפה ואנדוכתרי, A slave who has achieved his liberty through writing on a *tabula* or *πίναξ* (tablet), is duly manumitted; but not one for whom the writing is on a cap or **vindicatoria*. ▽ TosRid ad loc (edLiss, Jerusalem 1977, 53): ואנדרכתי, אנדרכתן. // YGit 4. 4, 45d43: הרנירק טיאונוס (↓), and Avadim 3. 11: אנטוקטא (↓).

Jastrow, REJ 7 (no 13), 1883, 150-52; Pineles, Darko shel Torah, Vienna 1861, 75; Brüll Jahrb 4, 1879, 112; idem, ibid 5, 1883, 119; Krauss, LW 1, 268; idem, TA 2, 99; Juster, Les Juifs 2, 83-84; AC 8 Add 27; ACSup 36a; Jastrow 81b.
For the fullest explanation and discussion, see Urbach, Papers of the Institute of Jewish Studies London, Jerusalem 1964, 59-60 = Zion, 25, 1960, 172. The Pehl etym in AC 1, 140ab is rejected by Bacher, ZDMG 42, 506. Soo too reject Dalman 121b.
See OhGGit 39 (ThGHarkavy 185). Note *vindiator*: liberator, in Maigne D'Arnis 2302 (VetGl); *οὐϊνδικάριος*, IGRom 3. 801. 20, 802. 25 (Syllium), slave emancipated by *vindicta*, LSJSupple 111b; Mason 73a; Cameron, AJP 52, 1931, 262.

Cf ↓ **אנטוקטא** and **הרנירק טיאונוס**.

אגדיקוס ↑ אנדיקוס

אנטוקטא (64) rod for symbolic gestures in manumission: *οὐινδίκτα* ← (*manumissio*) *vindicta*

Avadim 3. 11, edKircheim 30, edKanievsky 172: ... **יוצא באנטוקטא**, [A slave] achieves his freedom by the *vindicta* ... Partial // BGit 20a: **אנדוכתרי** (↑), and YGit 4. 4, 45d43: **הרנירק טיאונוס** (↓).

Jastrow, REJ 7 (no 13), 1883, 150-52; Krauss, LW 1, 267-68; Pineles, Darka shel Torah, Vienna 1861, 75; Brüll, Jahrb 5, 1883, 119.
See Berger 767 sv Vindicta, perhaps from *vim dicere, vis dicta*.
On T instead of D, see Gignac 1, 81-82; eg *ἐντεκάτης* (for *ἐνδεκάτης*) SB 5273, 487 CE, *κοντούκτορσι* (for *conductor*) OBeattyPanop 1. 60, 63?, 298 CE. For *οὐι(ν)δίκτα*, see LSJSupple 110b, citing PGnom 21. 64 (II CE). Cf DuCange 187: *βενδίκτα*.

Cf ↑ **אנדוכתרי** (with bibl), and ↓ **הרנירק טיאונוס**.

אנטיגרפון (69) copy, of a document: *ἀντίγραφον*

EstR 3. 14: **אנטיגרפון דאגרתא** (sic), copy of the letter, or imperial edict (transl **פתשגן הכתב**, in Est 3:14). So too in // (new) version of MidAbbaGurion, RabinovitzGM 169_{30}; TrgEst 3. 14: **ין~**; read: **ן~**.

Löw apud LW 2, 643 and 656b [read: *ἀντίγραφον ο* 69] rejected this identification, presumably because he was not aware of the form with *~ον*. However, it is well attested; see LSJ[9] 154b sv *ἀντίγραφος* II, LSJSupple 16a: *ἀντίγροφον;* Lampe 152a, 1; Syr: **אנטיגרפון**.
This word is to be distinguished for **אנטיגרפא** (∇ **י~**, **ין~**, **ה~**, **יה~**) in GenR 67. 6, 761_4, 762_1, and in YalkGen 115, 564_{44}, where it means "a written reply": *ἀντιγραφή* (LW 2, 68-69).

Syr: **אנטיגרפון**, PnS 256, Bruns-Sachau 23_{24}, 25_2.

אנטידיקוס ↓ אנטידיקון, אנטידו

אנטידיקוס (69, 599) adversary in a suit: *ἀντίδικος*

MechRashbi 219_{24}: **נעשה להן אנטידיקוס נגד אויביהם**, he serves as an adversary against their enemies. // MGEx 23. 22, 545_{21} = Gaster Maasiyot LXV, 40_7.
GenR 82. 8, 985_7: **שהקב"ה דן את האומות מיושב מדקדק בדין ומאריך, ואחרכך הוא עומד ונעשה אנטידיקוס כנגדן**, for the Holy One blessed be He judges the nations seated punctilious as to the law and with patience. And afterwards he stands up and becomes an adversary against them. ▽ **אנטיריקוס**, **אנטידיקי**, read: **אנטידיקוס**. // YalkGen 136 (700_{24}), ibidIs 396, MachIs 3. 13, 29_{29}: **אנטיריקוס**, MachJoel 4. 11, 39: **אנטידו**, read: **אנטידיקוס**.
GenR 100. 9, $1294_{8\ 9}$: **מה, אני נעשה אנטידיקוס לאבא?**, What, shall I become an adversary to my father? ▽ **קנטרוקוס**, **אנטירוקוס** // PRK 126a, 271_8; YalkGen 162, $857_{50\ 51}$: **אנטירקוס**, read ~ד~; MGGen 50. 21,879_6; *Mishnat R. Eliezer* 131_9; **אנטריקוס**, read ~ד~.
PRK 122b, 260_8: **מעשה באשה אחד שכיבדה לדיין ... והלך אנטידיקוס שלה וכיבדו ... למחר אתת ואשכחת דינא הפוך ...**, Once there was a woman who "honoured" (ie bribed) the judge ... and her adversary went and "honoured" him ... Next day she came and found the judgement had been reversed (against her.). ▽ **אנטירקוס**, read ~ד~, **אנטידיקון**: *ἀντίδικον* (acc), **אנדיטקוס** (metath), read: **אנטידקוס**. // YalkIs 391.
DeutR 5. 6: **שאם רוצה הדיין להושיב אנטידיקון יושיב**, read: ~ין, pl, that should the judge wish to seat the adversaries, he may do so. Cf // TSanh 6. 2, 424_4, BShevu 30a: **להושיב שניהם**. (Or perhaps: *ἀντίδικοι*, pl.)
EstR 1. 12: **אפילו אנטידיקוס של בית אבא לא נדונו ערומים**; read: **אנטידיקי**, Even the adversaries of my father's house were not condemned while naked — *ἀνβίδικοι* (pl). // AbbaGurion 1. 12, 165, MsCamb 33: **אנדידיקי**: *ἀντίδικοι*. ▽ **קטידיקי(ן)** (cf ↓ **קטידיקון**). (Or perhaps for קוס~ read קים~, pl.)
AgBer 23. 3, 47: **יצר טוב שאין לו אנטידקוס**, the good inclination which has no adversary.
AgBer 63 (64) 2, 128: **שונאין זה לזה ואנטידיקין**, hating one another and being adversaries.

In GenR 100. 9, $1294_{8\ 9}$ the ▽ **קנטרוקוס** and **קנטירוקוס** should be read: **קנטרדקוס**, a mongeral form meaning *contradictor*, opponent (OLD 434b sv), formed out of *contradico* (OLD ibid sv) under the influence of **אנטידיקוס**.

In LevR 27. 5, 631_5 (apparat), according to MsParis 149 we find: **מפני שיש להם אנטיקוס רודפים אותם. כיצד? הנץ אחר התורים ובני יונה**, For they (the birds) have an adversary who chases after them. How so? The hawk [pursues] the turtle-doves and pigeons. Perhaps we should read: **אנטי[די]קוס**, opponent, adversary, or perhaps pursuer(?).

The form **אנדידיקי**, in AbbaGurion MsCamb, shows the $\tau > \delta$ change, influenced by the following τ

and the preceding ν; see Gignac 1, 81-82, for many examples, such as: εἰδώδω[ν] (for εἰδότων), δευδέρας (for δευτέρας).
BCohen, Jewish and Roman Law, New York 1966, 656, referring to Modrzejewski, JJP 6,1952, 245n52; Mm47a; ArndtGingrich 73b. See also MMoreshet, Bar-Ilan 11, 1973, 200.

Syr: אנטידיקא, PnS 265, Schulthess 13b.
Cf ↓ קטידיקון.

אנטיכריסיס (69) agreement allowing the creditor the right to use a pledge (usually usufruct of land) in lieu of interest: ἀντίχρησις

YBM 6. 7, 11a 40: הדא אנטיכריסיס רבית, *Antichresis* is considered usury; or, Does not this *antichresis* involve usury?

See AEhrman, Sinai 54/4-5, 1964, 177-84, and BCohen, Jewish and Roman Law, New York 1966, 437 (= MarxJubVol, New York 1950, 183), explaining: does not the hiring out of the pledge lead to the possibility that the pawnee may get more than the value of the loan and delay returning the surplus, which will be usury. Cf AGulak, History of Jewish Law — Talmudic Law 1, Law of Obligation and its Guaranties, Jerusalem 1939, 72 (Hebrew).
For *antichresis* in Roman law, see Dig 20. 1. 11. 1, and the discussion of Taubenschlag[2], 286-91 and Berger 364a.
Prof Modrzejewski refers me further to HKupiszewski, "L'Antichrèse en droit hellenistique", AnnHistDroit 27/2, 1975, 57-65 (Polish). And concerning the question of *antichresis* and *ribbit* (usuary), he refers to AWeingort, Interêt et crêdit dans le droit talmudique, Paris 1979, (which is the latest study on *ribbit*, but does not cite this Yerushalmi passage).

אנטלר ↓ אנטילרות, אנטילר

אנטידיקוס ↑ אנטיריקוס, אנטיקוס

אנטלר (72) one who has been authorized: ἐντέλλαρ<ιος>

YSanh 2. 1, 19d40: וימנה ליה אנטלר? הגע עצמך שנפלה לו שבועה, ואנטלר בשבועה?, Let him appoint for himself someone who he has authorised? Imagine he became obligated to take an oath, could the authorised person take [his] oath? ▽ SY $256_{25\ 28}$: אנטילר.

The reading אנטילר is borne out by a number of later occurances of this word in mediaeval (Palestinian) documents. Thus, Assaf, Mi-Sifrut ha-Geonim, Jerusalem 1933, 207_{10}, published a document from Ramleh, dated 1015, which reads: (↓ אפיטרופוס) אפטרופוס ואנטילר. Similarly, MAFriedman, Jewish Marriage in Palestine 2, Tel-Aviv & New York 1981, 455, published a document from Tyre from the XI cent (no 59 line 14): [ל]אַפִּטְרו[פ]וס ואנטילר. JMann, The Jews in Egypt and Palestine under the Fāṭimid Caliphs 2, Oxford 1922, 356, document from 1034: כתב

אנטלירות (sic, according to correction in Assaf, ibid 205), letter of attorney. Additional material and references in Assaf, Tarbiẓ 9, 1937, 16, 196; idem, Mekorot u-Meḥkarim be-Toldot Yisrael, Jerusalem 1946, 62_{11}: האנטילר; idem, apud Meḥkerei Ereẓ-Yisrael, Jerusalem 1953, 112-16, etc. Lieberman, GH 10, referring to papyrological material where the phrases *ἐπιτρέπομεν καὶ ἐντείλομεν σοι* (PMasp 1, 198 no67124_6), and *ἐντέλλομαι σοι /καὶ ἐπιτρ/έπω* (Mitteis, GrUrk 1, 1906, 38_6) are to be found. He further compared this with the Syr: **אפטרופא או אנטליקן** *(ἐντολικόν)*, in Bruns-Sachau 10, sect 30, meaning power of attorney (from Leges Saeculares, Land, AnalectSyr 1, 38). See further Friedman ibid 458; N. Rakover, Ha-Sheliḥut ve-ha-Harsha'ah ba-Mishpat ha-Ivri, Jerusalem 1972, 89.
(Contra Krauss, BZ 2, 1893, 521, idem LW 2, 72a: *ἐντολάριος;* Levy 1, 109b-110a, AC 1, 146b, Jastrow 84a sv **אנטלי** [he emends thus]: *ἐντολεύς.*).

אנטריס a counter-statement (raised by the creditor in objection, should an attempt be made to collect a pledge): *ἀντίρρησ<ις>.*

YGit 4. 6, 46a31: ר' יצחק דהבן הוון ליה עבדיה. ערקין לבנותהון (read: כנותהון). אתא שאל לר' אימי, ואורי ליה: אוני (↑) אסור, אנטריס שרי, אפרכורים (↓) צריכא, R. Isaac Dihava had some slaves who ran away to join their old associates. He came and asked R. Immi who taught him [the following ruling]: Outright sale (*ὠνή*) is forbidden; sale reserving the right to raise a counter-statement (*ἀντίρρησις*) is permitted; surrender without document (*παραχώρησις*) requires further consideration. Read: אנטריס[ים].

Urbach, Papers of the Institute for Jewish Studies 1, 78n181 (= Zion 25, 1960, 181 n. 178), where he further explains that R. Immi permitted sale by *ἀντίρρησις*, inasmuch as the vendor in this case reserved the right of entering a courtclaim. (Contra LW 2, 72a sv **אנטרדוס**; Epstein, Tarbiẓ 8, 1937, 316-17, who emended to: אנט[יכ]ריס[ים] (↑): *ἀντίχρησις*). For loss of *-is*, cf ↓ **אפרכורים.** For *ἀντίρρησις* see PO 68. 11 = MChr 228. 11 (131 CE) – *ἀντίρησιν;* Preisigke 1, 139; Taubenschlag[2], 505, 534-35; Kupiszewski, JJP 18, 1974, 229-35.

אילוגין ↑ אנלגין

אנקלווסים [אנקלינטוס] (75) period of tenancy, lease: *inquilinatus*

YBM 8. 11, 11d35: ..... המשכיר בית לחבירו וביקש למוכרו, אמר ר' אמי: לא על דעת שזה ימות ברעב. ר' זירא ור' הילא, תריהון מרין: מכל קנוי לו, אלא דו אמר ליה: שיבקיה עד מלא אנקלווסים דידיה, He who leased a house to his fellow, and wished to sell it [during the period of tenancy], R. Ammi said: [He did] not [lease it] thinking he would die of hunger, (ie, he does not have to starve because of his tenant, and if he has to sell it to survive, he may do so). R. Zera and R. Hila both said: It will certainly belong [to the purchaser, after such a sale], but he (the vendor) should say to him (the purchasor): Let him (the lessee) stay on until his lease expires

(Pnei Moshe). ▽ MsL אנקלופיס ,אנקלווסיס (Aggur 26), אטולמוס (Nimukei Yosef BM), אנקלוסים (Lewin, Ginze Kedem 4, 1930, 14), אונקלאה (Mordechai BM). Read אנקלינטוס. (Note // YPes 4. 9, 31b 48: (↓) ר' זעורא ר' לא אמרין: מיסתיוסים כאוני (אוני ↑) היא ונקנית במקח.)

Jastrow 88a. (Contra LW 2, 75b: ἐγκέλευσις, which does not have the right meaning; Levy 1, 144b: ἀνάκλησις; AC 1, 158b: ἔγκλησις, already in Aggur 26n133; Schorr, He-Ḥaluẓ 13, 1889, 113: ἐνοικιολεπτάς: remainder of rent.) For ▽ see Ratner, Terumot 60, and Pesaḥim 70, ACSup 40a. For *inquilinatus* see Souter 209a (Tert), and cf Berger 503a.

אנקלומה (75) complaint, reproach: *ἔγκλημα*

DeutR 9. 3: אין אדם יכול ליתן לפניו אנקליטין (אנקליטון read = I **אנקליטון** ↓), אין אדם יכול לומר לפניו אנקלומא, A person cannot place before Him an appeal (*ἔκκλητον*). A person cannot level against Him a complaint. // EcclesR 8. 8 (edprinc): אין מי שיאמר אני קלומה, read: אנ<י>קלומה.

לומר/יאמר (לפניו) אנקלומה seems to mean: to level a complaint, perhaps against legal procedure (?). (Contra Jastrow 88a: ἐκκαλοῦμαι: A person cannot say before Him: I appeal; and so too Schlatter 60, despite the remarks of JHOliver in AJP100, 1979, 557; AC 1, 159a: ἀνάκλημα, etc.) On η > υ see LW 1, 87 (where some of the examples require correction; thus קרונה is not κρήνη but κρουνα, Hesych, see Sperber, SC 14, 1978, 126-27, etc); Gignac 1, 264-65, numerous examples. See further MM 179b-180a.

אנקליטון I (76) appeal (to higher authority): *ἔκκλητον*

GenR 49. 9, 510_{14}, 511_{1}: בשר ודם תולין לו אנקליטון מדוכס לאיפרכוס, מאיפרכוס לאיסטרטלטיס. ואת מפני שאין לך מי יתלה לך אנקליטון, לא תעשה משפט?, [In the case of] flesh and blood, they suspend an appeal from the *dux* to the *eparchus*, [and] from the *eparchus* to the *στρατηλάτης*. But You, because You have no one who could suspend their appeal for You, will you not do justice, (ie there is no higher instance of appeal above You). ▽ אונקליטון, read: ~אינ; אנקליטין, read: ~טון; סנקליטון (see discussion below); **אנקריטירין** (↓). // YalkGen 83, 378_{82}: ▽ אנקלוטי אנקליטון.

TanḥLev Tazri'a 7 (edprinc): לשלטון שהוא יושב בדין ומבקש לזכות או לחייב, הוא מתירא ממי שהוא גדול ממנו, שלא יתנו עליו אונקליטון לקומוס; read: אינקליטון, A governor who sits in judgement, and wishes to declare a person innocent or guilty, fears him that is greater than himself, lest they complain with an appeal to the *comes* ... ▽ edprinc and Venice: שנקליטון; perhaps read: ~אנ, or ~אינ, or = סנקליטון. // TanḥBibid 9, 37: אנקליטון. (יתנו, thus edprinc, and edVenice 1549. But edMantua 1563 onwards corrupted to ירננו.)

EcclesR 8. 8: (**אנקלומה** ↑) אין מי שיתלה אנקליטון, ואין מי שיאמר אני קלומה, There is no one who can suspend an appeal, nor anyone who can level a complaint. // DeutR 9. 3: ליתן לפניו אנקליטין, read: ~טון, to place before him an appeal.

See Sperber, Bar-Ilan 16-17, 1979, 14-15, (Schlatter 61). The Gk spelling is usually *ἐκκλ~*, but appears as *ἐγκ~* in Hesych (Latte 2, 9_{27}). The spelling ~אונ, read ~אינ, would show that we are dealing with *ἐκκλ~*, and not *ἀνακλ~*, as some scholars suggested, (eg Buber, TanḥB ibidn 56).
The word is found with two verbs: ~שלא יתנו עליו א (Tanḥ Tazri'a, DeutR 9. 3: ~ליתן לפניו א), and ~תולין לו א (GenR 49. 9; ~שיתלה א, EcclesR 8. 8). These Two usages correspond to: *interponere appellationem*, or *ἔκκλητον ἐπιδοθῆναι* (CodIust 7. 62. 36, in Gk epitome), and cf *appellatione pendente* (CodIust 7. 62. 9; cf ibid 7. 62 tit). See also Mason 42.
As to סנקליטון (and שנקליטון?), this seems to be a case of the prosthetic *sigma*, so common in all forms of Gk. See Pantelidos, Byzantinisch Neugriechische Jahrbücher 6, 1927-28, 373-81, and my remarks in Sinai 82, 1978, 162. For ס = ש, see my comment in Byzantion 48, 1978, 245.

This word is to be distinguished from אנקליטון II ↓.
Cf ↓ **אנקריטירין**

אנקליטון II (76) liability to charge, chargeable situation: *ἔγκλητον*

DeutR 2. 29: והוא נתפס באנקליטון, and he is caught in a blameworthy situation; or: one making him liable to a charge. // YalkGen 77 (303_{81}), and ibid Ex 167 (31_{43}): אנקליטון, ▽ אנקלימון (MsOxf), followed by Mussaf (AC 1, 159ab) אנקליטין (edLivorno etc). Probably in all cases read: אנקליטון.

אנקלימון, if not a corrupt of ~טון, may represent *ἐγκλήμων*, *~ον*, liable to a charge. (Contra Krauss, LW 2, 76a: *ἐγκλήματα*; AC 1, 159ab: *ἔγκλημα*, *ἀνακάλημαν*, cf DuCange 68; SachsBeiträge 1, 18; Schlatter 60.)
For *ἔγκλητον*, see PMasp 97 ii 5O, VI CE; PTebt 27. 14, II BCE, PTebt 1. 27. 4, 113 BCE. Cf MM 179b-180a sv *ἔγκλημα*.

To be distinguished from **אנקליטון** I ↑.

אנקלסיא (76) writ of seizure, from: *ἐνεχυρασία*

TBB 11. 5, 413_{25}: אנקלסיא, שלא מדעת המלוה. אבל אין כותבין אלא מדעת הלווה, A writ of seizure [may be written] without notifying the creditor, but it may not be written without notifying the debtor.
TBM 1. 7, 371_{33}: אונקליטיא, בזמן שהלווה מודה יחזיר למלוה. ואם לאו לא יחזיר לא לזה ולא לזה, A writ of seizure [that was found], when the debtor admits (its correctness), it should be returned to the creditor. But if not, it should be returned neither to the one nor to the other. ▽ אונקילוסיא, MsVienna and edprinc; Aggur 26: אונקליסיא, adding: פי' שטר חוב, meaning a bill of endebtedness. Read: אינקילסיא.

Jastrow 88a (which requires slight correction); Lieberman (private communication Jan 1981).

(Contra Lieberman, GH 7: ἔγκλησις [= ἔγκλημα], and Krauss, LW 2, 76: new *form* *ἐγκλησια. Despite the attractiveness of these suggestions, they must be rejected, in view of the attested meanings of ἔγκλησις. See also Lieberman, TR 2, 104 and 149.)

Lieberman further points out (ibid) that there is no need for emendation (contra Jastrow ibid), since χ > ק is not uncommon, see LW 1, 100 (and Gignac 1, 89-90, 92), and the R > L interchange is extremely common. For ~אי = ἐ, see Gignac 1, 274.

On ἐνεχυρασία in the papyri etc, see Preisendanz 276n21 (with bibl), 527, 534-35.

אנקריטיריון decision of examining tribunal: *ἀνακριτήριον

GenR 49. 9, 510$_4$ according to MsVat 30 (72b): בשר ודם תולין לו אנקריטיריון מדוכוס לאיפרכוס ומאיפרכוס לאיסטרטילטיס, Flesh and blood have the tribunal's decision suspended from (ie may appeal against) the *dux* to the *eparchus* and from the *eparchus* to the στρατηλάτης (*dux exercitus*). ▽ printed ed and Mss: אנקליטון (↑).

Sperber, Bar-Ilan 16-17, 1979, 15-16. See LSJ[9] 997a sv κριτήριον 2b and Mason 64a, and LSJ[9] 109b sv ἀνακριτήρ, ἀνκριτήρ (Dor).

Cf ↑ אנקליטון I

אסטו (78) Be it: ἔστω ← *esto*

YShev 4. 2, 35a40: אמר לון: האסטו שרא לכון מרדי, He said to them: Be it you were permitted to plough. // YSanh 3. 6, 21b7. (The *heh* at the beginning of ה־אסטו is the definite article.)

Esto (and later ἔστω) is found frequently as a legal and religious term, as in: *probe factum esto*, be it permitted, *ius fasque esto*, be it permitted by law, etc.

Lieberman, AAJRJubVol (= PAAJR 46-47, 1979-80), 1980, 379-80, referring to Nock, HTR 32, 1939, 83ff = Essays on Religion and the Ancient World 1, Oxford 1972, 481ff. (Contra LW 2, 78a: σίττε or σίττα, Krochmal, Yerushalayim ha-Benuyah, Lemberg 1867, 109a: *hasta*; SchönhakMil 5b: *justus*; N. Brüll, Jahrb 1, 1874, 130: ἴσθι, or ἰσταθω; Schorr, He-Ḥaluẓ 8, 1869, 122: Ἀσταδής; Levy 4, 241a: *heus tu?*, accepted by Guggenheim, Leshonenu 39, 1975, 62; AC 1, 167b: *iste*; Jastrow 328b: a Samaritan word, comp סטי (972a) and ה- : Oh, ... the perversion (of the Law); LGinzberg, apud ACSup 428b-429a sv אסטן: ἀσύνατος.)

אסטטיונר ↓ סטטיונר

אספיקולא ↓ ספיקולא

אספקטרין ↓ סקבטרין

אספקלטור ↓ ספקלטור

איסקבטיריי ↑ אסקפטריא, אסקבטריא, ~רין, אסקבטור

ספקלטור ↓ אספקלטור

אפיטרופיא ↓ אפוטרופא

אפיטרופוס ↓ אפוטרופין, אפוטרופים, אפוטרופוס

אפוכי (~כיתא) (100) (1) pardon, quittance, (2) reward (3) receipt: *ἀποχή* → *apocha*

(1) GenR 42. 3, 407$_{6\ 7}$: ... בו ביום נטלו ישראל איפכי על עוונותיהם, On that selfsame day Israel received pardon for their sins, (ref to Lam 4:22, "The punishment of thine iniquity is accomplished, O daughter of Zion..."). ▽ אפכי, אופכי, אפוכי, read in all cases אפוכי, אפופסין (↓). // LamR 4. 22, 154: איפוכי, ▽ אפוכי; NumR 13. 5; EstRProem II ad fin; RuthRProem ad fin: אופנין, ▽ edprinc: אפוכין (pl); PR 5, 20a: אפוכי; Ve-Hizhir 2, 104: אופיא; read: אופכיא?; TanḥLevShemini 9, from edMantua 1563 onwards: אפופסין (↓ אפופסים) (not in edConstantinople 1520-22); MGGen 41. 1, 690$_{19\ 20}$: איפכי; LevR 11. 7, 237$_{40}$: איפכי, אפכה, ▽ איפוסא, איפופסין MachJoel 4. 18, 45: אפיכיפין (perhaps read: אפופסין, ↓ ~סים), אפוכי.

(2) LevR 34. 1, 774: כ"ב פעמים כתיב "אשרי", ומכולן לא נטל איפוכי אלא זה בלבד. ומה איפוכי נטל? "ביום רעה ימלטהו ה'", Twenty-two times is it written "Blessed is he"; and from all of them he took no reward, except from this one alone. And what reward did he take? "The Lord will deliver him in time of trouble" (Ps 41:2). ▽ איפונין, איפוכין, read: איפוכין (pl), אפוני, אפרכו, read אפוכי. // YalkPs 740: איפוכין; MachPs 41. 5, 1. 241: איפוסין, read: איפוכין (pl).
LevR 34. 16, 813$_{4}$ (edVilna): אית בר נש יהב מגן? אפוכי דידיה הן היא? א"ל: גבי דוד מלכא, דכתיב, "פזר נתן לאביונים, צדקתו עמדת לעד", Does then a person work for nothing? Where is your reward? He said to him: With King David; for it is written "He hath dispersed, he hath given to the poor; his righteousness endureth for ever" (Ps 112:9). ▽ אפוסיתא, MsLondon (Margulies' main text), אופתיתא איפוכיתא, אפוכיתא, read in all cases: אפוכיתא; אפוני, read: אפוכי. // YalkLev 665: אפוכיה ▽ edprinc: איפוכיה; ibidIs 485 (354): אפוני; MachIs 58:12, 234$_{7}$. But PR 25, 127a: האוני: *ὠνή* (cf ↑ אוני), the reading preferred by Margulies, ad loc. Ar (Ac 1, 150a) and MsMunich 117: אנונא: *annona*, yield; (Kalla Rabbati, edHigger 208, word absent). (Could אפותיתא in MsOxfNeubauer 2335 be influenced by *ἀπόθετον*, store, treasure, hence: reward – a non-attested meaning?)

(3) YelamdNum 15:40, Ar (AC 1, 216a), GrünhutLikkutim 4, 38a n29: משל לבעל הבית שהיה שוקל בארנוניות וכותב אפכיות. א"ל אביו: הזהר באפכיות האלו, שכל חייך נתונין בתוך ..., It is like unto a landlord who used to receive *annonae* (produce) and write out receipts. His father warned him: Keep these receipts carefully, for your whole livelihood is dependent on them. // NumR 17. 5. But TanḥNumShelaḥ 15, edMantua onwards reads: אנפריות. ▽ edConstantinople: אפריות, read: אפכיות?

The form אפוכיתא seems to be a new Sem fem formation from אפוכי; cf אוני ↑ → אוניתא, טימי ↓ → טימיתא.

The forms איפוכין, איפכי, איפוכי (pl) may be mistakenly influenced by ἐποχή, suspense of payment etc. Cf Syr: איפוכי, אפוכי, אפוכא: ἐποχή, PnS 332. On the other hand, there are several examples of ἀπο~ becoming איפו~, as in איפופסין, see ↓ אפופסים.

The word אפוכי has two pl forms, masc אפוכין, and fem אפכיות. On אפוכי meaning "reward" (2), see Rosén, JSS 8, 1963, 62-63.

On YelamdNum 15:40, see Jastrow 100b, "and writing agreements of converting (security for case of forfeiture)". Such a meaning is unattested.

The reading in Tanḥ edMantua 1563 appears to be a learned emendation (by the scholarly editor R. Ezra b. Isaac of Fano), the word meaning some kind of deed to pay up in instalments: ἀναφορά (cf LSJ[9] 125b sv ἀναφορά II 7, and MM 39b, Jastrow 87b, where the meaning is probably correct, but the etym — 87a, Sem נפר, פרר — may be rejected outright).

See also LamentR 3. 13, 127: בני אפוכי ▽ אפוכו. // EstR 1. 1: בני אכפייה ▽ edprinc: אוכייפי? See Jastrow 25a. (אפוכו: ἀποχύ = ἀποχή, PMich 197. 24, 123 CE, Gignac 1, 264?) The text remains unresolved.

אפולוגוס council for the defence: [*]ἀπολόγος (?).

Rosenthal Piyyutim 86, 25_{18}: צהיל הוה ליביה דמשה וחדי דהוה אל רחום אפולוגוס דדה, Happy was the heart of Moses, and he was overjoyed that the Merciful Lord was her council for the defence. ▽ אפולגוס.

Rosenthal 93, 121. This is an artificial formation from ἀπολογία, (not grammatically correct). Such a form with this meaning is unattested in classical lexica.

אפוסיתא ↑ אפוכי

אפופסים ↓ אפופסין, אפופסים, אפופסים

אפופסים (~סין) (101—102) sentence, verdict: ἀπόφασις (~σιν, acc) → *apophasis*

YRH 1. 3, 57a 51, 52: צדיקים ... כבר נטלו איפוסי של חיים ... רשעים ... כבר נטלו

איפופיס שלהן; read: איפופסים, The righteous ... have already received their verdict of life ... The wicked ... have already received their own verdict ... ▽ SY $145_{1\ 2}$: איפופיס, אָפוֹפִים.

LevR 20. 10, 468_1: נטלו אפופסין שלהן למיתה, They received their verdict of death. ▽ איפופסין, אפופסין, איפופסים, read: ~סים, MsMunich 117: אפופסכת; read: ~סים. // NumR 2. 25; TanḥLevAḥarei 6, ibidB 8, 64, PRK 173b, 397_9, MGLev 10. 1, 220_{21}: פפסון ▽ פופסון, אפופסון, read: אפופסין. (In Sifra 44d this word is absent.)

ExR 18. 5: ... ידע אותו הסניגור שנצח. התחיל לשבח את הדיין שיוציא אפופסין; The attorney [for the defendant] realized he hd won [the case]. So he began to praise the judge, [urging him] to give the verdict ...

PR 44, 183a: בשר ודם, משמוציא איספוסין, אינו יכול לחזור בו; read: אפופסין, Flesh and blood, after pronouncing the verdict, cannot go back on his [word].

LevR 21. 1, 473_8: מוציא אפופסים שלו מיתוך פיו; read: ~סים, He has pronounced his verdict. // (= PRK Buber 174b); MidPs 27. 3, 224, MachPs 27. 5, 1. 179.

TanḥLev Va-Yikra 6, B 11, 7: נתן אפופסין ... gave the verdict.

TanḥEx Shemot 13: שנטלו אפופסים; read: ~סים, they received [the] verdict. // YelamdEx 3. 1, apud Ar (AC 1, 229c); LevR 11. 7, 237_5 in apparat: איפופסין. ▽ MsOxf 147: איפוסא; other readings איפכי (cf ↑ אפוכי); MachJoel 4. 18, 45: אפיכיפין; read: אפופסין (spelling influenced by אפוכי above in same passage).

TanḥBLev Va-Yikra 15, 9: נתפשו שניהם ועלו לבימה (↑ בימה), ונתן איפופסין לבן דעת, They were both sought and brought up before the tribunal, and he gave a verdict (i e pardon) to the sobre one.

DeutR, Lieberman 11: בא ליתן לו איפוסין; read: איפופסין, He came to give him the verdict. // PR 46, 187b: ניתן פאופרי; read: נטל אפופסי׳.

MidPs 92. 3, 403; MachPs 119. 44, 2. 224: איפופוסין.

DeutR 1. 6: נוטל איפופסין (ref to Lev 20:10), He receives the [death] sentence. // Yalk Deut 795.

PRK 187a, 454_9: ונוציא עליו אפופסין: we shall pronounce the verdict on him.

YSota 7. 5, 21 (17)d 40, 41: נטלו איפופסין שלהן למתה, they received their death sentences. // ExR 2. 4; CantR 4. 4; NumR 1. 8: אפופסים, read: ~סים; YelamdNum 1. 1, apud Ar (AC1, 229c), GrünhutLikkutim 4, 1b; TanḥBNum 7, 8; TanḥLevShemini 6, B 10, 28; YalkIs 363_1 ibid Ps 796; MachIs 60. 12, $245_{13\ 14}$. (Cf BShab 89a, and see Derasha be-Shevaḥ ha-Torah edAptovitzer, Jerusalem 1940 (Sinai 7), 37 n284.)

MidPs 9. 13, 89: מיד הביא הקב״ה פורפוריא שלו ודן אותם ונותן להם אפופסין, Forthwith the Holy One blessed be He donned his purple and judges them, and gives them [the] verdict.

MidPs 106. 6, 456: בא לחתום בקולמוס ליתן אפופסין, He was about to sign with the

read pen (*calamus*) to give the verdict. // MachPs 106. 63, 2. 168: איפופסין; YalkPs 864: איפופסיא, read ~ין.
LevR 6. 1, 128_6: // YalkProv 961. LevR 6. 2, 130_4 // MachZeph 5. 1: אפופ סים, read: אפופסים. MidPs 52. 5, 285. Tanḥ BEx Beshalaḥ 4, 56. // YalkEx 225 (226) 248_{73}: איפיפורין, read with MsOxf: אפופסין. TanḥLev-Tazri'a 9. YelamdGen 3. 1 apud Ar (AC1, 229a), GrünhutLikkutim 6, 106 YelamdEx 7:8–9, apud Mann 1, 99_{19}. YelamdNum 21. 21, Ar, GrünhutLikkutim 4, 59a. YelamdNum 27. 16, Ar and ibid 76a. YelamdDeut 1. 1, Ar and ibid 5, 87b.
See also Josef Kara's commentary to Lament (Kaufmann Festschr 1900) xiv, Lament 3:27: איפוספסין. ▽ איספוספסין, ibidxxiii n17.

There are two basic forms, (a) nom sing ~סים, (b) acc ~סין. (Cf ↓ קילווסין.) The word has been variously corrupted. Thus ~סין was thought to be a pl term and (possibly) substituted by ~סים. Or this was a miscopying of ~סים.
Sometimes the word is written ~איפו, apparently because it was thought to begin with ὑπο~. Note also examples of haplology and haplography. See Mason 25a, Souter 20a.
פורפוריא in MidPs 9. 13, 89 refers to the *toga purpurea* (LW 2, 435b–436a), the toga of kings. (cf my remarks in Sinai 79, 1976, 55).
אפופסרת in LevR 20. 10, 468, according to MsMunich 117, should perhaps be emended to ~סות, an unusual fem pl ending for this word.
PR 46, 187b: ניתן פאופרי ▽ edPrague: ליתן פאופרי'', is puzzling. Above we have given the editor's emendation (followed by Krauss in LW2, 102a, and Jastrow 101a.) which is not wholly convincing.
באיפרכוס in MidPs 17. 5, 128 // YalkPs 670: בהפרכוס, has nothing to do with our word, (contra Jastrow 101a). See LW2, 231b sv הפרכוס.

Syr: אפופאסיס, אפופסיס, אפפסיס, PnS 336.
Cf ↑ אפוכי.

אפותיסיס (117) supposition, assumption: *ὑπόθεσις*

DeutRLieberman 18: אפותיסיס לא קטלת, ובמה קטלת? On the assumption that you did not kill, but what did you kill with? (ie, a trick question on the part of a judge or interrogator,aimed at luring the defendent into implicating himself.) // DeutZ (Likkutim, ed Buber) 21, MachPs 37. 13; 1. 227, which latter reads: אפותיתוס, read: אפותיסיס. (The word is not found in DeutR 1. 17.)

Kohut, AC 8, Add 5a; Lieberman, DeutR ibid n18. (Contra Brüll, Jahrb 8, 1884, 147 n1; LW 2, 117b). See further Buber, Likkutim ibid n19; idem, Bet Talmud 4, 1885, 275; Rosenthal, Tarbiẓ 40, 1970-71, 179-80. (See also LW 1, 194 and correct accordingly.) LW ibid cites another example of this word from CantR 1. 9. However, that has nothing to do with our word; see Rosenthal, Tarbiẓ ibid 178-82: איפתיסיס (sic with Mss) = *ὑπτίωσις* = *supinatio* = a turning on one's back. (Contra Schönhak, Mashbir 1, 30a: *ἀβοηθησία;* Jastrow 58b: *ἱππόθορος*.)

אפותיקי ↓ אפותיקו, אפותיקאות

אפותיקי, הפותיקי (102-03, 231) (1) pledge, mortgage (2) deed of mortgage: *ὑποθήκη*

(1) MGit4. 4: ... עבד שעשאו רבו אפותיקי לאחרים, A slave whose master pledged him as security to others ...

TShev 8. 6, 201_{20}, 72_{31}: המלוה את חבירו ... בשטר שיש בו הפותקי, He who lends his fellow ... with a document containing a mortgage [obligation]. ▽ אפתקי, הפותיקי.

TKet 4. 14, 69_{45}, 265_{13}: עשה לה בית או שדה הפותיקי לכתובתה, He mortgaged a house or field to her *ketuba* (marriage document). ▽ אפותיקי, הפותיקי. (הפותיקו in Zuckermandel ed, looks like a misprint.)

Ibid 11. 1, $92_{4\ 5}$, $273_{2\ 3}$ ... אפילו עשתה מקצתה הפותיקו ... , even if she mortgaged [only] part of it ...▽ אפותיקי.

Ibid 11. 8, 95_{37}, 273_{30}. Ibid 12. 3,96_{24}, 274_{21}. YYev 7. 1, 8a 22. BBK 11b. Ibid 96a.

MechRashbi Ex 19:1, 137_{7}: לא עשיתיה הפותיקי, אלא נתתי מתן שכרה בצדה, I did not mortgage (the Torah), but gave a reward for keeping it.

(2) ExR 31. 6: לא תאמר לו: טול לך מנה ועשה מהם פרקמטיא וכתוב לי אפותיקי על שדך או על כרמך. למחר הוא מפסיד הפרקמטיא ואתה נוטל את שדהו או את כרמו, Do not say to him: Take yourself a hundred *denarii* and do business with them, and write a mortgage [document] on your field or on your vineyard. Tomorrow he will lose his business, and you will take his field or his vineyard.

TShab 8. 13, 32_{36}, 120_{17}: שטרי דייתיקי ואפותיקאות, writs of testament and mortgage [documents]. ▽ הפתקאות (pl).

TBM 1. 8, 372_{1}: הפותיקאות ומתנות, בזמן שהנותן מודה, יחזיר למקבל, Mortgage deeds and presents, when the donor admits [that he gave them], should be returned to the recipient. Cf BBM 19a: אפותיקאות ▽ הפותיקאות (pl).

The text in the MechRashbi seems to be saying that when one observes the commandments of the Torah, one is not merely repaying a prior debt (on mortgaged property, as it were), but meriting real reward. However, the // in Mech 206_{5} reads: פנגוס, with further // MGDeut 33. 2, 751_{2}: בטכס (=

MidTan 209), perhaps read: פנוכס; YalkMachIs 45. 19, 156$_{28}$: פוגוס, read פנגוס, YalkIs 325, etc, see LW 2, 464a, with bibl. Add: Hoffmann, MidTan ibid n400: *φέναξ*, ACSup 328b: היפו[פ]תנגוס: *ὑποφθεγγώς*. But Krauss, MGWJ 49, 1905, 93, prefers reading in MechRashbi. It would appear that there were two parallel traditions, one in Mech and //, which is as yet unclear as to its meaning, and the other in MechRashbi: *ὑποθήκη*.

This word is not to be confused with אפותיקי: *ἀποθήκη*, store-house, LW 2, 102b, sv אפותיקי I. However, see FragmTrgKlein Gen 24:10 (P): וכל שפר אפותיקי נ"א דיותיקי, and all the best *store-houses?* or: *deeds of mortgage;* another reading: testaments (↓ דייתיקי).(Transl: "and all the *goods* of his master".) ▽ אפותיקיה. Klein 252 was not sure which אפותיקי was meant. However, the alternative tradition: דיותיקי, in addition to the fact that all these "goods" were on his master's ten camels, makes it clear that it is "deeds", *ὑπο~*, that our text is talking of.

For bibl on this institution see NRakover, Oẓar ha-Mishpat 423-24; Berger 490; Taubenschlag[2] 277-85. See also Gulak, Oẓar ha-Shetarot 235-38; idem, Toldot ha-Mishpat be-Yisrael 1, Jerusalem 1939, 53-61.

Rashi (BBK 11b) and Ar (AC 1, 248a) give as popular etym: אפה (sic) תהא קאי, |the payment| will be from here.

Lat: *hypotheca.*
Syr: אפיתיקי, אפתיקא, PnS 338, 353.

אפיטרופוס ↓ אפטורפלין

איפטייה ↑ אפטייה, אפטיא

אפיטרופיא ↓ אפטרופא

אפיטרופוס ↓ אפטרופסין, אפטרופסים, אפטרופוס, אפטרופולין

אפיטרופסות ↓ אפטופסות, אפטרופיסת

אפיטרופוס ↓ אפיטרופא, אפטרפס, אפטרפין, אפטרפוס

אפיטרופוס (~אפו) (103-04) (1) guardian, trustee (usually of minors, orphans) (2) administrator (of estate, etc) (3) governor, procurator: *ἐπίτροπος*

(1) MGit 5. 4: אפטרופוס שמינהו אבי יתומים, A guardian who was appointed for orphans by their father ... TBB 8. 12-13, 409$_{26\ 29}$. Ibid 17, 410$_{46\ 47}$.
MBK 4. 4: בית דין מעמידין להם אפוטרופוס, The court appoints them a guardian.
Ibid 4. 7: שור האפוטרופוס, The ox of a guardian.
BPes49b: אין ממנין אותן (עמי הארץ) אפיטרופוס על היתומין, ואין ממנין אותן

אפיטרופוס על קופה של צדקה, One does not appoint them (ignorant people) as guardian for orphans, and one does not appoint them trustee for a charitable fund.
ExR 46. 5: ... משל ליתומה שהיתה מתגדלת אצל אפוטרופוס, It is like unto an orphan girl who was brought up by a guardian ...
SifDeut 11, $19_{5\ 6}$: אפיטרפס. ▽ אפטוריס, אפיטרופוס, אפטרופוס.
YKet 9. 6, 33b 7: אפטרפ׳, אפטרפוס.
TKet 1. 6, 59_{47}, 261_{22} // YKet 1. 8, 25d 8: אפיטרופוס; BKet 13b: אפוטרופוס; BḤul 11b; BNid 30b.
GenR 98. 2, 1250_{7}: עשאו לאפוטרופוס על בניו, He appointed him as a guardian over his children.
MidPs 78. 17, 355 // ibid 105. 10, 452; PRK 64b, 127_{11}; YalkPs 820; ibidEx 186, 108_{59}.
YBM 3. 3, 9a 47: והוא שנתן לו רשות לעשות בה אפיטרופא, And it is a case when he gave him permission to appoint an guardian for her, (Aram term).
BBM 39a: אפיטרופוס, ~פא.
BGit 52b. TBK 4. 4, 352_{6}. YTer 1. 1, 40b 45-50. MBB 3. 3: והאפיטרופין pl. TOhol 17. 4, 615_{14}: האפיטרופין. TShek 1. 8 202_{26}, 174_{13}: אפיטרופין. ▽ אפטרופין. MPes 8. 1: אפטרופסים. ▽ ~פסין, ~פין. // TPes 7. 3, 176_{11}, 166_{17}: אפיטרופין. ▽ ~פוס; YPes 8. 1, 35d 37: הפיטרופין. TBeẓa 4. 9, $303_{43\ 44}$, $208_{10\ 11}$: אפטרופין. ▽ אפטרופוס, אפוטרופוס, אַפְטְרְפוס. TYev 9. 2, 28_{18}, 250_{23}: אפיטרופין. TTer 5. 7, 130_{29}, 33_{7}: אפטרפין. MShevu 7. 8: והאפוטרופין // YelamdDeut, apud Koveẓ al Yad, NS 6/1, 1966, 66.
Common in Gaon lit with this meaning, e g Shaare Ẓedek 9b 9ff, 65a מ״ז; Cassel 5ab; Coronel 48; Assaf, Toratan shel Rishonim 2, 9, 13 etc. See Gulak, Oẓar ha-Shetarot 140-48; Shetarot le-Rav Hai, edAssaf, 49 etc.

(2) YBM 5. 7, 10c 29-30: ישראל שמינה גוי אפיטרופא ... וגוי שמינה ישראל ... אפיטרופא, A Jew who appointed a Gentile as administrator ... and a Gentile who appointed a Jew as an administrator ... // TBM 5. 20, $382_{26\ 27}$: ישראל שנעשה לגוי אפיטרופוס או סַנְטֵר ... A Jew who became an administrator or *saltuarius* for a gentile ...
TrgYGen 41:40 (and MsNeofiti): אפיטרופוס על ביתי (transl: על ביתי). TrgJGen 43:19 (and MsNeofiti): אפיטרופוס על בית יוסף (transl: על בית יוסף).
Also FragmTrgKleinGen 39:4 (and TrgY), 39:14.

(3) GenR 6. 4, 43_{4}: למלך שהיו לו ב׳ אפיטרופים, אחד שלט בעיר ואחד במדינה, Like aking who had two governors, one ruled over the city, the other over the countryside. ▽ אפוטרופסים // YalkGen 9, 30_{2}: אפוטרופסין, ▽ אפטרופולין edprinc,

אפטרופין MsOxf; MGEx 24. 14, 559_{13}: אפוטרפין (see below): MidPs 24. 5. 204: אפיטרופין // YalkPs 697. (Cf GenR 50. 12, 530_7 edprinc: פיטרופין, cf ↓ פטרון.)
TBB 2. 10, 400_{15}: זה אפיטרופוס שממונה על ידי כולן. שאין שבחו של מלך להיות שנים עשר משמשין אותו, אלא שנים עשר משמשין את האחד והאחד משמש את המלך, This is the governor who is appointed by all of them. For it is not seemly for a king to have twelve [people] attending him. Rather the twelve attend one, and the one attends the king.
BShab 121a: מפני אפיטרופוס של מלך, because of the king's governor.
BSuk 27a: אפוטרופוס של אגריפס המלך, King Agrippa's governor.
SifNum 103, 102_{15}. SifDeut 306, 331_2: אפוטרופים ▽ ~פסין, ~פוס.
PRK 95b, 161_7: אילין אפוטרופיא דנפקין לקריית' ובזין לאריסייה, These procurators who go out to the villages and extort (taxes) from the tenants;(Aram pl term). // TanḥDeutRe'e 10: אפטרפס, perhaps read: ~פס' (= ~פסין). ▽ edprinc: אפטרופא.
(// in ExR 31. 17 has: הגמונים ודוכסים ואפרכין.)
LamR 5. 12, 157: אפטרופא. ▽ אפיטרופא; (Aram sing term).
MGEx 32. 11, $684_{5\ 6}$: משל למלך ששלח אפיטרופוס, It is like unto a king who sent a governor. (Source of this text unknown.)
Mech 17. 14, 182_{13}: קלידיקוס מבטל על ידו ... אפטרופוס גוזר גזירה, When the procurator issues a decree, [only] the *chiliarch* (tribune) can make him revoke it. (Read: כלירכוס with MssOxf and Munich.)

TrgYGen 41: 34 (and MsNeofiti): אפוטרופין על ארעא (transl: פקידים על הארץ), governors over the Lord. ▽ FragmTrgKlein (v): אפיטרופו (sing, though MT pl).
Ibid 4: 35 (not in MsNeofiti): תחות אפטרופין דפרעה, under the governors of Pharoah. Trg1Est 1:8, ibid 2:3.

The word is extremely common and appears in a variety of forms: sing, ~אפי, ~אפ, ~אפט, ~פוס, ~פא (Aram sing term); pl, ~פים, ~פין, ~פסין, ~פיא (Aram pl term). The confusion between ~אפי (ἐπι~) and ~אפו (ἀπο~) occurs in Rabbinic Graecitas, e g, אפומליטים for ἐπιμελητής (LW 2, 106b). Cf LW 1, 194 (which, however, requires some correction; thus אפותיסים is not ἐπίθεσις, but ὑπόθεσις, cf ↑ אפותיסים).
The form הפיטרופין in YPes 8. 1, 35d37, is an example of aphaeresis of ἐ~ (LW 1, 123, ibid 2, 104a). Cf Gignac 1, 320: τοῦ 'πιτρόπου (for ἐπιτρόπου), PMerton 26. 13, corr 11, 15, 16 (274 CE), and cf Syr: פיטרופא, Brockelm 565b.
On Mech 182_{13}, see Frankel, MGWJ 3, 1854, 192-93, (which, however, requires correction).
On FragmTrgKlein 41:34, see Klein 252, and corr meaning.
See also BacherTanJer 94 for an interesting false etymology relating the word to πατήρ and παῖς.
As to אפטרופולין in YalkGen 9, 30_2 and אפטורפלין in MGGen 24. 14, 559_{13}, this should be corrected to אפטרופסין, with Mss and //. (Contra LW 2, 103b = פטרובולי, AC 1, 212b: πᾶτηρ πόλις. See also Levy 1, 140a.)
See Joüon 466; Mason 49ab; MM 249b; ArndtGingrich 303b.

Lat: *epitropus*, Souter 127a.
Syr: אפיטרופא, אפטרפא, אפטרופה, PnS 340, 1032; פיטרופא, Schulthess 16b, Brockelm[2] 565b.
Palm etc, LidzbarskiHb 224, CookGloss 24: אפטרפא; DISO 21: אפטרף, and see MGBertinelli Angeli, Nomenclatura pubbica e sacra di Roma nelle epigrafi semitiche, Genova 1970, 133.
Arm: *epitropos*, Hübschmann 120.

Cf ↓ אפיטרופיא, אפיטרופסות, and ↑ אנטלר

אפיטרופיא (אפא~) (105) female guardian, administrator; new form from אפיטרופוס: *ἐπίτροπ<ος>* (with fem term)

MKet 9. 6: ... ולא נעשית אפיטרופיא ... ואם נעשית אפיטרופיא, and she was not made a guardian ... But if she was made a guardian ... ▽ אפטרופא, אפוטרופיא, אפיטרופא, פו~, פיה~.
TKet 9. 3, 87_{18}, 271_{21}: אין האיש משביע את אשתו עד ... שיעשנה אפיטרופיא, A man may not exact an oath from his wife, unless he ... makes her a guardian, etc.
YKet 9. 6, 33b 3-5: אפיטרופא, אפטרפוס, read א~.
BBB 144a: אפטרופא.

The Gk *ἐπιτροπία* and Syr אפטרפיא (PnS 340) have a different meaning, an abstract noun meaning "protection, guardianship". The form ו~ may be an abbreviation for וס~ (?).

Cf ↑ אפיטרופוס

אפיטרופיא, אפיטרופין ↑ אפיטרופוס

אפיטרופסות[0] (105) guardianship, trusteeship; new form from אפיטרופוס: *ἐπίτροπος*

TKet 9. 3, 88_{23}, 271_{25}: יצא מאפטרופסותו, he ceased to be a guardian. ▽ אפטרופיסתו, אפיטרופסותו.
TBB 2. 5, 399_{30}: יצא מאפיטרוסותו, read: מאפיטרופסותו.

The omission of the P in TBB may be a scribal error. But it may also be a reflection of the phenomenon wherein consonantal clusters are simplified in colloquial speach, commonly expressed in the omission of P before S, (Gignac 1, 65).
Also found in Gaon Lit, eg GaonHark 76, 77, 79, 134; Müller, MizMaarav 3a.

Cf ↑ אפיטרופוס

אפיטרפס ↑ אפיטרופוס

אפיסטון not trustworthy, treacherous: *ἄπιστον* (acc)

GenR 46. 10, 468_3 (according to MsParis 149): בשעה שיצא למלחמה, עשו לו סיעה אפיסטון, וירד מלאך והצילו, At the hour he went out to war, they (his enemies) made him (set him up) a treacherous escort, and an angel came down and saved him. ▽ פיסטון, פסטון, פושטון, פשטון, פוסטון. // YalkGen 82, 338_{26}: פסטון, with gloss: פירוש מערב, meaning an ambush.

Most readings have פיסטון with slight variations. This has been variously interpreted. Thus Löw, apud GenR adloc: *σεπτόν, septum* (most unlikely, and rightly rejected in ACSup 331a). Krauss, LW1, 230-31, 2, 468b sv פסטון explained it as *φοσσᾶτον, fossatum*. This on basis of comparison with TanḥLevTazria 9, B ibid 12, 40 (// YalkKings 230; פטשק; MachP 5. 15, 1. 34: הפסטין): כשבא מלך ארם להלחם בישראל, נתייעץ בעבדיו, ועשה להם פיטסים, ▽ פוטיסין, פוטסים, reading: פוסטון, where such a meaning makes good sense. (For such a metath see ↓ פיסטים.) In this he rejects Ar (AC 6, 378a sv פסט), explaning "ambush," as gloss in Yalk, but with etym; DeLara and Mussaf (AC ibid): *πεζῖται*; Fürst 174b: *πέζοι*; Brüll, Jahrb 1, 1874, 74: *ἀπόστατοι*; SchönhakMashbir 2, 54b: *πεζάταιριοι* (read: *~ροι*). Levy 4, 70a follows Mussaf, while Jastrow 1184a follows LW (who is, however, rejected by Basher apud ACSup ibid). Krauss' interpretation is further borne out by glosses in Tanḥ: בורות, pits or ditches, and in YalkKings: חפירות, diggings. (Buber's emend in MachPs, and his interpretation based on a gloss in Tanḥ edMantua: פי' כדים וקנקנים: *πίθος*, LW2, 440b-441a, may be rejectd outright.) Note further SIRappoport's identification with *πιστόν* (?) apud AC 6, 378a; (not in Erech Millin).
Whatever this word be, it is clear that אפיסטון in MsParis is *ἄπιστον*. סיעה אפיסטון may perhaps be compared and contrasted with סיעה של בני אדם כשרים in BKet 15a.

Cf ↓ פיסטון, פיסטים

אפיטרופוס ↑ אפיטרפס

אפיקלין (25) officials attending on a magistrate: *ὀφφικ<ιά>λ<ιοι>* ← *official<es>* (with pl term)

YelamdNum 23. 7 (apud Ar, AC 1, 231b, GrünhutLikkutim 4, 66a): לאשה שהכעיסה בנה וקבלה והיתה סבורה שמא בדברים הוא מיראה. שלח אפיקלין ובלשיין. כיון שראתה אפיקלין, הפליגה בדבר, Like unto a woman whose son angered her and she complained [before the magistrate], and she thought he was frightening her with [idle] words. When he (the magistrate) sent *officials* and policemen [to fetch her son], she changed her story. ▽ אופיקילין (ACSup 57b) // LevR 27, 6, 635_4 according to Ar (AC ibid): ... חמיתה דדאין במרזובתא ובמגלבין [ובאפקלין], חלת אפכת מיליא, When she saw he was judging [people] (or torturing them) with fire, pitch and whips, and through the *officials*, she began to change her story. (But // NumR 10. 1; CantR 5. 16; PRK 76b, 155; TanḥLevEmor 10, TanḥB ibid, 13, 92; MGGen 45. 3, 762; YalkMich 554, do not have this word.)

PerlesES 111, also noting that PnS 344 gives Syr אפיקילא, *regii ministri*,as "Sonat ἐπικλεής". Lieberman, JQRNS 35/1, 1944, 15-16, especially n102. He refers one to Cabrol, Dictionnaire etc II, 1111 n10, for information on the role of the *officiales* as investigators, searchers, torturers and arresters. (Contra AC 1, 231b: φάκελος,' following Levy 1, 148a, who in turn followed SachsBeiträge 2, 181 to 116.)
For *officialis*, see OLD 1243a sv officialis 2 (eg Dig 36. 4. 5. 27 etc).

Gk loanword ὀφικιάλιος (or more usually ὀφφ~), see LSJSupple 112a, Sophocles 827a, Lampe 990a, DuCange 1069, Mason 73a.
Syr: אופפיקיליאוס, PnS 86; אפיקלא Brockelm[2] 42b; (אפיקילא PnS 344).

אפירטין ↓ פירטין

אפוכי ↑ אפכיות, אפכה

אפרגל ↓ פרגל

אפרכורים [אפרכוריס] cession (*cessio*), withdrawal from holding (here: agreement to transfer slave, or land, in place of sum agreed upon): *παραχώρησ<ις>*

YGit 4. 6, 46a 31: ר' יצחק דהבן הוון ליה עבדיה. ערקין לבנתהון (read: כנותהון). אתא שאל לר' אימי, ואורי ליה: אוני (↑) אסור, אנטריס (↑) שרי, אפרכורים צריכא, R. Isaac Dihava had some slaves who ran away to join old associates. He came and asked R. Immi who taught him [the following ruling]: Outright sale (ὠνή) is forbidden; sale reserving the right to raise a counter-statement (ἀντίρρησις) is permitted; surrender without document (*cessio, παραχώρησις*) requires further consideration. Read: אפוכורים[ים].

Urbach, Papers of the Institute for Jewish Studies 1, 78 n181 (= Zion 25, 1960, 181 n178), following Epstein, Tarbiẓ 8, 1937, 317-18; Ostersetzer, ibid 9, 1938, 395-97. (Contra LW 1, 116a; Levy 1, 151b; AC 1, 240b; Jastrow 109a.)
For loss of *-is*, cf ↑ **אנטריס**. But perhaps in both cases read 'ריס (= ~סא or ~סיס).
For the prosthetic *aleph*, see LW 1, (122), 140: אפרדוכסוס in NumR 10. 5: *παράδοξος* (LiebermanGH 153), LW 2, 114a. See further Preisigke 2, 262; Taubenschlag[2], 228-29, 417-18; Berger 387b.

Syr: פרכוריסא, PnS 3264, Bruns-Sachau 21_2.
Cf ↑ **אנטריס**

אפותיקי ↑ אפתקי

אקוליתוס in good order: *ἀκολούθως*

[Not strictly a word found in Rabbinic lit, but included because of its interest.]

Berliner, Kovez al Yad 9, 1893, 4 citing a Palestinian marriage document (Ms Paris, BiblNatHeb 188, 611) = Gulak, Ozar ha-Shetarot 36: ובנימוס (↓) מיושר אקוליתוס, and in good order, *akolythos*.

Assaf, Sefer ha-Shetarot 59: בין בנימוס אומי עלמא בין בדיניהון דמרינן ורבנן אקוליתוס, where according to the law of the nations of the world, or according to the laws of our leaders and Rabbis, in good order.
Mann, Jews 2, 96_{10} (marriage document from Mastaura 1022) שריר וקיים אקוליטוס, ibid n2 (T-S 16 375): ובין בדיניהון דמרינו רבנו אקוליתוס.

For a full discussion and numerous additional ref see M. Friedman, Jewish Marriages in Palestine – A Cairo Geniza Study. 1, Tel-Aviv New York 1980, 44, 479-80; Kaufmann, MGWJ 41, 1897, 219-20; Rosenthal, P'raqim 1, 1967-68, 198-99 n61. (Contra Epstein, GKE77; Mann ibid, suggesting: *ἀκωλούτως*: unhindered; Gulak, ibid n7, suggesting: *aequalitas*.) Cf Gil, JNES; 1973, 318–20; Reinach, Mélanges ... Schlumberger (1924), 130.

For *ἀκολούθως*, see PRainer 1. 146 (VI CE?); Lampe 63b (citing HomClem 15. 9). The change from *ου* to *yod* (i) is due to an *ου* > *υ* interchange (see Gignac 1, 214-15), as is evident from the Lat form *acolythus* (DuCange 41 sv *ἀκόλουθος*, Maign D'Arnis 63b; but cf Souter 3b: *acolūthus*). The better spelling has a *tav*.

Cf Syr: אקולותיא, קאלותיא: *ἀκολουθία*, PnS 360, (and cf Gignac 1, 308: *ἀκλούθως*, etc).

ארכי ↓ אריכות

ארכיון ↓ ארכון

ארכי, ערכי (130, 418-19) (1) court, magistrates office, (2) archive, public records office: [*]*ἀρχή* (= *ἀρχεῖον*)

(1) MidPs 3. 3, 35: הדיין הזה בזמן שארכי שלו מקולקלת, אין עומדין לפניו בטכסיסי שלהן, אלא משונין ומטולטלין. הצריכין לעמוד דרך ימין עומדין דרך שמאל. הצריכין לעמוד דרך שמאל עומדין דרך ימין. וכיון שרואין ארכי שלו מתוקנת, עומדין בטכסיסי שלהן. התחיל אומר: אילו היתה ארכי שלי מקולקלת, לא היה כל אחד ואחד עומד בטכסיסו. התחילו "ויהי דוד בא עד הראש" הן כמו כן, והודו לו. אימתי?, This judge, when his office is disordered, they do not stand before him in the right array, but all strange and confused. Those who should be standing on the right stand on the left, and those who should be standing on the left stand on the right. But as soon as his office is orderly, they [too] stand in the right array. He began saying: Were my office to be disorderly, everyone would not be standing in his rightful place. They began likewise, and agreed with him. When? "And it came to pass that when David had come to the top ..." (2 Sam. 15:32). // YalkSam 151. (Note the clever word-play on ἀρχή = ἀρχεῖον and ἀρχή meaning "first place, sovereignty", suggested by עד הראש, "to the top" in 2 Sam ibid.)

In the form ערכי etc:

BGit 88b (line 22), according to MsMunich: היה ר' טרפון אומר: כל מקום שאתה מוצא ערכאו' של גוים, אע"פ שדיניהם כדיני ישראל, אי אתה רשאי להזקק להם, R. Tarfon used to say: Everywhere you find gentile courts, even though their laws are like the laws of Israel, you may not use them. ▽ printed ed: אגוריאות ↑ // MGEx 21. 1, 459_{21}: אורכיות, ▽ ארכיות, ארכאות. (TanḥExMishpatim 6: אגוריאות (sic edprinc), Sheiltot 2, Mirsky 1, 23_{12}; MachIs 1. 17, 12_{40}: אנגריאות, read: אגוריאות. Cf ↑ **אגוריאות**.)

BSanh 23a: בערכאות שבסוריא, concerning the [local] courts in Syria. // YSanh 10. 2, 21a10 (pl).

BGit 9b: והא ערכאות של עובדי כוכבים דפסולה דאורייתא הוא, But is not [a document from] a court of idolators disqualified by Biblical law?

BGit 19b: שטרא פרסאה דעביד בערכאות של כותים ... , a Persian document drawn up in a gentile court.

TanḥDeutShoftim 1, Bibid 1, 28: שאסור לישראל לומר לגוי: לך עמי לערכאות שלכם, For it is forbidden for a Jew to say to a gentile: Go with me to your (ie gentile) courts. // YalkPs 888.

TrglChron 2:17: מטול דזריז ית חרצוי בסיפא למסייעא ית דוד בערכאה, For he girt his loins with a sword to aid David before the court.

(2) NumR 9. 7: אף מי שהיה חתום עד בארכי ישנה של צפורי, Also he who was signed as a witness in the old archive of Sepphoris. // Ar, AC 1, 287a: ארכי. But // MKid 4. 5 = BKid 76a: ערכי.

EcclesR 1. 4: אלו נכנסין לארכי ואלו נשמטין מן הארכי, These (names) are entered in the records office, and these are omitted from the records office.

YGit 1. 5, 43d 4: קול יוצא בארכיים, a voice (a known fact) goes out of the archives, (pl).

YMK 2. 4, 81b 39: מראה לו כיסין של דינרין והגוי חותם ומעלה לארכיים, He shows him purses [full] of *denarii*, and the gentile signs and registers [the documents] in the public records office. Partial // in TMK 2. 1 (1. 12), 368_{36}, 230_{7}: לוקחין מן הגוים בתים ושדות ... מפני שהוא כמציל מידם, וכותב ומעלה בערכיים ..., One purchases from gentiles houses and fields ... because he is, as it were, recovering [them] from them, and he writes and registers in the records offices. ▽ ערכאין. // TAZ 1. 8, 461_{4}: בערכים ▽ ערכאים; BAZ 13a: בערכאות; BEruv 47a, 47a; BMK 11a.

TAZ 6. 2, 469_{21} according to MsVienna: וכותב.ומעלה בארכים, and he writes and registers in the records offices. ▽ בערכיים, בערכאין. Cf TBM 1. 17, 385_4: וכותב ומעלה בערכאים.

MGGen 47. 22, 792_{10}: נכנס לבתי האריכות והוציא הטמסון (↓ טימוס) שלהן, שפלוני ממשפחת פלונית ופלוני ממשפחת פלונית, והיה ידען, He entered into the offices of the archives and took out their register, [in which was written] that so and so is of the family of such and such, and that so and so is of the family of such and such, and he knew them. ▽ האורכיות, (pl form).

TrgJosh 15: 15, 16; Judges 1: 11, 12: קרית ארכי (transl: קרית ספר).

In the form ערכי etc:

SifNum 117, $135_{2\,4\,5}$: למלך בשר ודם שהיה לו בן בית, ונתן לו שדה אחת במתנה, ולא כתב ולא חתם ולא העלה לו בערכיים. בא אחד וערער כנגדו על השדה. אמר לו המלך: כל מי שירצה יבוא ויערער כנגדך על השדה. בוא ואני כותב ואני חותם ואני מעלה לך בערכיים ..., Like unto a king of flesh and blood who had a member of his household and gave him a field as a present, and he did not write [any document] nor sign [it] nor register [it] for him in the records offices. Someone came and contested the ownership of the field. The king said to him: Whosoever wishes may come and contest against you for the field. Come and I will write and sign and register for you in the record offices. ▽ בערכים, בערבים, בעדים, read: בערכיים. // Ibid 119, 143_5.

TBB 8. 2, $409_{7\,8\,9}$: כתב והעלה להם בערכאים, זכה להם הערכיים, He wrote and registered for them in the registry offices, the registry offices took possession for them. ▽ ב/ה־ערכים, also ערכאין, ערכיין in lines 8-9.

MGit 1. 5 (BGit 106b): כל השטרות העולים בערכאות של עכו״ם ... אע״פ שחותמיהם עכו״ם כשרים ..., All documents drawn up in the registry offices of idolators, even though they are signed by idolators, are valid ... // TGit 1. 4, $247_{27\,30}$, $324_{1\,4}$ ▽ בערכיות; BGit 9ab, 11a.

BGit 44a: ... מותר ליטול את דמיו וכותב ומעלה בערכאות שלהן, One may receive his worth in money and write and register in their record offices ...

EcclesR 1. 4: ״האבות״ — אבות? אלא אלה נכנסין לארכ׳ ואלה נשמטין מן הארכ׳, "[the chiefs of] the fathers" (Num 36:1) – Fathers [would have sufficed] (ie without "the")? But [to tell you] that these enter the records and these are omitted from the records.

See also BNed 22b: ... וספר יהושע שערכה של ארץ ישראל הוא, and the book of Joshua, for it is the record of ownership (?) of the Land of Israel. ▽ MsVat 110: שעירכה. (But may be from Heb ערך, order, "arrangement of the Land of Israel," JastrowDict 1118b.)

The two spellings ארכי, ערכי alternate regularly. See LW 1, 14 for *aleph-'ayin* interchanges, and cf the alternating forms אוניתא —, עניתא (↑ אוני). The primary spelling is surely that with an *aleph*. The spelling with an *'ayin* may be influenced by the Heb root ערך, to arrange etc, with its strong legal associations. So too it has been shown that the term עורכי הדיינים in MAvot 1. 8 ▽ ערכי, ארכי, אורכי; ARN I, 10, 43; YKet 1. 1, 29a52; BKet 52b, 86a; and cf GenR 50. 3, 519$_4$ (↑ ארכי יודיקי). // STGen 19. 1, 32: ערכי הדיינים, which is not directly related to our word, and where ערכי (עורכי) is an alternative spelling for ארכי~: ~*ἀρχι* ... (LW 2, 130a, sv ארכי I, chief, chief judge), is clearly influenced by the verb ערך, used in a legal context in the prayer to the High Holidays – לאל עורך דין. See EYKutscher, Words and Their History, Jerusalem 1961, 89-91 (Heb); SSharvit, Tractate Avot according to the Genizah (unpublished MA thesis, Bar-Ilan 1963, Heb), 37-38; HYalon, Studies in the Hebrew Language, Jerusalem 1971, 154-55 (Heb). But see Lieberman's remarks in Erchei 1, 1972, 108 (to Kutscher ibid44) on the influence of the *resh* on *aleph-'ayin* interchanges, with numerous examples, and see also JJHess, Zeitschrift für Semitistik, 2, 1923, 219-23.

Note alternative pl forms, in masc: ין~, ייך~, אין~, אים~, יים~, and fem: אות~, יות~. Cf LW 1, 181-82 for numerous examples of this phenomenon. It should here be noted that the pl form often refers to a single building in which the documents are housed, and thus corresponds to the Gk *τὰ ἀρχεια*.
Our word should not be confused with ארכי I and II in LW 2, 130a.
On NumR 9. 7, see BacherMeliẓa 26$_{44}$ and ed note ad loc.
On קרית ארכי in TrgJosh etc, see SachsBeiträge 2, 190.
On בערכאה in Trg1Chron 2:17, see Jastrow 119a: registration of legitimacy, citizen's list. However, I have followed LevyTrgWb 2, 245a, followed by LW2, 419a.
On the function of the public records office, see AHMJones, The Greek City, Oxford 1940, 239-40, 357 n55. See also MM81ab.
See also Lieberman's remarks in AAJRJubVol (1928–29 / 1978–79) (= PAAJR 46–47, 1979–80), 375, on the courts in the diaspora entitled by the Talmud ערכאות and not בתי דין, which were recognized by the government, and were supposed to judge according to Jewish Law.
Not to be confused with ארכי meaning "sovereignty", "office" (LW2, 130a sv ארכי II).

Syr: בית ארכא, PnS 385.
Cf ↑ **אגוריאות**

ארכי יודיקי (130) chief judge: *ἀρχι ἰουδικη (from *archijudex)

GenR 50. 3, 519$_4$: אותו היום מינוהו (ללוט) ארכי יודיקי, That day they appointed him (Lot) chief judge. ▽ (ה)דיינים(ן), עורכי (cf ↑ ארכי), ארקי.

Krauss, BZ 2, 1893, 534. (Contra Perles ES 135: *ἀρχίδικος*, Jastrow 568a sv יודקו, who reads: ידיקין, pl *judices*; cf AC 4, 1116 sv ידקי).
For the form ארקי: *ἀρκι (= ἀρχι)*, see CGL 3, 297$_{65}$: *αρκιιερευς*, ibid 70: *αρκιραβδουκος*, etc.
For ~*κη* term, see Krauss, LW 1, 236. Note that such mongrel forms are common in mediaeval Lat, e g: *archijurare, archijustitiarus, archiminister*, etc, (Maigne D'Arnis 195). See also Mason's discussion 113 et seq. As to ▽ עורכי הדיינים, this is under the influence of MAvot 1. 8, where there too are to be found ▽ עורכי — ארכי (↑). See the remarks of EYKutscher, Words and their History, Jerusalem 1961, 90 (Heb).

Cf ↓ ארכיקריטיס, which has an equivalent meaning.

ארכיון (130) (1) office of magistrate, i e court-house (2) public record office, archive: *ἀρχεῖον, archi(v)um*

(1) EstR 1. 3: להדא ארכיון דגדר, שהמלך יושב לדין מלמעלה וכל העם יושבין לפניו על הארץ, Like the courthouse of Gadara, where the king sits in judgement up on high, and all the public sit before him on the ground.

(2) PRK 27a, 48_3: מה עשה עמלק? ירד לו לבית ארכיון של מצרים ונטל טימסיהם (טימוס ↓) של שבטים, שהיה שמם חקוק עליהן ..., What did Amalek do? He went down to the office of the archive of Egypt and took the register of the tribes, in which their names were inscribed ... ▽ ארמון, ארגיון, ארכוון, read: ארכיון. // TanḥDeutTeẓe 9; אכיון; Bibid 13, 41; YalkDeut 938 (edprinc): ארכוון. (Not in partial // in PR 12, 52a.)
ExR 5. 14: אמר להם: המתינו לי עד שאחפס בספר שלי. מיד נכנס לבית ארמון שלו, והיה מביט בכל אומה ואומה ואלהיה ... אמר להם: חפשתי שמו בבית גנזי, ולא מצאתי אותו; read: ארכיון (parallel to בית גנזי), He said to them: Wait for me while I search in my book. Forthwith he went into his office of archives and looked at every single nation and its gods ... He said to them: I have searched for his name in my records office, but have not found it.
TrgYDeut 3:11: ... הא היא יהיבא בבית ארכיון ..., she is placed in the archive ...

(On EstR 1. 3, see ISHorowitz, Palestine and the Adjacent Countries 1, Vienna 1923, 192 n17, and reject.)
Mason 26a; ArndtGingrich 111a, DuCange 129 sv *ἀρχεῖον* 3.

Syr: ארכיאון, PnS 385 (suggesting *ἀρχείων* pl?)
Cf ↑ ארכי

ארכיליסטיס ↓ ארכי ליסטים, ארכי לוסטוסין

ארכיליסטיס (131) robber-chief: *ἀρχιληστής*

MechEx 15: 10, 90_6: לערבי ליסטים שהיה עומד אחר פלטירו של מלך; read ~ערכי, like a robber-chief who was standing behind the king's palace. // MGEx 15. 10, 302_9. GenR 48. 6, 480_{12}: לארכיליסטיס שמרד במלך, like a robber-chief who revolted against the king. ▽ ~ים, ארכי ליסטים, ליסטים (↓ ליסטיס). // MGGen 18. 1, 284_{14}: ליסטים (↓); MachHos 3:5, edGreenup, JQR NS 15, 1924-25, 163; so too in Baḥya's Kad ha-Kemaḥ, edChavel 181.

Ibid 75. 3, 882_2: לארכיליסטיס שישן בדרך, like a robber-chief who slept by the wayside. ▽ ארכי ליסטוס, read ~ים, ארכי ליסטים etc. // YalkGen 130, 643_{72}: ארכי ליסטס; ibidProv 961: לסטים (↓ ליסטים); MGGen 30. 4, 559_{18}: לכלב, like a dog! Ibid 77. 2, 911_3: לארכיליסטיס נדמה לו, he appeared to him in the likeness of a robber-chief. // CantR to Cant 3:6; YalkGen 132, 655_{18}; MachObadiah 5:18, 14: ארסליסטיס, read: ~ארכי. But TanḥGenVa-Yishlaḥ B7, 165: רועה, a shepherd. Ibid 38. 7, 356_{10}: ארכיליסטיס. // YelamdDeut, Kovez̩ al Yad 6/1, 1966, 72_{28}. DeutR 4. 5: זה הנער עתיד להיות ארכי ליסטים, This youth is destined to be a robber-chief.

~ערכי in MechRashbi represents the influence of the common ארכי > ערכי change. See ↑ **ארכי**. YalkEx 255, 345_{15} read: איסקלסקיטון, with MsOxf (bearing out Krauss' suggestion, LW1 131a, 87b): *σχολαστικόν*. Reject readings in edprinc etc: ארכי לוסטוסין, ארכילסוטוטין, which look like our word but make little sense in the context. ארכיסטרטגוס (LW2, 131b) in modern edd is a learned emendation.

See also LW2, 131a sv ארכיסטיס, that ארכי ליסטיס in MidSam 20 (124) is a corrupt emendation, and should read with // ארכיסטס: *ὀρχηστής*.

The word is common in later Gk, e g, JosBJ 1. 10. 5; PsCallisth 1. 36, PMasp 2 iii 22 (VI CE). See ArndtGingrich 112b. Cf similar *λῄσταρχης*, *~ος* (Hesych, Latte 2, 594_8: *λῄσταρχος· ἀρχιλῃστής*), and CGL 2, 56_{20}: *ducatus latronum. ἀρχηλῃστείας*.

Cf ↓ **ליסטים**

ארכיליסטיס ↓ ארכיסטס, ארכיסטיס, ארכי ליסטס, ארכילסוטוטין

ארכיקריטיס (130, 568) chief judge: **ἀρχικρίτης*

GenR 50. 3, 519_5 (MsBritMus): ולוט היה ארכיקריטיס שלהם, And Lot was their chief judge. ▽ Ar (AC 7, 196a): ארכי קריטיס .// YalkGen 84; LTGen 19: 1, 1. 86: ארכי (ה)דיינים(ן); STGen 19: 1, 32: ערכי, (cf MAvot 1. 8, and cf ↑ **ארכי**).

**ἀρχικρίτης* = *ἀρχιδικαστής*, and has the equivalent meaning to ארכי יודיקי (↑).
See EYKutscher, Words and their History, Jerusalem 1961, 90 (Heb).

Cf ↓ **קרטוס**, and ↑ **ארכי יודיקי**, which has an equivalent meaning.

ארכיון ↑ ארמון

ב

◇בורדילין (144) cudgels, lashes (for punishment): *βούρδουλ<ας>* ← *burdill<us>* (+ pl term)

PRK 81b, 178_7: מאה בורירילין אתה לוקה, one hundred lashes will you be lashed. ▽ ברדילך, בורדלין, בודולין Ar (AC 2, 185b), בורלילך, read: בורדילין. // YalkEx 225 (250_4) בורלידין, metath, read: בורדילך; but MsOxf reads: בורלולין, read: בורדולין. (// in MechBeshalaḥ 1, 86_{17}, MachRashbi 49, MGEx 14, 5. 257_{16} have Heb: מכות; MidProv 27. 2, 101: מכות, מלקיות; TanḥBExBe-Shalaḥ 8, 57, ve-Hizhir 1. 38: מגלבין, see above introduction n2.)
NumR 13. 4: ... וחמת שוטיא וברדליא והיא מדחלא, and she sees whips and lashes, and she is afraid. // LevR 15. 4, 327_2 apparat MsOxfNeub 147: בורדלייא, MxOxfNeub 2355: ~ביר (read ~בור); Aggur 36 (citing LevR): ברדלא. (Main reading in LevR ibid: מגלבייא, see above introduction n 2.)

Sachs Beiträge 2, 88 n87, and PerlesES 90, following Mussafia, referring to DuCangeLat 1, 781. Cf DuCangeGk 221 sv *βουρδουλίζειν*, (*βουρδουλισμός*). The first appears to derive from the Gk form *βούρδουλας* (modern Gk; Dalman² 64a gives *βουρδούλη*); the second from the Lat form *burdillus*. As to the etym of *burdillus*, one may reject Jastrow 149b: corrupt of *flagellum*, cf פרגל(↓), so also Buber, PRK 81b n35 (and in Aggur 36 n266), who emends כורדולי: *κορδόλη* (as suggested by DeLaraKK), and so also Schönhak 48b, Levy 1, 203a; cf AC 2, 185b. DuCange 221 explains: vox formata e *Burdonibus*, baculis ita dictis ... Cf ibid211 sv *βόρδων*. See also Krauss, Dvir 1, 1923, 92. See most recently ESRosenthal's detailed discussion in Irano-Judaica, ed SShaked, Jerusalem 1982, 123 n45.

בטאריקי ↓ קטאדיקי

ביא (148) (1) injustice: (2) perforce: (1) *βία* (2) *βίᾳ*

(1) GenR 93. 6 (10), 1155_2 בייא את עביד לנו, You do us an injustice. ▽ מעביר ... עלינו ... בייה, ביה, בזה // YelamdGen 44:18, apud Ar (AC 2, 45a); LTGen ibid., 1. 215 adds: לשון יוני ביאה לשון אונס; YalkGen 150 (151), 807_{99}: MGGen ibid 754_{19}; TanḥBGen Va-Yigash 6, 205, ibid ExShemot 18, 10; ibidLevShemini 5, 24; ibidDeutDevarim Add 1, 3; YelamdDeut 14:1, apud Ar (AC ibid): ביאה אתה מעביר עלינו.
ExR 20. 10: שמא אני מעביר בייא על ברייה, Do I (God) cause injustice to any creature?

ExR 27. 9: אם רואה אדם מעביר בייא על חבירו ולא ממחה בידו, הוא נענש עליו, If a man sees someone doing his fellow an injustice, and he does not rebuke him, he is punished for it.
YelamdGen, Bereishit ad fin, apud Ar (AC ibid), Grünhut Likkutim 6, 19a, no 55: ביאה עוברת עלינו, We are being done an injustice.
GenR 12. 10, 108_5: אין כל מקום ומקום שאין לו ממונה על ביה שלו. אגדיקוס (↑) במדינה ממונה על ביה שלה, אגבה בסטס (↑) במדינה ממונה על ביה שלה, There is no place which does not have an authority responsible [to redress] injustice. The *ecdicus* in his city is responsible [to redress] injustice; the *agba bastēs* in his city is responsible [to redress] injustice. ▽ בייה, ביא, בית, read: ביה. // YalkPs 794; MachPs 68. 7, 1. 327; YḤag 1, 77c54 abbrev; MidPs 114. 3, 471.
YelamdLev 13:24, apud Ar (AC ibid): צווח אני ביאה עליהם, I cry out "injustice" against them, (cf ACSup 83b).
LevR 17. 7, 387_8: בייא בייא, (a cry) "injustice, injustice!" // LamRProem 22, 17; DeutR 2. 20: בייא רבא לעלמא, a great injustice to the world; YalkEzek 346: בייא בא לעלמא, injustice comes upon the world.
BYoma 69b: בייא בייא (on Neh 9:4: ויזעקו בקול גדול, "And they cried with a loud voice"). // BSanh 64a.
(2) YNed 3. 3, 32a 28: כורוסתי בייה; read: כורדסתי, to give a present perforce, *χαρίζεσθαι βίᾳ*.

(1) AC 2, 44b-45a explains YelamdLev as a cry of woe or pain, *vae, οὐαί*. This may possibly be the case in BYev 97b: בייא בייא, not cited above, but unlikely for the other sources.
As regards GenR 12. 10, Jastrow 158b—159a suggests *via*, late Gk *βία*, highway, road; LW 2, 148b sv ביא I suggests *βία*, livelihood, sustenance. Reject both. See Wartzky, Leshon ha-Midrashim 190-210.
See further WDahlman, "*Ἡ βία* im Rechte der Papyri," DissCologne, 1968, on the specialized legal meanings of this word in Egyptian papyri, (cited by JModrzejewski, Archiv für Papyrusforschung 26, 1978, 208).
(2) LiebermanGH 34, cf ↓ כורוסתי.

ביא ↑ בייא, ביה, ביאה

בילאטירין council-chamber, *curia: βουλευτηρί<ο>ν*

YelamdEx 4:18, apud GS 1, 48_{15}: אותה השעה נכנס הא' בתוך בילאטירין של מדין, והתיר למשה את נדרו, At that hour the Lord entered into the council-chamber of Midian, and released Moses from his vow.

Ginzberg ad loc; but cf ibid31 where he suggests as alternatives: *πρατήριον* or *πραιτώριον*, suggestions which may be dismissed.

Syr: בולוטריון, PnS 467 (Brockelm[2] 63a). Cf Palm: בילוטא: *βουλευτής*, CookGloss 29, LidzbarskiHb 235.

בילה, בילון ↓ וילון

בימא ↓ בימאות

בימה (150) (1) elevated platform serving as seat of judge or tribunal, place of judgement (2) judicial tribunal (3) stage, elevated platform, for public meatings, etc: *βῆμα* (→ *bema*)

(1) SifDeut 9, 17_9: מלך בשר ודם יושב על בימה שלו, דן להריגה לחניקה ולשריפה, A king of flesh and blood sits on his platform, and issues sentences of death by the sword, strangulation, fire. // MGDeut 3, 24, 62_{19} (= MidTan 17); YalkDeut 814.
SifDeut 27, 44_2: מלך בשר ודם יושב על בימה שלו, מתירא הוא מפני דיתוכוס שלו שלא יחזירנו, A king of flesh and blood sits on his platform [judging and] he fears lest his successor will reverse [his judgements]
Mech 13. 21, $82_{5\ 6}$: ... פעמים שהיה דן על הבימה ... שנפטר מן הבימה, At times he would judge on the platform ... When he left the platform ...
ExR 30. 11: המלך יושב בבימה ... , the king sitting on the platform. Ibid41. 3: וישב על הבימה ודנו וחייבו, and he sat on the platform, and judged him guilty.
NumR 16. 21: למלך שעלה על בימה שלו לדון, like a king who ascended his platform to judge ...

GenR 76. 7, 905_4: אתה יושב על הבימה ודן, you sit on the platform and judge.
SifDeut 343, 394_6: ללוטייר (**ריטור** ↓) שהיה עומד על הבמה, Like an advocate who stood on the platform [of the tribunal]. ▽ עובר על בהמה (reject). Read: הבימה. // YalkDeut 951, MGDeut 33. 2, 749_{24} (= MidTan 208): בימה.
THul 2. 24, $503_{19\ 23}$: ... העלו אותו לבמה לדון read: לבימה, They took him up to the [judgement-]platform to be judged ...
YelamdEx 2. 15, Ar (AC 2, 107b): העלו את משה לבימה להרגו, They took Moses up to the platform to execute him.
TanḥExShemot 10. IbidLevVa-Yikra 6, B11, 7: העלום לבימה ... נתן אפופסין, They were taken up to the [judgement-]platform ... He gave a verdict. (Cf ↑ **אפופסיס**.)
DeutRLieberman 19. // Mach 37. 13, 1. 227; Buber, Likkutim 21. (See Lieberman ibid n6.) ExR 15. 12 (↑ **אילוגין**). Ibid30. 7. EcclesR 1. 8.
TanḥNumShelaḥ 12: ... למלך שעלה אדם אחד לבימה שלו לדון ... , Like a king before whose [judgement-]platform a person ascended to be judged ... // Bibid 22, 69; MannBible 2, 148, YalkNum 744. (Cf ↑ **אילוגין**.)

TKelBM 10. 6, 589_4: ... הכוסיות שבבמה הרי אלו טהורין, the chairs on the (judges') platform are pure ... Probably one should read: בבימה, as the passage continues to discuss the גרדין, read גרדון (↓), *gradus*.

(**2**) LevR 13. 5, 291_7: ... כאילו מצעת בימה ... , ... as though she sets up a tribunal ... // GenR 65. 1, 713_6; YalkPs 830; MidPs 80. 6, 363: כימיה, (but Ms ו: בימיה); MachPs 80. 25, 2. 46 (citing GenR ibid).
GenR 37. 2, 345_2: בימה של רשע, the tribunal of the wicked. (But // MachPs 72, 1. 40: עשו הרשע, which reading Buber preferred, ibid n4.)
YRH 1. 3, 57b 13, 15: העמידו בימה, יעמדו סניגורין (סניגור ↓) יעמדו קטיגורין (קטיגור↓) ... העבירו בימה, יעברו סניגורין, יעברו קטיגורין, Set up a tribunal, [and] let the defence attorneys stand forth [and] let the prosecutors stand forth ... Remove the tribunal [and] let the defence attorney be removed, [and] the prosecutors be removed. // PRK, 53b-54a, $102_{10\ 12}$; PR 15, 77a; MidPs 81. 6, 367; MachPs 81. 18, 2. 50; YalkEx 190, 123_{46}, ibidPs 831; MGEx 12. 1, $169_{6\ 8}$:

(**3**) MSota 7. 8: בימה של עץ, a wooden platform, (sic MsKaufmann). ▽ MsDeRossi 984: במה. // TSota 7. 13, 195_{112}, 307_{20}: ובימה של עץ היתה באמצע, and a wooden platform was in the centre. ▽ במה. // YSuk 5. 1, 55b 3; BSuk 51b.
YYev 12. 13, 13a 24: עשו לי בימה גדולה, They made me a large stage. // GenR 81. 2, 969_5, 971_5.
GenR 41 (42). 5, 410_4: בימה גדולה, a large platform. // Ibid42 (43). 5, 419_9, according to Mss in apparat; EcclesR 4. 13. (But // in TanḥNum Be-Haaloteḥa 9, B 17, 53; NumR 15. 14; YalkProv 961 ad init, have: כסא, a throne.)
MAZ 1. 7: ובימה (LW 2, 119b) ואצטדיא, and a *stadium* and a public platform. // BAZ 16ab.

Pl PRK 84a, 184_1: כסאות, chairs. But MsSafed: בימאות, platforms. (questionable reading). (// in CantR 4. 12. TanḥBExBe-Shalaḥ 5, 56; YalkEx 225; Ve-Hizhir 1. 36: תיבות ומגדלים.)
BMeg 32a: הלוחות והבימות, the planks and the platforms (in a synagogue). ▽ MsM: במות. // YMeg 3. 1, 73d 53: בימה ולווחין.
Cf Ar (AC2, 108b).
Note further MechYitro 192_9: ... תפסו את משה והעלוהו לבימה וכפתוהו והניחו הסייף על צוארו, they seized hold of **Moses** and brought him up to the "platform", and bound him and laid the sword across his neck. ▽ some Mss omit the word לבימה. Here the word בימה is used in the sense of *gradus*, the platform upon which the *defendant* is placed (↓ גרדון), whereas, strictly speaking, the בימה is usually the *judge's* platform. Lieberman (in JQR 35, 1944, 13 n83, 15 n77) notes that Gk sources too at times use the terms *βῆμα* and *gradus* indiscriminately.
(**1**) On TKelBM 10. 6, 589_4, see TR 3, 66.
On SifDeut 27, 44_2, see LW2, 198a: *διάδοχος*, Ziegler 155 n3: *δούκας*, Krauss MT 5 1, 160 no379 n5: *ἱερατικός*.
(**2**) On MidPs 80. 6, see KraussMT 5, 44 no75 n4.

On the various meanings of בימה, see Krauss PR 111–12, Lieberman, JQR 35/1, 1944, 13, Ziegler 111 n3, Perles, MGWJ 21, 1872, 132 n2 (Thron u Circus). On בימה — במה, Grünbaum, ZDMG 42, 1888, 254, and Jastrow 162a. See also BacherMeliza 50_{212}: ב' נומה, ibid51_{232}: בנומה; idem HebPers 78 n2 (?). (See also DeutRLieberman 19, and ed note 135.)
Meanings (1) and (2) are not always clearly distinguishable.
See further MM 109ab, Joüon 466, ArndtGingrich 139b, Lampe 296a sv *βῆμα* B.
Cf ↓ **גרדון**.

Lat: *bema*, $Souter_{29_a}$
Syr: בים, בימא, באם, באים, באימא, PnS 519, באמא, Brockelm[2] 68a: בימא, Schulthess 24b–25a.

פלסטיר ↓ בליסטרי

בימה ↑ במה

בנפקין ↓ בני פיקון

◇**בנפקין** (160) right of a person privileged by law (concerning the protection of his character: *βενεφίκ<ο>ν* ← *beneficium*

TanḥBNumKoraḥAdd 2, 96: לשושבינה של בת המלך שביקש בני פיקון מן המלך. אמר למלך: אם אינך תובע בני ייקון שלי, אף אני אומר ..., It is like unto the sponsor of the kings' daughter, who claimed satisfaction on the grounds of his privileges from the king. He said to the king: If you do not stand up for my legal privileges, then I shall say ... Read as the word: בניפיקין. // Ar (AC5, 367a sv נפק, GrünhutLikkutim 4, 42b, citing Yelamd, cf ibid 2, 127a): בניפיקין; NumR 18. 12 (a fuller version, deriving from a more accurate version of Tanḥ-Yelamd): בניפקין שלך (read שלי). (Not in // in Tanḥibid 8; Yalkibid 752; MannBible 2, 153, from YalkTalmudTorah.)

Jastrow 177b, whose definition seems more accurate than that of other lexica, who all agree as to the etym (except Fürst 84b–85a: *veneficus*. See also SachsBeiträge 1, 92). See Lampe 295b; Berger 327b; LSJSupple 30b: *βενεφίκιν*, PFlor 298. 49 (VI CE).
The best reading is surely our reconstructed one: בניפיקין, (which is how Krauss etc listed it).
The meaning we have given is based primarily on the context. It does not find precise attestation in the classical sources. However, closely related meanings are given in the lexica.
Cf בניפיקרין (LW2, 160a): *beneficarii.*

בורדילין ↑ ברדליא

קרטיס ↓ ברטיסן

בריות [בריוין] (152) brief order: *βρέουιον* ← *brevis (breve)*

PR 42, 177a: המלך מבקש להראות כמה אוהבו מכובד עליו. נתן בריות שיפתח הפילקיות; read בריוין, The king wishes to show how much he honours his friend. He gave an order to open the prisons (↓ **פילקי**). ▽ edPrague: בירין', read ביריוין.

Fürst 87b, who corrects בריות to ברייה, or בריויות *βρέβια*, *breve* (pl), followed by Krauss, LW ibid, explaining as a brief [royal] letter. The meaning of *brevis, breve*, is any kind of brief document, list etc, (OLD 241-42; Berger 377b). A common meaning is *epistola* (DuCange 226), but the meaning *mandatum* is listed in Maigne D'Arnis 355. The word appears in a number of Gk transl, the commonest *βρεβίον*, but also *βρέβειον*, *~ιον*, *~ουιον*, *υϊον*, Sophocles 318b; PLond 2. 41, 4. 9 (IV CE). See also Gignac 1, 69 and 232.

ג

גמיקון ↓ גהיקן

גממסות ↓ גמומסיות

גמיקון ↓ גמיקום, גמיסקין, גמיסקון, גמיסיקון, גמיטוס

גייס לוקס ↓ גוים לוקין

גייס לוקס (312) Gaius [and] Lucius, as fictitious names of witnesses and villains: *Γαϊ<ο>ς, Λούκ<ιο>ς* ← *Gaius, Lucius*

YTer 10. 7, 47b 30: ואילין אגרתא, לא גייס לוקס כתיב בהן, and as to those letters (of divorce), are not Gaius [and] Lucius signed in them? // YAZ 2. 10, 42a 35-36: גוים לוקין, read: לוקיס (גיוס or) גייס.
YGit 1. 1, 43b 4: גוים לוקין חתומין עליו, Gaius [and] Lucius are signed in it (in the letter of divorce). Read: גייס לוקיס.
PR 21, 107ab: גייס מן גודר ולוקים מן סוסיתא, Gaius of Gadara and Lucius of Sussita (Hippos) (two villains, adulterers and murderers). Read: לוקיס.

Lieberman, Texts & Studies, New York 1974, 412 (= Annuaire, 9, 1949, 412), citing Plutarch, QuaestRom 30, 271E: *οἱ νομικοὶ Γάιον Σήιον καὶ Λούκιον Τίτιον ... παραλαμβάνουσιν*, The jurists employ the names of Gaius Seius and Lucius Titius (as fictitious names). He adds (ibid); "This statement is, of course, corroborated by many instances in the Digest, but, as I have learned from Prof ABerger, Gaius and Lucius do not occur as fictitious names either of witnesses or of villains ... It is evident that the Rabbi(s) used the Roman legal terms current in the East." See also idem TK 8, 790 (and MAFriedman, Tarbiẓ 52, 1982 663 n13). (Contra Krauss, LW 2, 312ab sv לוקוס 2): *Λύκος*; Fürst 132b; Levy 3, 490b; cf Jastrow 236a.) Cf LW 2, 171b 603b sv גייוס, (and BGit 11b: לוקוס ולוס, LW 2, 311b sv לוס?).
גוים לוקין, lit: punishable gentiles, is probably a conscious distortion of these two typically gentile names, (just as אוך גליון, gospel falsehood, is a cacophemistic adaptation of *εὐαγγέλιον*, LW 2, 21a, Jastrow 27b).

Syr: גאיוס, PnS 633, BB 442.

גמיקן, גמיסקוס (~ון) (178—79) marriage contract: *γαμικόν* (neut), **γαμισκος* (nom), *~ον* (acc)

The term appears in a number of different forms, which have been set out here as follows: (1) גמיקן (2) גמיסקוס

(1) גמיקון
PRK 52b-53a, 101_{15}: למלך שנשא נשים הרבה, ולא כתב להן לא גמיקן ולא איפטייה (†). וכיון שנשא אשה בת טובים ובת גניסין, כתב לה גמיקן וכתב לה איפטייה ..., Like a king who married many women, but did not write them either a marriage contract or the era (*ὑπατεία*, i e make a significant date of these marriages). But when he married a woman of noble descent and good family, he wrote her a marriage contract and the era ... ∇ גמיקון, גמיקיאן Ar (AC 2, 311a). // PR 15, 76b: גהיקין, גהיקן, כתובה, גהיקן; read: גמיקון, גמיקן (? or ~קין, pl ? or *~κι<ο>ν*); AgEst 2. 16, 23: גמיקין; YalkEx 190, 122_{23}: גמיקון; ibidEst 1053.

(2) גמיסקוס
ExR 32. 2: מה אשה זו אינה יכולה למרוד בבעלה אלא ברעה היא יכולה לכפור בו. למה? שאין ביניהן גמיסקין, Just as this woman cannot rebel against her husband, but only against her companion can she deny him. Why? Because there is no marriage contract between them. Read ~קון, (or perhaps ~קין, **γαμισκι<ο>ν*).

ExR 47. 2: משל למלך שנשא את האשה וכתב לה גמיסקוס משלו ... אלא עשה לה גמיסקוס, ולואי אתן בו ידי. הה"ד "ואכתוב על הלוחות", Like a king who took to wife a women, and wrote her a marriage contract of his own ... Rather make you the marriage contract, and would that I could put my hand (i e signature) to it. As it is written, "And I will write on the tables" (Deut 10:2). ▽ Ar (AC 2, 311a): גמיקן: *γαμικόν* (see above), גמיסקין (read ~ון, or ~ין = ι<ο>ν). // TanḥBExKiTissa 17, 117: גמיטוס. ▽ גמוטות, גוויטוס, read: גמיקוס (nom sing); YalkEx 405 (404), 771_4: גמיקום (sic edprinc) read: גמיקוס (see above).

YelamdGenBereshit adfin, apud Ar (AC 2, 311a): לא נתחתם גזר דינם של דור המבול עד שכתבו גמיסיקון לזכר ולבהמה, The sentence was not drawn against the generation of the flood, until they wrote marriage documents for men (i e between two men) and with animals (i e legitimized formally such deviant relationships). Read: גמיסקון. // TanḥBGen Bereshit 33, 24: קמיסמסין. ▽ קמיסקסין; ibid21, 16: גמיקיסוס, (metath) read: גמיסיקוס (גמיסקוס). For a different text tradition in other //, see ↓ **גממסות**. Ar (AC 2, 311a n4): גמומסיקון, is perhaps: גממיסקין, with geminated *mem*. Cf ↓ **גממסות.**

The word appears in two main forms: *γαμικόν*, ~*ος*, and *γαμισκός*, ~*ον*.

The two seem to be quite interchangeable, *γαμισκός* = *γαμικός*, with medial *sigma*, so common in all stages of Gk. See Mayser 1/1[2], 180; Gignac 1, 131; Pantelidos, ByzNeugrJahrb 6, 1927-28, 373–81; and cf Sperber, Sinai 82, 1978, 162. (Note also the form *γαμίσκω* = *γαμίζω*, ArndtGingrich 1506.) Cf ↓ **פטריקון**.

גמיקין in AgEst etc may be **γαμικι*<*ο*>*ν*, *γαμικι*<*όν*> + Arm pl term, or a scribal error for גמיקון.

As to the ~קמיס in TanḥBGenBereshit 33, 24, they need no emendation. See, e g, BGU 975. 17–18 (45 CE): *κάμοι* (for *γάμου*). See Mayser 1/1[2], 143–44; Gignac 1, 77. קמיסמסין and קמיסקסין seem to be corrupt from קמיסקין. The ~ין term may represent ~*ι*<*ο*>*ν*, or a scribal error for ~ון.

The phenomenon of parallel forms with nom and acc term (~וס, ~ון) is common in Rabbinic Graecitas, (see ↑ **אפופסיס**).

גמיסיקון is an example of vowel development. See Gignac 1, 310-12; e g: *χαριτίνων* (for *χαρτίνων*). PBerlLeihg 9. 1, BL iii 29 (240/41 CE), etc.

For *γαμικόν* meaning marriage contract; see PO 903. 17 (IV CE), and see BCohen's note in his Jewish and Roman Law, New York 1966, 376. (Jastrow's transl, 253a, "did not order on their behalf a record of the nuptial act ..." is unnecessarily complex.) Note that the "unwritten marriage," *γάμος ἄγραφος* (see above ExR 32. 2), was only a provisional union (see MM 121b, Taubenschlag[2] 115–19), as opposed to the *γάμος ἔγγραφος* with its contract which was binding. See Ziegler 337.

Cf ↓ **גממסות**

גמיקון ↑ גמיקן, גמיסיקוס

גממסות ↓ גממטיות

◇**גממסות** (178–79) marriage contracts; from [*]*γάμος* (*γάμου* [*ὁμολογία*]) (+ fem pl term)

LevR23. 9, 539_5: אלא על ידי שכתבו גממסות לזכר ולבהמה, ... until they wrote marriage contracts for [unions between] male[s] and with animal[s]. ▽ גמססיות, Ar (AC 2, 311a), also גמומסיות (ibid n4), גמומסיקון (ibid, cf ↑ **גמיקון**), גמסיאות, גומסיות, גממטיאות, גממ׳, גלימסאות, נימוסיות MsParis 149 (↓ **נימוס**). // GenR 25. 2, 248_6: גמומסיות. ▽ גממוסיות, גמוסיו׳, גימוסיות, גממטיות, גמומוסיות (Geniza fragm, MSokoloff, The Geniza Fragments of Bereshit Rabba, Jerusalem 1982, 117_{20} [Heb]); YalkGen 44, 153_{56}: גממטיות. All these readings appear to be varying degrees of corrupt of a basic גמוסיות and גממוסיות (~סות), a Hebraized fem pl of *γάμος*. For a different textual tradition in other //, see ↑ **גמיקון**.

These forms derive from *γάμος* with different kinds of pl term (~ות, ~יות, etc), and with geminated *mems*. On such gemination see CGL 3, 511_{62}: gammos *nuptiae;* Mayser 1/1[2], 193; Gignac 1, 157–58; Psaltes 128. גמססיות in Ar (AC 2, 311a) may be an example of a geminated *sigma* (Gignac 1, 159), but is more likely to be a scribal error.
For *ὁμο(λογία) γαμου*, see PTebt 1. 104 (92 BCE); for *συγγραφὴ γάμου*, PO IV 713. 12 (97 CE). See MM 121ab, ArndtGingrich 150b.

Cf Syr: גמוס, BB 499.
Cf ↑ גמיקון

גניסיסים [גנוסיסים] judicial investigations: *γνῶσις* (+ pl term)

Sefer ha-Maasim, ed Mann, Tarbiẓ 1/3, 1930, 9_{21}: ואם רצו להניח, עושין עליה גניסיסים על מה שידוע שבין ידיה [כדי ש]לא תבזבז, And if (the heirs) wish to leave her (the widow, to live in the deceased husband's house, where she receives her maintenance from his possessions, rather than paying her the ketubah), they make investigations as to what is known to be in her hands, [so that she does] not waste it. Read: גנוסיסים. (The word **שידוע** may be an internal gloss.)

Mann adloc n9. *γνῶσις* in this sense is the equivalent of Lat *cognitio*, (see Berger 393b–394a).

Syr: גנסס, גנוסיס (different meaning), PnS 750, Brockelm[2] 126a.

גרדום ↓ גרדון

גרדון, (~ום) (183) (1) small platform (usually raised one step) on which the accused is questioned (and at times tortured as part of questioning), (2) court-tribunal, platform on which court-tribunal sits (= **בימה** ↑ : *βῆμα*): *γράδον* ← *gradum* (acc sing)

(1) TKelBM 10. 6, 589_4: והגרדין טהור, שאינו אלא ישיבת צער, and the *gradus* is pure, for this is only a sitting of pain (i e torture). Read: ~ון (LiebermanTR 3, 66).
TanḥBExBe-Shalaḥ 4, 56: נטל השבאי ותלאו בגרדק, התחיל לצער אותו, He took the captor and had him suspended in the *gradus*, and started to torture him.
PRK, 118b, 245_{14}: נטלו ותלאו בגרדון, He took him and had him suspended in the *gradus* ▽ Ar (AC 2, 359b): ~ום, // MachZeph 1. 5, 9: גורדון.
YTaan 4. 8, 6961: תליין בגרדון, ... he had them suspended in the *gradus*. // EcclesR 3. 16; LamR 4. 13, 49 (cf BGit 57b).

(2) MAZ 2. 17: אין בונים עמהם בסילקי גרדום ואצטדיא, One does not build with them (i e idolators) a basilica, a *gradus*, and a stadium ... ▽ ~ון MsKaufmann. Explained in BAZ 16b (by Babylonian Amora early IV CE): בסילקי ... של גרדום, i e a basilica for holding court procedures (questionings etc). ▽ גרודוס, גרדוס; *γράδος: gradus* (nom sing), see MsJTS, edAbramson 156b-157a.
BAZ 16b: כשנתפס ר׳ אליעזר למינות, העלוהו לגרדום לידון, When R. Eliezer was arrested for *Minut* (i e Christianity), he was brought up to the *gradus* (i e the tribunal) for judgement. ▽ MsJTS: גרדוס: *γράδος*. // YalkProv 938: גרדום. But // THul 2. 24, 503_{19}: לבמה; EcclesR 1. 8: על הבימה (cf ↑ **בימה**).
BShab 32a: כמי שהעלוהו לגרדום לידון, שכל העולה לגרדום לידון, אם יש לו פרקליטין גדולים (↓ **פרקליט**) ניצול, ואם לא אינו ניצול, Like one who goes up to the *gradus* for judgement. For anyone who goes up to the *gradus* for judgement, if he has powerful attorneys, he may be saved. But if not, he will not be saved. // YalkJob 919.
BRH 18a: שנים שעלו לגרדום לידון, two who went up to the *gradus* for judgement.
EcclesR 3. 17: ליסטים עולה לגרדון, ור׳ עקיבא עולה לגרדון, A robber (↓ **ליסטים**) goes up to the *gradus*, and R. Akiva goes up to the *gradus* (Ref to Eccles 3:17 "... God shall judge the righteous and the wicked".) ▽ edprinc: נרדון, read: גרדון.

LamentR 1. 13: לגרדום. ▽ edBuber 77: גירדה. MrPMandel (Jerusalem) kindly supplied me with ▽ from Mss: printed ed and two Spanish Mss (299 מ and 495 ק) have: גרדום; Buber, Parma 1400 have: גידרה; Sienna 18.vi. x has: נירדים; 164 א: גיבושים; Parma 1408 גידורי (?); London 1076: גידורים (?).
The meaning of the passage is unclear and the variety of ▽ further complicates matters. Clearly there is more than one textual tradition here. The reading גרדום may be explained if we assume that the text was originally adjoined to Lament 3:62, containing the words: כל היום as in ibid 1:13, thus, "the lips of those that rise up against me, and their device against me all the day," describing questioning techniques (see Lieberman, JQR 35, 1944, 24—27). In addition I believe there was another (corrected?) reading on 1:13: גירדה, meaning "prison". For Lieberman, GH 32 n62, found בית גירדא in EcclesR 4. 14, transl: בית הסורים (Eccles 4:14, "prison"), being an Aram transl of בית משיכה = בית הסוהר, jail. (גרר = משך, to take to jail, or into captivity, Lieberman, ibid 31 n62.)

This word is found in three forms: גרדון: *γράδον*, גרדום: *gradum*, and גרדוס (גרודוס): *γραδος* (or *gradus*).
The forms גרודום and גורדון reflect an *α* > *ο* interchange; see Gignac 1. 286—87; Mayser 1/1², 37 n4; Psaltes 5—6. For ~גרו >גור, cf טרולוס > טורלוס (Sperber, Bar-Ilan 16/17, 1979, 30 n47), *Κροκόδιλος* > *Κορκόδιλος* in papyri (Gignac 1, 314—15, with many other examples).
Lieberman, JQR NS 35, 1944, 13—15, 20; (cf Krauss, Dvir 1, 1923, 112). Lieberman shows that *gradus* = *catasta*, and that עלה לגרדום = *ascendere gradum* = *ascendere in catastam* (14), where לתלות בגרדום = *suspendere* (or *levare*) *in catasta* (15). And ibid13 n83 he writes: Although *βῆμα* (↑ בימה) and *gradus* are etymologically the same, they usually designate two different objects. But the sources sometimes use them indiscriminately".
For *γράδος* see LSJSupple 35b, Sophocles 337b, and cf TDrew-Bear, Glotta 50, 1972, 66.

Cf ↑ בימה

גרדון ↑ גרדוס

ד

דיאטגמא ↓ דאטגמא

דיוקטא ↓ דאיקוטטה

דיאטגמא ↓ דוגמיות

דוסים [דיסים] written request, petition: *δέησις*

PRK 167b, 382₁₃: לשנים שהושיטו דוסים למלך, Like unto two who presented a petition to the king. Read: דיסים. ▽ כירסים, הדסים. Read the latter: הדסים, the petition. // MGNum 14. 20, 221₁₇: דוסים, (with gloss: פ' ענין אגרת, meaning: a letter); YalkNum 744: הדסים.

Lieberman, apud Mandelbaum 382, 475. The spelling דוסים perhaps influenced by *δόσις*, bequest, contribution. הדסים perhaps under influence of story told of R. Zeira in YBer 1. 1, 2d bottom. כירסים perhaps **χρεσις*, or **χρειсις*, from *χρεώ*, meaning, "a request". Note Hesych, edLatte 1, 410₂₃: *δέησις· παράκλησις ἢ χρεία*. For similar example of such metath, כירסים in כריסים, see Gignac 1, 314—15; *χρότου* — *χόρτου*, *κροκόδιλος* — *κορκ*~, etc. (Reject Rabinowitz' suggestion, MGNum adloc.) See Sperber, Sinai 87, 1980, 152—53 (Contra KraussPR 83, idem TA 2, 38, following SachsBeiträge 1, 82: *μυρτηφόρος*.)
On *δέησις*, see DeissmannBS 250—51, MM 137b; ArndtGingrich 170b—171a.

Syr: דיסים, PnSSupple 89a, Brockelm² 160b.

דיפורין ↓ **דופרן**

טולמיסן ↓ **דטלמסן, דטולמיסן**

דיאטגמא ↓ **דיאגטמאות**

דיאטגמא (196) edict, decree: *διάταγμα*

SifDeut 33, $59_{9\ 10}$: "אשר אנכי מצוך" — שלא יהיו בעניך כדיוטגמא ישנה שאין אדם סופנה, אלא כדיוטגמא חדשה שהכל רצים לקראתה, "Which I command thee" (Deut 6:6) – that they should not be in your eyes like an old edict which no one regards with respect, but like a new edict to which all rush [with interest] ▽ **כדיוטגמא**, כדיוטוגמא. (But // in PRK, 102a, 207_1: כפרוזדגמא, YalkEx 27, ibidProv 960; MachProv 22. 2, 31a: כפרוזדיכמא; MGEx 19. 1, 373_{14}; cf ↓ **פרוזדוגמא**.)
LevR 1. 10, 25_1: משל לדיאטגמא כתובה ומוחתמת ונכנסה למדינה, אין בני המדינה נענשין עליה עד שתפרש להן בדימוסיה של מדינה, It is like unto an edict [which was] written and sealed, and brought to the city; [but] the people of the city are not punished over it (i e for not keeping it) until it has been promulgated to them in the public place of the city. ▽ **לדיטגמא, לדיאטוגמא, לדיטוגמא, לדיוטגמא, לדיודיגמא,** ללדיא טוגמא. // CantR 2. 3: לדיוטגמא; YalkLev 432: דיטגמא.
LevR 27. 6, $638_{1\ 3}$ according to MsParis 149: ... קרית שמע דיוטגמא שלי הוא, The recitation of the Shema is my edict. ▽ פרוסדוגמא, etc. Cf ↓ **פרוזדוגמא**.
YelamdGen Mi-Keẓ, apud Ar (AC 3, 37a): ... שלש דיטגמאות פירש יוסף, Joseph promulgated three edicts. (But // TanḥBGen Mi-Keẓ 17, 202: שלש פרוסטגמאות, cf ↓ **פרוזדוגמא**; GenR 91. 4, 1126_3: ג' גזירות גזר; EcclesR 9. 15, EcclesZ 150.)
ARN II 8, 24: ופרס דיוטגמא ואמר: כל מי שימצא גונב יהא יודע שדינו דין, And he promulgated an edict saying: Anyone who is found stealing, let him know that his punishment is [so and so]. // GenRabati 2. 21, $34_{14\ 16}$: ופירש (ופרש) דייטיגמא.
ExR 30. 5: משל למלך שהיו לו י' בנים, ומרדו בו, ובטלו י' דיוטגמאות שלו, It is like unto a king who had ten sons, and they rebelled against him and abolished ten of his edicts.
ExR 30. 16: אמר המלך: לא קראת בדיוטגמא שלי שכל מי שנוגע באיקונין שלי הוא אבד?, Said the king: Did you not read in my edict that anyone who touched my image is lost (i e punishable by death)?
DeutR 5. 14: ... היה פורש דאטגמא בכל מקום שהיה הולך לכבוש בו, He would promulgate an edict in each place he went to conquer. Sic printed ed and MsParma 1240/12. ▽ MsMunich 229. 2: דיטגמא. (But // in DeutR Lieberman 101: פרוסטיגמא, cf ↓ **פרוזדוגמא**; YShev 6. 1, 36a 44: **פריסטיגיות** ↓.)

PanimAḥerim II, 63: ... וכיון שנתפרסו דיוגמוטאות של מלך במדינה; read דיוטגמ(ו)אות, and as soon as the king's edicts were promulgated in the city. (The metath is probably a scribal error.)

Trg1Est 3:14: דיטגמא דכתבא (transl: פתשגן הכתב). Ibid 4:8: דיטגמא כתב גזירתא (transl: פתשבן כתב הדת): Ibid 8: 13, edSperber 201: כתבא ודייתיגמא(transl: פתשגן הכתב).

Trg2Est 3:15: ודיטגמא איתפרסמת בשושן בירתא (transl: והדת נתנה בשושן הבירה), read: אתפרסת (Ar, AC 3, 37b): and the edict was promulgated in the city of Shushan.

Ibid 4:2: מאי כתיב בדיטגמא דפרס מלכא אחשורוש, What is written in the edict which King Ahasuerus has promulgated?

GenRabbati 49. 9, 236_{14}: ... רצונך ידעו, שכבר עברה דיאגטמאור שלך לא יהא אדם מתפלל עד ל' יום כי אם לפניך, They knew your will, for your edict has also passed through [stating] that for thirty days none should pray but before you. Read: דיאטגמא (the metath being a scribal error). Or perhaps: עברו דיאטמאות?

MidPs 118. 12, 485: "סבבוני כדברים", שהוא עתיד לפרוש ריש גמיות למדינות להוציא כרוזות, שנאמר "קראו זאת בגוים, קדשו מלחמה", read: דיטגמיות, "They compassed me like bees (*ki-devorim*)" (Ps 118:12): For he will promulgate edicts in the cities to give out announcements, as it is written "Proclaim ye this among the Gentiles; Prepare war ..." (Joel 4:9). ▽ edprinc and edd: דוגמניות, so also Ar (AC 3, 196), דגמטיות על המדינות להוציא חיילות, edicts in the cities to raise soldiers, דגמטיא, דיגמטיות, דוגמטיות (readings influenced by דוגמא, *δόγμα, δόγματα*, cf LW 2, 187b–188a). The exegesis is based on a play on כדברים "like bees", vocalised *ki-devorim,* as though it were *ki-devarim,* like words, statements, commands. // MachJoel 4. 9, 37: דוגמוטיות.

Pl: YShevu 7. 9, 38a 37: אנן משלחין דיאטיגמתין. אין אתא, הא טבות. ואין לאו, אנן מחליטין נכסוי, We send out edicts. If he comes, good. And if not, we sequester his properties. // YKet 9. 10, 33b50: דין מוגמרין, read: דיוטגמתין. (Double-plural of דיאטגמא.)

On פרס, פרש דיאטגמא, to promulgate an edict, see Lieberman, JQRNS 35, 1944, 6–7, especially n40, idem GH 399 n4, and Löw apud Krauss, LW 2, 188b.

On די~ for ~דיא, cf Gignac 1, 318 *δί* for *δι<α>*. Cf. Syr. Common in Rabb Graecitas; cf ↓ דיגטסים.

On ~דיו for *δια~*, see LW 1, 165 (87), no doubt influenced by common prefix ~דיו. (And cf Gignac 1, 286–7.)

דאטגמא in DeutR 5. 14 is probably to be emended: דיאטגמא. However, it may also represent **δαταγμα*, since the *ι* following the *δ* is sometimes omitted in papyri etc. See Gignac 1. 75. e g: *δακόσια* (for *διακόσια*) PGen 48 = PAbbin 60, 14 (346 CE), etc. On דיטגמא, see Gignac, 1, 318. The form די(א)טוגמא noted above (▽ to SifDeut 33, etc) is explicable on the basis of the *a > o*

interchange found in this period. See Gignac 1, 287, e g: *πρόστογμα* (for *πρόσταγμα*), PLips 64 = WChr 281. 34, corr 43 (368/9 CE.). דירדיגמא (▽ to LevR 110) reflects $\tau > \delta$ interchange (Gignac 1, 82–83), and the influence of דיגמא: *δεῖγμα*, *digma* (LW 2, 187b), and cf LW 1, 88.
On DeutR 5. 14, see ACSup 342b sv פרסטגי, and reject Bacher's suggestion to emend.
On MidPs 118. 12, 485, see Buber's n25 adloc, followed by Brüll, Jahrb 4, 1879, 117, (*διατάγματα*), and Löw apud Krauss, LW 2, 188b. (Contra Krauss LW 2, 188a svv דוגמטא, דוגמניות: *δόγματα*; AC 3, 19b: *δόγμα*; Levy 1, 377b: *τάγμα*; Fleischer apud Levy 1, 439b: *διώγματα*; Jastrow 283a corrects to הגמוניות, cf 331b sv הגמוניא; Fürst 94a: *διαγνώμη*.) Löw rightly points to the use of the verb פורש as connected with the *διάταγμα*. להוציא חיילות is probably a "learned" emendation. Other Mss have: גרוזות, חרוזות (whence: חיילות?), pointing to a primary reading: כרוזות.
See on this term, Wilcken, ZSav 42, 1921, 128–33; Katzoff, AuN II/13, 1980, 819–820; MM 15–5a; ArndtGingrich 188ab; Mason 36b, 127.

Syr: דיטגמא, PnS 880.
Cf ↓ דיגטסים, פרוזדוגמא

דיאתימון [דיאתימין] (197), I disposed by will: *διεθέμην* (aor mid of *διατίθημι*)

TBB 9. 14, 416_{21}, according to edprinc: רבן שמעון בן גמליאל אומר: הכותב דיותימין בלעז הרי זו מתנה, Rabban Simon b Gamliel says: He who writes *διεθέμην* – I willed – in Greek, it is a present (i e despite the fact that *διεθέμην* is in the past and not the present). ▽ דייתיקי (↑), but reject this reading (TR 2, 147–48). Probably we should read דייתימין.
YBB 8. 8, 16c 14, 15: תני: רבן שמעון בן גמליאל אומר: אף הכותב דיאתימון בלעז הרי זו מתנה. ר' חנין בשם ר' יהושע בן לוי: חיזרתי על כל בעלי לשונות לידע מהו דיאתימון, ולא אמר לי אדם דבר, We have learned (in the Tosefta): Rabban Simon b. Gamliel says: Also he who writes in Greek *διεθέμην* – I willed –, it is a present. [Said] R. Ḥanin in the name of R. Joshua b Levi: I went round to all the linguists to find out what דיאתימון meant, and no one could explain me a thing. Read: דיאתימין.
Sefer ha-Maasim, Epstein, Tarbiẓ 1/2, 1930, 42_{18}: כתב בכתב דייתיקי למעלן משם מתנה, ולמטן הוטל שם לשון אידייתמין ... ?, He wrote in a testamentary document, above as a present, and below was written there the formula אידייתמין – *διεθέμην*, I willed ... ? (I e, the document was written at the beginning as a present, and later on as a will. Although the question as to the status of such a mixed document is not given, presumably it would be ruled as a present. Cf MBB 8. 5.)

Jastrow 294a; Gulak, Tarbiẓ 1/4, 1930, 144–45, citing papyrological formulae: *τάδε διεθέμην*, etc; followed by Lieberman, TR 3, 147–48, idem, GH 20 n76. (Contra Epstein, Tarbiẓ 1/2, 42 9: *διάθεμα*, following ZFränkel, Mevo ha-Yerushalmi, Breslau 1870, 7b; so too Krauss, BZ 2, 1893, 541–42, idem LW 2, 197a; SachsBeiträge 1, 152; Levy 1, 392a. Perles ES 110, following DeLara, emends דיותסין: *διάθεσις* (~*ν*), followed by FPerles, BZ 10, 1901, 305, and so AC 3, 48b. [Lonzano,

Maarich 31, reads דיאטיגמא; *διάταγμα*?] Cf ZMPineles, Darkah shel Torah, Vienna 1861, 133–34, citing earlier bibl.)
The spelling ... דיו may be a scribal error for ~דיי, or it may be a dialectic phenomenon; cf דיוטגמא: *διάταγμα* (†) (LW 2, 195b), דיוביט: *διαβήτης* (ibid 198b), דיוטי: *δίαιτα* (199a), דיוטרין: *διαιτητήριον* (199b).
The ~אי in אידייתמין is the well-known Rabbinic prothesis; see LW 1, 136–40. (Cf CGL 2, 577_3: Diathima <*distributio*>.)

דייתיקי ↓ דיאתיקי

◇**דיגטסיס** **[דיטגסיס]** (197–98) imperial constitution: *δι<ά>ταξις*

Trg2 Est 2:8: ... כד שמע מלכא, כתב בדיגטסיס, When the king heared, he wrote in an imperial constitution ... ▽ דיגנוסיס edLagarde 242; דיטגסיס Mussaf (apud AC 3, 37b).

LevyTrgWb 169b; Löw apud Krauss, LW2, 1980; already suggested in Mussaf, apud AC 3, 37b, see Kohut's n5 ibid. The metath is probably a scribal error (cf Gignac 1, 59). The x > gs interchange is understandable in terms of the "origin" of this word *διάταγμα*, a much commoner term in Rabbinic language, and in view of the oft-found *κ* > *γ* interchange. See LW1, 7, 108, and cf ↑ **אגדיקוס**. *δια*~ is often elided into ~די— *δι'* (cf Gignac 1, 318), and cf ↑ **דיאטגמא**.
As to the reading דיגנוסיס, clearly corresponding to: *διάγνωσις* and seen by some scholars as the primary one (Krauss, LW2, 197b–198a; Jastrow 295b), it would have to bear the (rare) meaning "decision". Cf *διαγνώμη*: decree, and see MM 155a sv *διάταγμα*; ArndtGingrich 188b; cf PnS 868: דיאגנוסטיקי (?): *διαγνωστική*. See further Mason 36b.CGL 3, 276_{44}: *διάταξις constitutio*.

Syr: דיאטכסיס, דיטכסיס, PnS 869; Brockelm² 150b.
Cf ↑ **דיאטגמא**

דיגטסיס ↑ דיגנוסיס

דיהכסיס document of proof: *δεῖξις*

YelamdGen 33:12, apud YalkTalmudTorah by Jacob b. Ḥananel Sikili: ולא הניחו זה את זה עד שעשו דיהכסיס. וחתם זה בדיהכסיס של זה וזה בדיהכסיס של זה. אמר ר' אחא: לולי דיהכסיס שעשה עשיו ליעקב, היה נוחל עשיו עם יעקב לעתיד לבא, And they (Jacob and Esau) would not leave one another until they had drawn up document[s]. And the one signed upon the document of the other, and the other on the document of the first. Said R. Aḥa: Were it not for the document which Esau drew up for Jacob, Esau would have inherited with Jacob in the World to Come.

Cited in MannBible 1, 324; Ha-Ẓofeh me-Ereẓ Hagar 3, 1913, 20; BatMid 1, 159. The identification

was first given by Löw, cited by Poznansky, Ha-Ẓofeh ibid n1, and followed Mann ibid n411. (Contra Wertheimer, BatMid ibid n2.)
Jacob b. Ḥananel Sikili (of Sicilian? ancestry) lived in Cordoba Spain and then Damascus in the later XIII and early XIV cent. YalkTalmudTorah on Gen was completed probably in the second decade of the XIV cent, while he was still in Spain. See Encyclopaedia Judaica, Jerusalem 1971, 14, 1530–31.
כס is a regular form of transliterating ξ. See LW 1, 6. However, the orthography יה for ει is somewhat puzzling, and may indicate that the ει was pronounced as a long ι (ί). See Gignac 1, 189–91, (but cf ibid 325).

דיאטגמא ↑ דיוטגמא, דיוגמוטאות

פילקי ↓ דיוטא

דיוקטא prosecutor; *διώκτ<ης>* (+ Aram term)

EcclesR 3. 6, according to reading in Responsa Rivash 442: וקרב עליהון גבי דיוקטא דקיסרין, And he complained against them before the prosecutor of Caesarea. ▽ Reading in printed ed (edprinc etc): אנטיפוטא: *ἀνθύπατος*, proconsul. LevR 5. 6, 118_7: עליבא מדינתא דאסיא פטגריטוס ויוזקטטא דחדא עיינה, סניגורה מקטרג בדיני נפשין, Ill-fated is the city whose doctor suffers from *podagra* (gout), whose prosecutor is one-eyed [Cyclops], and whose advocate prosecutes capital cases. ▽: ודאיקטוטא, ודאי קושטא etc. // YalkLev 469 (edprinc): ודאיקוטטה; read: ודיוקטטה(א) = דיוקטא.

Schlatter 60. Lieberman, Sefer ... Yalon 228, (contra idem, apud LevR 872, who had suggested **ἰσοκτίστης*: craftsman skilled in making equal pairs of instruments; cf Perles, JQR 16, 353; AC 2, 53b; ACSup 20b; Levy 1, 70b; LW 2, 40b and reject). Reading אנטיפוטא influenced by YMeg 3. 2, 74a 41. On the one-eyed [Cyclops] see Lieberman ibid228. Or perhaps: *διοικητής*: governor, thus equivalent to אנטיפוטא: *ἀνθύπατος*. One may also note the word דיחתו (LW 2, 203a) in CantR 2. 15, explained by Krauss (and accepted by Löw) as being *διῶκται*. Cf LW 1, 155. However, the whole passage remains unclear (see Lieberman GH 5 n30), and this identification is questionable.

דיוקני (202–203) document authorizing an agent with power of attorney to receive money as payment of debt, or return of deposit, containing inter alia, name of agent, *his description*, and signature of witnesses: derived from *εἰκών, εἰκόνι<ον>* → *iconi<on>*

BBK 104b: אמר רב יהודה אמר שמואל: אין משלחין מעות בדיוקני, ואפילו עדים חתומים עליה. ור׳ יוחנן אמר: אם עדים חתומים עליה משלחין, Said Rav Judah said Samuel: One may not deliver [trust] money to an agent on the basis of a power of attorney containing the description of the agent, even if the witnesses are signed on it (i e who witnessed the agent's being granted power of attorney and can identify the signature). R. Yoḥanan said: If the witnesses are signed on it, one may.

For the Gaonic discussions of this term, see OhG BK 80–83, 159, R. Ḥananel, ibid 100. For further usage in Gaonic period, see JMann, The Jews in Egypt and in Palestine under the Fâṭimid Caliphs, 2, Oxford 1922, index 415 sv דיוקני.

Ostersetzer, Tarbiẓ 11, 1939, 39–55, discusses in detail the legal content of this term, comparing it with Hell-Rom documents called *εἰκονικά – iconica*, containing detailed descriptions of persons involved in the document. Cf MM 183b sv *εἰκών*. (Contra Jastrow 297b: figure in place of signature; AGulak, Das Urkundwesen im Talmud, Jerusalem 1935, 145 n2: copy of document, Worman, JQR OS, 19, 1907, 727 n1.)

As to etym, see Löw apud Krauss, LW 2, 202b–203a, equating דיוקני with commoner דיוקן, image (preceding entry in LW ibid), and explaining it as deriving from *εἰκών* (– *εἰκόνιον*). He discusses at length the problematic *dalet*, comparing initial *gy* (= *dj*) in Hungarian etc; unconvincing. It may be noted that Nöldeke and Frankel (LW 1, 199) could not explain this phenomenon, (also LW 2, 202b sv דיוקן). Cf LW 2, 212a sv דיקינתון: *ὑάκινθος*, ibid 605a, and Ostersetzer ibid 41. Löw also suggests a possible popular influence of Sem דייק: to be accurate. The initial *dalet* remains problematic. (Contra AC 3, 47b: *δύω- εἰκών*, Doppelbild; Levy 1, 395a; Krauss, LW 2, 202b, compares with preceding entry דיוקן, image, for which he offers two alternative etym: *δείκανον*, which may be rejected [Löw, LW 2, ibid], or *εἰκών*. In LW 1, 199, he cited Nöldeke and Fraenkel, who equate דיוקנא with Syr: דוקנא, *εἰκόνα*. See also Krauss, BZ 2, 1893, 502–504. SachsBeiträge 1, 45 on דיוקנא: *δείκανον*, subsequently rejected for *εἰκών*, ibid 2, 50.)

דיאתימון ↑ דיותימין

דייתיקי ↓ דיותיקי

דיוקטא ↑ דיחתו

דיאטגמא ↑ דייטיגמא, דייטגמא, דיטגמא

דיקי ↓ דייקי

דייתיקי ↓ דייתיקא, דייתוקי

דייתיקי (197) will, testament: *διαθήκη*

MMK 3. 3: ואלו כותבין במועד ... דייתיקי, מתנה ... And these may be written out during the mid-festivals, ... testaments, [deeds of] gift ...

MBM 1. 7: מצא ... דייתיקי ... הרי זה לא יחזיר, If [a man] found ... a will ... he should not return [it].

MBB 8. 6: ... מי שמת, ונמצא דייתיקי קשורה על יריחו, If a man died, and a will was found bound to his thigh ...

TBB 11. 6, 413_{26}: דייתיקאות והפותיקאות (↑ אפותיקי) ומתנות ... אין כותבין אלא מדעת המקבל, Testaments and deeds of mortgage and [deeds of] gifts ... one does not write out, except with the agreement of the recipient (pl).

YBM 1. 8, 8a 45–46: שאין אדם מצוי לפגום דייתיקן שלו, For a man is not likely to make his own testaments defective (pl).

YSanh 9. 6, 20c 40: כל דייתיקי שבטלה מקצתה בטלה כולה, Every testament part of which was annulled, is completely annulled. // CantR 5. 11; LevR 19. 2, 420_{6} (slightly different formulation).

BBB 135b: דייתיקי מבטלת דייתיקי, One (later) testament cancells another (earlier) testament // Ibid 152b; YBB 8. 16, 16b 59.

TBB 8. 10, 409_{24}: איזו היא דייתוקי (read: דייתיקי)? הדא תהא לעמוד ולהיות, What is a testament (*diatheke*)? Let this [document] endure and persist. (Popular etym.) // YPea 3. 9, 17d 57: תהא לי להיות ולעמוד; BBB 135b: דא תהא למיקם; BBM 19a.

TBB 8. 9, 409_{21}: ... בריא שכתב דייתיקי, שכיב מרע שכתב נכסיו במתנה, A healthy person who wrote a will, [and] a dangerously sick man who wrote his properties as a present ... // YPea 3. 9, 17d 55.

YBer 5. 2, 9b13: בדייתיקי נתתיו לאברהם? במתנה נתתיו לו, Have I given it to Abraham by testament? (i e something which may be changed or cancelled). I have given it to him as a donation (i e which cannot be cancelled). // YTaan 1. 1, 63d 12; GenRabbati 110_{2}: בדיאתקי נתתי ... מתנה, I gave ... as a donation by testament. (This reading prefered by the ed.)

YShevu 7. 9, 38a 32: בהדא דייתיקי, ... a case of a testament ...

GenR 59. 11, 637_{13}: "וכל טוב אדוניו בידו" ... זו דייתיקי, "for all the goods of his master were in his hand" (Gen 14:10) ... This means a testament (i e that he had bearing witness to the transfer of all his master's properties to his control). // TanḥBGenVa-Yeẓe 3, 145: דיתיקי (vocalized in MsVat: דְיַתִיקִי); AgBer 46 (45), 92: דייתקי; LTGen 24. 10, 1. 108 (with folk etym); STovGen ibid 1. 78; MGGen ibid, 394_{11}: דיאתיקי; TrgNeofiti ibid: דייתיקא; Ar, AC 3, 55b. (PRE 16, 37a: כתב אברהם כל אשר לו ליצחק ירושה, ונטל הכתב ונתנו ביד אליעזר עבדו.)

GenR 61. 6, 664_{2}: קבורה ודיאתיקי, burial and will. ▽ דייתיקי, דאתיקי, דייתקי. // YalkGen 110, 500_{19}; MidPs 1. 5, 6; YalkPs 612.

GenR 96, $1200_{1\ 2}$: אין לודר עושה דייתיקי ... ומי עושה דייתיקי? בני חורין, A gladiator does not make a will. Who makes a will? Freemen. // AgBer 82 (81), 156; YalkGen 157, 832_{95}; BHM 2, 73.

TanḥGenLech 8: דיאתיקי. IbidVa-Yeḥi 8: היכן דיתיקי שלהן והאוני(אוניז) שלהן?, Where is their testament and deed of sale? // TanḥB ibid 8, 217; GenR 9b, 1201_{2}.

TanḥNumNaso 2: ... עומד הבעל וכותב לו דייתיקי מכל נכסיו ומורישו ונוחלו, The husband stands up and writes him a will on all his properties, and gives it as inheritance ...// NumR 9. 12.
TanḥDeutVa-Etḥanan 4. NumR 2. 8: דייתיקי יש בידן מיעקב אביהם, They have a testament from Jacob their forefather.
MGDeut 3. 23, 58_{22}: לחולה ... וישב וכתב דיאתיקי לבניו, Like a sick man ... and he sat down and wrote a will to his children.
Yelamd, apud YalkDeut 793, GrünhutLikkutim 5, 86a: אמרו בניו ללבלר: ברר לנו דייתיקי, His children said to the scribe: Pick the will out for us.
FragmTrgKlein(P) Gen 34:10: אפותיקי נ"א דיותיקי, deeds (↑ **אפותיקי**), another reading: testaments. (Transl: טוב, "goods.")
TBB 9. 14, 416_{21}: הכותב דייתיקי בלעז, read with edprinc: דיותימין (↑ **דיאתימון**).

See also Sefer ha-Maasim, edEpstein, Tarbiẓ 1/1, 1930, 47_{17}; idem, edRabinowitz, Tarbiẓ 41, 1972, 292_{15}, 293_{10}; Shetarot le-Rav Hai, edAssaf, 29.
See further BacherTanJer 95–96.
On the orthography ~דיא, with the ā in the middle of the word (not usual in Palestinian orthography, other than in foreign words), see SokoloffGeniza 64.
There is quite a literature on the Gk *διαθήκη*; see MM 148–149a; ArndtGingrich 182ab; (Joüon 466); add EBammel, NTS 6, 1959/60, 813, and GDKilpatrick, ZNW 68, 1977, 263–65.

Syr: דיאתיקי, דיאתקא, דיתיקא, דיתיקי etc, PnS 873.
Lat: *diatheca*, CGL 5, 335_{60} (*testamentum*), etc.
Arm: *diatik*, Hübschmann 89, Brockelmann, ZDMG 47, 1893, 35.

דייתיקי ↑ דייתקי

דימוס I (205) release, pardon: *dimis<sio>*

YBer 9. 6, 14 (13)b 25: כשהוא נותן דימוס הכל מקלסין אותו. וכשהוא נותן ספקולא **(ספיקולא ↓)** הכל מרננין אחריו, When he grants a pardon, all praise him. [But] when he gives a death sentence, all murmur against him. // LevR 24. 2, 550_4, ▽ דמים; Yelamd apud Ar (AC 3, 87a), Grünhut Likkutim 50, 90b; YalkPs 843 adfin; MachPs 92. 26, 298: נימוס, read: דימוס; MachPs 101. 2, 2. 122 (citing LevR 24. 2); MachIs 5. 16, 44_{30}.
MidPs 100. 2, 425: בשעה שאינו מודה נותן לו ספיקולא (↓). בשעה שהוא מודה נותן לו דימוס, When he does not admit [to his guilt], he gives him the sentence. When he does admit, he gives him a pardon. // PRK 159a, 356_3. (Cf YalkPs 854.)
PRK 334_{5-7}: ... יצא בדימוס לפני הקבה, He went out with a pardon before the Holy One blessed be He. // DeutR Lieberman 11 (partial //); LevR 29. 1, 669_4:

דימיס, ▽ דימוס, דומיס; MidPs 119. 44, 2. 224; PR 46, 188a; YalkNum782; MGGen 1. 26, 58_4.

EcclesR 11. 1; נמצא נוטל דמים כפי שניהם; read: ... דמיס מפי ... , So he receives pardon from both of them. ▽ מפי // AgBer (98) 49, 98: נוטל דימוס מפי שנים.

MidPs 31. 6, 239: ונותן לצדיקים דימוס שיכנסו לגן עדן, and He grants the righteous pardon, so that they should enter the garden of Eden.

PRK 189a, 458_{16}: שנטלו הנפשות דימוס שלהם ביום הכיפורים, The souls receive their pardon on the day of atonement.

AgBer 22, 55: נתן לה דימוס ולא נשרפה, He granted her pardon, and she was not burned. Ibid 83 (82), 159.

MGEx 8. 11, 123_4: בשעת רווחיה עביד דימוס, and when his situation eases, he feals pardoned.

Lieberman, DeutR 11 n9. The more accurate form of the word would seem to be: דימיס: *dimis<sio>*. However, the commoner form דימוס is influenced by דימוס II (↓) *dim<iss>us*, with which it was frequently confused, which in turn was influenced by דימוס: δῆμος (LW 2, 204b–205a). See also Souter 105a.

Cf ↓ דימוס II

דימוס II (205) released, pardoned: *dim<iss>us*

THul 2. 24, 503_{22}: דימוס, הרי אתה פטור, [You are] pardoned; behold you are released. // BAZ 16b: דימוס, פטור אתה; EcclesR 1. 8; YalkProv 938.

YShev 9. 1, 38d 27: שמע ברת קלא אמרת: דימוס ואישתיזבת, He heared a [heavenly] echo saying: [You are] released, and have been saved. // GenR 79. 6, 942_1: דימיס (sic MsBritMus and Vat60), *dimis<sus>;* PRK 88b, 192_4: דימיס (sic MsOxfNeubauer 151 (1)); EcclesR 10. 8; MidPs 17. 13, 134; MachPs 17. 25, 1. 100, EstR 1. 9 (3. 7 edVilna): דימוס ואתפשת; YalkGen 133, 679_{17}: דמוס, ▽ MsOxf: דימוס.

Lieberman, JQRNS 35, 1944, 21 n140; Krauss, LW 1, XXI n1; AC 3, 86b–87b; Fürst 100b–101a. (Contra Levy 1, 396ab svv, דימוס II–III: δειμός, δημοσσόος, cf Fleischer ibid 442a; Jastrow 300a sv דימוס II: δῆμος; AC 3, 84a: θέμις [strangely enough left without comment in ACSup], and cf ibid 87 n5.)

We note two parallel forms: דימוס, the commoner one, and דימיס, probably the more original one. The (secondary) form דימוס was presumably formed under the influence of דימוס: δῆμος (LW 2, 204b–205a), a word commonly found in Rabbinic literature, by way of haplography. See Mayser 1/1[2], 218–19; Gignac 1, 313.

There are two homonymes that should be distinguished from one another, דימוס I: *dimissio* and דימוס II *dimissus*. Rabbinic lexica have hitherto not made this distinction.

Arab: *dimṣ*, Vollers, ZDMG 51, 1897, 298.
Cf ↑ דימוס I

דימיס ↑ דימוס I and II

דיאטגמא ↑ דין מוגמרין

דוסיס ↑ דיסיס

דיסקפלינא ↓ דיסקיא פלניא

◇**דיסקפלינא** (209–210) rule of orderly conduct, discipline: *disciplina*

YelamdLevVa-Yikra adfin, apud Ar (AC 3, 102b–103a): הפולח הזה יודע נימוסי ודיסקפלינא שלי, This soldier knows my law (↓ **נימוס**) and my rule of orderly conduct. (Absent in partial // in TanḥLevVa-Yikra 6, YalkLev 464, Ar, AC 6, sv $פגן_2$.)
PanimAḥerim II 5. 9, 72: ללמד בו אדם דיסקיא פלניא;read: דיסקיפלינא, to teach man the rule of orderly conduct.

On PanimAḥerim see Buber n155 ibid. The corruption is meant to mean something like "a full double-pouched bag"!
On Yel, Lieberman, apud LevR Margulies 873, remarks that נימוסי ודיסקפלינא corresponds exactly to the formulation in Galerius' (Lat) edict (Lact, de mort pers 34) as found in Gk transl in Euseb (HE 8. 17. 6) *κατὰ τοὺς ... νόμους καὶ τὴν δημοσίαν ἐπιστήμην*, where *ἐπιστήμη* translates the Lat *disciplina*. (Cf ↓ **פסטמא**.) See Berger 438b. Note *disciplina* also corresponds to Gk *τάξις*, Souter 106b. (See also CII 1, no215: *δισκειπουλειναι = discipulina*.)

Cf ↓ פסטמא

◇**דיפורין [ריפודין]** (192) unilateral dissolution of a marriage: *ῥεπούδι<o>ν* ← *repudium*

GenR 18. 5, 166_8: אמר ר׳ יוחנן: אשתו מגרשתו ונותנת לו דיפורין, his wife divorces him and gives him a [letter of] divorce. ▽ דופורין, דיופרין, ריפורין (edprinc). But read with MsVat 60 (fol 61a): ריפודין, (and perhaps this is the reading in MsVat30 too). // YalkGen 25, 88_{20}: דופרן.
YKid 1. 1, 58c 18, according to MsLeiden: ר׳ חונה רובה דציפורין: ... או ששניהן מגרשין זה את זה. ר׳ יוחנן אמר: דיופרין, R. Ḥuna of Sepphoris: ... or they both divorce one another. R. Yoḥanan said: A *repudium*. (Corrected in Ms to: ר׳ יוחנן דצפרין, and hence to edprinc and subsequent edd.) Read: ריפודין.

Perles, BZ 10, 1901, 35 (on GenR), noting that this suggestion was already given by David de Pomis, Ẓemaḥ David, Venice 1587, 215b; Jastrow 287a. (Contra Blau, Jüdische Ehescheidung, 1, 57 n2, preferring other suggestion: דיפורין: *διαφερνή*, double dowry given as punishment, a view cited by Löw, apud LW 2, 192b, and supported by many readings, but refuted on legal grounds by BCohen, Jewish and Roman Law 384–85, Cohen's argument accepted by Lieberman, Biblical and Other Studies, edAltman, 1963, 133 n48.)
On YKid, see Lieberman, Tarbiẓ 2/2, 1931, 239, and idem, YK introduction 18. The mistaken reading was presumably influenced by ר' חונה רובה דציפורין in the preceding line.
Berger, 676, explains that the dissolution is made either by an oral declaration before witnesses, or by a letter, or through the intermediary of a messenger who transmits to the other party the wish that the marriage be dissolved. נותנת לו ריפודין means, presumably, "she gives him the *libellus repudii,*" the written form of the divorce.
For *ῥεπούδιον* see PO 129. 1 (VI CE); cf Sophocles 968b; DuCange 1290; Lampe 1216a. Form *ῥιπούδιον* in PLips. 39 = MChr. 127. 10 (390 CE), Gignac 1, 251.

Syr: ריפודין, PnS 3893, Bruns-Sachau 8_{10} etc.
Cf ↓ **רדופין** (which is the same word in a different form).

דיקאליקוס ↓ דיקולוגוס

דיקו ↓ דיקי

[0]**דיקולוגוס** (211) pleader, advocate: *δικολόγος*

LevR 29. 7, 676_5: מני לך דיקאליקוס פלוני ואת זוכה לפני בדין, Appoint yourself so and so as an advocate, and you will win your case before me. ▽ Ar (AC 3, 125b): דקליקוס.But other Mss. and // have **ניקולוגוס** ↓.
YalkNum 738, citing Yelamd: שני דיקולוגין היו עומדין לפני אדריינוס. אחד מהם מלמד על הדיבור שהוא יפה, ואחד מלמד על השתיקה שהיא יפה, Two advocates stood before Hadrian. One of them argued that speach is [most] worthy, and the other argued that silence is [most] worthy. // YalkProv 946: דיקליקין; Orḥot Ẓaddikim, chap 21, edEshkol 138.

For *δικολόγος*, see EdDiocl 7. 72; CGL 3, 514_{21}: dicologos *causidicus*, etc. The ק instead of ג, ~ליקוס for ~לוגוס, is not uncommon; see Gignac 1, 77, (and cf ↑ **אגדיקוס**). The form ~**דיקא** may correspond with *διακαιολόγος*, advocate, (CGL 3, 276_{61}).

Cf ↓ **ניקולוגוס**

דיקי (211–12) (1) justice, cause, right (2) penalty, punishment (3) vengeance: *δίκη*

(1) GenR 45. 5, $452_{1\ 2}$: ... תבוע דיקי דידי, Plead my cause (or: demand justice for

me). ▽ דקיון, דיוקון, דיקיון (↓). // YalkGen 79 ad init, $321_{26\ 27}$: דקיון, ▽ דיקיון (↓), דיקי. LTGen 16. 5, 1. 73: דיני דיני, read: דיקי דידי. Cf below (**3**).
Pl: GenR 9. 13, 73_{12}: שהיא תובעת דיקיות שלבריות, for she demands the rights (or pleads the causes) of [her] creatures. ▽ דקיון (cf ↓ **דיקיון**). // YalkGen 16, 46_3, ibidIs 462 (324): דקיון; MachIs 45. 12, 153_{27}: רקיון, read דקיון.

(**2**) CantR 2. 7: ... אין הקב"ה מעמיד מלך חנף על אומתו עד שגובה דייקי שלה, The Holy One blessed be He does not set a tyrannical king over His people until He [decides] to claim penalty from her, (ref to Is 32:1). ▽ edprinc: ריקי. Read: דיקי.

(**3**) ExR 19. 4: ועשיתי דייקי שלהם בבני, I exacted their vengeance against My children. Read: דיקי. // MachZach 2. 15, 34.
NumR 22. 2: אינו אלא דיקו שלכם שגרמו לי להזיק אותן, It is only your [plee for] vengeance that caused me to harm them (ref to Num 31:2, "Avenge the children of Israel on the Midianites"). Read: דיקי. // TanḥNumMatot 3, edprinc: הרי הריני ריקו שלכם, edMantua 1563: ... הריני ואתם זיקו שלכם מתבקשים, read (?): אינו אלא דיקי שלכם מתבקשים, it is only your cause being taken up (... that caused me to harm them, cf above **1**). TanḥB ibid 3, 158: דין שלכם מתבקש; YalkNum 785: דין. Read: דיקי, (or gloss on דיקי, where original loanword fell out).

The many meanings of the Gk *δίκη* are listed in LSJ[9] 430ab. Meaning (3), vengeance is listed there IV 3. See further MM 163b; ArndtGingrich 197b.
On TanḥMatot 3, see Jastrow 305a. The form זיקו may be influenced by להזיק ibid.
The form דייקי may reflect the *ι* > *ει* interchange, found frequently in papyri. See Gignac 1, 190–91; eg: *τειμήν* (for *τιμήν*), etc.
Note that דירין cited in LW 2, 212a, from YRH 1. 3, 57b 27, has nothing to do with דיקי. Likewise reject Jastrow 305a, and 176a sv במגנימין, who also reads דיקין. See LiebermanTK 5, 1022–23, who emends to דירדין: *δειράδι<ο>ν*, ridge of chain of hills. Perhaps emendation unnecessary, and דירה (א~), sing, is *δέρα* (= *δειρά*), which Hesych, edLatte 1, 419_{61}, explains thus: *ὑπερβολὴ ὄρους. οἱ δέ σιμὰ τῶν ὀρέων*, that is the ridge of the hills, (see editor's note ad loc). Cf LSJ[9] 375b sv *δειρή* II. However, it should be noted that SY 147_2 reads דִידין.

Syr: דיקא, PnS 890, (and דיקים: *δίκης*, ibid 891, and דיקי? ibid 891 sv דיקוס).
Cf ↓ **דיקיון**

דיקיון (216) justice, cause: *δίκαιον*

GenR 45. 5, $455_{1\ 2}$: **תבוע דיקי** (↑) **דידי**, Plead my cause (or: claim justice for me). ▽ **דקיון, דיקיון, דיוקון**, read **דידיון**. // YalkGen 79 ad init, $321_{26\ 27}$: **דקיון**. ▽ **דיקיון**.
GenR 9. 13, 73_{12}: **שהיא תובעת דיקיות** (↑ **דיקי**) **שלבריות**, for she pleads the causes of [her] creatures. ▽ **דקיון**. // YalkGen 16, 46_3, ibidIs 462 (324), MachIs 45. 12, 153_{27}: **רקיון**, read: **דקיון**.

GenR 10. 5, 78_9: לתבוע דיקיון שלו, to plead his cause. // YalkJob 901: דקיון.
MachIs 45. 12, 154_8: רקיון, read: דקיון.
GenR 22. 12, 218_5: לתבוע דיקיך של הבל, to claim justice for Abel. ▽ דקיון, דקיונו, דין (presumably gloss), דמו, his blood (influenced by GenR 216_4?). // YalkGen 38, 131_1: דינו ▽ דקיון, TanhBIntroduction 157 (from MsDeRossi 261): לתבוע דיוקנו; read : דיקיונו.
NumR 20. 15: וכי דקיון של אתון בא מלאך לבקש מידו?, and did the angel come to plead the cause of the ass? (דקיון there contrasted with עלבון, insult, humiliation.)

לתבוע דיקי(ון) is a literal translation of *δίκας αἰτεεῖν*. See Lieberman, JQR 36, 1946, 353 n185, (and KraussPR 114).
דיקיוס appearing in the lexica is based on the reading in YalkGen 16, edFrankf/M, and has no basis in Mss and early edd (Theodor, GenR 74).
On *δίκαιον* see Mason 37b, MM162ab, ArndtGingrich 195a, Lampe 369a.

Cf Syr: דיקאיוס, PnS 890 sv דיקאנוס.
Cf ↑ דיקי

דיקיות ↑ דיקי

דיקליקין ↑ דיקולוגוס

דיתיקי ↑ דייתיקי

דמים ↑ דימוס

דקיון ↑ דיקיון

דקליקוס ↑ דיקולוגוס

דקמסיות ↑ אורקמסיא

ה

אסטו ↑ האסטו

אוני ↑ הוניות

אפותיקי ↑ הפתיקי, הפתקאות, הפותקי, הפתיקאות

הרנירק טיאונוס [הוינדקטיונוס] (64) form of manumission by *vindicta:* **οὐινδικατίωνος* ← **vindicationis*

YGit 4. 4, 45d 36: מַנַיין היוצא בכיפה ובהרנירק טיאונוס ובחרות של מלכים?, Whence [do we know that a slave] achieves his liberty by [manumission with] the cap, or the **vindicationis* or by the 'freedom of kings'? Thus in MsL and edprinc. Perhaps read: הוינדקטיונוס or ~יס. // BGit 20a: אנדוכתרי (↑) and Avadim 3. 11: אנטוקטא (↑).

See LW 1, 268 and ↑ **אנדוכתרי** with full bibl. For *vindicatio,* see Maigne D'Arnis 2302: *redemptio praedii* (?), or perhaps through misunderstanding of *vindicatio in libertatem* (cf Berger 766b). Or more simply, an abstract noun created from *vindicta* is quite likely. On the genitive form, see LW 1, 69–70 for examples. The ה is not a digamma as Krauss suggested (LW 1, 268). Indeed ה for digamma seems unattested. Thus הרדיקינוס (LW 1, 62) should not be cited as an example; see LW 2, 222ab; Lieberman, TK 1,106, suggesting *ἀνδρογίγας* (?). (Cf Dalman[2] 121b and correct.)

Cf ↑ **אנדוכתרי** and **אנטוקטא**

ו

וילון (235–236) curtain, which separates the court from the public (when proceedings are held in secret: *βῆλον* ← *velum*

GenR 36.1, 334₂: "והוא ישְׁקִיט ומי ירשיע". דרש ר' מאיר: הוא ישקיט מעולמו ויסתר פנים מעולמו. כדיין שמותחים בילה עליו ואין יודע מה נעשה בחוץ, "When he is undisturbed, who can then condemn" (Job 32:9). R Meir (mid II CE) interpreted it [thus]: [When] he is undisturbed about His world and hides his face from it.

Like a judge in front of whom curtains (*vela*, pl) are stretched, and he does not know what is happening without. ▽ בילן, וילן: *βῆλον*, sing; כילה, read: בילה pl (influenced by כילה Sem curtain, canopy. Jastrow 632a). // LevR 5. 1, 99_1: ולון, וילון; YalkJob 908: וילון. (// in YalkPs 680: פסליון, MidPs 10. 5, 95: פליטין; see ↓ **פסליון:** *παστόν* [?], curtain.)

DeutZ (apud BuberLikkutim, from YalkDeut 815): משל למלך שהיה יושב בבית דירתו מסביר פנים לכל בני פלטין. וכיון שנכנס איפרכוס שלו התחיל מזדעף. גזר ואמר: עשו בימה (↑), פרסו וילון, שאני יושב בדין. א"ל איפרכוס שלו: מרי המלך, לכל בני פלטין עשית פנים יפות. וכיון שנכנסתי פרסת עלי (בימה) [וילון]. עלילה אתה מבקש לי?, It is like unto a king who was sitting in his house, showing friendliness to all members of his imperial household. When his *eparchus* entered, he began to rage. He decreed, saying: Make me a *bema* (platform for judgement, ↑ **בימה**), and stretch the curtain, for I am sitting in judgement. Said his *eparchus:* My Lord the king, to all your household you show friendliness. But when I enter, you stretch the curtain. Are you seeking a pretext for me (i e, to punish me. See continuation, where Moses says to God: And you condemn me to death?!).

Lieberman, JQR 35, 1944, 17–18, explains first text as indicating that it is not the trial that is *intra velum, in secretario,* but the deliberation of the judge on the sentence. The *velum* (or *vela*, pl) is (are) drawn before him, so that he no longer see what is going on in the crowd, and need not heed possible condemnation by the public. See further ibid n116 (and 19 n125) for ref to patristic lit on the drawing of the curtain during the liberation. E g, Acta Claudii, Asterii etc (TRuinart, Acta Sincera 2, 142 n9): Lysias introgressus *obduxit velum* et post exiens ex tabella recitavit sententiam. Cf Berger 693ab sv *secretarium.*

The second text reflects (IV CE?) judicial procedure (cf Berger ibid).

The reading בילה, *vela* (pl) suggests that there was sometimes more than one curtain. See also KraussPR 112; Ziegler 105. בימה in DeutZ maybe a corrupt for בילה (pl).

There is, of course, a very specialized meaning of *velum*, which is common in Rabb lit, and means any kind of curtain. It appears in a variety of forms, e g: וילון, ווילון, בילון, בילן, etc. See LW2, 235b–236a (where, however, several entries have been confusedly put together).

Gk translit: *βέλον* and *οὐῆλον*, LSJSupple 30b, etc. On Rabb translit, LW1, 47.

Syr: וילא, ואלא, ולא, PnS 1062.

Cf ↓ **קנקנים, פסליון**

וילון ↑ ולון

ז

זיטמא ↓ זוטימיא

זיטיטוויס ↓ זיטיוטוס, זיטיוטויס, זיטוטוות

◇**זיטיטוויס [זיטיטוס]** (246) one sought for (to be put to death), "wanted": *ζητητός* (sc *θανεῖν*), **ζητευτός*

GenR 32. 1, 289: הסיר (נ"א: התיר) קונעתו ועשאו זיטיטורס, כמי שהוא מת דמו מותר ואשתו מותרת, (Doeg) removed (David's) wife (or: permitted her [to remarry]), and declared him sought for, like one who is (legally) dead, [that] he may be killed and his wife free (to remarry) ▽ זיטיוטים, זיטוטים, זיטיוטוס, זיטיטיוטים Vat 60, etc. Read in all cases: זיטיטוס. // Ibid 38. 1, 351_7: זיטוטוות. ▽ זינטטיוטוס, זיטיוטוס, זיטיוטים etc, read: זיטיטוס; YalkPs 631; MachPs 5. 18, 1. 36: זיטיוטים.

Jastrow 393a (which requires slight correction) ref to Tobit 1:19: *ζητοῦμαι ἀποθανεῖν*, and BTaan 29: מתבקש, meaning: wanted (for execution). The alternative form offered **ζητευτός*, borne out by many readings, is not attested in Gk lexica, but is quite likely in view of the (poetic) form *ζητεύω* (= *ζητέω*). See also Gignac 1, 229, on *ε* > *ευ* changes in papyri. Cf Levy 1, 527b, AC 3, 283a. (Contra SachsBeiträge 1, 125–26; Fürst 114ab: *ζημιωτός* – an unattested word.)
As to the strange forms זיטיטיוטים and זינטטיוטוס, see Mayser 1/1², 219–20, Gignac 161 (on gemination and dittography) and cf ↑ **אילוגין**. The *nun* in ~זינט is perhaps an example of a nasal insertion before a stop; see Gignac 1, 118, eg *οὔντος* (for *οὗτος*) PMich 228. 14 (47 CE)?

זיטמא (246–47) blameworthy conduct: [*]*ζήτημα*

NumR 4. 8: לטרפיסטים (read: ~יס) של מדינה שנמצא דבר של זיטמא, the money changer of the city in whose conduct was found a blameworthy matter.
LevR 20. 10, 468_2: ונמצא בשושבינים שלו דבר שלזינימון, and in his groomsmen was found a blameworthy matter. ▽ של זיטימא, MsMunich 117, של שמצא, transl, Ar (AC 3, 284b, 306a): זיטימא, זינימון. // PRK 173b, 397_{11}: זינו מייא, ▽ זינומייא, זינימון; NumR 2. 25: דבר של לוגמיא(?); TanḥBLevAḥarei 8, 64: זוהמא; so too YalkNum 625; (TanḥLevAḥarei 6: דבר מקולקל, also in edprinc, transl); MGNum 3. 4, 16_{15}: זוטימיא, ▽ זוטימא. Read: זיטימא, זיטימיא, זיטימון (?).

Buxt 662; cf Perles, MGWJ 16, 1867, 298; Buber, TanḥLevAḥarei 64 n121; Levy 1, 528a; AC 3,

306b—307a, and 384b; Mandelbaum PRK adloc; Löw, apud Krauss, LW 2, 246b—247a. (Contra Krauss LW 2, 246b—247a, who unnecessarily divides the material into two entries, suggesting one to be *βλασφημία*, cf LW 1, 316—17; Fürst 114a: *ζημιώδης*.)
On NumR 2. 25, see LW 2, 304b, again suggesting *βλασφημία*, rightly rejected by Löw 658b. No better is Jastrow's suggestion, 694b: *λαγνεία* or *λάγνευμα*, lewdness, nor AC 5, 16b—17a: *λῦμα*, dirt. We tentatively suggest emending to: **זטמיא**, cf below, variant (2).

The variants exhibit a number of different readings: **(1)** **זיטמא** and **זיטימא**, *ζήτημα* **(2)** **זהמא** in Tanḥ and Yalk should perhaps be read: **זוטמא**, cf MGNum. **זוטימא**, and cf Syr: **זוטמא**, *delictum* PnS 1116 **(3)** **זיטימי(י)א**, (corrupt forms: **זינומייא**, where the *tet* was broken up into *nun-vav*, **זוטימיא**, read: **זיטימיא**, **לוגמיא**, read: **זיטימיא** ?) corresponds with **ζητημια*, a form created by analogy with *ζημία*, and other *~μα* endings. (Cf ↑ **אכסיוכא**.) Such vowel development is often found in Rabbinic Graecitas (cf ↓ **מיסתיוסים**, Sperber, Sinai 87, 1980, 151—52), and in papyri, see Gignac 1, 310—11, eg *ἡμέρια* (for *ἡμέρᾳ*) in BGU 1039. 3 (Byz), etc. **(4)** **זינימון**, perhaps **זיטמון**, **ζητημον*? (Jastrow 393b suggests reading: **זיטיסין** = *ζήτησις*. Perhaps *~σιν*, acc?)
The Gk *ζήτημα* usually means judicial inquiry, subject of dispute, etc (see LSJ[9] 756a). However, the meaning "blameworthy conduct" found in Rabbinic Graecitas is paralleled by the Syr: **זטמא**, meaning *reprehensio*, *vituperium*, PnS 1115—16, (and **זוטמא** *delictum*, ibid).

Syr: **זוטמא**, **זטמא**, PnS 115—16; also **זאטמא**, **זאטימא**, **זיטימא**, Brockelm[2] 194.

זיטמא ↑ זינימון, זינומייא, זינו מייא

זמיון expense, loss, damage: *ζημιον (= ζημία)

Teshuvot ha-Geonim [ha-Keẓarot], edJerusalem 1960, 30 no72: **נשבע חמיו שנגנבו ולא פשע בהם ונפטר, והזמיון על הבעל כשקבלן בצאן ברזל**, His father-in-law swears that they were stolen, and that he was not negligent [in his care] for them, and he is exempt, and the expense [falls] upon the husband, if he received them as inalienable goods. (Also cited in Tarbiẓ 2/4, 1931, 109).
Ibid 78 no275: **וגרם לו חבישה וזמיון**, and he caused him imprisonment and damage.

Cf Lewin, Tarbiẓ ibid n2. And cf LW 2, 247ab sv **זימיא**: *ζημία* (Syr: **זימיא**, PnS 1117), meaning a tax in Rabbinic literature. It should be noted that the neut dim term *~ιον* is very common in later and Byz Gk; see Psaltes 271—76. Furthermore, there are numerous examples of fem nouns being given this neut term; eg *κριθίον* (from *κριθή*), *φιάλιον* (from *φιάλη*), *δοκίμιον* (from *δοκίμη*), etc.

ח

◇חלף סידרה (252) water-clock, used to time speeches in law-courts. adaptation from: *κλεψύδρα* → *clepsydra*

GenR 49. 24, 514_4: (↓ סניגור) חלף סידרה מלאה מים. כל זמן שהיא מלאה מים הסניגור מלמד. פעמים שהדיין מבקש שילמד הסניגור, והוא אומר הוסיפו בתוכה מים, A water-clock full of water. As long as it is full of water, the attorney for the defence pleads. Sometimes the judge wishes the attorney for the defence |to continue| to plead. And he says: Add water to it. ▽ סרדה~, קדירה~, סדרא~, סודרא~, סידרא חלוף, etc. // YalkGen 83, 381_{17}.

Time allotted to speakers in Athens was called *ὕδωρ*. First "water" went to the accuser, second to the accused, third to the judge. Length of time, i e amount of water depended upon importance of case. A special officer (*ὁ ἐφ' ὕδωρ*) watched the *clepsydra*, stopping it whenever a document was read. A speaker not bound by time was called *δίκαι ἄνευ ὕδατος*, one bound, *δίκαι πρὸς ὕδατος*. According to a law introduced by Cn Pompeius the same system was used in Rome, with an officer to stop the *clepsydra*. Pliny (Epist 2. 11) related that on one important occasion he spoke for nearly five hours, twelve large *clepsydrae* having been granted him by the *iudices*. But the case was so important that four more were added. See Smith's Dict of Gk and Rom Ant 1. 973a, 975b; Mommsen, Römisches Strafrecht, 1899, 428; Lieberman, JQR 35, 1944, 27; KraussPR 114. The term regularly appears as two words (see ed note in GenR adloc), and is a (conscious) Hebraization of the Gk, meaning literally "change of water." This in itself is sufficient to explain all the phonetic peculiarities here (κ > ח, ψ > fs; cf LW1, 12, 107, much of which is unnecessary). However, the ▽ סודרא~, if not simply an error for סידרא~, may reflect knowledge of the Gk original ~*ψυδρα*. Not additional Hebraization in ▽ קדירה, Heb pot, urn.

ט

◇טולמיסן (268) he dared: <*ἐ*>*τόλμησεν*

YKet 7 adfin 31d28: על דטלמסן למגע בסמה דמטרונ׳, Because he *ἐτόλμησεν* (dared) to seize (*ἅψασθαι*) *σώματος ματρώνης* (the body of the matron) // GenR 40. 2, 389 = 52. 13, 553_7: על דטולמיסן למקרב למסנה דמטרונה, because he dared to touch the shoe of the matron. (Partial // to GenR in TanḥGenLech 5, B8, 67.)

LiebermanGH 30–33; idem in Biblical and other Studies, edAAltmann, 1963, 133, who shows that the whole sentence: *ἐτόλμησε(ν) ματρώνης σώματος ἅψασθαι* is a verbatim quotation from a Roman legal source, in Gk, forbidding the seizure of a matron for unpaid debts, for which the punishment was corporal punishment. He cites ValMax, Facta et Dicta Memorabilia II 1, London 1823, 234, which reads: *in ius vocanti matronam corpus eius attingere non permisserunt*, which, in turn, is a Lat transl of a Gk law, which later formed the basis for Justinian's Nov 134. 7, 9, which fixes punishments for such deeds. On the ▽ in GenR see Lieberman GH 33–34 n77.
See LW 2, 268a, and 397a sv סמא (where Krauss is to be accepted and Löw rejected); AC 3, 37b–38a, 4, 35a sv טלם2; Levy 2, 161b. SCohen, ZDMG 79, 204, finds טלמסן in Samaritan too. However, the significance of this entry is not so much in the single Gk word (or words) but in the fact that a whole sentence in Gk from a Roman law has survived in Rabbinic writings. (Note, however, that GAlon, Meḥkarim 2, 261–63, has called into doubt the legal character of this statement. But his argument is more polemic than it is convincing.)

טימוס ↓ טומוס

טומטייה appraisal, assessment: *τιμητεία*

Avadim 2. 5 (Kirchheim 27, Kaniewsky 118) Higger 57_{49}: אין קונים שני עבדים כאחד, שאין עושין טומטייה בשני עבדים, One may not purchase two slaves in one go; for it is forbidden to make an appraisal of two slaves. (The meaning seems to be that each individual slave – we are talking of a Jewish bondsman, *'eved 'ivri* – has to be bought at his own specific price. One may not buy slaves in bulk, and later assess the value of each one. See Kaniewsky's second explanation, ibid 118–19.) ▽ טומריא.

See PerlesBeiträge 41–42.
Kirchheim knew only the reading טומריא, and in his notes adloc (3) suggests several explanations, none of which are satisfactory. AC 4, 45a sv טומריא, suggests *τιμωρία;* however, the meaning is unsuitable to the context. Likewise, the Pehlevi Tīmār (ibid) is rejected in ACSup 203a. We have preferred the other reading, found in MsHalberstam-Epstein, as giving a better sense.
As to the *υ* > *ι* interchange (~טום – *τιμ*~), cf ↓ טימי.

Cf ↓ טימי

טומטייה ↑ טומריא

טיטראון instrument of torture: **τιτρωον* (?)

LevR 32. 1, 735_7, according to emendation in MsMunich 117: מה לך לוקה בטיטראון, why are you being struck with an instrument of torture (?). ▽ MsMunich before emendation: בפראגין, main reading בפרגל (↓ פרגל) // MechYitro Ba-Ḥodesh 6, 227_9: מאפרגל; Ve-Hizhir 1. 50: מכף רגל, read: מאה פרגל; MidPs 12.

5, 109: בפרוגין; LTEx 20. 6, 1. 136: מאה פרגול; YalkEx 292, ibidZach 581; ibidPs 659; MachPs 12. 24, 1. 76: meaning lashes or a hundres lashes.

Main reading פרגל (↓): *φραγελ|λιον|*, *flagellum*, scourge.
**τιτρωον*, perhaps from *τιτρώσκω*, an instrument of injury, torture, like *τρωτήριον*, wounding instrument (Lampe 1418a), rather than simply a corruption of one of the forms of the main reading. (I now reject my own earlier idea of relating this word with *τιτράω-τετραίνω*, to performate, something like *τετραῖον*, which Hesych, explains as a kind of bird, some kind of pecker?)

Cf ↓ פרגל

טימי ↓ טימהא

טומוס, טימוס (263) (1) roll (of sheets of papyrus stuck together) (2) register (of names): *τόμος* → *tomus*

(1) TBK 9. 31, 366_8: היכה באחד ידו בנייר בפנקס ... ובטומוס של שטרות ▽ בידיו, נותן ארבע מאות זוז ... מפני שמכה של ביזיון היא ..., If he hit him backhandedly with paper with a *pinax* ... and with a roll of deeds that was in his hands, he gives him four hundred *denarii* (lit: *zuz*) ... because this was a demeaning blow. ▽ בטימוס (LiebermannTR 2, 100). // MachPs 3. 21, 1. 26: בטמוס; SifraEmorPerek 20, 104d: ובטימסמירות, read: ובטימס ניירות, a roll of papers, ▽ MsVatAssemani 46, 467: ובטימסניירות – Ravad adloc: ובטומוסנירות (sic), explained ibid: טומוס ניירות; YBK 7. 1, 6b 23: בטומוס שבידו; YalkLev 658: ובטומוס שטרות. (Cf MBM 1. 8: תכריך של שטרות, and cf below.)
TShab 13. 4, 58_{17}, 129_1: טומוס של ברכות, a roll of benedictions. // BShab 115b. (But // YShab 16. 1, 15a 30, and Soferim 15. 4, 276_{24}: תכריך. Cf above.)

(2) YHor 3. 7, 48a 53: אע"פ שנתנו אחרים יותר ממך, כתבנו ראש טימוס, Even though others donated more than you, we have written you up |at| the top of the register. // LevR 5. 4, 113_1: בראש טומוס, ▽ טמוס, טימוס. But YalkDeut 884 and ibidProv 956 have: כתבנו בראש, with our word omitted. DeutR 4. 8 in a rather free reworking has: ועשינו אותך ראש פרק.)

GenR 25. 1, 238_2: אינו נכתב בתוך טומוסן של צדיקים, אלא בטומוסן שלרשעים, He is not written in the register of the righteous, but in the register of the wicked. ▽ טימוסן, טמוסן, טימוסין, (ניתווסיק, נתווסיק?). // YalkGen 42, 145_{90}; ibidChron 1072; GenRabbati 36_4: נימוסין, read: טימוסין.
PRK 27a, 48_4: מה עשה עמלק? ירד לבית ארכיון (↑ ארכיון) של מצרים. נטל טימסיהם של שבטים שהיה שם שמם חקוק עליהם ..., What did Pharaoh do? He went to the

archive of Egypt, took the register of the tribes in which their names were inscribed ... ▽ טמסיהם, טימוסיהם, טימוסין, טומסיהם etc. // TanḥDeut Teẓe 9, Bibid 13, 41; YalkDeut 938. (But PR 12, 52a has a free rendering: סיפר ייחוס שמותם של ישראל.)

MGGen 47. 22, 792_{10}: מה עשה יוסף הצדיק? נכנס לבתי האריכות (↑ ארכי) והוציא הטמסון שלהן, שפלוני ממשפחת פלונית ..., What did Joseph the righteous do? He went into the offices of the archives and took out their register, [in which was written] that so and so is of the family of such and such. ▽ הטפסון, read: הטמסון. // Ibid introduction 25; ▽ בטימסון (corrupt from טמסק pl, ?).

YSanh 17. 1, 28a 8: אף שמותיהם פרחו מתוך טמסותיהם, So too their names flew out of their registers. (Note fem pl term.)

ExR 15.10: הוציא הנמוסין ופשפש בהם ולא מצא שם את השם הזה; read: הטימוסין, He took out the registers and searched through them, but did not find there the name. (// in TanḥEx Va-Era 5; Bibid 2, 19; YalkEx 175 have: דיפתרא: *διφθέρα*, LW 2, 211a, while ExR 5. 14 has: בספר שלי, in my book. And cf BHM 3. 45, Alpha Beta de R. Akiva ק', which reads: דלוסקא של כתבים, edWertheimer, BatMid 2, 390: דלוסקום, cf LW 2, 213b.)

Note that LamentR 2. 2 (and cf Buber 106 n105): טימסן. // YTaan 4. 8, 69a 41: קטמוס have nothing to do with our word. (Contra LW 2, 263b; Jastrow 1350a; AC 4, 44a.) Cf Levy 2. 155a, (and LW 2, 264a) *τῖμος*, a tax (? asterisk unnecessary, as this form is attested, see LSJ[9] 1974b). Or perhaps metath, קמטוס: *κομιτής* on **comitus*, mayor or representative of city (?).
On the form טימוס with the *o* > *ι* interchange, see LW 1, 88–89, and cf ↓ נימוס, where we have suggested that the main (Rabbinicized) form is טימוס, and the secondary, less frequently attested. טומוס is a "purist" deviation from the main form.

Syr: טומסא, PnS 1443.
Arm: *tom, toms*, Brockelmann, ZDMG 47, 1893, 10–11, Hübschmann 459. (*τομάριον* has survived in Arm *tomar*, Brockelmann ibid, and Hübschmann 458, and in Arabic, cf Vollers, ZDMG 51, 1897, 299, and Fraenkel 251, also citing Aethiopic from Dillmann 1217.)
Cf ↓ נימוס

טימוס ↑ טימוסמירות

טימי (~מין, ~מיתא) (264) (1) worth, value, price (2) reward satisfaction: *τιμή* (~*μήν*, acc)

(1) YBer 9. 1, 12 (11)d 46: למרגליתא דלית לה טימי, like a precious jewel that has no price (ie is priceless). // MidPs 19. 2, 164.
YPea 1. 1, 15d 49: אמר ליה: מה! אנא שלחית לך מילה דלית לה טימי, He said to him: What! I sent you something priceless ... // GenR 35. 4, 333_{10} in apparat;

YalkJosh 31; ibid Prov 934; Sheiltot Ekev 163, edMirsky 5, Deut 18_{45}.
GenR 2. 2, $15_{4\ 5\ 8}$: ... למלך שקנה לו ב׳ עבדים, שניהם באוני (↿ אוני) אחת ובטימי אחת, Like a king who bought himself two slaves, both on one deed and for one price. // GenRabbati 1. 2, $36_{20\ 21}$; YalkGen 4, $12_{76\ 78}$ 13_{81}.
GenR 11. 4, 91_{8}: ... הוה הדין מסיק ליה בטימי והדין מסיק ליה בטימי עד דמטא בי״ב דינרין, ... the one raised the price, and the other raised the price, until it reached twelve *denarii*. (// PR 23, 119a has: ... והוה דין מעלי ליה, without our word.) This text is cited in Shibbole ha-Lekket 307, 288, and Tanya 78. (CfTurOraḥḤayyim 604 for a different version, without our word.)
LevR 28. 6, 763_{5}: ובכמן הות טימיה?, And how much is its price? ▽ טימי דידיה. // EstR 10. 4 (to 6:10): טימיה; AgEst 6. 11, 63: טימא; AbbaGurion 6, 40: טימיה; PRK 71b, 144_{4}: טימי, ▽ טומי, טימא, טימיה; PR 18, 93a: טימי; YalkLev 643; ibidEst 1058.
LevR 30. 1, 692_{2}: בכמה הות טימי דידיה? How much is its price? ▽ MsParis 149: טיימיה. // PRK (179a), 404_{4}: טימין (not pl, but acc: τιμήν), ▽ טימי, טומין, טומי; MGLev 23. 40, 654_{10}; YalkNum 651: טימין. PRK cited in Arugat ha-Bosem 2, 172: טימין. (// in CantR 2. 3. (2) has: כמה היא טבא, sic edprinc.)
EcclesR 11. 9: אייתי טימי מה דאכלת, Bring the value (i e pay) of what you ate.
TrgYGen 21:33: ... והוו בעיין למתן ליה טימי די אכלו ושתו, and they wished to give him the price of what they had eaten and drunk ...
TrgPsJ 23:15: קבל מני ארע דטימין דילה ארבע מאה סלעין דכסף, Receive from me (i e buy) a [plot of] land whose price is four hundred *selaim* of silver. (טימין is not pl, but acc: τιμήν.)
TrgPsJNum 20:19: דמי טימיהון, their price.
TrgPsJNum 24:14: ... בבציר מן טימיהון ... , ... for less than their price ...
TrgProv 31:10: יקירא היא מן כיפי טבתא טימהא, Her price is more costly than precious jewels, (transl: מכרה).
1 Chron 20:2: ... דהות טימין דידה, whose price was ... (τιμήν acc).

Secondary sing form: טימיתא:
YShek 5. 6, 49b 11: ... הא לך טימיתה קופד, Here is the price of meat for you (i e the sum covering the cost of the meat). ▽ SY $132_{16\ 17}$: טימתה, טימיתה. // YPea 8. 9, 21b 31: הילך טימיתיה.
YTaan 1. 4, 64b 45: וזבנית חמרי ויהבית לה טימיתיה, and I sold my wine and gave her the price (i e the income). Ibid line53: טימיתיה.
YSanh 17. 2, 28b 13: והוא מפריש טימיתיה לע״ז, and he donates its value to idolatry.
LamentR 1. 1, 44: ... פסק טימיתהון, he fixed their price ...
LevR 2. 1, $245_{1\ 2}$: ... מזבין ליה ושתי בטימיתיה חמרא, he sells it and drinks wine for

its price ... ▽ בטימיותיה, בטמיותיה, בטומיתיה. // EstR 5. 1; MachProv 23. 31, 44b: בטימיתיה; YalkProv 960.
RuthR 3. 4 (to 1:17): ומה דהוא עביד טימיתא, תיסב, and whatever price it fetches, take. // EcclesZ 2. 8, 119: טימתיה. (Reworked in ExR 52. 3 and YalkProv 964 without our word. Also cited in MnHm as deriving from MidHashkem; see Enelow, HUCA 4, 1927, 329.)

(2) Trg1Est 3:8: ולמלכא לית ליה טימי מנהון, and for the king there is no reward from them (transl: שוה).
Trg1Est 5. 13: וכל דא ליתיה טימי לותי, and all this gives me no satisfaction (or: is of no worth to me, meaning **(1)**).
Trg1Est 7:4: טימין, reward (~*μήν*, acc).

See also RosenthalPiyyutim 2_{25}.
As to טימי דרומי in YAZ 3. 3, 42d 26, read: טיכי; thus LW 2, 263ab sv טיכי; Lewy, ZDMG 47, 1893, 118; Epstein, Tarbiẓ 3, 1931, 19_{11} and n11. (Contra SchwabVocabulaire 136.)
For טיימיה in ▽ to LevR 30. 1, 691_2, cf *τειμήν* (for *τιμήν*) in the papyri; Gignac 1, 190. As to the forms טומי, טומיתיה, rather than simply brushing them off as scribal errors, they may possibly be explained as examples of *ι* > *υ* interchange; eg *τυμίου* (for *τιμίου*) in PLond 390 (ii, 332) 2 (VI–VII cent), etc (Gignac 1, 269–70). Cf ↑ **טומטייה**: *τιμητεία*. (שומי in LamentR 4. 2, 142 should perhaps be emended to: טומי, or is from Sem שומא, assessment. Printed ed ibid has: דמי, money, price.)
טימין is almost certainly an acc form (LW 2, 264a) and not a pl form (contra LevyTrgWb1, 300b). The existence of two parallel forms, one nom sing and the other acc sing, is not uncommon in Rabbinic Graecitas. Cf ↑ **אפופסיס**, with form ~סין, and ↓ **קילווסין**, with form ~סיס.
As to טימיתא, this is a new Sem fem formation from טימי. For similar examples of such fem formations, cf אוניתא from **אוני** ↑ , אפוכיתא from **אפוכי** ↑
For the related term אטימיטון: *ἀτιμήτον*, priceless, see LW 2, 29b.
See DeismannLAE 323–24; MM 635ab; ArndtGingrich 825ab.

Syr: טימא, טימי, PnS 1461. Cf BrunsSachau index sv *τιμή*.
Cf ↑ **טומטייה**.

טימי ↑ טימיתא, טימין

טימוס ↑ טמסותיהם, טמסון, טימסן, טימסיהם

טילמיסן ↑ טלמסן

פיסטיס ↓ טפוס

י

דיוקטא ↑ יוזקטטא

כ

כורוסתי [כורזסתי] (284?) to give a present: *χαρίζεσθαι*

YNed 3. 3, 38a 28: כן אורחה דבר נשא מימור לחבריה: כורוסתי בייה?, read: כורוסתי, Is it the way of man to say to his friend: [*ὁμολογῶ*] *χαρίζεσθαι* [*σοι*] *βίᾳ*, i e, I give [you] a present perforce.

LiebermanGH 34, who shows that *ὁμολογῶ χαρίζεσθαι σοι* ... is a common legal phrase used in deeds of gifts, ref Preisigke sv *χαρίζομαι*. (Correcting Jastrow 160b sv בייא II; AC 4, 338a: *χαρίζεσθαι ποίει;* rejecting AC 2, 45b: *βρῶσθι βαιὸν*, first suggested by BrüllJahrb 1, 1874, 131, and followed by Levy 2, 413b. Krauss, LW 2, 284a, refers to כירי. However, it is not quoted in כירי I–IV, 280b–287a. Hence our question-mark.) For *χαρ~* > ~כור, *a* > *o*, see Mayser 1/1², 37–38, Gignac 1, 286–87.

Cf ↑ ביא

כירו מניקייה ↓ כידו ומניקיא

בימה ↑ כימיה

כירו מניקייה ↓ כירומיניקייה, כירומנקיהן, כירומניקיא, כירו מניקיא, כירומניקאה

כירומניקייה, כירו מניקייה (286) fetters, handcuffs, manacles: *χειρομανίκια* (pl)

YSanh 11 (17) 2, 28c 48: מהו "בח[ו]חים"? בכירו מניקיא, What is "ba-ḥoḥim" (2Chron 33:11 – "in fetters")? In handcuffs; sic MsL and edprinc. // PRK 162a, 365_3: בירומי ניקיא, בידי ומניקייה, כורו מיניקיא ▽ כירו מיניקייה, Ar (AC 4, 332a): כרומנקיא, corr acc; Trg2Chron 33:11: בירומנקיא ▽ נקייה~; RuthR 5. 6 (to Ruth 2:14): כירומניקאה, sic edprinc.

AgEst 5. 14, 56: אם בכפר מתקיא תשליחהו, כבר נתפלל מנשה בן חזקיה ויצא, If you throw him in fetters, Manasseh son of Hezekiah already prayed and went free; read: בכרמניקיא, (cf YSanh ibid and //). // AbbaGurion 5. 14, 36 has מולא (see LW 2, 325b sv מולי).

CantR to Cant 4:8: בקרקומניקיאה, read: ~בכירו (?), (transl בזקים, "in chains", Is 45:14). ▽ edprinc: בכרקומיניקיאה. // SederOlamRab 23, edRatner 102: בכידו ומניקיא, ▽ edMilikowsky (1981), 337–38$_{29\ 30}$: כירה מהניקיא.

Trg2Chron 36:6: בכירומנקיא (transl בנחשתים, "in fetters"), is gloss to בשושלוון דנחשא, "in chains of bronze". ▽ ~מנקיהו.

Krauss, LW 2, 286a explains: *χειρομάνικον*. But Löw, adloc, explains: ~*μανίκια* (pl), noting that Soph 732a knows *μανίκιον*, and ibid 505a *ἐπιμανίκια*. Krauss ibid concludes that **χειρομανίκιον* is unattested in Gk lit, and therefore gives asterisk. However, it is recorded in DuCange872 sv *χειρομάνικον*. For the meaning metal handcuffs, as opposed to simply sleaves or cuffs (Soph ibid) see DuCange ibid. This too is the meaning of Lat *manicae* (OLD 1073a sv).

The ref to מניקת ראש in LW ibid, from PRE 43 (Luria 102a, Higger, Ḥorev 10, 1948, 225 and ▽ 286 n53: מקיבת) should be seen as part of sv מניכא, LW 2, 343b–344a, and does not belong here. It is interesting to note that most of the Rabb sources recognize the two distinct components of this *word: χειρ~* hand, and *μανίκια*, dim of Lat *manica*, sleave or fetter.

כמס (292) bridle with hook (placed in and/or over mouth of convict before he is led to execution): *χάμος*

PRK 159b, 357$_9$, 358$_1$: ללסטים שהוא נידון לפני הקוסטינר (↓), בתחילה הוא קורא אנלגין (↑ואילוגין) שלו. ואחר כך הוא מכה אותו, ואחר כך הוא נותן לו כמס, ואחר כך נותן לו פרקולה (↑), ואחר כך יוצא ליהרג ... ואחר כך הוא נותן להם כמס, "צרור עון אפרים וגו׳", Like a robber who was tried before a *questionarius*. At first he reads his *elogium*, then he flogs him, then he gives him the bridle-hook, then he gives him the *periculum* (sentence), and then he is led to his execution ... And then He gives them the bridle-hook, [as it is written] "The iniquity of Ephraim is bound up ..." (Hos 13:12). // YalkHos 532: כמס; MachHos, JQRNS 15, 1924–25, 212.

Lieberman, JQRNS 35, 1944, 44–48; already suggested by PerlesES 89. Lampe 1512b, Sophocles 1160a, DuCange 1729 (and cf ibid 1723 sv *χάβος*) equate this word with *κημός:* muzzle, which was placed *over* the mouth. This is borne out by some Byz sources (Lieberman ibid 44–45), as well as being supported by the verse in Hos ibid (צרור: bound up). However, Lieberman rejects this identification, and brings sources (eg Peter of Alex, Canon Epist 14, early IV CE) to show that the *χάμος* was placed *ἐν τῷ στόματι* (Peter of Alex ibid), *in* the mouth. He thus equates the *χάμος* with the Lat *hamus* (OLD 785bc): hook. It would seem that the *χάμος* – *chamus* (Maigne D'Arnis 483: *frenum*) is a bridle with a crooked bit like a hook (hence, Hesych: *χαμόν· καμπύλον*), which is placed

both over and/or in the mouth. It both binds the mouth (cf Hos ibid) and tears it. Cf also Krauss, Dvir 1, 1923, 100.
This word is not to be confused with קומוס (contra LW 2, 292a, and reject Löw's suggestion ibid), which appears in TTehorot 11. 3, 672_{16}, according to reading of Rashi (M ibid 9. 9, cf Lieberman TR 4, 99): תוחב בהן הקומוס, ▽ :בו הקוסמין ... , he inserts (or sticks) the *komos* into them. Read: קימוס: *κημός:* hook (contra TR ibid). Thus *χάβος* = *κημός*, Sch Ar Eq 1147, and cf above (Lieberman, private communication). Cf Syr. כימוס: *κημός*, PnS 3603, כאמא, PnS 3458.

אכסוריא ↑ כסוריא

כירו מניקייה ↑ כפר מתקיא

קרטיס ↓ כרתיס, כריסטן, כרטיס, כרטוסה

ל

ריטור[0] ↓ לאיטר, לאיטור
לגטון
לגטון (304) bequest, legacy: *ληγᾶτον* ← *legatum*

BSanh 91a, according to Ar (AC2, 273a): נתן אברהם מתנות. אב שנתן לגטון לבניו ושיגר זה מעל זה, כלום יש לזה על זה כלום?, Abraham gave (the sons of the concubines) presents. If a father made a bequest to his children in his lifetime, and sent them away one from the other, has the one any claim against the other? ▽ edd: אנטין, אגטין, MsM: שכתב גיטין (see RabbinoviczVL ibid 252 n70). // YalkGen 110, 503_{69}: לגיטיך, לגיטיון ▽ אגיטון; MGGen 25. 5–6, 417_{8}: גטות.
Pl: TanḥGenNoah 14, B20, 47: ואברהם התחיל ... ובליגטא ... ובליגטא (זהו מתנה) מנין? שנאמר, "ולבני הפילגשים אשר לאברהם נתן אברהם מתנות", And Abraham was the first (in the Bible) ... and in [the making of] legacies ... And in legacies (this is a present – internal gloss), whence [do we know this]? For it is said, "But unto the sons of the concubines, which Abraham had, Abraham gave gifts" (Gen 25:6). //MGNum 3. 32, 25_{4}: ובמלונטא ▽ ובלונטה (influenced by ובפונדק above in same line, פונדק = מלון); read: ובליגטה, MannBible 1, 305 (from Yelmd apud YalkTalmudTorah of Sikili): ובליגטמא = *legatum* (+ Aram pl). ליגטא, ה~, is *legata*, pl, explaining מתנות, presents in Gen ibid.

See AC 2, 273a sv גט and n12; LW2, 304b; Jastrow 692a; Levy 2, 473b. The readings גטוט, גיטין, are determined by the context which speeks of sending them away from one another.

לגיטין may be *$\lambda\eta\gamma\alpha\tau\iota o\nu$, (not $\lambda\eta\gamma\alpha\tau i\omega\nu$, Lampe 799a, or *legatinum*, OLD 1013b). $\lambda\eta\gamma\hat{\alpha}\tau o\nu$, BGU 1. 327. 6; $\lambda\varepsilon\gamma\acute{\alpha}\tau o\nu$, Lampe 799a, DuCange 796. Note CGL 4. 254_4: *legata donata*.

Syr: ליגטון, PnS 1938; לגטא, BB 941; cf BrunsSachau 8_{16}, 14_{15} etc.
Cf ↓ לוקטור

זיטמא ↑ לוגמיא

ריטור[0] ↓ ליטור, ליטול, לוטייר

◇**לוקטור** (304) one who leaves a legacy: *legator*

GenR 61. 7, 666_8: והא כתיב, "ויתן אברהם את כל אשר לו ליצחק". אמר: ואיכן הוא לוקטור? אמר לו: "ולבני הפילגשים [אשר לאברהם נתן אברהם מתנות]", And surely it is written, "And Abraham gave all he had unto Isaac" (Gen 25:5). He said: And how, [then], was he one who left a [valid?] legacy? He replied: "But unto the sons of the concubines [which Abraham had, Abraham gave gifts]" (ibid 6). (Commentaries explain that if he gave *all* to Isaac, and left nothing to his other children, the legacy, will, would not be valid, ref BBB 131b, see Theodor ad loc.) ▽ לו קטור, לוקא טור, ליקטור, נותן לבני קטורה (learned emend, followed by Jastrow 701a), שטר שילוח שחילק בין בניו (internal gloss, with original word lost?), MsVat 60: לזקטור. // YalkGen 110, 501_{40}: ליזקטור. Read: לוקטור (?).

Suggested by Krauss LW2, 304b sv לגטון (↑). AC5, 58a prefers: *legatarium* = *legatum* (see Souter 229a), cf Syr: ליגטרא, BrunsSachau 14_{15}. The text remains difficult, and this interpretation uncertain. Cf AC2, 273a; Levy 2, 524b.

Cf ↑ לגטון

◇**לו קיבוסת** (527) plagiarist, corrupt. from: $\lambda o\langle\gamma o\rangle\kappa\lambda\acute{\varepsilon}\pi\tau\eta\varsigma$

YSanh 10 (18) 7, 30d 28: חנניה בן עזור נביא אמת היה, אלא שהיה לו קיבוסת והיה שומע דברים שירמיה מתנבא בשוק העליון ויורד ומתנבא בשוק התחתון, Ḥananiah b. Azur (see Jer 28:1 et seq) was a true prophet, but he [became] plagiarist. For he used to hear what Jeremiah prophecied in the upper market, and then go down to prophecy in the lower market; read לו[גו]קלבתס?

LiebermanGH 161–62, following Löw (LW 2, 527b), finds confirmation of this suggestion in Mishnat R. Eliezer, edEnelow 117_{16}: היה מגנב דברים, he would steal words (cf MT 13. 3, 67 = 270_{15}), meaning he was a plagiarist. The homily is based on Jer 23:30, "the prophets ... that steal my words". $\lambda o\gamma o\kappa\lambda o\pi i\alpha$, $\sim\varepsilon i\alpha$, is known from antiquity (LSJ[9] 1056b, Soph 719a), so that $\lambda o\gamma o\kappa\lambda\acute{\varepsilon}\pi\tau\eta\varsigma$, attested only in modern Gk (Koumanides, Synagoge neo lexon 611 sv), must have

existed in the parlance. (Contra Krauss, LW ibid; *κυβισμός*; Tur-Sinai, apud BenIehuda 11, 5707: *loquax*, inter alia; Jastrow 1354a, from Syr כפס, PnS 3695; AC 7, 59b: *κυβίστησις*, similar to Bacher, apud ACSup 357a; Levy 4, 239b: *κίβδηλος*, *~λιά*, see Fleischer ibid 479b, etc.)
The corrupt may (partially) result from the omission of the *gamma*. See Gignac 1, 74; eg, *λοογράφου* (for *λογογράφου*) POxy 53. 5 (3126 CE). The *lamda* is also sometimes omitted; see Gignac 1, 107. The splitting up of misunderstood loanwords is a common phenomenon in Rabbinic texts. See my remarks in Bar-Ilan 16/17, 1979, 20—21.

לוקים, לוקין, לוקס ↑ גייס לוקס

ליסט, ליסטא, ליסטאה, ליסטאי, ליסטום, ליסטיא ↓ ליסטיס

ליסטיא, ליסטיות ↓ ליסטייא

ליסטיי, ליסטייא, ליסטים, ליסטין, ליסטסייא ↓ ליסטיס

ליסטייא (~טות, ~יות, ~יותא) (315) robbery, banditry: *λῃστεία*

TSanh 9. 7, 429_{23}: ... ואחד יצא לליסטייא, ואחר זמן נתפס זה שיצא לליסטיא והיו צולבין אותו על הצלוב, and one [of them] left for [a life of] robbery. After a time, the one who had left for [a life of] robbery was caught, and they crucified him on the crucifix. // Bibid 46b: **ליסטייא**, sic MsM etc (Rabbinovitz VL 137 n3), ▽ printed ed: לסטיות (see below); MachPs 26. 14, 1. 176: **ליסטיא**.
YBB 9. 4, 17a 7: **אדם שיצא לליסטייא**, a man who left for [a life of] banditry.
YHor 3. 3, 47c 28: מכאן ואילך בליסטייא היו נוטלין אותו, from here on, they would take it by robbery. ▽ **~טיא**.

Additional forms (Hebraized): **ליסטות, ~יות**:

SifDeut 313, 355_{8}, 356, apparat: במקום הצרות, במקום גייסות, במקום לסטיות, in a place of troubles, in a place of marauding troops, in a place of banditry. ▽ **לסטות**, הליסטים, לסטים (↓ **ליסטיס**). (Explains "in a waste howling wilderness," Deut 32:10.)

BKid 30b: כל שאינו מלמדו אומנות מלמדו לסטות. לסטות ס"ד? אלא כאילו מלמדו, Anyone who dies not teaches his son a trade, teaches him robbery. Do you really mean "robbery"? Rather,it is as though he teaches him robbery.
BYev 25b: שנתפס על ידי ליסטיות, ... who was arrested on account of robbery.
BSanh 46b: **ואחד שיצא לליסטיות**, and one who left for [a life of] robbery. ▽ **ליסטיא** etc (see above).

Additional form (Aramaicized): לסטיותא:

BBM 84a: לסטאה בלסטיותא ידע, A robber (↓ **ליסטיס**) knows his trade (lit: robbery, ie he knows the nature of dangerous weapons). ▽ בלסטאה (RabbinovitzVL 240 n50), perhaps read: בלסטיאה.

Syr: לסטיותא, PnS 1959, (cf מלסטיותא ibid).
Cf ↓ **ליסטיס**

ליסטיס (**~טים**, **~טאה**) (315–16) robber, bandit, brigand, highwayman: *ληστής → lestes*

Heb sing:

MBM 7. 9: הלסטם הרי זה אונס, A brigand counts as an unavoidable accident, ▽ הליסטים.
TYev 4. 5, 244_{27}, 11_{24}: ליסטים אחד, a robber. ▽ לסטם. // Yibid 2. 11, 4a bottom; Bibid 25b.
YBer 9, 13 (12)b 4: חד ליסטים, a robber.
YKet 2. 10, 26d 33: אשת ליסטים כליסטים, the wife of a robber is like a robber. // PRK 80a, 176_5: ליסטים, ▽ ליסטים, לסטס. (Cf BAZ 39a.)
BEruv 53b: ליסטים כמותך כבשוה, robbers like you trod it out (i e this path).
GenR 22. 6, 211_3: לליסטים שפוף שהיה יושב על פרשת דרכים, Like an enfeabled highwayman who set at the cross-road. // YalkGen 36, 124_2, ibidPs 840.
PRK 182a, 410_{13}: לליסטים שהוא יושב בפרשת דרכים ומקפיח את העוברים והשבים, Like a highwayman who sits at the cross-road and robs the passers by. ▽ ליסטים. // LevR 30. 5, 702_2: ~יס; MidPs 26. 5, 217; YalkLev 651; ibidPs 703; MGLev 23: 40, 656_6: ליסטום, ▽ ליסטים.
TanhDeutKi-Teze 9, Bibid 12, 40: כליסטים, like a robber. ▽ ~יס, ~יך.
MidPs 59. 4, 302: אתה השיאתני לליסטים שלך, You married me off to your bandit.
EcclesR 3. 17: ליסטים עולה לגרדון, A robber goes to the *gradus* (↑ **גרדון**).
EcclesR 7. 26: ליסטים ... נפיק ומקפח בליליא וזיין בניה ובנתייה ביממא, A robber ... who went out to rob by night, and who fed his son and daughters by day.
GenR 20. 7, 191_8: אשה ... שהיתה נשואה ללסטם אחד, A woman ... who was married to a bandit. ▽ לסטיס, Ar (AC 5, 21ab): לווטס, (see below).
MGGen 27. 1, 465_1: כלסטיס ▽ ליסטים.
ליסטים מזויין, an armed robber. See BBK 57ab, 80a, 114ab, BBM 22a, 93b, 95a, BBB92b, BTem 15b, YShek 2. 1, 46c 29. (It is a subject of controversy whether his legal status is that of a גנב, *ganav*, a stealthy thief, or a גזלן, *gazlan*, an overt

robber, there being a difference in the obligation on the part of a bailee to make good a loss caused by such a robber.)

Heb pl:

(Often the incorrect suffix ~ים was thought to be pl; hence pl forms: ~ים, ~ין.)
Mech to Ex 19:4, $208_{4\ 5}$: ובאו לסטים, and robbers came.
Ibid 22:9, 303_5: ששבוהו לסטים — "או נשבה", "or be driven away" (Ex 22:9) – that it was stolen by robbers. ▽ ליסטים, ~ין.
SifNum 25, 31_7: גלחוהו ליסטים, brigands shaved his |head|.
MBer 1. 3: וסכנתי עצמי מפני הלסטים, and I endangered myself on account of bandits.
MShab 2. 5: ... המכבה את הנר מפני שהוא מתיירא ... מפני לסטים, He who snuffs out the candle, because he fears ... bandits ... ▽ ליסטים. // Bibid 18a; Yibid 2. 5, 5a 17, which adds: מפני ליסטים של סכנה, because of dangerous bandits.
MBK 6. 1: או שפרצוהו לסטים, or that bandits broke in. ▽ ~ליס.
Ibid 10. 2: גזלו לסטים את כסותו, Robbers stole his suit.
MBM 7. 9: למקום גדודי חיות ולסטים, to a place of wild animals and brigands. (Cf BBer 29b.)
MKid 4. 17: שאומנותן אומנות לסטים, for their trade is the trade of robbers. ▽ MsKaufmann: לֶיסְטִים (sing).
TTaan 2. 12, 218_{14}, 334_{76}: לסטין, ▽ ליסטים, ~ין. // BTaan 22b.
BShab 10a, BPes 12b: מאכל לסטין, the meal of robbers (taken late, because they are up at work all night, and sleep late).
LevR 9. 9, 186_5: כיתות כיתות שלליסטין, hoards and hoards of robbers. ▽ ~ים. // YalkLev 493. (Cf Ve-HizhirLev 34b: של אנשי זעף ...) (Cf Krauss PR 280 on this text.)
BBeẓa 15a: רוב לסטים ישראל נינהו, the majority of robbers are Jewish.
TrgYGen 21:13: לעם ליסטים, to a nation of robbers.
TrgJud 5:11: לסטין.

Additional forms Aramaicized sing: ליסטיא, ~טא, ~טאה:

LevR 30. 6, 702_4: איתצייד ההוא ליסטיא, that robber was caught. ▽ ליסטא, ~טאה. // PRK 182a, 411_2: ליסטא, ▽ ~טאה, לסטס (see above); MidPs 26. 5, 218; YalkLev 651; ibidPs 703; MGLev 23:40, 656_9: לסטיא ▽ ליסטא,
BBM 84a: לסטאה בלסטיותא ידע, A robber knows his trade, (robbery, ↑ ליסטייא).
EcclesR 7. 26: ליסטאה, a robber.
EstR 1. 12: הן דליסט את מקפח תמן מצטלב; sic edprinc, read: דליסטאה, Where the robber robs, there he is crucified. ▽ modern edd: ליסטאות? // TanḥExTeẓaveh 11,

B 7, 100: מקום שהליסטים מקפח שם הוא נתלה, The place where the robber robs, there he is hung; YalkPs 808; ibidProv 935 (both latter from Tanḥ).
BSanh 106b: פנחס ליסטאה, Phineas the robber.

Aram pl: לסטאי, ~יא, ~ייא, etc:

YShek 5. 1, 48d 3: גנבתה ליסטאי בליליא, ... robbers stole her (R. Pinḥas b. Yair's donkey) by night. // YDemai 1. 2, 21d bottom: ליסטיי, (probably ליסטיי' = ליסטייא); GenR 60. 8, 648_5: לסטאי; ARN 1. 8, 38: לסטים; YalkGen 109, 488_{28}. PRK 165b, $377_{3\ 5}$: ... עלון להון לסטיא ... אזלון להון ליסטייא ..., Let the brigands come ... The brigands came ... ▽ ~אי. // YalkHos 533; Arugat ha-Bosem 2. 96: ליסטין. (Not in // in YTaan 3. 8, 66d 37.)
TrgJob 4:11: לסטיא ▽ ליסטייא, ליסטסייא.
Ibid 5:5: לסטיסין.

YSanh 5 (12) 1, 22c 56: ליסטים both in MsL and edprinc. But MsAssis (Tarbiẓ 46, 1977, 41_4) has: אלסים, read אלסים, which is the better reading. See ed note adloc. (See LW 2, 57a sv אלסים.) This corruption may be explained by ref to an interesting intermediate stage found in EcclesR 3. 9, edHirshman (unpublished JTS doct diss, 1982) line 163. There the main reading is אליסים (▽ ~איל), but MsJTS 5529/2 has אליסטס. (For added τ after *sigma*, cf SB 7662. 13, late II CE: *προφεστίονα*, for *προωεσσίωνα, professio;* Gignac 1, 66). From אליסטס to ליסטס is an easy transition.
GenR 20. 7, 191_8 according to Ar (AC 5, 21ab): לווטס, according to Theodor (from Löw via Fraenkel) is *λῶταξ*, flute player. (Contra AC 5, 25ab: *leutus*, slave mortgaged to land; LW 316a, reading: בוליוטיס; Levy 2, 482b: *λιτός, λειτός*, simple, which latter is apparently related to Syr לוטסא, PnS 1934–35, explained as *lanista*, and in lex *scurra*, according to PnS perhaps related to *λώταξ, mendicus*. See on this PnSSupple 180a sv לטס, citing VitMon 89. 10: לוטסא וזניתא, lewd men and harlots. This connection was first pointed out by Fraenkel, ZA 17, 1903, 87. Reject Brüll, Jahrb 8, 1887, 85: *εἱλώτης*, Helot. See also PRE 46, 109b: לייטי ישראל?)
In EcclesR 1. 1, the printed edd have בולווטוס (= *βουλευτής*, LW2, 140b) and so too // CantR I.I. 9: בליוטוס. However, edprinc has לווטוס, and Mss show the following ▽: MssOxf 164. 2, Munich 4. 356 xii: ליסטים (and so too Pugio Fidei 512), MsJTSMic 5529/2: לוסטוס ס"א בוליות, MsVat 291. 12: לוטוס (edHirshman line 18). Hirshman rightly notes that ליסטים is out of place in this context and explains MsJTS לוסטוס as *λῷστος*, a good friend (LSJ[9] 1069b sv *λωΐων*; cf Hesych, edLatte 2. $617_{17\ 18}$). We may add that the reading לוטוס in MsVat may reflect the loss of the medial *sigma* before τ; see Mayser 1/1[2], 1979, and Gignac 1, 131 n2. Clearly in all cases ליסטים should be emended to לוסטוס.
On ליסטס in LevR 32. 5 //CantR 4. 12, see LW2, 311b sv לוסטוס = *Justus* (cf ibid 280a)?
ליסטטירין in CantR to Cant 6:4 is not *ληστήριον*, robbers' den, attractive though this suggestion be, (Jastrow's 709a). The whole passage remains obscure. (LW 2, 379a: *στηθάριον*, but, following SachsBeiträge 2, 105, Fürst 152; Levy 3, 500a: *σταθερός;* Fleischer, ibid 722a: *στατήριον;* Brüll, Jahrb 7, 1885, 61 and AC 6, 37a: *statura*. All rejected by Löw LW ibid.) HJacobson, (private communication, Feb 1982), suggests convincingly: **λιστόταυρ<ος>*, *~ον*, (*~ιν*), a bull which is worshipped, ie an Apis-bull of gold.

This is an extremely common word, found in post Talmudic texts as well, (e g Pirkei Rabbenu ha-Kaddosh, edSchönblum 19b). Note the variety of forms, in Heb and Aram, alternative pl forms etc. The fact that a verbal form was created out of this word (↓ **לסטם**) is a further indication of the extent to which it became rooted in Rabb parlance. For Arab, see Fraenkel 284 (Vollers, ZDMG 51, 1897, 303).

Cf MM 375a; ArndtGingrich 474; Joüon 467.

Lat: *lestes*, CGL 5, 506_{30}.

Syr: ליסטיס, PnS 1959; לסטיא, לסטא, PnS 1958.

Cf ↑ **ארכיליסטיס, ליסטייא** ↓ **לסטם**[0]

ליפון, what remains to be proved: *λοιπόν*

Hilchot Ereẓ-Yisrael min ha-Geniza, edMargulies 29_6: והיכמה דאין אית בו מום, בלא ליפון הוא משתריי למתאכלה, And when it (the firstborn animal) has a blemish, without further ado it may be eaten

Ta-Shma, apud Margulies, ibid 37. *λοιπόν*, lit: remainder. But see LSJ[9] 1060b sv *λοιπός* 2: *λοιπόν* [*ἐστι*]: it remains to show, etc. This is a post-Amoraic word, probably belonging to the Byz period.

לסטאה, לסטאי, ↑ ליסטיס

לסטות ↑ ליסטייא

לסטיא ↑ ליסטיס

לסטיותיה ↑ ליסטייא

לסטייא, לסטים, לסטין, לסטיסין, לסטם ↑ ליסטיס

לסטם[0] (316) practise robbery, rob, deriv verb formed from ליסטיס, ~ים, corresponding to: *ληστεύω*

TanḥExShemot 1: ישב בפרשת דרכים והיה מלסטם את הבריות, He sat at the cross-road and robbed people. // ExR 1. 1.

BBB 123a: איש רע הוא מלסטם בריות, a bad man [who] robs people. (See Rabbinovitz VL 343 n30.)

BSanh 72a: ויוצא לפרשת דרכים ומלסטם את הבריות, and he goes out to the cross-road and robs people. // YalkDeut 930.

The verb is in the *piel* form.

Syr: ליסטי, PnS 1958.
Cf ↑ ליסטיס

ליסטיס ↑ לסטס

מ

מטלון (332) mine, as place of punishment, to which a criminal is condemned (for life): *μέταλλον* ← *metallum*

NumR 7. 3: מלך בשר ודם יש לו מטלון של טרודין, אף האלקים יש לו מטלון שלטרודין, שנאמר "וישלחו מן המחנה כל צרוע וכו׳", A King of flesh and blood has a place of punishment for banished (criminals), so too the Lord has a place of punishment for the banished, as it is said, "that they put out of the camp every leper, etc" (Num 5:2).
DeutR 2. 30: אמר המלך: אילו בטובתו שיברה היה נהרג. עכשיו שלא בטובתו, יטרד למטלך, Said the King: Had he broken it (the king's image) intentionally, he would have been executed. But now that he broke it unintentionally, he shall be banished to the mine. ▽ late edd: ין~, read: ון~.
Ibid 6. 12: תיטריד למטלון, let her be banished to the mine.

The primary meaning of the Lat *metallum* is a place where metals are found and quarried. The secondly meaning, a place of punishment.
מטלך של טרודין and יטרד למטלון corresponds to the Lat *in metalla damnatio,* or *ad metalla condamnatio* (cf SeutCal 27. 3). Criminals were condemned to work in a mine, or quarry, for life, and this not only involved rigorous labour, but also being kept in fetters. As a consequence it was considered the severest punishment after the death penalty (cf above DeutR 2. 30). *proxima morti,* nearest to death. See Berger 581b sv *metallum;* Krauss, Dvir 1, 1983, 95.
Not to be confused with מטלייה (contra Krauss, LW 2, 332a, AC 5, 122a); see Löw, LW ibid, and Levy 3,88b.

Arm: *metalk'*, Thumb, BZ 9, 1900, 423.
Syr: מטלך, מטאלך, PnS 2078, Brockelm², 382ab.

מיסתיוסים [מיסתיוסיס] (338) lease; **μισθιωσις* (= *μίσθωσις*)

YPes 4. 9, 31b 48: מיסתיוסים כאוני (↑) הוא ונקנית במקח, Lease (*μίσθωσις*) is like sale (ὠνή), and is acquired in a purchase. (The meaning is that sale does not cancel tenancy; cf // in YBM 8. 11, 11d 35 (↑ אנקלווסים). ▽ מִיסְתִיוֹסִיס (GS 1, 443_{18}), מסתיוסיס (Ittur 50a). Read: ~יס.

See Gulak, Le-Ḥeker Toldot ha-Mishpat ha-Ivri bi-Tekufat ha-Talmud 1, Jerusalem 1929, 116; Lieberman YK 448. (Jastrow 28b requires some correction.) For ▽ see Ratner 70.
On ιω for ω, cf Gignac 1,310—11, for examples of such vowel-development, eg: συνηγόριων (for ~ων), PThead 15. 2. 19 (280—81 CE). There are a number of similar such examples among Rabbinic loanwords, eg *ἀξιωμια, *ζητημια, etc, (cf ↑ אכסיומא, זיטמא). See Sperber, Sinai 87, 1980, 151—52.
On μίσθωσις see Taubenschlag[2], 354—55.

פרגל ↓ מפרגל

פרנה ↓ מפרוני

נימוקו ↓ מתנמקין

נ

◇**נוטי נוטומי [טימי׳ טימ׳ (נו)]** (355) a deposit which must be returned in its original form, a deposit the value of which must be returned: *θέμ<α>* (or *θῆμ<α>*) *τιμή*

YMaasSheni 2. 5, 53c 29 edprinc: והן נוטי נוטומי; read: והן נו טימטימי, it is one whether it be a deposit which must be returned in the form in which it was deposited, [or] a deposit the value of which may be returned. ▽ MsVat: ניטומטומי; read: נו טומטומי.

Lieberman, Tarbiẓ 3/3, 1932, 337—38. According to him נו is to be separated from נו — טי, and goes with הן, meaning: והן הוא = והנו, and this is, i e either a θέμα (or τῆμα) or a τιμή. (Contra LevyTrgWb 2, 109a sv ניסא, chief silor, ναύτης; Levy 3, 356a sv נוטי, something like *nota, notum*; LW2, 355b: *noti not<iss>imi*; AC 5, 322a: *nota notamen*; Löw, apud LW 2 ibid: *Νόστιμοι*; Jastrow 886b: prob a corrupt tautography of: והוא שליקט מיכן ומוכן ... (?); SchönhakMiluimm 45b: *nota notumi*. On θέμα cf TDrew-Bear, Glotta 50, 1972, 74—75.

Cf ↑ טימי

נוטרין (356) written statement informing authorities of crime, denunciation (made by police official or private informer): **νοτωριον* ← *notorium*

ExodR 31. 13: משל למי שרצח והביאוהו לפני השלטון. כיון שקרא את הנוטרין שלו, אמר: עד עכשיו חי?!, It is like unto someone who committed a murder, and they brought him before the ruler. As soon as he read the statement indicting him (*notorium*), he said: [What,] is he still alive?!

Krauss, LWibid, sees ין~ as Aram pl form, comparable with *notoria* (sc *epistola*). Maarich 5 sv נוטריא:אלוגין = *notoria*. (Contra Jastrow 886b: *notaria*, indictments. However, note Souter 267a sv *notaria* 2,often corruption of *notoria*. Similarly AC 5, 336a; Levy 3, 356ab.)
On *notorium*, see Souter 267b, citing Paul, Dig 48. 16. 6, CodIust 9. 2. 7, SymmEpist 10. 4. Cf Berger 599b. On *νοτωρία*, see Lampe 923a, citing MAgap 3. 1 (early IV CE).
Not to be confused with נוטר, נוטרין (pl): *notarius*, scribe, shorthand writer (LW 2, 355b–256a sv *נוטר).

נימוס ↓ נומוס

נומיקה jurist, scribe: *νομικ<ός>*

MGDeut 5. 6, 102_9: אנכי ... אנא נומיקה כתבית יהבית, "Anochi" (I am, Deut 5:6) ... [The *notarikon*, i e the letters of this word corresponds to the initial letters, of] ... I, the scribe, or jurist (i e Moses), wrote [and] gave [the ten commandments]. But // in BShab 105a, PRK 222_{11}, PR 21, 105a, Midrash Aseret ha-Dibberot (BHM 1, 63) etc, read: נפשי, instead of נומיקה, i e I myself wrote [and] gave. AgBer 36, 72: "איה סופר" — איה הן הנמקין שלו, "Where is the scribe"? (Is 33:18). Where are his *notarii*? נמקין: *νομικοι* – pl.

MGDeut cited by Hoffmann, MidTan 20n*. Moses as *nomika* discussed by Lieberman, GH 212, citing Samaritan Memar Marqah (Heidenheim, BiblSamaritana 3, 114) נומיקה; *iuris prudens;* also = סופר, *notarius*, as in AgBer (GHibid n272, as already Löw, apud Krauss LW2, 361a). Cf Syr: נומיקא, scribe, PnS 2323. And see CGL 3, 531_{13}: *nomikos iuris peritos, iuris consultus, iuris prudens*.
A different possibility is that נומיקה: (*τὰ*) *νομικά*, according to Lampe 918b, sv *νομικός* 1a, teachings of the Law, books of the law, (and cf Syr: נמקא, PnS 2385). Accordingly, we would translate: I wrote [and] gave the Law (i e the ten Commandments). Note that glosses in MGibid explain נומיקה as כתב ואגרת בלשון ארמי, (ed note ad loc). According to this, our statement would correspond to the following one, in the name of R. Judah b. R. Simon (line 10 ibid): אנכי נתתי כתבתי עשרת הדברות. For a different pl form, see Lieberman ibid n272: נומיקים, from SJMiller, The Samaritan Molad Moshe 60_{12}.

Cf ↓ נימוקו

ריטור⁰ ↑ ניטור

נומוס, נימוס (359–60) (1) law (2) custom, practise (3) legal act (of warning carried out by c...) required in order to claim debt or surity (4) religion: *νόμος* → *nomos*

(1) MGit 6. 5 (= BGit 65b): עשו לה כנימוס, Do for her as is [required by] the law (or custom?). In MssMunich and Vat130 to BGit ibid a gloss is added: עשו לה כדת. MsKaufmann vocalizes: כְּנִימוֹס.
YBer 5, 9a 29: בנימוסיא דברייא, according to the laws of the peoples (Aram pl).
YRH 7. 8, 59c 44: בנימוסון אינון עסיקין, they are engaged in their laws.
YRH 1. 3, 57b 1: פרא בסיליוס או נומוס או גריפוס, For the King the law is not written (i e not binding). ▽ SY 145_{19}:אוגְרֶפוֹס, ibid 152_{14}: אַגְרָפוֹס. // LevR 35. 3, 820_6: פרא בסיליוס נומוס אגרפוס. ▽ נימוס, בומוס read: נומוס; Aggur 25: פרא יוסלי אוס אונימוס אגריפוס, read: פרא וסיליוס. (Absent in YalkLev 670, TanḥEx Va-Era 722.) = *παρὰ βασιλέως* (*ὁ*) *νόμος* (*οὐ γραφος*? or) *ἄγραφος*.
LevR 7. 6, 161_1: נומוס הוא וקילוסין (↓ קילווסיס) הוא שכל מי שמתגאה לפני המקום אינו נידון אלא באש, It is the law and the decree that anyone who is haughty before the Lord, is punished by burning. ▽ נימוס // YalkLev 480; נימוס; MachZach 2. 9, 21; ibidPs 73. 21, 2. 5; Ar (AC 5, 346a).
GenR 93. 5, 1155_3: בנימוסות שלנו כת׳, "שלם ישלם, אם אין לו ונמכר בגנבתו", In our laws it is written "For he should make full restitution; if he have nothing, then he shall be sold for his theft" (Ex 22:2). ▽ בנמוסותינו. // MGGen 44. 18, 755_{18}; YalkGen 150, 807_2. (Cf TanḥBGen Va-Yigash 5, 205.)
NumR 8. 4: בנימוסות שלנו כל מי שמכתיב את עצמו סגרון למלך, הוא כופר באבותיו, According to our laws, anyone who registers himself *sgron* (?) to the king, denounces his forefathers. // PR 23, 121b: בנימוסיות.
AbbaGurion 3. 12, 31: דתיהון ונימוסיהון, their religions and laws.
TrgO, PsJ and Neofiti 1 Lev 18:3: ובנימוסיהון, and according to their laws, (transl: ובחקתיהם). Ibid 20:23: ובנימוס (transl: בחקת). TrgY and Neofiti 1 Num 23:9. Trg1Kings 17:13. 1 Sam 8:9. Ibid 10:25. Ezek 20:25. Prov 1:8. Ibid 31:26. Ps 1:2. 1Est 3:8.
Maalat ha-Middot 66 (in name of Midrash): מה בין נימוסות אלקינו לבין נימוסות האומות, What is the difference between the laws of our Lord and the laws of the nations?

(2) MechBeshelaḥ Va-Yehi Parasha 7, $140_{6\ 7\ 8}$: בנימוסי מלכות, according to the customs of royalty. // MechdeRashbi 89_{15} = MGEx 15. 9, 301_{22}: מפני נימוס מלכות.
GenR 48. 14, 491_5: עלת לקרתא עביד בנימוסא, when you enter a city, behave according to its customs. // ExR 47. 5: בנימוסיה.

GenR 67. 6, $762_{5,6}$: את יש לך נימוסות, והוא יש לו נימוסות, You have [your] customs, and he has [his] customs. ▽ נימוסים, נימוסיות. // YalkGen 115, 564_{51}: נימוסים. (Levy 3, 387b suggests: *νόμισις*; reject.)
ExR 15.27: עשר המכות הביא עליהם בנימוס המלכות, The ten plagues He brought upon them after the manner of the royalty, (i e according to royal strategy). (But // in PRK 66b, 132_{3}; MGEx 10. 3, 150_{15} etc., have בטכסים: *τάξις*, battle arrangements, cf LW 2, 267ab.)
ExR 25. 7: ועובדי כוכבים רואים מנהגים ונימסין, and idolators will see their practises and customs. ▽ ונימסין, read: ונימוסן.
NumR 18. 8: בדרכי הגוים יש נימוסין הרבה, In the ways of the gentiles there are many customs. // TanḥNumKoraḥ 5; Bibid11, 89: ונימתרין, read: נימוסין. ▽ MsVat 34: נימוסין; YalkNum 750.
SifraAḥarei Perek 13, 86a: שלא תלכו בנימוסות שלהן, בדברים החקוקין להם, כגון תיטריות וקרקסאות והאסטריות, that you should not behave according to their practises, things which have become firmly established (literally: engraved) among them, such as theatres, circuses and arenas (? cf Jastrow 92b). (Ref to ובחקתיהם in Lev 18:3.)
LevR 23. 9, 539_{5}, according to MsParis 149: נימוסיות, (instead of גמוסיות in other readings, which is correct). Cf ↑ **גממסות.**
TrgNeofiti 1 Gen 19:1: בנימוס דארעא, according to the custom of the land.
TrgYGen 19:3: כנימוס כל ארעא, according to the customs of all the land. TrgYGen 34:1. FrgTrgEx 1:19. Trg1Sam 2:13.

(3) TTer 2. 11 114_{42}, 27_{30}: וגוי שמישכן שדהו לישראל, אף על פי שעשה ישראל נימוסי עליה ..., and a gentile who mortgaged his field to an Israelite, even though the Israelite carried out the measures which the law requires concerning it (the field, i e sent warnings to the debtor before claiming the surity). Read: נימוס'. ▽ MsV: נימוסות. // BGit 43b (see below).
TAZ 3. 16, 464_{28}: אם עשה לו הגוי נימוסות, יצא בן חורין, If the gentile took the measures which the law requires regarding him (the slave), he achieves his liberty. // BGit 43b (see below).
BGit 43b: ת״ר: לוה עליו מן העובד כוכבים, כיון שעשה לו עובד כוכבים נמוסו, יצא לחירות. מאי נמוסו? אמר רב הונא בר יהודה: נשקי. מתיב רב ששת: ... ועובד כוכבים שמשכן שדהו לישראל, אע״פ שעשה לו נמוסו, פטורה מן המעשר. ואי ס״ד נשקי, שדה בת נשקי היא? אלא אמר רב ששת: זמן, We have learned in a baraita: If the gentile borrowed against him, (i e using the slave as surity), as soon as the gentile took the measures which the law requires regarding him, he achieves his liberty. What is the measure? Said Rav Huna bar Judah: *Nashki.* Rav Sheshet raised the

following objection: ... and a gentile who mortgaged his field to an Israelite, even though he took the measure required by the law concerning him, it is free of tithes. And if you suggest *nashki*, is a field subject to the *nashki?* But said Rav Sheshet: Time. ▽ MsM: נימוסי, read: נימוס', (= either נימוסו or נימוסות). MsOxf 368 reads: ואי ס"ד נמוסו נישקי. Ar (AC 5,346a) reads: ורב ששת אמר: נימוסו — זמן, כגון שקבע לו זמן אם לא אפרענו עד הזמן, יהיה העבד קנוי לגוי, And Rav Sheshet said: The measures required by law – time, as when he fixed a time [limit], that if I will not pay up to [that] time, the slave will belong to the gentile.

(4) BMeg 12b: מרדכי מוכתר בנימוסי היה [כעדי], Mordechai was adorned with his religion (divine law) [as an ornament]. (CfRabbinowitz VL adloc, 53–54 n300–400.) // AgEst 2. 5, 18: נימוסין; THGLyck, no17, 10a: בנימוסו (= OhGMeg 16); Ar (AC 5, 346a); YalkEst 1051: בנימוס.

See also ExR 15.10: הנמוסין, which should, however, be read: טומוסין, cf ↑ טימוס. Likewise נימוסן in GenRabbati 36_4 should be read: טימוסן.
The word is extremely common in later Rabb Heb, and in modern Heb in sense of habit, good manners etc.

(1) On YRH 1. 3, 57b1 and //, cf LW 2, 12b sv אגרפוס, KraussPR 134; Baer, Zion 21, 1956, 28; Ginzberg, apud ACSup 420a; Lieberman GH 28–29, 110 n2 (= Greek 37, 144 n2); idem, apud Biblical and other stud, edAltmann, 128–129; idem, KS 14, 1937–38, 222; GAlon, Meḥkarim 260–61. Note וסליוס in Aggur, and cf vocalized spelling in SY ibid, always VASILEŌS. Note further that in several Mss in LevR the difficult (?) word בסיליוס was written twice, once correct, and once in a corrupt "correction". Eg, MsVat 32 (Margulies apparat 821): בכל יום בסיליוס, or in MsMunich 117: בסיליאוס בר סיליאוס. See also AC 1, 30a, and ibid 2, 132a.
On GenR 93. 5, 1155_3: בנימוסות שלנו כתיב, see LW 1, 218.
(2) For the phrase נימוס המלכות, cf *νόμος βασιλικός*, and see the discussion on this in Deissmann LAE 362 n5, and MM 105b sv *βασιλικός* ad fin.

(3) נימוס in this meaning corresponds to *τὰ νόμιμα (τοὺς νόμους) ἐπιτελεῖν* of the papyri. See Gulak, Toldot ha-Mishpat ha-Ivri, 1939, 152–56; Lieberman, TK 2, 315–16; Urbach, Papers of the Institute of Jewish Studies 1, 1964, 70–71. (Contra Perles, MGWJ 37, 1893, 372: מנימוסי: *manumissio*; ZKahn, Die Sklaverie nach Bibel und Talmud, Prague 1888, 131; Levy 3, 400b, Sem; Büchler, REJ 48, 1904, 132–36; Osterzetzer, Tarbiẓ 8, 1937, 312–15; BCohen, Jewish and Roman 441 n50 *νομή*: *possessio*; Rapaport, apud AC 5, 346b, regular meaning of law; so too Pineles, Darkah shel Torah 77 etc. See LW 2, 360b–361a, addition bibl.)
(On נישקי ▽ נשקי, in BGit 43b see AC 5, 395a, MedLat *nosca = armilla*, or *nusca = fibula;* Levy 3,454a, Heb נשק, cf OhGGit, R. Ḥananel 30; so too Jastrow 942a. See LW 2, 360b–361a; but see Krauss, TA 2, 494 n608, accepting the suggestion of Büchler, REJ 48, 1904, 132–36.)
(4) Levy 3, 621a; Jastrow 682b sv כתר: faith.
The meaning "religion' derives from the more primary meaning "divine law"; see Lampe 920a, sv *νόμος* IIc. (Contra Perles, MGWJ 37, 1893, 370: *τόμος;* Krauss TA 1, 657 n918; ACSup 280b; ornament.)

There are two forms of this word: נימוס, the main form, and נומוס a less frequent form. Similarly טימוס ↑ and טומוס. See Perles, Beiträge 40–41. There is a considerable literature on this word, on its form (with i), on the Arabic *namus* etc. See Lagarde, Mitteil II, 358 n1; Fleischer, ZDMG 12, 1858, 701–02 n3 (apud Nöldeke); Sprenger, ibid13, 1859, 690–701, and 14, 1860, 294; Beurmann ibid 16, 1862, 564 (on Maltese); Fraenkel, ibid 52, 1898, 299 n1 (on *o* > *ι* interchange) etc. See the detailed discussion in LW 1, 309–12 (where some of the references need correction), and note the dissimilation of the initial o in the Syr form. In the final analysis it seems clear that the main form is the (Rabbinicized) נימוס (*nimos*, as vocalized in MsKaufmann, later altered to *nimus* in accordance with Heb grammar). נומוס seems to be a "purist" form, which deviates from main form. (Similarly in the case of טימוס ↑.)
On נימוס in Palestinian marriage documents, see MAFriedman, Jewish Marriage in Palestine 1, Tel-Aviv & New York 1980, 472–475.
See further Taubenschlag, JJP 11, 1948, 67–73 (= Opera Minora 2, Warsaw 1959, 107 et seq); MM 105b sv *βασιλικός* ad fin, on *νομος βασιλικός*, (Deissmann LAE 362 n5); MM429b; ArndtGingrich 544–45.

Lat: *nomos* (which, however, has quite different meanings, see OLD 1187c).
Syr: נמוס, נמוסא, PnS 2383–84; נימוס, Schulthess 123ab.
Palm: נמוסא, Cook 81, LidzbarskiHb 323; DISO 179.
Arm: *nomos*, H294.
Arab: *namus*, Fraenkel 278.
Cf ↑ טימוס

נימוס ↑ נימוסיות, נימוסות, נימוסא

נימוקו (361) his juris prudence, his knowledge or skill in law; from *νομικ<η>* (sc *τέχνη*) (with third person masc sing term)

ARN I 18, 69: (ל)ר' יוסי נמוקו עמו, R. Jose has skill in law. // BEruv 14b, 51a; BGit 67a; BBK 24a; BBech 37a: נימוקן. ▽ נמוקו; MGEx 19. 14, 386_{26}: נימקו; ▽ נימוקו, נמקי, נמקו.

See LSJSupple 105a sv *νομικός* 2. citing GVI 2021. 3 (Amasia 1/11 CE). Cf Levy 3, 388a, *νομική*. See the long discussion in Krauss, LW 2, 361ab. (Contra Jastrow 405b, constr of נעמוק, עמק, depth, penetration; AC 5, 347b, and Perles ES 37. Pehlevy etym rejected in ACSup 280b. However, see ESRosenthal apud Irano-Judaica, edSShaked, Jerusalem 1982, 93 n25, 132, ref to OhG to BK 115, R. Hananel, and Ginze Kedem 5, 1934, 81: דר' יוסי נמקו (!) עמו — תורתו עמו, מלשון פרסי שקורין לכתב נמקא, JBarth, Ha-Kedem 3, 1, apud ACSup ibid, suggests Akkad etym, from *nemēqu*, wisdom, *maqtal* of עמק. This too may be rejected, primarily on semantic grounds. Krauss, LW ibid: *νομικός*, following Mussaf *νομικόν*.) AC 8 Add 60 cites MG[Gen 24. 58, 408_{13}]: רשעים מתנמקין, explaining this to be a verb formed from נימוק. However, the meaning is not altogether clear, it may mean "to be uncertain", and derive from Sem נמק. Cf BenIehuda 7, 3680b.

Cf Syr forms from *νομικ<ός>*, נומיקא PnS 2323, נמיקא ibid2385.
Cf ↑ נומיקה

נימוקו ↑ **נימקו**

נימוס ↑ **נימתרין**

ניקולוגון ↓ **ניקולוגוס**

ניקולוגוס (~ון) one who wins in court: **νικολόγος* (*~ον*)

PRK 153b, 340_1: אם מבקש אתה לזכות לפני בדין, מני לך ניקוליגוס פלוני, ואת זכיי לפני בדין, If you wish to win your case before me, appoint yourself so and so as a "winning attorney", and you will win your case before me. ▽ ניקיאלוגוס, ניקלוגיס, ניקלוגוס, ניקולוגוס. Cited in Ar (AC 5, 380b). // LevR 29. 7, 676_5 in apparat: ניקולונין, (corrected דיקליקוס), ניקוליגון, ניקוליגוס, קוליגוס, פקו לי גוס (explained **פרקליט** ↓). Printed ed: דיקאליקוס (cf ↑ **דיקולוגוס**). Read in all cases: ניקולוגוס, ~גון. YalkLev 645, edprinc: ניקולוניס; ibidNum 782: ניקולוגוס.

Lieberman, apud PRK 475 (and 340). To be distinguished from **דיקולוגוס** ↑. (Contra LW 211b; also reject Jastrow 908a, suggesting: **νεικολόγος*, pleader in a law-suit.) Rokeaḥ sect. 200, 87 cites LevR, reading: ביקולוגוס; read: ~ני.

Cf ↑ **דיקולוגוס**

נימוקו ↑ **נמוקו**

נומיקה ↑ **נמקין**

ס

סקבטרין ↓ **סויקטרים, סווקטירים**

סטטיונר (379) military police officer: *στατιωνάρ*<*ιος*> ← *stationar*<*ius*> (sc *miles*)

GenR 26. 2, 245_8: לעתיד לבוא עושה מלאך המות סטטיונר שלכם, In the future He will appoint the Angel of Death officer in charge you (Nations of the World). ▽ אסטטיונר; PsRashi adloc reads: מיטטור (see LW 2, 331ab): *metator*, which clearly does not fit this context.

ExodR 51. 8, cited in Ar (AC 4, 32b) as from YelamdNum 14:12, GrünhutLikkutim 4, 32b: סטטיונר בראתי אותך על אומות העולם, I have appointed you officer over the Nations of the World. ▽ איסטטיונר, Ar ibid. //MachPs 50. 22, 1. 275: קנטיאון ↓.

στατιωνάριος, IGRom 1. 42 (Puteoli II CE), etc. See Lampe 1251b, Mason 85b, DuCange 1430. (cf Sophocles 1006b, different meaning). On the *stationarius*, see OHirschfeld, Kl Schrift. 596ff., Jones LRE 3, 149 n114, Berger 714b.

Cf ↓ סנדטור and קנטיאון.

סימפון, סמפון (389) postscript to document, codicil, special stipulation within a written contract: *σύμφων<ον>*

MBM 1. 8: אם יש עמהן סמפונות, יעשה מה שבסמפונות, If there were postscripts to the documents, let him act in accordance with the postscripts (pl). // TBM 1. 9, $372_{5,6}$: סימפונות.
TBM 1. 13, 372_{13}: סימפון שיש עליו עדים, יתקיים בחותמיו, A codicil which has witnesses should be honoured according to its signatures. // BBM 21a; BSanh 31b.
YGit 1. 6, 49a 18: ... סדר סימפון כן הוא, The formula of the codicil is as follows, (here discussing a marriage contract). // YEruv 3, 21b 16.
YBB 10. 1, 17c 28: סמפון כתוב מלעיל וסימפון מחיק מלרע, A postscript written above, and a postscript erased below ...
YKid 3. 2, 63d 25–52. Ibid 3. 3, 64a 8.

Note משום סימפון and סימפון בעבדים ליכא in BKet 57b–58ab, and BKid 11a was regarded by Krauss, LW 2, 389b sv סימפון II, Levy 3, 513a, and Jastrow 982a, as *σύμφωνον*, explaining: the bodily defect of a woman or a slave not stated in the contract annuls the agreement. However, Fleischer, apud Levy 3, 723a and AC6, 75b explain it as some kind of disease, from *σύμπτωμα*, symptoms of disease, hence: the disease itself. This is more likely – note Löw's rejection of Krauss' explanation in LW 2, 677b, index –, and the loss of the *τ* in *σύμπ<τ>ωμα* is quite usual in papyri. See Gignac 1, 67, e g: *ἑπακοσίους* (for *ἑπτα*~), PO 243 = MChr 182. 35 (79 CE). Not to be confused with סימפון: *σίφων* (LW 2, 389b sv סימפון III). For Gaonic lit, see Sefer ha-Shetarot of Al-Barceloni, edHalberstamm 67 for popular etym: ולשון סימפון הוא סימון פון, דבהאי סימפון האי ענין אם הוא פרוע ... או לאו. ויש אומ' מלשון סמפוניא האמורה בספר דניאל. Ibid 99. See also Tanḥum Yerushalmi's Dict, edHShay (unpublished diss 1975) 2, 141–42.
τὸ σύμφωνον, agreement (Philo), ArndtGingrich 788–89 *σύμφωνον*, agreed upon, CodIust8. 10. 12. See also MM 598–99 (on *ἐκ συμφώνους* by agreement, 1Cor 7:5). Taubenschlag[2] 296: "In the Byzantine period new terms appeared such as ... *σύμφωνον* (n24 for ref) ... Sometimes ... its use is restricted to special stipulations within a written contract." This, indeed, is the main meaning in Rabbinic lit. See Gulak, Tarbiẓ 5/2, 1934, 126–33; idem, Urkundenwesen 41–42; idem, Toldot ha-Mishpat be-Yisrael ... 1, 1.

Lat: *symphona*, DuCange 1479 sv *συμφώνησις*.
Palm etc: ספון, DISO 196 (LidzbarskiHb 330).

סיקה פנטיון false accuser,calumniator: *συκοφαντέων* (particip form from ~*τέω*)

MidTanDeut 33. 8, 215: סיקה פנטיון נעשה לאחיו, He became a calumniator against his brother. Read: סיקופנטיון. // SifDeut 349, 408_5: סקיפנטים (↓).

Hoffmann adloc n40. Or perhaps: **συκοφαντιον* = *συκοφαντία:* calumny, i e calumny was practised against his brother (?). What is clear is that this word should be distinguished from סקיפנטים in the parallel text in SifDeut ibid.
The *heh* of סיקה־ looks somewhat suspect, appearing as it does in the middle of a word (after we have read the two parts as one). סיקהפנטיון could represent a possible **συκαφαντ*, since the *o* > *a* interchange is not uncommon, and could occur here. See Gignac 1, 287–88; eg *συκάμ|ω|ρ<ον>*, for *συκόμορον*, in PO 1925. 13, 14, 19, 23, 43 (VII CE). Could the original reading have had an *aleph*, and when the word was split a *heh* was substituted? Alternatively, read with a *waw*, ~סיקו, which was incorrectly copied as *heh*, when the word was split.

Cf ↓ סקיפנטים

סקרדין ↓ סיקרוקין

סיקריקון (392) (1) confiscation by authorities (regarded by the people as [legalized ?] robbery) (2) law concerning purchase of confiscated property (3) property confiscated by government authority (4) confiscator, or usurping occupant of such property: **σικαρικόν*

(1) BGit 55b: דין סיקריקון, the law of confiscation – *sikarikon*. (And see below 4.)

(2) MGit 5. 6: לא היה סיקריקון ביהודה בהרוגי מלחמה. מהרוגי מלחמה ואילך יש בה סיקריקון, The [law of the] *sikarikon* was not applied in Judaea until [the period of] "the slain in battle". From [the period of] "the slain in battle" onwards [the law of] *sikarikon* does apply there.
TGit 5. 1, $257_{59, 62}$, $328_{5, 7}$: ארץ יהודה אין בה משום סיקריקון ... מין המלחמה ואילך יש בה משום סיקריקון. גליל לעולם יש בו משום סיקריקון, The land of Judaea has not [the status permitting the application of the law of] *sikarikon*. From the war onwards, she does have [the status permitting the application of the law of] *sikarikon*. The Galilee always has [the status permitting the application of the law of] *sikarikon*.
YGit 5. 6, 47b 13: התקינו שלא יהיה סיקריקון ביהודה, They enacted that [the law of] *sikarikon* should not apply in Judaea.
Ibid lines 17–18: המטלטלין אין בהן משום סיקריקון ... , [The law of] *sikarikon* does not apply to movable properties.

Ibid lines 18–19: ... חכירי בתי אבות אין בהן משום סיקריקון, [The law of] *sikarikon* does not apply to hereditory tenant farmers.

(3) TAZ 3, 16, 464_{29}: (עבד) שנפל לו בסיקריקון, יצא בן חורין, If he inherited (a slave) who was confiscated property, he goes free ...

(4) MGit 5. 6: ... הלוקח מסיקריקון ... , לקח מסיקריקון וחזר ולקח מבעל הבית, If he bought [a field] from the confiscator ... He bought [a field] from the confiscator, and then from the [original] owner ... // TGit 5. 1, 257_{62}–258_{67}, $328_{7\ 11}$, YGit 5. 6, 47b 13–17, BBB 47b.

MBik 1. 2: ... והסקריקון והגזלן ... , the confiscator and the robber ... // SifDeut 297, 317_{2}: סיקרקון; Mech 23. 19, 335_{9}: סקריקון ▽ סיקריקון; MGDeut 26. 2, 583_{19} (= MidTan 26. 2, 171).

TTer 1. 6, 108_{22}, 25_{27}: ... בעלי בתים סיקריקון, owner-confiscators ...

MMach 1. 6: מפני הסיקרין, but EpsteinGK 128_{6} reads: הסיקריקון, the confiscators.

YGit 5. 6, 43b 16–17: תפתר שבא סיקריקון וגזל וחמס. לא הספיק לכתוב תרפו, עד שבא סיקריקון לכל העולם, You may explain this as a case where a confiscator came and robbed and extorted [land]. He did not manage to write out a binding document before confiscation (meaning 1) came to the whole world.

**σικαρικόν* derives from *σικάριος* = Lat *sicarius* (from *sica*, dagger + *arius*) meaning: assassin, murderer (JosAnt 20. 8. 10 al, ActAp 21. 38; MM 574b, ArndtGingrich 757b). *σικάριον* = *sica*: dagger in POxy 1294. 8 (II–III CE). The form **σικαρικόν* parallels *ληστικόν:* piracy, from *ληστής*. Since government confiscation of property was regarded by the people as a form of robbery, or banditry, they called it, and its official legal formulation and the practitioner of it, **σικαρικόν*. The usages seem to be local, deriving from a term which reflects public opinion of this practise: [*πρᾶγμα*] *σικαρικόν*, מילא דליסטיותא, banditry.

Lieberman, TK 8, 841, following Krauss BZ 2, 1893, 511–12. There is a considerable literature on this subject, and many other etymologies have been suggested. Eg: Graetz, Jahresbericht d Breslau Sem, 1892; Rosenthal, MGWJ 1898, 1–6, 57–63, 111–16; Elbogen, ibid 69, 1925, 249–57; Feist, ibid 71, 1927, 136–40 (from: *συγκρίνω*, to judge -*νόμος συγκρίνων*); Gulak, Tarbiẓ 5, 1933, 23–27 (from: *σὺν κηρυκι*, [sold] at a public auction); Safrai, Zion 17, 1952, 50–64 (*ius sicaricum*), and so AC 6, 122b; Rokeaḥ, Tarbiẓ 35, 1966, 125–31 (*νόμος σικαρικῶν*); Gil, RIDA 3/17, 1970, 45–53, especially 47 (from *συγχώρησις*, *cessio*); Jastrow 986b (a disguised form of *καισαρίκιον*, property confiscated by the Roman government). However, Krauss-Lieberman's interpretation remains the most convincing.

On MMach 1. 6, cf LW 2, 392–93 svv *סיקר, סיקרא, סיקריקון, whence confusion of readings.

On TTer 1. 6, see LiebermanTK 1, 297.

Note further that מיני סיקריקון, in YBeẓa 1. 9, 60d 27, is not *σαχαριχηνός* (as suggested by Krauss, LW 2, 392b), but should be read סִיקָמְרִיקוֹן with SY 172_{16}: **συκομορικον*, fruit of sycamore (cf *συκομορίτης*). (See Lieberman, cited by Franzus, in his ed of Eleazar Azikri's commentary to YBeẓa, 1957, 113, and Sperber, Bar-Ilan 16/17, 1979, 13.) The mistake, already found in MsLeiden (and cf RatnerVL ad loc 13), no doubt evolved under the influence of our word.

סיקריקון ↑ סיקרקן

טולמיסן ↑ סמה

סימפון ↑ סמפון

סמפניא ↓ סמפיא

◇**סמפניא** (470) conspiracy: *σύμπνοια* or *συμπνοιή*

MidPs 12. 1, 104 (edprinc and edd): **ונמצאו בני אדם עסוקין בהדי סמפניא**, and as a result people will be involved in conspiracy. ▽ סימפוניא (maybe corrupt from: סימפנויא), הוסמפניא (read: ~הס?), הוסתיא, חוסתנייא, סמניונא (read: סמפונא?). // YalkPs 659: סמסוניא, read: סמפופיא (or **ספסופא**↓); MachPs 12. 4, 1. 72: בההיא סמפניא; MachMid (Lauterbach, apud Occident&Orient, Gaster-Vol, 1936, 371): סמפיא, read: סמפ[נ]יא.

•
Lieberman, Sefer ... Alon (1970) 229, 234. (Contra Fürst, apud Buber, MidPs ibid 104 n8: *συμφωνία;* Krauss LW2, 470a: *ψήφισμα;* Levy 3, 493b sv סופיסטא: *σοφιστής;* AC 6, 106b, place name: *Soufsafeh*, NeubauerGéographie 271.)
CGL 2, 443_4: *συμπνοια conspiratio*; ibid 112_{53}: *conspiratio συμπνοή*.

Cf ↓ **ספסופא**

סניגוריא ↓ סנגורייה, סנגוריא

סניגור ↓ סנגורן, סנגורק, סנגורים

סניגרון ↓ סנגרון

סנדטור [סטטנר?] executioner: *στατιωνάρ<ιος>* ← *stationar<ius>*?

RavPoalim 23, citing an (unknown) Midrash: **ויפקד אותו להיות סנדטור ... ויצו המלך להסנדטור**, And he appointed him to be an executioner (*? sandator*) ... And the king ordered the executioner (*sandator*) to behead him. Perhaps read: **סטטנר?**

Gloss adloc has תליין, שר הטבחים, hangman, executioner. (Contra Ginzber, Legends 6, 169 n2, who emends to קוסטינר (↓): *quaestionarius;* but in MGWJ 78, 1938, 28, he suggests: *συνδαίτωρ*, table companion.) Or perhaps read: סטטור: *stator*: vizier; see Souter 387a (citing SSExod 15:4, apud Rufin Orig Exod 6:3).
The Midrash is cited in the name of R. Nathan (Nathan ben Solomon) Spira (Spiro), the famous

Polish Kabbalist (c 1582–1633), best known for his classic of Ashkenazi Kabbalah, Megalleh Amukkot, Cracow 1637. It is a strange passage describing the birth and early life of the biblical Joshua bin Nun in terms of the Oedipus story. The source and origin of this Midrash remain unknown. Neither is it known in which work of R. Nathan Spira it is to be found.

Cf ↑ סטטיונר

סנדרי, סנדראות, סנדריות, סנדרייתא ↓ סנהדרין

סנדרנא (401) (leading?) members of council (i e of *synhedrin*); new formation from *סנדר (= סנהדרין) with pl term, corresponding to: *σύνεδρος*

CantR 4. 4: על ידי מי נעשית מלחמת מדין? על ידי "שני שדיך" על ידי סנדרנא משה ופנחס, By who is the war against Midian waged? By "Thy two breasts" (Cant 4:5), by the *synedroi*, Moses and Phinehas.

Cf LW 1, 63, 191; Levy 3, 553; AC 6, 84a. Contraction (syncope) from *סנהדרנא. (Contra Jastrow 1005a, who suggests a corrupt dittography of ע"י שני שדיך, and Fürst 157a: *σύνθρονος*.) The context suggests that these are more than simply members, and more likely heads of the *sanhedrin*. *σύνεδρος*, JosAnt 14. 172; ArndtGingrich 794a. On the loss of the interaspiration cf LW 1, 63, and the form: סנדרי (↓ סנהדרין).

Cf ↓ סנהדרין

סנהדרין, סנדרי (401–02) (1) supreme court or council of seventy or seventy-one members (2) smaller (provincial) court usually of twenty-three members (3) learned council of academy (4) cœlestial council of angels (5) name of a treatise in the Order Nezikin in the Mishna, Tosefta and the Palestinian and Babylonian Talmuds: *συνέδρι[ο]ν* → *synhedrium*

(1) MSanh 1. 6: סנהדרין גדולה היתה של שבעים ואחד, the supreme court had seventy-one members. // BSanh 16b.

YSanh 1, 19c 20: סנהדרין שבלשכת הגזית, אף על פי שהיתה של ע"א, לא היו פחותין מכ"ג, The court in the hall of hewn stone, even though it had seventy-one members, did not have less than twenty-three members.

MSanh 4. 3: סנהדרין היתה כחצי גורן עגולה, the court was [seated] in a half circle. // T ibid 8. 1, $427_{8\ 9}$: סנהדרי; Yibid 1, 19c 30.

MMid 5. 4: לשכת הגזית, שם היתה סנהדרי גדולה של ישראל יושבת ודנה את הכהונה, The hall of hewn stone, where the great council of Israel was seated and judged the priesthood.

TSanh 3. 10, 420_2: סנהדרין נוהגת בארץ ובחוצה לה, The *sanhedrin* function in the land [of Israel] and outside it. // MMak 1. 10; BMak 7a.
TSanh 2. 15, 418_6: אין המלך יושב בסנהדרין, The King does not sit [as a member] in the *sanhedrin*.
MechEx 21:14, 264_{15}: סנהדרין בצד מזרח, The *sanhedrin* on the east side ...
SifraKedoshim Pirka 10, 91c: סנהדרי, סנדריות (pl). ▽ MsVat 410: סנהדרין, סנהדריות.
SifNum 92, $92_{5\ 14}$: "שבעים איש" — שתהא סנהדרין של שבעים, "seventy men" (Num 11:16) — That the *sanhedrin* should consist of seventy [men].
BSuk 51b: כנגד ע"א של סנהדרי גדולה, like the seventy-one of the great *sanhedrin*
PRK 184b, $415_{6\ 9}$: ... סנהדרין גדולה של ישראל, the great *sanhedrin* of Israel. ▽ סנהדרי. // LevR 33. 2, 759_4.

TSota 15. 7, $240_{50\ 51\ 54}$–$241_{60\ 65}$, $321_{26\ 27}$: סנדרי, סנהדרין. ▽ סנהדרי
GenR 98 (99) 8, 1259_2: ... סנהדרין שהיא מכה ורודה, *Sanhedrin* which beats and chastises ... Ibid 97, 1219_5, 1220_6: סנהדרי, ▽ סנהדרין; ibid 98 (99) 10, 1261_2, etc.
YSanh 1, 18c 15: ... הני סנהדרין שראו את ההורג, These *sanhedrin* (i e members of the *sanhedrin*) that saw the murderer. (The ~ין term seen as a pl form.)
BRH 31a, BAZ 8b: ... גלתה סנהדרין ... , the *sanhedrin* was exiled ...
MidPs 78. 12, 352: רישא דסנהדרין, the chief of the *sanhedrin*.
TrgYNum 25:4, TrgPs 140:10, Trg1Chron 5:12: (ריש סנהדרי(ן, chief of the *sanhedrin*.

TrgPsJGen 28:3, ibidNum 7:85. Trg1Chron 4:12: סנהדרין רבתא, the great *sanhedrin*. TrgPsJNum 25:7: סנדרי. Trg1Chron 18:17: סנדרי רבתא. Trg2Est 1:2. TrgPs 69:1. TrgPsJLev 24:12: סנהדרייתא (Aram pl). TrgPsJNum 9:8: לרישי סנהדרייתא, to the chiefs of the *sanhedrins*. FragmTrgKlein (V) Ex 15:27, Num 21:18, 25:4, 33:9; (P) Lev 19:26, Num 21:18, 25:4. (Transl: ראשי עם, "heads of the people", in Num 25:4.) Etc.
ER 11 (10) 53–54: בסנהדרין אינם מדברים שיחה בטלה לעולם, In the *sanhedrin* they never indulge in pointless conversation
Ibid 12 (11) 57: סנהדרי גדולה, the great *sanhedrin*.
KallaRabbati 12. 15, 211_{49}: מרדכי מזקני סנהדרין היה, Mordechai was one of the elders of the *sanhedrin*
MidTadshe 10 (Taraklin ed, Warsaw 1924, 15) = BHM 3, 174, OM 479a, AEpstein, Mi-Kadmoniyot haYehudim (= Kitvei R. AEpstein, 2) 154: שבעים סנהדרין היו מבית ראשון עד בית שני, There were seventy *sanhedrins* between the first and the second Temples. (Seen as pl because of ~ין term. Cf above.)
Cf also MidPs 4. 4, 44. MidSam 19. 3, 102. Ibid 25. 3, 123; 29. 3, 135 etc.

(2) MSanh 1, 6; וכמה יהא בעיר ותהא ראויה לסנהדרין, And how many people must there be in a city so that it require a *sanhedrin?*
TSanh 3. 7, 419_{19}: מניין לְסַנְהֶדְרִי קטנה של עשרים ושלשה, Whence do we know of a small *sanhedrin* of twenty-three?
MSanh 1. 5: אין עושין סנהדרין לשבטים, אלא על פי בית דין של שבעים ואחד, One does not appoint a *sanhedrin* for the tribes, but by [the decision of] the court of seventy-one.
SifDeut 144, 198_{2}: "בכל שעריך" — בא הכתוב להקיש סנהדרי קטנה לסנהדרי גדולה, "In all thy gates" (Deut 16:18) – the verse came to compare (or: draw an analogy between) the small *sanhedrin* and the great *sanhedrin* (above 1).
TanḥExKiTissa 26: סנהדראות מבני לוי, *Sanhedrins* of the house of Levi (pl).
CantR 3. 7: סנהדריות (pl).

(3) SifNum 131, 172_{13}: עמד מתוך סנהדרי שלו, He left his *sanhedrin*. ▽ ~ין, סנדרי.
SifNum 78, 73_{17}: שהיו יושבין בסנהדרין, they would participate in a learned council.
GenR 98 (99) 12, 1262_{11}: אלו מאתים ראשי סנהדראות שהיו משבטו של יששכר, These are the two-hundred council-heads who were of the tribe of Issachar, (or maybe: heads of provicial court, cf (2) above). ▽ ~יות.
TrgPs 45:1: סנהדרין של משה, Moses' council.
Trg1Est 5:9: בסנהדרין דעבדת להון אסתר, in the council which Esther appointed for them.

(4) ARN I, 20, 72: הושיב לו משה סנהדראות של מלאכי השרת, Moses appointed for himself courts of the angels of service.
Ibid 32, 93: לא הושיבו סנהדרין בארץ, אני מושיב להם סנהדרין במרום, They did not appoint a court on earth. [So] I shall appoint a court in heaven.

This word in its various forms is extremely common throughout all classes of Rabbinic lit. A fanciful homiletic etym for the word appears in LTNum 11. 16, 202: מה לשון סנהדרין? סין — זה תורה שנתנה בסיני. הדרין — שמהדרין התורה במדרשה, ומיפים ומישרין הכתוב זה עם זה, What is the etymology of *sanhedrin*? *Sin* – This is the Torah which was given at *Sinai. Hadrin* – For they beautify (*mehadrin*) the Torah with its exegesis, and make good and harmonious one verse with another. (Note that the *sin*–Sinai exegesis does not necessarily presuppose the knowledge of the Gk prononciation of *syn*hedrin, but is more likely a characteristic example of the freedom in Rabbinic exegesis.)
We have noted (above) that the ~ין term was sometimes seen as a pl form, so that סנהדרין meant *sanhedrins*. Perhaps for this reason the sing form סנהדרי evolved. From this the form סנדרי (separated in LW 401ab sv סנדר) evolved (see LW 1, 183), through a loss of the interaspiration (ibid 63, and cf Gignac 1, 135).
On סנדרי see Lieberman TK 8, 1973, 764, that this form is common in Palestinian and Gaonic sources.
Other pl forms: ~יות, ~אות (cf ibid 101). On סנ~ – σνν (i e υ > α interchange), see LW 1, 20, 86,

and cf Mayser 1/1² 124: σv (= σύν). On ין~ for ~ιον, see ibid 92, 164–65, and cf Psaltes 47–48. On Trg1Est 2. 21: ומרדכי יתיב בסנהדרין דתקינת ליה אסתר (transl: ומרדכי יושב בשער המלך), see LW 1, 217, and 2, 402b (perhaps a stool, cathedra?). More likely, read סנהדרי': συνέδρα = Lat *statio* (Hesych, LSJ⁹ 1704a) = post (sentinel post).
סנהדרוס in Sefer Raziel 42a is the name of an angel: σύνεδρος.
See MM 604ab; ArndtGingrich 793b–794a, with bibl; DittSyll³ index; Schürer³ II, 193f (= English ed II, 1893, 169 n461f); Mason 89ab. There is a considerable literature on this subject. The most up-to-date and comprehensive work on the *sanhedrin* is HMantel, Studies in the History of the Sanhedrin, Harvard University Press 1961 = Meḥkarim be-Toldot ha-Sanhedrin, Tel-Aviv 1969, with full bibl.

Lat: *synedrium*, Souter 410b.
Syr: סנדריק, PnS 2674; סונהדריון, BB 1338 (transcr).
Cf ↑ **סנדרנא**

סניגור (403–04) attorney for the defence: *συνήγωρ

[Frequently coupled with **קטיגור** ↓: prosecutor.]

BRH 26a: אין קטיגור נעשה סניגור, A prosecutor cannot serve as an attorney for the defence. // BBer 49a; YYoma 7. 3, 44b 43; PRK Buber 177b; YRH 3. 6, 58d 21; MGLev 16. 4, $_{211}$ (not clear whether // with independent formulation, or from independent but similar source).
LevR 21. 10, 490$_3$: שלא יעשה סניגור קטיגור, Let not the prosecutor become the attorney for the defence, (partial // to YYoma 7. 3, 44b 43 above).
BḤag 13b: קטיגור יעשה סניגור?, Will the prosecutor serve for the defence? // BKid 5a; Mann, HUCA 14, 1939, 342$_{17}$.
YSuk 3. 1, 53c 16: אי לו לזה שנעשה סניגורו קטיגורו, Woe is he whose defence becomes his prosecutor. // Lev 30. 6, 704$_2$; PRK 182b, 412$_2$; MidPs 26. 5, 218; TanḥLevEmor 18, ibidB 26, 98; YalkLev 651; MGLev 23. 40, 656$_{20}$.
GenR 49. 12, 514$_5$: חלף סידרה (↑) מלאה מים. כל זמן שהיא מלאה מים, הסניגור מלמד. פעמים שהדיין מבקש שילמד הסניגור, והוא אומר: הוסיפו בתוכה מים, A water-clock full of water. As long as it is full of water, the attorney for the defence pleads. Sometimes the judge wishes the attorney for the defence to [continue to] plead. And he says: Add water to it. ▽ (↓) שילמד סניגוריא. // YalkGen 83, 381$_{17}$.
ExR 18. 5: מיכאל וסמאל דומין לסניגור וקטיגור עומדין בדין. זה מדבר וזה מדבר. גמר זה דבריו וזה דבריו, ידע הסניגור שנצח ..., Michael and Samael are like an attorney for the defence and a prosecutor [that] stand in court. The one speaks and the other speaks. The one concluded his case and the other likewise. [Then] the defence attorney knew he had won ...
TanḥGenVa-Yera 8: מבקש להם סניגור שילמד עליהם זכות, ונותן שביל לפני הסניגור,

He seeks a defence attorney for them who will plead their cause, and makes a path before the attorney.
TanḥBGenVa-Yeẓe 2, 145: כשיעמדו הכל בדין, היא סניגורין שלו ומלמדת עליו זכות, when they all stand for judgement, she (the Torah) will serve as his defence attorney and plead his cause. Perhaps read: **סניגורון** ↓. // AgBer 45 (46). 2, 91: **היא** סניגור שלו, she shall serve as his defence attorney.
ExR 43. 1: הסניגור הטוב מסביר פנים בדין. משה אחד משני סניגורין שעמדו ללמוד סניגוריא (↓) על ישראל, והעמידו פנים כביכול כנגד הקב"ה, A good defence attorney [usually] acts pleasantly in court. Moses was one of the two defence attorneys who stood up to plead the defence of Israel, and they, as it were, presented themselves as opposition to the Holy One blessed be He.
MidPs 106. 6, 456: למלך שכעס על בנו, בא לחתום בקולמוס ליתן אפופסין (↑), וחטף לו הסניגור הקולמוס מידו. כך "להשיב חמתו השחית", Like a king who was angry with his son, He was about to sign with the reed pen (*calamus*), when the attorney snatched the reed pen out of his hand. Thus, "to turn away His wrath, lest He should destroy them," (Psalms 106:23). // YalkPs 864; MachPs 106. 63, 2. 168.

Pl:

MechRashbiEx 23:1, 214_{8}: שלא ידברו סניגורין לפניהם, that advocates should not speak before them (the judges; i e that the judges should first hear the case from the plaintiffs' mouths, and not through the agency of lawyers). // MGEx 23. 1, 531_{6}: סניגורין, סניגירין ▽ סניגרין. (Reworked version in RMeyuḥas to Ex 23:7, edGreenup, Budapest 1929, 87: אזהרה לדיין שלא יעמיד סניגוריאה בדין, שהן מדברין דבר שקר, A warning to the judge that he should not set up advocacy (sic) in court, for they speak falsehood. Cf ↓ **סניגוריא**.)
YRH 1. 3, 57b 14, 15: העמידו בימה (↑), יעמדו סניגורין, יעמדו קטיגורין ... יעברו סניגורין, יעברו קטיגורין, Set up a tribunal, [and] let the defence attorney stand forth, [and] let the prosecutors stand forth ... Let the defence attorneys be removed, [and] let the prosecutors be removed. But for // PRK 53b–54a, $102_{10\ 12}$ with slight ▽ ; PR 15, 77a; MidPs 81. 6, 367; YalkEx 190, $123_{46\ 48}$; ibidPs 831; MGEx 12. 1, $169_{6\ 8}$, see ↓ **סקיפטורין**. (But // in MachPs 81. 18, 2. 50: **סניגורון** ↓.)
MidPs 141. 1, 530: למי שהיה לו דין לפני השלטון. ראה שיש לכל סניגורין לדבר עליהם. קרא אל השלטון ואמר לו: בבקשה ממך, הכל צריכים הם לסניגוריהם. אני אין לי סניגור, אין לי מי שידבר עלי. אתה הדיין ואתה הוא הסניגור, Like unto one who has a case before the ruler. He saw that everyone had defence attorneys to plead for them. He called to the ruler, saying: Please, everyone needs their defence attorneys. I have no defence attorney. I have no one who will plead for me. You are the judge, and you will be my defence attorney.

The word is very common in early and later Rabb lit. On GenR 49. 12 and the water-clock, see Lieberman, JQR 35, 1944, 27, referring to Mommsen, Römisches Strafrecht, 428, and ↑ **חלף סידרה**.
The form **συνήγωρ* parallels *κατήγωρ*, on which see ↓ **קטיגור**.
On the form ~סנ for *συν~*, see LW 1, 86. Cf ArndtGingrich 797a
Note that סניגורים in YSanh 17 (10) 2, 28d 38 is probably *singularii* (LW 2, 399b; Fürst 157a; contra Levy 3, 551b, suggesting *sanguinarii;* AC 6, 82a suggesting: *σύγχορος* or *συνοικουρός*). So too סניגורים (sic) in YelamdNum 10:2, apud Ar (AC 6, 20a), GrünhutLikkutim 4, 19a, is probably *singularii* (Jastrow 1004b), rather than *signarii* (LW 2, 380b sv סינגורים!). Incidentally, the usual Rabbinic form סנגלרין corresponds closely to the Gk form *σιγγλάριος* (on which cf Gignac 1, 309).

Syr: סניגרא, סנגרא, סנאגרא, PnS 2672.
Cf ↓ **סניגורון, סניגוריא, סניגוריא, פי סניגוריא, קטיגור**

סניגורא ↓ **סניגוריא**

סניגרון ↓ **סניגורון**

סניגוריא (~יה) (404) defence, advocacy on behalf of another's cause: *συνηγορία*

YTaan 2. 4, 65d 7: ואין להם מי ילמד עליהם סניגוריא. אתה תהא מלמד עליהם סניגוריא, They have no one who will plead defence on their behalf. You will plead defence on their behalf. ▽ SY 176_9: ~יה.
LevR 23. 9, $540_{3\ 6}$: לוט עומד מדבר עליהם סניגוריה ... סניגוריא, Lot stands advocating on their behalf ... ▽ סניגורייה. // GenR 26. 5, 249_5: סניגורייה. ▽ ~יא; ibid 50. 5, $522_{3\ 4}$; YalkGen 44, 54_3.
PRK 164a, 370_9: דלא יתעביד סניגוריא קטיגוריא (↓), that the defence should not turn into prosecution. // YalkHos 532, (Arugat ha-Bosem 2, 95).
ExR 15. 29: שנים עומדים בפני המלך, אחד מלמד קטיגוריא (↓) שלו, ואחד סניגוריא שלו. לא כל המלמד קטיגוריא מלמד סניגוריא ... אבל הקב"ה אינו כן. הוא מלמד סניגוריא, הוא מלמד קטיגוריא, Two men standing before the king, one prosecutes and one pleads his defence. Not all who prosecute plead defence ... But the Holy One blessed be He is not so. He pleads defence, and He prosecutes.
Ibid 38. 8: משל לבן מלכים שהיה פדגוגו נכנס ללמד סניגוריא על בנו, It is like unto the son of a king whose tutor would come [before the king] to plead his son's defence.
Ibid 43. 1: משה אחד משני סניגורין (↑ **סניגור**) שעמדו ללמד סניגוריא על ישראל, Moses was one of the two defence attorneys who stood up to plead the defence of Israel.
TanḥGenVa-Yera 8: מיד התחיל אברהם ללמד עליהם סניגוריא, Forthwith Abraham began to plead their defence.

TanḥExTissa 17: סנגוריא. Ibid 32: סניגוריא. Ibid Lev Kedoshim: סניגוריא.
PRK 196a, 438_{10}: סניגוריא. ▽ סניגורא.
CantR 8. 14: התורה נכנסת ומלמד סניגוריייא (sic edprinc): The Torah enters and pleads the defence. ▽ סניגוריא. // YalkDeut 950; ibidSam 151.
PR 10, 38a: סניגורא, read: סניגוריא.
R. Meyuḥas to Ex 23:7, edGreenup, Budapest 1929, 87: אזהרה לדיין שלא יעמיד סניגוריאה בדין, שהן מדברין דבר שקר, A warning to the judge that he should not set up advocacy (sic) in court, for they speak falsehood (i e he should hear the case directly from the plaintiffs and not by the agency of lawyers). This is a reworking of the text in MechRashbiEx 23:1, 214_8 (cf ↑ **סניגור**).

The text in R. Meyuḥas is somewhat problematic (with the uncomfortable transition from the sing abstract noun to pl). But the interpretation (and source) is clear; see MMKasher, Torah Shelemah 19, 322. The orthography there, ~ריאה, may reflect mediaeval Gk usage, since R Meyuḥas undoubtedly knew Gk. He was Macedonian (or from elsewhere in the Balkan); see Cheval's ed of his commentary to Job, New York 1969, introduction 3–4.
PR 40, 171b has: ... השופר סניגורת לכם, which should surely be read: סניגור[י]ה, the *shofar* (ram's horn) is advocacy on your behalf. (Contra LW 2, 404b sv סניגורית, a female advocate; LW 1, 189.) Note that the following word in that passage is also corrupt: לסס for לכם. (No evidence for such a form from נימורת in YPes 4. 9, 31b 52, as edprinc has נימורה, and GS 1, 433_{22}: נומירה: *νούμερα, numerus*, LW2, 356b. See LiebermanYK 443–44.)
Common in both early and later Rabbinic lit.
For סניגוריא II in LW 2, 404ab, see ↓ **פי סניגוריא**. See Lampe 1327a.

Syr: סנאגרותא, PnS 2672–73.
Cf ↑ **סניגור**, ↓ **קטיגוריא**, **פי סניגוריא**

סניגוריא ↑ סניגורת, סניגוריאה

◇**סניגרון** (404), advocate, attorney for the defence: *συνήγορον* (acc term)

BShevu 30b: מניין לדיין שלא יעשה סניגרון לדבריו? ת״ל — ״מדבר שקר תרחק״, From whence [do we know] that a judge must not make himself advocate for his own words (i e cause)? You may learn from [the verse] "Keep thee far from a false matter" (Ex 23:7). ▽ MsMunich: דבריו סנגרון, perhaps meaning, "he shall not make his own word an advocacy (abstract noun) [for himself]? R Ḥananel reads: סניגורן, explaining: מליץ יושר, attorney for defence. // MGExod 23:7, 535_7: סניגרון ▽ סניגורין (↑ **סניגור**) פי׳ מליץ; YalkEx 352, 616_{35}: סניגורן.
TanḥBLevẒav 1, 12: בלעם הרשע היה סניגרון של אומות העולם, Baalam the wicked was advocate for the nations of the world. But // in Tanḥ ibid 1: סניגורן (not in edprinc, but from edMantua 1563 onwards); so too in YalkLev 479: סנגורן (sic edprinc).

MidPs 20. 3, 174: באותה שעה נמצא סנגרון של ישראל משתתק, At that hour, the attorney of Israel is silenced. // RuthR ad init: סניגרון (sic edprinc, later edd: סניגורון, probably emended).
TanhBGenVa-Yeze 2. 145: היא סניגורין שלו ומלמדת עליו זכות ... , she (the Torah) will serve as his defence attorney and will plead his cause. Read: סניגורון. But // in AgBer 45 (46) 2, 91: סניגור (↑).
MachPs 81. 18, 2. 50: העמידו בימה (↓), והעמידו סניגורון וקטיגרון (קטיגור ↑), Set up a tribunal, and let the defence attorney stand forth and the prosecutor. (But // in YRH 1. 3, 57b 14, 15 has סניגורין, pl of **סניגור** ↑, which seems the more original reading. For // in PRK 53b–54a, $102_{10\ 12}$; PR 15, 77a; MidPs 81. 6, 367; YalkEx $123_{46\ 4}$; ibid Ps 831; MGEx 12. 1, $169_{6\ 8}$ see ↓ **סקיפטורין**.)

Note the angel names סנגרון, סנגרי and סניגרון in SchwabVocabulaire, 200, 202.
On the acc term, see LW 1, 71, and cf ↑ **גרדון** and **אפופסיס**.
On the meaning of the word in BShevu 30b, see MMKasher, Torah Shelemah 19, New York 1959, p. 322.

Cf ↑ **סניגור**, ↓ **קטיגור**

סנסן [סנדין] tablet (on which laws are written): *σανίδι<ο>ν*

MidCant, edGrünhut 4a: **אם על הגזרה באת, כבר נכנסה מדת הדין לפני הקב"ה, ובידו** **סנסן אחד, וכתוב עליו "וגנב איש ומכרו ונמצא בידו"**, If you have come in connection with the edict, stern judgement has already entered before the Holy One blessed be He with a tablet (*σανίδιον*) in his hand, and written on it [is], "And he that stealeth a man, and selleth him, or if he be found in his hand, [he shall surely be put to death]" (Exod 21:1b). Read: סנדין.

Sperber, Leshonenu 33, 1969, 74–75, 320. The scribal error came about due to the fact that (in Sefardi calligraphy) the *yod* was written inside the *dalet* forming something that could be mistakenly read as a *semach*. (Cf Lieberman TR 3, 74, idem TK 1, 106 n19, idemGH 115 n30.) The form סנסן is influenced by the Biblical and Rabb word סנסן, leaf of palm tree (Jastrow 1008a).
Note that the dim term *~ιδιον* does not necessarily the diminutive nature of the object in later Gk. See Psaltes 271, 276.
For *σανίδιον* see DuCange 1331 sv *σανιδι: tabula, Σανίδιον*. (Cf LW 2, 404b sv סניס; AC 6, 80b sv $סן_5$; RosenzweigWohnhaus 8 n9, explained as *σανίς*, to be rejected. See Löw, LWibid 612b; ACSup 297b, Arab etym. Ginzberg, MGWJ 78, 1934, 27–28, also to be rejected.)

סנקלטירי, ספוקלטריא, ספוק לטרייה ↓ ספקלטור

סקרדין ↓ ספיטרון

ספיקולא (407–08) death sentence *σπέκουλα ← [*]*specula*

YBer 9. 6, 14b (13b) 26: מלך בשר ודם כשהוא נותן דימוס (↑) הכל מקלסין אותו. וכשהוא נותן ספקולה הכל מרננין אחריו ..., A king of flesh and blood, when he grants a pardon, all praise him. [But] when he gives a death sentence, all murmur against him. // LevR 24. 2, 550_5: ספיקלא. ▽ MsOxf Neubauer 147: ספקולייא, ספיקיא, ספקלא; YelamdDeut ad init, apud Ar (AC 3, 87a): ספיקלא (= Grünhut, Likkutim 5, 90a: ספקיולא, read: ספיקולא); YalkPs 843 ad fin; MachPs 92. 96, 2. 98: אספקלריא (perhaps read: אספקלייא?); ibid 101. 2, 2. 122 (citing LevR 24. 2); MachIs 5. 16, 44_{31}: ספיקלא.

YelamdLevAḥarei, apud Ar (AC 6, 109b): נתן להם ספקולא, He gave them the death sentence.

MidPs 9. 13, 89: עשה עצמו דיין, ודן אותו שיתנו לו ספיקולא, He set himself up as judge, and sentenced them that they be given the death sentence. ▽ סקילה, read: ספקילה. // YalkPs 643: ספקו, read: ספקו׳ = ספקו[לה]; MachPs 9. 15, 1. 57: סקילה, read: ספקילה.

TanḥGenHayyei 3: עשו לי אספתון (read: אספתין), שאם ימרדו העבדים ישמעו מפי ספקולא, Prepare me the swords, so that if they rebel, they will hear from me the death sentence. // ExR 15. 22: אספיקולא.

GenR 79. 6, 942_1: ספיקולה, הוות מיתצדה, (He heared a heavenly voice call:) "The death sentence," and it was caught. ▽ ~לא, ספקולא. // PRK 88b, 192_4: 10. 8: ספיקלא; EstR 1. 9 (3. 7); MachPs 17. 25, 1. 100: ספי קלא, (but MidPs 17. 3, 134: אפופסין ↑); YalkGen 133, 680_1; (Tosafot AZ 16b, and Recanati KiTeẓe which latter has: שפיקולא).

NumR 7. 3: מלך בשר ודם יש לו ספקולא, אף הקב"ה יש לו, שנאמר, "מות יומת הנואף והנאפת", A King of flesh anbd blood has the death sentence [at his disposal]. So too the Holy One blessed be He has it, as it is said "the adulterer and the adulteress shall surely be put to death" (Lev 20:10).

MidPs 100. 2, 425: בשעה שאינו מודה נותן לו ספיקולא, [And] when he does not admit [the charge], he sentences him to death. ▽ ספקו. // MachPs 100. 1, 2. 121: ספקו; MachProv 28. 12, 75b: ספקו; read: ספקו[לא]. (But // in PRK 159a, 356_3; YalkPs 854; YalkProv 961 ad fin; MGEx 8. 11, 123_3: פרקולא, with slight ▽. So too MachProv 28. 12, 76a: פיקולא is probably to be read: פרקולא, or פריקולא, as it is quoted from PRK ibid. Cf ↓ **פריקולא**.)

MidProv 6. 20, 57; ... ואני עומד (בגזירה (gloss: בספיקולא שלך ליום הדין לעתיד לבוא, And I will insist on the death sentence for you in the future. // MachHos 14. 2, 5: בגזירה ספיקלא.

Specula here from *speculator*, meaning "executioner" (cf ↓ **ספקלטור**). The spelling with the *yod*,

ספיקולא, may be influenced by *spiculum*, javelin, but not necessarily so as *epsilon* is frequently transcribed with a *yod* (LW 1, 17, and cf Gignac 1, 251, that Lat e is sometimes transcribed by *ι* in loanwords eg: *πρίγκιψ — princeps, μάγκιψ — manceps*, etc). (Contra Jastrow 1014a. On ExR 15. 22, see Brüll, Jahrb 4, 1879, 112: *speculum*, Levy 1, 129a: *σφάκελος = φάκελος*.)
The form סקילה, which we have emended to ספיקלה, is, of course, influenced by the Bib Heb סקילה, stoning.
On PRK 356₃, see Lieberman, JQRNS 35. 1944, 33–34.
As to NumR 9. 20 // YSota 1. 4, 16d 48: ספסליה ▽ MsVat: סבסליה, which Krauss, LW 2, 408a wished to emend to ספקלה, see AC 6, 106a, it is from: ספסל, bench, (and cf Berger 720a)?
בית ספיקריא in YBer 9. 2, 13 (12)c 68, ▽ ספוקלרין, אספקולרין, איסקוריא etc (Ratner 201) is not *specula* (as suggested by Krauss, LW 2, 408c sv ספיקליא), but probably a form derived from *specus*, cavern, ditch, trench, such as **specularia*, **specaria?* Cf AC 6, 110b–111a.
The form ספקולייא noted above may represent a vowel development; see Gignac 1, 311, and cf ↑ מיסתיוסים. אספקלריא in MachPs 98. 26 is probably influenced by **אספקלריא**: *speculare, σπεκλάριον*, mirror (LW 2, 93ab), but may derive from a form: אספקלייא, again showing a vowel development.

Cf ↓ ספקלטור

ספיקולה ↑ ספיקולא

סקיפטורין ↓ ספיקטורין

ספיקלא ↑ ספיקולא

ספיקלטור ↓ ספקלטור

ספסוניא ↑ סמפניא

◇ספסופא [ספנוסא] (408) conspiracy: *σύ<μ>πνευσ<ις>* (+ Aram term)

YTer 8. 10, 46b 48, 53: ר' איסי איתציד בספסופה ... זעיר בר חנינא איתציד בספסופא, R. Isi was caught [involved] in a conspiracy ... Ze'ir bar Ḥanina was caught [involved] in a conspiracy. ▽ MsVat: ~פה in both cases.
EcclesR 11. 1 (edprinc): לבתר יומין איתצדון יהודאי בהדין ספפאסא, After some days Jews were caught [involved] in a conspiracy. ▽ edd: ספפסא. Read throughout: ספנוסא.

Lieberman, Sefer ... Alon (1970), 229, 234. The two texts are partial // to one another, as already noted by R. David Luria, EcclesR ad loc. Lieberman (ibid n43) points out that ספנוסא was (mistakenly) seen as masc ספנוס + *aleph* (definite article); hence: ... הדין.
(Contra Krauss LW2, 408c: *Σπασίνου (χάραξ)*, following PerlesBeiträge 1893, 30, rejected by Löw

ad loc; AC 6, 106b: place name *Soufsafeh,* NeubauerGéographie 271; Levy 3, 493b sv סנפיסטא: *σοφιστής;* Jastrow 1015a, from אספס', (אסף!) CGL 2, 443_2: *συμπνευσις conspiratio.*

Cf ↑ סמפניא

ספסופא ↑ ספפסא, ספפאסא, ספסופה

ספיקולא ↑ ספקולייא, ספקולה, ספקו

סקיפטורין ↓ ספקטורין

ספקלטור ↓ ספקלאטור

ספקלטור, also **אספקלטור** (92–93, 409) (1) executioner (2) overseer: *σπεκ<ου>λάτωρ ← spec<u>lator*

(1) SifNum 91, 91_{19}: אמר לספקלטור: הרגני עד שלא תהרוג את בניי, He said to the executioner: Kill me before you kill my children. ▽ לסקלפטור, לאיספקלטור (metath). // SifZutaNum 11. 15, 271_7; MGNum 11. 15, 174_4 = GasterMaasiyot LXXVI, 51_{12}.

ARN I 38, 114: והיו מתחננין לאספקלטור ... הרגני תחילה ..., And they begged the executioner ... Kill me first ... // Ibid II 41, 115; MachZach 13. 7, 121: ... פלטור לאיספ', read: לאיספקלטור, or לאיספ<פ>לטור.

BShab 108a: לשני בני אדם שנתחייבו הריגה למלכות. אחד הרגו מלך, ואחד הרגו איספקליטור, Like two people who were condemned to death by the imperial authority. One [of them], the king executed; the other, the executioner executed. ▽ MsMunich: אספקלטור, AggTalm: **אספליטור.**

NumR 20. 14: מלך בשר ודם משלח ספקלטור להרוג את האדם ..., A king of flesh and blood sends off an executioner to kill a man ... // TanḥNumBalak 8; TanḥBibid 12, 138; YalkNum 785.

EcclesR 10. 11: לפיכך נעשה (נחש) ספקלאטור לכל פורצי גדרות, For this reason the snake was made executioner of all who break through the fences" (i e sin against Rabbinic ordination) (sic edprinc). // LevR 26. 2, 591_4 in apparat (in printed edd, but not in Mss): ספקלטור.

LamentR 2. 1, 98: שלשה דברים היה משמש אותו המלאך: ספקלטור ... כד"א "החרימם נתנם לטבח", That angel served in three capacities: an executioner ... as it is said "He hath utterly destoryed them, He hath delivered them to slaughter" (Is 34:2). // YalkEzek 349: ספיקלטור.

EcclesR 12. 7: "לפתח פה ברצח" — ספק לא טורין (sic edprinc): "to open the mouth in the slaughter" (Ezek 21: 27) – Executioners (pl). // LamentRProem 23, 20: ספקלטרים ▽ ספיק ליטורין; YalkEzek 361: ספקלטורים (edprinc).

NumR 19. 26: ... ואין אדם מקלס לאיספקלטור שלו, And a man does not praise his own executioner. // TanḥNumḤukkat 21, TanḥB ibid 48, 127; YalkNum 764: לספקלטור.

CantR 8. 6: קפיק ליטור (sic edprinc), read: ספיקליטור.

PRE 48, 115b: סנקלטירי פרעה היו מחנקין את ישראל בקירות הבית; read: ספקלטורי, Pharaoh's executioners would choke the Israelites in the walls of the houses (i e by building them into the walls of the houses). ▽ אספלאטורים, edHigger, Ḥorev 10/19–20, 1948, 238, ספקלטורים, ibid 293 n88 (pl). // YalkEx 167, 46_{78}: ספקלטורין; ibidDeut 826: ספיקלטורין.

YelamdBalak, apud Mann, Bible 2, 162 (from Sikili's Yalkut Talmud Torah): ספקלוטור.

Seridei Tanḥ-Yelmd, edUrbach, Koveẓ al Yad NS 6/1, 1966, 16: איספקלטור.

TanḥExShemot 10: ... ולספקלטרין (pl).

Panim Aḥerim II, 6. 1, 76: וספקלטור.

MGGen 37. 1, 622_9 according to Ms ש in apparat: ספקלטור, (פטריקוס: *patricius* in text).

MGLev 10. 2, 223_{20}: מיד אמר לספקלטור וחתך את ראשו. Forthwith he ordered the executioner, and he cut off his head.

TrgNeofitiGen 40:3: רב אספקלטוריא, transl שר הטבחים, chief of the executioners.

TrgNeofitiGen 37:36: רב ספקליטיריה // TrgYI ibid: אספקלטוריא; TrgYIIibid: ספוקלטריא (pl), (read ~ספיק?); FragmTrgKlein (N): ספוקלטריא, (V) ספוק לטרייה.

TrgIIEst 5:2: אספקלטורי דמלכא, the king's executioners (pl).

(2) EcclesR 9. 18: ספקלי — "אליקים בן חלקיה אשר על הבית", read: ספקל' = ספקלטור, "Eliakim, Ḥilkiah's son, which was over the house" (Is 36:3) – [The] overseer.

סקלפטור in ▽ to SifNum ibid may be meant to represent something like "father (פטור – *pater*) of stoning (from Bib Heb סקל, to stone). Cf ↑ **ספיקולא.**

For קפיקליטור in CantR 8. 6, see Luria ad loc, ad PerlesES 12.

On PRE 48, 115b, see Luria and loc n67, and GFriedlander's ed, 381 n5 (contra AC 6, 89a: *συγκλήτωρ*). See also Jastrow 1008b.

In MachZach we read: לאיספ', which should be completed: לאיספקלטור, or perhaps: איספלטור, since earlier in the same line we read: שקבל את [פלטור] (פגעו) פגעו. is correct; see // in ARN ibid. פלטור looks like the second half of איספ[ק]לטור, that get separated from its abbreviated fellow. On the possible form איספלטור, cf BShab 108a according to Agg Talm: אספליטור, and ▽ to PRE 48: אספלאטורים. For such a loss of the K before L, see Gignac 1, 65; eg: *κελήρωμαι* (for *κεκλήρωμαι*), SB 7032 = PMich 189. 35 (75 CE) etc.

There are two main forms of this word, one with the prosthetic *aleph* (cf LW 1, 136–40, especially

138), and one without (ibid 140). Invariably, in all its forms the u of *speculator* has been lost, just as in ספקלריא and אספקלריא: *specularia* (ibid 25), and cf ↑ **ספיקולא**. The form σπεκλάτωρ is attested; see REG 72, 214 no260 (Tomi), and cf Souter 383b. The form ספיקלטור is parallelled by the Lat *spiculator* = *speculator* (DuCange 1420, Schürer 1[5], 427 n89; but see Souter 384b, who thinks these two words probably differ).

Speculator had the primary meaning of "investigator, examiner"; then "scout, courier," and then "executioner." See MM 582b; ArndtGingrich 769a; Sophocles 1003b; Lampe 1248a; DuCange 1420. For the meaning (2) "overseer" or "guardian", see Souter 383b, and hence "bishop" (ibid and Maigne D'Arnis 2088). (Reject Jastrow 1017a, who suggests ספיקלי is a corrupt from פילקס: φύλαξ – *excubitor*!) Cf HAMusurillo, Acts of the Pagan Martyrs, Oxford 1954, 65, 213.

See Schürer 1[5], 471–72 n89–90.

Syr: אספקולטרא, ספקולטרא, PnS 312, 2698.
Cf ↑ **ספיקולא**

ספקלטור ↑ ספקליטיריה, ספקלי, ספקלטרים

סקבטרין written document: [*]σκεπτ<ώ>ρι<ο>ν ← [*]*exceptorium* (?)

LevR 21. 2, 407_3: "[אם תקום עלי מלחמה] בזאת [אני בוטח]" — א"ר לוי: בסווקטירים שכתב לנו משה בספר תורה לזקיני, "וזאת ליהודה ויאמר", "[Though war should rise up against me,] in this [will I be confident]" (Ps 27:3). Said R Levi: In the written document which Moses wrote in his Torah to my forefather – "And this is the blessing of Judah, and he said ..." (Deut 33:7). ▽ סקבטרין, סויקטרים, סקווטורים, טווקבירים (read: סווקטירים), קוטרים (cf ↓ **קרטים**). // Ibid 478_6: **איספיקטורין** (↑). ▽ סקנטריין (read: סקבטריין), סקווטורים, etc; ibid 474_7 and 480_2 according to MsMunich 117: סקנטריין (read: סקבטריין); PRK 175a: סקווטרים (= LevR 21, see Mandelbaum's note PRK 400_3); MachPs 27. 5, 1. 179: סויקטרים, אספקטרין (corrected by Buber in both places to: סקווטרים).

This host of variants fall into two major categories, with slight ▽ : (a) סוו(פ)קטרין, i e SPECTORIN (= *σπεκτ<ω>ρι<ο>ν ← *spectorium*), or (b) סקוו(ב)טרים, i e SCEPTORIN. We would suggest SCEPTORIN as the primary reading, and all the rest as orthographic ▽ and metath etc. Since איסקבטֹרִיי (↑) is a scribe, *[ἐ]σκεπτωρ (and cf ↓ **סקיפטור**), it would seem reasonable that [E]SCEPTORIN is a written document, i e [*]*exceptorium* [*]σκεπτώρι<ο>ν. Indeed these forms exist, but with other meanings, eg σκεπτώρι<ο>ν, mirror, LSJSupple 133b (citing PMasp 340[V]. 40), and σκεπτούρι<ο>ν = *exceptorium*, cistern, Lampe 1236a.

A // tradition (noted above) reads: **איסקיפטורין** (↑), written judgement, etc.

Yet a further (parallel) tradition appears in a number of sources; MidPs 27. 4, 225: **אכסיטורין** = ibid 102. 2, 430, ▽ **אסיטורין**; ibid 84. 4, 371: **אגיסטרון**, = ibid 86. 1, 372; MachPs 84. 18, 2. 60: **אניסטרון** (read: **אגיסטרון**); ibid 86. 3, 2. 65: **אגיסטרין**; ibid 102. 6, 2. 126: **אגוסטרין**. See Buber's discussion in Oẓar Ḥochmah 1, 7b, and again in PRK 175ab n158, and MidPs 224 n39, and LW 2, 11a:

ἐξιτήριον, a parting message (cf Lampe 418a sv *ἐξιτήριος*, ref AnastAnt *redit* (p251), and similarly Schlatter 61–62). Further // in YalkSam 126, and ibidPs 706, omit the difficult word.
On parallel traditions, see my remarks in Bar-Ilan 14–15n 1977, 34–37.
The ב and וו (= v) for *π* is the result of a two-stage consonantal change, each stage being well attested in Rab Graecitas: P > B > V. On P > B, see Krauss LW1, 97–98 and Gignac 1, 86–87, and on B > V, ibid 98 and ibid 68. Cf ↑ **איסקבטירי** for a similar example of this.
The secondary reading SPECTORIN is probably the result of metath (LW1, 114–15), under the influence of the similar sounding **σπεκτ<ω>ρι<ο>ν*, meaning: a (written) decree (?). On **σπεκτωριον* deriving from Lat **spectorium* see Souter 383b: *specto*, to issue a decree. (For a homonym see EpsteinGK 76_1: איספיקטורין: **espectorin* = **expectorium* = *pectoralium*, meaning corset.)

Cf ↑ **איסקיפטורין**

סקבטרין ↑ סקווטריס, סקווטורים

איסקריטור ↑ סקיווי פטריי

ספיקולא ↑ סקילה

סקיפטורין (410) scribe of the court: *σκέπτωρ* ← *sceptor* (+ pl term)

PRK 54a, $102_{10\ 12}$: ... העמידו בימה (↑) ויעמדו סניגורין (↑ **סניגור**) ויעמדו סקיפטורין ויעבירו סקיפטורין, set up a tribunal, and let there be advocates, and let there be scribes of the court ... and let the scribes of the court be removed. ▽: סקפטורן, קפטורין, מקיפטורין. Read: סק(י)פטורין. // PR 15, 77a: סקפטורים; MidPs 81. 6, 367: ספיקטורין; YalkEx 190, $123_{46\ 49}$: ספיקטורין, ibid Ps 831 ספיקטורין; MGEx 12. 1, $169_{6\ 8}$: ספקטורין. Read: סק(י)פטורין. The // in YRH 1. 3, 57b 14 has: קיטיגורין (↓ **קטיגור**). And so too MachPs 81. 18, 2. 50: קטיגרון (↓).

Sperber, AJS Revue 4, 1979, 205–07. Cf Brüll, Jahrb 1, 1874, 178; Levy 3, 581b–82a; Jastrow 1020a; AC 6, 120b, suggesting *ἐσκέπτωρ*, *exceptor*. (Contra Sachs, Beiträge 1, 170, emending to ספקולטורים, *speculatores;* ↑ **ספקלטור**.) However, Thumb, BZ 9,1900, 435, constructed a form *σκέπτωρ* from the Arm, and not knowing it was attested gave it an asterisk. Actually, the form appears in ConstPorph, de Cer, PG 113, 322 (see Psaltes 253), and in Coptic (see Drescher, Le Muséon 89, 1976, 320–21). Similarly the Lat form appears in CGL 5, 389_3: *sceptor notarius*. Hence, there is no need for Mandelbaum's emendation (PRK ad loc): סקריפטורין, *scriptores*, which is against all the Mss evidence. (In this he follows JBöhman, Keẓad Maarichin, Berlin 1855, 4). The form סקפטורים should perhaps be read סקפטוריס: *sceptores* (?).
The word has the specialized meaning of a scribe specially attached to the magistrates, who not only writes out the *apologia*, but also announces it (Drescher ibid, Sperber ibid). See also Berger 461ab. The metath ~ספק ~סקפ (see LW 1, 113–15), is probably influenced by the more usual Lat element

spect~. See Gignac's remark 1, 59.
Syr has only the form אכסקפטרס, אכסקפטורס, PnS 189.

Cf ↑ סקבטרין, איסקבטיריי

סקיפנטים [סקיפנטיס] (411) false accuser: *συκοφάντης* → *sycophanta*

SifDeut 349, 408_5: סקיפנטים נסתקפת לו, You became a false accuser against him. ▽ סקיפסים, סקיפים, read: סקיפנטיס. // YalkDeut 954: תסקופים ניסתקפת; MidTanDeut 33. 8, 215: ... סיקה פנטיון (↑), (= MGDeut 33. 8, 764_1).

Jastrow 1020a. (Contra LW 2, 411a, suggesting: *συκοφαντ<ία>* + Heb pl term.)
נסתקפת may be a verbal form created out of the noun סקיפנט'. A similar such verbal form is found in SifDeut 242, 272_5: אילו לא יצאת בעיר, לא היה מסתקף לה, Had she not gone out of town (cf Deut 22:23), he would not have levelled false accusations against him. It may also be that this verbal form derives from Sem סקף. However, Torczyner (Tur-Sinai), Ha-Lashon ve-ha-Sefer I_1 (1955), 434–37 (and apud BenIehuda 10, 5046 n4, and 16, 7828 n3) claims that סקף is derived from the Gk *συκοφάντης*.
As to תסקופים in the Yalk, it has been erroneously suggested that it is an independent Aram word. See LevyTrgWb 2, 547b sv תסקופא; Levy 4, 656b (from סקף = עקף); but cf ibid 3, 581b sv סקף ad fin, and reject. See the discussion in ACSup 412a sv תסקופא, citing Bacher, MGWJ 50, 1906, 249, contra Krauss, ibid 49, 1905, 691, and Torczyner referred to above. (See also Güdemann, apud Fürst 159b, and reject.) Note Lieberman GH 31 n61, and Ginzberg, MGWJ 78, 1934, 30–31 (Sem).
On *σύκοφαντέω*, its meanings and possible etym, see MM 596ab; ArndtGingrich 784a; NLewis, JJP 9/10, 19565, 118–25; EHatch, Essays in Biblical Greek, Oxford 1889, 88–89.

Lat: *sycophanta (sūc~)*, OLD 1895a.
Cf ↑ סיקה פנטיון

◇סקרידין (411) imperial office, or council chamber, in which copies of statutes etc were filed: *σήκρητ<α>* ← *secret<a>* (+ pl term)

GenR 89. 7, 1094_3: ... שכן היה מוכתב בסקרידין של פרעה שאין עבד מולך, For so was it recorded in the *secreta* of Pharaoh that a slave cannot rule ... ▽ סקרידון, סקרירין, סקוטרין, סיקרידין, מקדידין (read: סקרידין), סינקתדרון (obvious emend: *συγκάθεδρον*, acc, LW2, 405ab), סינקרידין. // YalkGen 147, 772_{77}: ספיטרון ▽ סיקרדין, סיקררין; STovGen 41. 12, 252: סיקרוקין (read: סיקרדין); MGGen 41. 12, 702_2: דימוסין ▽ דימסון (+ *δημόσι<ο>ν*, LW2, 206, public building); RashiGen 41: 12: בנימוסי (↑ נימוס). (Absent in LTGen ibid, 206.)

Levy 3, 583b; LW2, 411b; AC 6, 122b–123a, (and cf ibid 4, 232 sv כלידר, n9).
Secretum (sing) has a variety of meanings: council chamber in a palace (Lampe 1230b, sv *σήκρητον*

2; Souter 369b), a court-house (Souter; DuCange 1346—47), office of notary, secretariate (Souter), etc. Here, however, the context demands something like a *tabularium* or *aerarium* (as suggested by Jastrow, see below), a central imperial archive ' which copies of laws, statutes, edicts and royal correspondence were kept (see Berger, 355a, 729a). *Secreta,* meaning *aerarium* is listed in DuCange, Glossarium Mediae et Infirmae Latinitatis 7, 386a, sv *secreta* 2, (not in Niermeyer, Blaise, GkDuCange etc).

The ▽ דון~ may indicate ~*τον*. T > D change is common; see LW1, 101, Gignac 1, 80—83; Psaltes 69—70.

(Contra Jastrow 1021b, who prefers reading: סקררין + *sacrarium,* which he explained as *aerarium,* though this meaning is unattested. *Sacrarium* in the later empire can mean imperial business room [Souter 360b] or a court-hall [Berger 688b]. However, the weight of textual evidence is against this reading being original. The orthography סיק~, moreover, points to *σεκ*~, *σηκ*~, and not *σακ*~. Perhaps the reading סקרירין was influenced by *sacrarium*?)

Cf Syr: סיקרטין, סיקריטון, PnS 2619. (Is the latter a correct reading? Cf Brockelm[3], 496a.)

סיקריקון ↑ סקריקון

ע

אוני ↑ עניתא, עינותא

ארכיליסטיס ↑ ערבי ליסטים

ארכי ↑ ערכי, ערכאין, ערכאים, ערכאות, ערכאה

פ

אפופסיס ↑ פאופרי

פילקי ↓ פולקי

פיסטון ↓ פוסטון

פיסטיס ↓ פוסיטיס

פרנה ↓ פורנה, פורנא, פורן

פרנך ↓ **פורניך ,פורנך**

פטריקון ↓ **פזמריקון ,פזמיקון**

איפטייה ↑ **פטייה**

פיסטיס ↓ **פטיסין**

פטרון (438–39) (1) an influential person who has undertaken the protection of another person, a patron (2) a person who has undertaken to protect the interest of a community (a country, municipality, etc.): *πάτρων* ← *patronus*

(1) YBer 9, 13 (12)a 27, 29: **בשר ודם יש לו פטרון. אמרו לו: הרי הוא יוצא לידון. אמר להן: אני מקיים עליו. אמרו לו: הרי הוא יוצא ליתלות. היכן הוא והיכן פטרונו?**, Flesh and blood has his patron. They said to him (the patron): A member of your household has been seized (by the authorities). He replied to them: I will protect him. They told him: Behold, he is going to judgement. He replied to them: I will protect him. They told him: Behold he is going to be hung. Where is he and where is his patron? (Rhetorical question, meaning: What good is his trust in a human patron?) Partial // again ibid: lines 42, 45, 47, 49, 52. // DeutR 2. 29.

Ibid lines 54, 56: **בשר ודם יש לו פטרון. אם באת עת צרה, אינו נכנס אצלו פתאום, אלא בא ועומד לו על פתחו של פטרונו, וקורא לעבד או לבן ביתו ...**, Flesh and blood has a patron. If troubles beset him, he does not enter suddenly (i e without prior warning) upon him, but comes and stands at the entrance of his patron, and calls the servant or a member of the household ... // DeutR 2. 29.

Ibid line 68: בשר ודם יש לו פטרון. אם הטריח עליו ביותר אומר: אשכח פלן דקא מטרח לי, Flesh has a patron. If he troubles him too much,he says: There is a fellow who troubles me much.

Ibid b 11, 12: **בשר ודם יש לו פטרון, ובאו שונאין ותפשו אותו על פתח חצירו של פטרונו. עד דצוח ליה, עד דהוא נפק, עברת חרבא על קדליה וקטלת ליה ...**, Flesh and blood [who] has a patron, and the enemies came and seized him at the entrance to his patron's courtyard, until he cries out and [his patron] comes out [to help him], a sword is passed across his neck and kills him ...

GenR 46. 3, $460_{5\,6}$: **אמר לו הקב"ה: דייך שאני אלהיך, דייך שאני פטרונך, דיו לעולמי שאני פטרונו**, The Holy One blessed be He said to him: Let it suffice you that I am your God. Let it suffice you that I am your patron. Let it suffice My world that I am its patron. (But in // TanḥBGenLech 25, 80 our word is absent.)

GenR 46. 9, $466_{2\,3}$: **אם מקבלין בניך אלוהותי, אני הווה להם לאלוה פטרון**, If your children accept My Lordship, I will be for them a patron-God. // YalkGen 82, 337_{6}.

GenR 63. 12, 696_{3}: מיניה ומן פטרוניה, from him and from his patron. (Difficult text, see ed note ad loc.) // YalkGen 111, 525_{1}.

TanḥBLevTazri'a 12,40: ... העושה פטרונו בשר ודם, He who makes flesh and blood his patron ... // YalkLev 556.

TanḥGenVa-Yeshev 8: אתה הוא פטרוני, אתה הוא בטחוני, You are my protector, you are my security.

PRK 109a, 221_{18}, 222_{1}: ... פטרונך אני מקיים עליך ... מה הפיטרון מועילה אצל הדין?, I am your patron [and] will protect you ... What good does the patron do at court? // RuthR 1. 1: דייך אני פטרונך ... אע"פ (sic edprinc) שאני פטרונך, מה פטרונא מהני בדינא?, Suffice it that I am your patron ... Even though I am your patron, what good does a patron do in court? TanḥBEx Yitro 15, 78; YalkEx 286, 441_{18}: מה הפטרון מועיל אצל הדיין?, What good does the patron do before the judge; (Partial // YalkPs 760, and TanḥBExVa-Era 1, 17, BHM 6, 100. And cf ExR 29. 4, abbreviated text referring to PRK or TanḥBYitro ibid, see Buber's note 87 on p78.)

LevR 27. 11, $646_{4\ 5}$: ... ולא היו יודעין שיש להן פטרון בשמים. אני איני עושה כן. אלא בתחילה אני מזדויג לפטרונן, ואחרכך אני מזדויג להן, ... And they did not know that they had a protector in heaven. I shall not do so. But first I shall attack their protector, and then attack them. ▽ לפטרוני'. // MidPs 2. 4, 26; PRK 79a, 159_{14}; TanḥLevEmor 13; B ibid 18, 95; EstR 7. 23 (to 3: 12); AgEst 3. 13, 36; PanimAḥerim I, 50; AgBer 2, 7; YalkGen 116, $565_{5\ 6}$; ibidZach 583; ibidEst 1055; MachZach 14. 3, 129; MGEx 1. 16, $19_{17\ 18}$.

ExR 11. 2: כאדם שאומר לחבירו: לא יטול פלוני בטאריקי (↓ קטאדיקי) זו, שפלוני פטרונו עומד עליהן (!), Like one who says to his friend: So and so will not receive this punishment, for such and such, his patron, looks after them (perhaps read: him).

ExR 14. 3: ... לפי שהיו פושעים בישראל שהיה להן פטרונין מן המצרים, For there were evil-doers among the Israelites who had their Egyptian patrons ... // TanḥExVa-Era 14.

CantR 5. 10: מה פטרון הוא מפטרונין?, What is this patron [better]than [other] patrons?

(2) YBer 9. 13 (12)b 16: מלך בשר ודם יש לו פטרון, שולט באיפרכיא אחת, אינו שולט באיפרכיא אחרת, A king of flesh and blood has a patron who rules over one province, but does not rule over another province. // YAZ 3. 1, 42c 50.

GenR 50. 12, 530_{7}: למדינה שהיה לה שני פטרונין, like a city which had two patrons. ▽ פיטרונין, פיטרופין (edprinc presumably emendation to פיטרופין[א], governor, cf ↑ **אפיטרופוס**, and cf GenR 6. 4, 43_{4}). // YalkGen 84, 392_{34}.

Note a very specific case of פטרון meaning father appears in GenR 93. 10, 1160_7: "וישימני לאב לפטרון בסיליוס — "[לפרעה], "And He hath made me a father [to Pharaoh]" (Gen 45:8) – Father to the king. ▽ ~לפיטרון, ~לפטרן, לפטרובסיליאוס. // (YalkGen 152, 813_6, just בסיליוס, and פטרון is missing.) MGGen 45. 8, 764_{17}, LTibid 218; STov ibid 1, 285. (Cf MannBible 1, 87_3: לפטיר = πατήρ, editor's n3 ad loc.) πάτρων βασιλέως = βασιλεοπάτωρ, a title of Byzantine nobility (Sophocles 301b; DuCange 180; cf Fürst 167b–168a).
Note further the personal name מ"ר יעקב בן מ"ר פטרון in THGHarkavy no 1. 2.
On YBer 9, ibid, and the phrase ... להתקיים על, see Lieberman, Tarbiz 3, 1932, 455 n5; idemGH 49.
On GenR 50. 12, 530 see Krauss, MT 5, 126 no288 n2, with bibl.
The form פיטרון shows the not uncommon A > I interchange; see LW 1, 88, and cf Gignac 1, 286.
See Berger 622a sv Patrocinium. (For a different legal meaning of *patronus*, see Berger 622b–623a.)
See Lampe 1053b; Mason 75a.

Syr: פטרון, פטרונא, פטרונוס, PnS 3095.
Cf ↓ פטרונה⁰, קלסטרא

פטרונה⁰ (439) (1) patroness (2) protectress: *patrona*

(1) MidPs 7. 3, 64: כשם שבאת הכושית פטרונתו של יוסף עליו בדברים, Just as the Aethiopian patroness of Joseph came to persuade him ...
(2) EstRProem 1. 3: יש לכם פטרונות. מה הם? "אלה דברי הברית", You have protectresses. Who are they? "These are the words of the covenant" (Deut 28:69) (Pl.)

Gk: πατρτώνισσα, Sophocles 866a.
Syr: פטרוניסא (פטרונא), PnS 3095.
Cf ↑ פטרון

פטריקא patrimony, heirloom: πατρική (sc οὐσία), or (τὰ) πατρικά

YelamdNum 21. 1, apud Ar (AC 6, 321b), Grünhut, Likkutim 4, 56a: יודעין אנו שיש להם מאבותיהן פטריקא ... שהן מתפללין ונשמעין, We know that they have [inherited] an heirloom from the forfathers ... that they pray and are answered. // YalkNum 764.

See LW 2, 439a, and AC ibid. However, there is no need to emend to ~קון (πατρικόν). For πατρική (sc ουσία), see eg Elon 1304; for (τὰ) πατρικά, AP 11. 75 (Lucill), in sing sense; CGL 2, 143_{25}: patrimonium οὐσία πατρική.

Cf ↓ פטריקון

פטריקון (439) (1) property inherited from father or ancestors, patrimony (2) something hereditory: πατρικόν

(1) GenR 49. 2, 499_7, 500_2: למלך שנתן אסייא לאוהבו. לאחר זמן ביקש המלך לקרץ מתוכו חמשה אילני סרק. אמר המלך: ואילו מן פטריקון שלו הייתי מבקש, לא היה מעקב, A king who gave an estate (*οὐσία*) to his dear friend. After a while, he wished to cut down five trees which bear no fruit that were in it. He said: And had I requested this from his ancestral estate, he would not have stopped me ... // MachAmos 3. 7, 22; YalkGen 82, 369_{42}.

GenR 95, 1234_{11}: פטריקן שלהם קנה. מה שקנו לעצמן לא קנה, He acquired their ancestral estates. He did not acquire that which they had acquired for themselves. (Pl,or read קון~, sing, referring to אדמת הכהנים, in Gen 47:22.)

(2) GenR 98. 6, 1258_2: שהיה פטיריקין שלו, ... because it was his inheritance. ∇ פטריקן, פטרונין (↑ פטרון). // MGGen 49. 8, 841_{17}: פטריקון; MidPs 18. 32, 160: פזמריקון; YalkGen 162, 855_{23}: פזמיקון ∇ פוזמיקין, פוזמיקון; YalkSam 163: פיזמיקון (sic edprinc); MachPs 18. 78, 1. 122: פיזמיריקן. Perhaps read all as: פוטריקון (?). YelamdNum 20:18, apud MGNum 20. 18, $370_{8\ 10}$: קול אחד אנו צווחין קמי ... קודשא בריך הוא, ומפיל לך ולחיילותיך לפנינו. למה? שהוא פטריקון שלנו, שנאמר "הקול קול יעקב". אמר להן: אתם בטוחין על קולכם. אף אני בטוח על פטריקון שלי, "ועל חרבך תחיה"., We raise our voice in a single call before the Holy One blessed be He, and he will fell you and your armies from before us. Why? For this is our heirloom, as it is written "The voice is Jacob's voice" (Gen 27:22). He replied to them: You rely on your voice. I too rely on my heirloom, "And by thy sword shalt thou live" (ibid 27:40). // Ar (AC 6, 321b), Grünhut Likkutim 4, 53b no20. (// in GenRabbati $231_{9\ 10}$ reads: ואנו מתגאים על מה שהורישו לנו אבותינו, and we are proud of what our fathers passed on to us. (Cf also MannBible 2, 88, Rashi and R. Baḥayye to Num 20:18.)

PerlesES 123. On פזמיריקן in MidPs and //, see LW 2, 439a and in ACSup 322a, that this is corrupted from פטריקון. We have suggested a possible form פוטריקון; see Gignac 1, 287 for *a* > *o* interchange (?) (Contra AC 6, 305a, suggesting Pehl etym, rejected in ACSup 322a. Jastrow 1150b writes: The corrupt may have arisen form a fusion of *φυσικόν* and its synonym *πατρικόν*. Unlikely.) Or perhaps this is an example of the insertion of a *sigma* (cf Mayser 1/1², 179–80, Gignac 1, 101, and cf ↑ גמיסקוס).

Cf ↑ פטריקא

פטריקון ↑ **פטריקן**

פטרמוניא patrimony: *πατριμωνία* ← *patrimonia* (neut pl from *~ium*)

RashiEzek 16:61, citing Tanḥuma (YelamdDeut 2:3, apud Grünhut, Likkutim 5,

93a): "ולא מבריתך", לא מפטרמוניא שליך, ... "but not by thy covenant" (Ezek ibid) – Not from your patrimony.

ACSup 324a sv פטריקון (contra Grünhut ibid n2). Note // TanhBuber Deut 5 sect 3: פרקמטיא: *πραγματεία;* CantR 1. 5: פרניך: *φερνή* (↓ פרנה). The precise meaning of *patrimonia,* private or personal possessions of the *paterfamilias* (OLD 1310c), is further reflected in the continuation of the homily: לא נתתיה לאברהם אבינו בברית בין הבתרים, I did not give it to our father Abraham at the "covenant of the halved pieces" (see Gen 15).
Note further Rashi's gloss ad loc: פטראמוניא בלע"ז, וכן קורין לכל דבר שיש לו לאדם מנחלת אבותיו.
πατριμούνιον, PFlor 320. 4 (IV CE), LSJSupple 117a; *πατριμόνιον,* Lampe 1052b, DuCange 1136; *πατριμώνιον,* Sophocles 865a (HMTod, Hermathena 60, 1942, 23, ACameron, AJP 52, 245).

Cf ↓ פטר מוניקא

פטר מוניקא patrimony: **patrimonica* (?)

Mahzor Vitry 320, sect 289, citing LevR (not found in our ed): הוה נקיט נכסי מפטר מוניקא דידיה, He would take possessions from his own patrimony. Read: פטרמוניקא.

ACSup 324a sv פטריקון. However, this form is unattested in the lexica, and is somewhat doubtful.

Cf ↑ פטרמוניא

פטריקון ↑ פיזמיריקון, פיזמיקן

פיסטיס ↓ פיטסין

פטרון ↑ פיטרן

פטרון, אפיטרופוס ↑ פיטרופין

פילקי (448–49) prison: *φυλακή*

PRK 182a, 411_2: בתר יומין איצטייד ההוא ליסטא (↑ ליסטיס) ואתייהב בפילקי, After some days that bandit was caught and placed in prison. ▽ בפולקי, בפלקי. // LevR 30. 6, 702_4: ואיחבש בפילקי. ▽ בסילקי, read: בפילקי; MGLev 23. 40, 656_9; MidPs 26. 5, 218: בפילקא; YalkLev 651: בפולקי. ▽ edprinc: בפילקי.
LevR 34. 12, 797_2: וחבש יתהון בפילקי, and locked them up in jail. // YalkLev 665: בסילקי. ▽ edprinc: בפילקי; ibidIs 482 (352): בפילקי; MachIs 58. 7, 230_7: בפילקי.
ExR 15. 16: נתנה בפילקי, He put her into prison.

ExR 30. 11: ... בעט בפלקי והוציא איסרין, He kicked (the door of) the prison, and let out the prisoners.
MGGen 27. 1, 463_{13}: חבשוהו בפלקי חשיכה, They locked him up in a dark cell. ▽ בסילקי, read: בפילקי.
AgBer 23. 48: בפילקי (קוסטריא ↓) וקוסטריא ... , and the warden in the prison.

Pl:

PRK 67a, 132_7: חבשן בפלקיות, He locked them up in jails. // PR 17, 89b: בפילקיות; MGEx 10. 3, 150_{20}, 151_8. (// in TanḥExBo 4, ibidB 4, 43, YalkEx 182: בבית האסורין.)
PR 42, 177a: ... שיפתח הפילקיות ... פיתח הפילקיות, that they should open the prisons ... opened the prisons ...

Krauss, LW 2, 448b cites additional instances of this word in MidPs 105. 8, 451 // YalkPs 663, but they do not belong in this entry. Ar (AC 6, 358a) also brings a verbal form פלק from this root, found in BGit 69a, in Aruch's reading, and in Geniza fragm (1), apud Feldblum's ed, line 15: פלקוליה (Ar), ופליקו ליה (Geniza fragm). Not in our text.
The form פולקי is a transcr. The form *pilki* exhibits syncope (with loss of unaccented *alpha* after the liquid, etc). See LW1, 121, and Gignac 1, 307: e g: OMich 147. 5 (III CE): *φύλκι*.
There would seem to be yet another Gk loanword found in Rab lit meaning prison, namely דיוטא, *διαίτα, diaeta*. This word, which is very common in Rab lit, normally means: chamber, or story (see LW 2, 199ab). However, in EstR 1. 1, ad init (edprinc) we read: "והיו חייך תלוים לך מנגד" — זה שהוא בתוך בדיוטא של קיסרין. "ופחדת לילה ויומם" — זה שהוא יוצא לדון. "ולא תאמין בחייך" — זה שהוא יוצא להצלב. "And thy life shall hang in doubt before them" (Deut 28:60) – This [refers to] one who is incarcerated (lit: placed) in the *diaeta* of Caesarea; "and thou shalt fear day and night" (ibid) – this [refers to] one who goes to be judged; "and thou shalt have none assurance of thy life" (ibid) – this [refers to] one who goes forth to be crucified.
The order of events described here suggests that *διαίτα* here is a (pre-court) jail, rather than the office of the *διαιτητής*, arbiter, (see Hesych, edLatte 1, 432_{34}: *δαιτητής, κριτής, βασανιστής*; DuCange 291; ArndtGingrich 192a). However, such a meaning, though closely related to the basic meaning "chamber", is unattested in Gk sources. On the other hand, it may be noted that this word appears with a rather forbidding overtone, as in the phrase דייטי התחתונא של שאול, the lowermost chamber in the netherworld (YYev 1. 6, 3a 37 and //).
MM 677b; ArndtGingrich 875b.

Syr: פיליקא, פילקא, PnS 3110, פולאקי (transc) PnS 3059, Schulthess 158b.
Arm: *p'iulakê*, Brockelmann, ZDMG 47, 1899, 28; Hübschmann 482.
Cf ↓ פילקרין

פילקרין prison wardens: *φυλακάρ<ης>* (+ Aram pl term)

MidProv chap 15, according to Geniza fragm (Rabinovitz, GM 227_{49}): מסרו ליד

שני פילקרין, He handed him over to two prison wardens. ▽ פקידים, in edBuber 80.

Sperber, Bar-Ilan 16–17, 1979, p 13. See DuCange 1708. (Contra Rabinovitz adloc n62: *φυλακή*.)

Cf ↑ פילקי

פיסטיס ↓ פיסטיא, פינוס

◇פיסטון (450) treaty made by exchange of assurances: *πιστόν*

ER (7) 8, 39: גדול פוסטון שעשה אלישע עם מלך ישראל יותר מכמה מלחמות שעשה יורם בן אחאב מלך ישראל. שנאמר "ויאמר מלך ישראל אל אלישע כראותו אותם: האכה אכה, אבי? ויאמר: לא תכה ... " ואומר, "ויכרה להם כירה גדולה". ואין כירה האמור כאן אלא שלום ... הא למדת שגדול פוסקין שעשה אלישע ..., Greater was the treaty which Elisha made together with the king of Israel, than several wars that Joram ben Ahab, king of Israel made. As it is stated, "And the king of Israel said unto Elisha, when he saw them, My father, shall I smite them? Shall I smite? And he answered, Thou shalt not smite them ..." And it says, "And he prepared great כירה (usually translated: provision) for them" (2Kings 6: 21–23). And כירה here is nothing other than peace ... From this you learn how great was the treaty which Elisha made ... ▽ edVenice: פיסטון, פיסטון (instead of פוסטון, פוסקין). Read thus. // YalkKings 231: פסקין (sic edprinc), read: פסטון, or פסטין = *πίστιν* (↓ פיסטיס).

עשה פיסטון corresponds to *τό πιστόν* (or *τὰ πιστὰ*) *ποιέσθαι* = *πίστιν ποιεῖσθαι*, eg Hdt 3, 8. See LSJ[9] 1408b sv *πιστός*, ibid 1408a sv *πίστις* III. (Contra ed ad loc, who relates our word to פיסקן in BSanh 44b, on which word see ACSup 331b; Löw apud LW2, 568b; Ginzberg, Legends 6, 348 n22). Not to be confused with פסטון; *φοσσᾶτον*, LW2, 468a.

Cf ↑ אפיסטון, ↓ פיסטיס

פיסטיס ↓ פיסטק, פיסטים

פיסטיס (~ין) (449–50) (1) trust (2) feigned transfer: *πίστις* (nom), ~*ιν* (acc)

(1) TKet 9. 2, 86c, 271_{10}: הרוצה להבריח נכסיה מבעלה, כותבן שטר בטפוס לאחר; read פסטיס, A woman, who wishes to withold her properties from her husband, may write them [in] a deed of trust to a third person (prior to her marriage; i e trusting that he will not keep the property for himself). בטפוס sic printed ed. ▽ MsVienna: בטפיה; MsErfurt: פסיס, with ט added above line, i e to read: פס[ט]יס; Geniza fragm: פסטס, read: פסטס. // BKet 79a: פסים. ▽ Ar (AC 6, 381b): פסיס. MidPs 19. 10, 168: ונוטלין זה מזה בפיטסין, ופורעין זה לזה בפיטסין, אין אחר שומע

בינידם; read: בפיסטין, They borrow from one another in trust (ie without a contract or witnesses), and pay each other in trust, and no one else is there to hear them. ▽ בפיסטין, כי פרוסין, edprinc: בפינוסין. // YalkPs 673: בפיסטים ▽ late edd: ~טיא, corrected to בפינוסין; MachPs 19. 9, 1. 128: בפטיסין; LevR 26. 4, 595_5 (in notes, added in late edd from MidPs): בפיוסין. Read throughout: פיסטין = πίστιν (acc), or פיסטיס, YalkPs, (and see below).

(2) TBB 23, 399_{25}: אם אמר: כתבתי שטר ונטלתי מעות, שטר פיסטיס הוא בידך, If he said: I wrote a deed [of sale] (on the pledge) and received the money (as a loan), [and] it is a deed of feigned transfer which you have in your hand ... (נטלתי, sic printed ed, MsVienna, and MsErfurt. But in MsErfurt corrected to לא נטלתי. נטלתי also in Responsa Maharit 112, but he emended to ולא נטלתי.) ▽ MsErfurt פסטים. // BB 154b: פסים. ▽ MsHamburg 165 (19): פיס. Read: פיס' + פיסטיס. YKet 2. 3, 26b bottom: נאמנים העדים לומר: שטר אמנה ושטר פוסיטיס הוא, Witnesses are credited when they say: It was a deed of trust or a deed of feigned transfer. BKet 19b: "אם און הוא הרחיקיהו" — זה שטר אמנה ושטר פסים, "If iniquity be in thine hand, put it far away" (Job 11:14) – This is a deed of trust or a deed of feigned transfer. // YKet 2. 3, 26c 1: פוסיטיס

On TKet 9. 2, see Lieberman TK 6, 325. = ὠνὴ ἐν πίστει, perhaps also translatable: deed of feigned transfer (meaning 2). Note that reading פסים may be an example of the omission of τ after σ; see Gignac 1, 66. E g: πισσικίου (for πιστικίου), PCairIsidor 48. 2, 4 (309 CE), etc.

On MidPs 19. 10, see Buber 168 n64, and Aruch's reading פינוס (AC 6, 371a), explained as *foenus, fenus,* and reject. (פינוסין is surely a corrupt of פיטסין, with the *tet* having been split up into *nun waw.* For the metath (~ts~ for ~st~) cf LW1, 113–15 (and Gignac 1, 314–15), and cf ↑ **אפיסטון**.) This meaning of πίστις is found in BrunsSachau 25_{14} no97: פסטס.

On TBB 2. 3, see Gulak, Toldot ha-Mishpat be-Yisrael 1, 63–64; Lieberman TR 2, 136. We are dealing with a case where a pledge was given with a deed of sale against a loan, on the understanding that if the loan was repaid the pledge would return to its owner; but if not the pledge would be sold by virtue of the deed of sale.

On BBB 1546b, see AssafTHG (1942) 150: explaining שטר פסים thus: [שטר] הברחה, שיש לו נכסים וכותב אותן משם ראובן להבריח אותן מבעל ח[ובו ... See further, Gulak, Ozar ha-Shetarot, 190–91 (from Sefer ha-Shetarot of Al Barceloni, 73 n51).

Concerning YKet 2. 3, it might be suggested that we have here a kind of explanatory gloss, suggesting a lexical equivalence of πίστις = אמנה. Attractive though this suggestion be, the textual evidence, the *waw* of ושטר פוסיטיס, and the order of the Gk *following* the Heb, points to these being two different kinds of document.

See BCohen, Jewish and Roman Law, New York 1966, 452 n96; Taubenschlag² 44–45; MM 515b; EHatch, Essays in Biblical Greek, Oxford 1889, 83–88.

The form פוסיטיס should perhaps be emended to פיסיטיס, and correspond to *πισιτις, an example of anaptyxis; see Gignac 1, 311–12.

Syr: פיסטיס, PnS 3119; פסטיס, BB 1504; (Brockelm[2] 581a).
Cf ↑ אפיסטון, פיסטון

פי סניגוריא [פיסקוסניגוריא] advocacy for the fisc, *φι|σκο|συνηγορία

LevR 6. 1, 127_7: הדא רוח הקודש פי סניגוריא היא מלמד זכות לכן ולכן, This Holy Spirit is advocacy for the fisc, pleading the cause of [both] this side and the other. ▽ פי׳ (MsOxf 147), כי. So too // in MGDeut 9. 16, 180_2, while DeutR 3. 11 has: משפסק סניגור, so too edLieberman 88. In all cases read: פי[סקו]סניגוריא.

Prof SLeiter, Jerusalem (private communication 1977). Note that apostrophe in MsOxf, פי׳, indicates abbreviation of first element. See Sperber, Bar-Ilan 16–17, 1979, 20–21.
φισκοσυνήγορος: advocatus fisci, PKleinForm 1025, PMasp 57 ii 23 (both IV CE).
See Berger 352b. (Also called *patronus fisci*, CGL 2, 472_{11}. Cf *ταμιείου γλῶττα, advocatio fisci* PhilostrVS 2. 29, 621; Mason 32a, and cf ibid 89b–90a.)

Cf ↑ סניגוריא

איפטייה ↑ פיפודיון

פרקולה ↓ פירקולא, פיקולא

פירטין (452, 108) pirates: *πειρατ<ής>* → *pirat<a?* (with pl term)

LevR 25. 1, 567_4: מתיירא אני מפני הליסטין (↑ ליסטיס) ובים מפני הפירטין, I fear the brigands on the road and the pirates at sea. ▽ אפירטין, printed edd, אפירוטין, אפטרופין (mistaken: ↑ אפיטרופוס), corr in Ms to אפוריטין, פראטיס (sing ~*της*?), פריטין. // YalkLev 615: אפריטין. (Not in // YalkProv 934.)
ExR 17. 5: למלך שבא עם בניו בים וספינות של פירטון מקיפות אותו, Like a king who came with his sons by sea, and pirate ships surrounded him; read: ~ין.
AgBer 34. 1, 66: משל לחובל גבור שהיה לו ספינה ... בא עליו פירטון ועמד והרג כולן, Like a brave captain who had a ship ... Pirates came against him, and he killed them all; read: ~ין.

Note: פורטין in DER 2, 11, edHigger 283_{29} // MidTalpiyyot, edJerusalem 1963, 174b (*dalet, anaf Devarim Ra'im*), is from Heb root פרט, and means "money-changers", (Higger ibid 105, contra LW 2, 452b).
On prosthetic *aleph* in אפירטין, see LW 1, 139–40 (and cf ↑ אפרכורים).

◇**פלסטון** (462) forged, counterfeit: *πλαστόν*

TSuk 2. 5, 262_{29}, 194_{8}, according to MsLondon (Add 27. 296): כותבי פלסטון, writers of counterfeit (document[s]). ▽ פלסתר, פלסטיר (↓)

YBM 5 ad fin, 10d 8: שעושין התורה פלסטרן ואת משה טיפש, for they make the law a forged [document] and Moses a fool. Sic MsL and edprinc. Probably one should read: פלסטון (but see below). // TBM 6. 17, 385_{6}: פלטר, (↓ פלסטיר).

YelamdNumKoraḥ ad init (apud Ar, AC 6, 356a, Grünhut, Likkutim 4, 42b): יודעין אנו שחנון ורחום הוא, שמא יתמלא רחמים על הללו, ויאמרו כל באי עולם: פלסטין היא תורתו של משה, We know He is forgiving and merciful. Perhaps He will be filled with mercy for those people, and all mortals will say: The Law of Moses is counterfeit. Read: ון~.

Yelamd apud YalkJer 321: שאני רואה את תורתכם פלסטרון ... אין דבר בתורה פלסטרון ולא דבר של שקר, אלא כל התורה אמת, I regard your Law as counterfeit ... There is nothing in the Law that is counterfeit, and there is nothing false (a gloss?), but the Law is true in its entirety. ▽ modern edd: ין~, read: ון~. The form *πλαστρόν* = *πλαστόν* (see below).

NumR 8. 4: ... והיו אומות העולם אומרים: תורתן של אלו פלסטון הוא, And the Nations of the World would say: Their Law is forged.

TanhBGenLech 10, 69: והוא אומר פלסטין הוא (פי׳ מזויף הוא), אתם עשיתם אותו, ואין אני מעמינו, and he says it is counterfeit (gloss, forged), you made (i e fabricated it), I do not believe it. Read: ון~. // GasterMaasiyot CLXX, 122q.

MGEx 10:28–29, 163_{1}: כדי שלא לעשות דבריך פלסטון, so as not to make your words false. (// ExR 18. 1: שלא ימצא בדאי, that he be not found a liar.)

The form פלסטרון: **πλαστρόν* = *πλαστόν*, with inserted R. The insertion of this liquid is not uncommon in Gk and Rabbinic Gk. See LW 1, 142; Mayser 1/1[2], 160; Psaltes 84; Gignac 1, 108; eg, *Φρέατρος* (for *Φρέατος*), POxy 1105. 10 (81–96 CE). It may therefore be that פלסטרן in YBM ibid also is a form of **πλαστρόν*, and need not be emended (?). See Levy 4, 55b–56a.

The primary meaning of *πλαστός* is "formed, moulded" – a meaning not found in Rabb usage, and the secondary metaph sense is "forged, counterfeit". See LSJ[9] 1412b sv *πλαστός* II. See also MM 516b, citing, as example of this secondary meaning, POxy II, 237. 8. 14 (186 CE). ArndtGingrich 672b.

Cf ↓ פלסטיר

פלסטור ↓ פלסטיר

פלסטיר (461) forgery, fraud: **πλαστήρ*

TSuk 2. 5, 262_{29}, 194_{8}: כותבי פלסתר, writers of forgery. ▽ פלסטיר, פלסטון (↑ = *πλαστόν*); Bibid 29a, ▽ GKedem 5, 1934, 174: בליסטרי; DER 2. 26, Higger 290_{78}.

TBM 6. 17, 385_6: עושין את התורה פלסטר ואת משה טיפש, for they (userers) make the Law a fraud, and Moses a fool. // YBM 5 adfin, 10d 8: פלסטרן (↑ פלסטון); Bibid 75b: משה חכם ותורתו אמת, Moses is wise and the Law truthful (euph).
LevR 19. 2, 420_6: משנה תורה עלה ונשתטח לפני הקב"ה: ... עקרני שלמה ועשאני פלסטור, שכל דייתיקי (↑) שיש שנים או שלשה דברים בטלין ממנה, כולה בטלה והרי שלמה המלך מבקש לעקור יו"ד אחד ממני, The book of Deuteronomy complained: ... Solomon has uprooted me and makes me a forgery. For a document (or testament, ↑ דייתיקי) of which two or three points are null is null and void in its entirety. And behold King Solomon wishes to uproot one *yod* from me. ▽ פלסטיר, פלסטר, פלסתר // TanḥExVa. Era 4. (Not in other //, such as TanḥBibid 2, 18; YSanh 2. 6, 20c 40; CantR 5. 11. 3; AgBer 76 (75) 2, etc.)
BBer 31b: ואי אתה עושה תורתך פלסתר, and Thou wilt not make Thy Law a fraud. ▽ פלסטר.
MidPs 52. 6, 286: ותעשה תורתך פלסתר, and your Law will become a fraud.
DeutR 11. 10: ואתה עושה תורתך פלסתר, and you make your Law a fraud.
BAZ 11b: סך קירי פלסתר (▽ Rabbinovicz VL 28 n200: בר), said to correspond to: אחוה דמרנה זייפנא, meant to mean: the brother (son?) of our Lord is a fraud (?). // MGGen 27. 41, 485_{17}: כך in some Mss.
See also MV 163_1: פלסתירא, RosenthalPiyyutim 24_{17}: פלסתיר.

LiebermanTK 4, (485 n2), 856; LW 2, 481b; Levy 4, 56a; AC 6, 356ab; Jastrow 356ab, who, however, divides into two categories: *πλαστήρ* = *~ης*, forger, and *πλαστήρ<ιον>*, forgery (?). (Contra MCohn, MGWJ 44, 1900, 569: *falsator;* Löw, apud LW ibid, comparing with Syr: פלסטס, PnS 3160, Brockelm[2] 575b: *φαλσάτας*, etc?)
On BAZibid, see Krauss, LW 2, 394a sv סך (with bibl), idem, MT 5, 163 n5, (following Brüll, Jahrb 1, 1874, 130), suggesting: *κάσις κυρίου πλαστήρ*, brother of Lord is a fraud.
The primary meaning of *πλάσσω* is to form, mould, (not attested in Rabb usage). A secondary metaph meaning, to counterfeit, forge, hence: *πλαστογράφος*, a forger, etc. Our form is, as yet, unattested outside Rabb literature.
The *tet* – *tav* interchange is common; Krauss LW 1, 4, Gignac 1, 92.

Cf ↑ פלסטון

פלסטיר ↑ פלסטר

פלסטק ↑ פלסטרן ,פלסטרק

פלסטיר ↑ פלסתר ,פלסתירא ,פלסתיר

פילקי ↑ פלקי

פסטמא (469) rule of orderly conduct, *disciplina*: <*ἐ*>*πιστήμη*

LevR 9. 8, 186: תהי פסטמא דילך טבא, ולית את דחיל מיניה, If your *disciplina* (public conduct) is good, you need not fear him. ▽ 'פסטמ, פיסטימא. // YalkLev 493: פשטמא; MGLev 7. 11, ed ENRabinowitz 140_{17}: אפסטמי; Ve-HizhirZav 34b: אפסטמא (with gloss: שורתך טובה).

Lieberman, apud LevRMargulies 873 (and already in Buxt 1766), explaining that *ἐπιστήμη* = *disciplina*. He cites EusebHE 8. 17. 6, who transl *disciplina* in Galerius' Lat edict (Lact, de mort pers 34) with this word. See Lampe 535a sv *ἐπιστήμη* II, and Berger 438b sv *disciplina*. The aphaeresis of the *ἐ*~ in some of the readings is very common. See Gignac 1, 319–20, LW 1, 123 (and ↑ **אכסוריא**).

(Contra LW 2, 469a; Fürst 175; Levy 4, 70a, Mussaf: *πίστωμα*; Jastrow 1194b emending to: פרגמטא; AC 6, 378b: *πίστευμα*; Lonzano 81: *στόμα*; KraussPR 280: *πιστευτής*; Löw, apud LW 2, 469a: *ἀπόστημα*.)

See CGL 2, 51_2, 311_{15}; 3, 25_{26}, 198_{28}: *ἐπιστήμι* (*epistini*) *disciplina*, etc.

Cf ↑ **דיסקפלניא**

פסטיס ↑ פסים

פסיפס (470b) vote of condemnation: *ψῆφ*<*ο*>*ς* (sc *καταγνώσεως*)

LamentR 2. 1, 98: "והתוית תו [על מצחות האנשים]" ... חתוכין ופספס; read: כתיטה בפסיפס, "And set a mark [upon the foreheads of the men]" (Ezek 9:4) ... Like the [letter] *theta* (*θ*) in the vote of condemnation, (*theta* being the first letter of *thanatos* – death, see below). ▽ edBuber: התורה פספס; Ar (AC 6, 383a): התיבה פספסן; YalkEzek 349: פספסין; Mussaf (apud AC ibid, citing Ms reading?): כתיטה בפסיפס (↓ **תיטה**[0]), read thus, or: בפספס.

Mussaf (AC ibid) writes (on Ar sv פסיפון): Also in Gk it means "judgement." For in the courts of the Greeks there were little stones called *ψῆφον*, and those who ruled guilty would put a black stone into the ballot, while those who ruled innocent [put] a white stone in. Or sometimes those who ruled guilty wrote the letter *theta*, because it is the first letter of *thanatos* (*θάνατος*), which means death ...
Lieberman GH 142 discusses the matter in detail, accepting Mussafia's reading, and rejecting the reading: חתוכין ופספס, probably influenced by חתיכה ופסיפס in SifZ 320_{16}, SifDeut 13, 21_{10} (see GH 57).

This is, of course, a very specialized meaning of פסיפס: *ψῆφος*, which means a piece of mosaic, voting pebble etc. See LW 2, 470a–472b (which requires much addition and correction). For this special meaning, cf LSJ[9] 2023a sv *ψῆφος* 5b, and cf OLD 1938a sv *thēta*, and Berger 727b sv *tabella*.

Cf ↓ **תיטה**[0]

◇פסליון [?פסטון] (473) curtain, which separates the court from the public (when proceedings are held in secret): *παστόν* (acc) (?)

MidPs 10. 5, 95: מה הדיון הזה (משהוא) [משהן] נותנין פליטין לפניו, עוד אינו רואה מה נעשה, Like this judge, after they stretch the curtain in front of him, he knows not what is happening without. ▽ פלסין. // YalkPs 650, Ar (AC 6, 380b–381a): פסליון, (פסקיון? in ZeitRaanan). משהן correct in Yalk. (// GenR 36. 1, 334_2; LevR 5. 1, 99_1; YalkJob 908: בילה, בילון, וילון, etc, *velum*, curtain, ↑ **וילון**.)

Both the context and the // in GenR and LevR etc make it quite clear that our text is speaking of a curtain. Indeed, Buber, MidPs 94 n28, suggested reading פפיליון: *papilio*, tent (LW 2, 474b–475a). However, Lieberman, JQR 35, 1944, 18 n113, quotes HGrégoire's opinion that we should read פסטון – the *tet* was resolved in לי –, meaning: a curtain. Lieberman himself suggested (ibid) possibly corrupt from *palla:* curtain. We may add that we find *πάλλιον = velum* (CGL 3, 92_{58}: belon. pallium; cf ibid 323_{30}: *πεπλος*; *παλλιον* etc). If we may posit the insertion of an intervocalic *sigma*, so common in all periods of Gk (see Pantelidas, BNJ 6, 1927–28, 430–31), we may reconstruct a form **παλσιον*, and require no emend in our Yalk reading. At all events, even if the etym and exact identification of our word remains problematic; its meaning is clear. (Reject LW 2, 473a, following Fürst 176a, who emended: פסליון לעיניו, explaining: *πασσαλεύειν ὀφθαλμούς*; AC 6, 310b: *fasciola*.) Lieberman (ibid 18–19) adds that the wording of the text indicates that this is not a trial that was held *intra velum, in secretario* (see Berger 693ab sv *secretarium*), but that the curtain was drawn in front of the judge for his deliberation, so that he would not see the public, nor heed any possible condemnation by the public.

Cf ↑ וילון, ↓ קנקנים

פסיפס ↑ פספסין, פספסם, פספס

פיסטון ↑ פסקין

אפופסיס ↑ פפסון

נימוס ↑ פרא בסיליוס

◇**פראדימוס** (479) [sitting] publically in judgement: *προ<όδῳ> δημοσ<ίᾳ>*

LevR 19. 6, 433_7: **וישב לו בפראדימוס**, and he sat for the examination publically. ▽ בכפר אדימוס, בכורדימוס, כפר אדימס, ביפר אדימס, ביפראדימם, בפרדימס, בפרדיאמוס (!) // YalkKings 249: פרדימס.

Lieberman, JQR 35, 1944, (41), 43–44; idem, apud LevR 876. (Contra LW 2, 479b: *παρὰ δήμῳ*, or **παράθεμις*? – This latter an impossible formation, see Zuntz, JSS 1, 1956, 133; Perles, Thron und

Circus des Königs Salomo 20, followed by ACAdd 6: *ἱππόδρομος*; AC 6, 412b: *πρόθεσις*; Fürst 80a: *παραδρομίς*.)

On the falling out of elements thought to be dittographic (haplography), see my remarks in Bar-Ilan 14–15, 1977, 27 n73; and cf Mayser 1/1[2], 217–19, and Gignac 1, 313.

פרא פרנון, פראפרנך (476–77) (1) the wife's additional settlement above the normal one, (2) that which the wife brings over and above her dowry: *παράφερνον*

(1) GenR 80. 7, 960_3: "הרבו עלי מאד מהר ומתן" — "מהר" פרנון (↓); "ומתן", פראפרנון, "Ask me never so much dowry and gift" (Gen 34:12) – "Dowry" (*mohar*), *phernon;* "and gift" (*u-matan*), *paraphernon.* ▽ Ar (AC 6, 431b): פרא פרנון; פראפורון, פור פראנון, פרפרנין, פרפר אינך, פרפראנון, פרא פורנך, פרא פראנון, פרא פורון. // YalkGen 134, 685_{15}: פרא פורנין. (On ין~, see ↓ **פרנה, פרנון**.)

Ibid 65. 14, 725_8: **... ואם לאו, הבא לי מפראפרנון שלי ... שכך הכתיב לה שהוא מעלה** לה שני גדיים בכל יום, ... And if not, bring me from my additional settlement ... For so he had written her (in her marriage document) that he would give her two kids a day. ▽ פרע פרנין, רפא פרנון, פרא פורנון, פרא פורכון etc. Corr acc. // YalkGen 114, 543_{84}: פרא פורנין.

YKet 5. 10, 30b 38, 41: מה מיפחות מפרא פרנון **דידה?** .. מפרא פרנון דידה פוחת, May one reduce [the payment also] from her additional settlement? ... (Pnei Moshe). From her additional settlement one does reduce.

Ibid 7. 7, 31c 5: מהו נסב מן הפרא פרנון שלה, May she take from her additional settlement?

YBB 10. 15, 17d 14: דלא יחזור ויעבדינן מטלטלין או פרא פרנון ולא משכח מרי חובא מתפס, so that he should not remarry and turn these (properties) into movables or the additional settlement, and the creditor will not find [anything] from which to claim [his debt]. // YNaz 5. 1, 54a 13: עבדה לון תכשיטין, עבדה לון פרה פרנון, he will turn them into jewelery (= immovables), he will turn them into an additional settlement.

(2) YGit 5. 7, 47b 31: אבל נכסים שהכניסה לו פרה פרנון גובה מאיזה שתרצה, But of the properties which she brought [him] in addition to her dowry, she may claim whichever she prefers. (see Korban ha-Edah.)

See ZFrankel, MGWJ 10, 1861, 118; LW 1, 213.

On ~פרא, with the ā in the middle of the word, unusual in Palestinian orthography other than in foreign words, see SokoloffGeniza 64.

(1) In GenR 80. 7, 960_3, the last two ▽ we have noted, פרא פורון and פראפורון, may represent [*]*παράφορον*, by a (mistaken) identification with *προσφορά, ἡ*, additional (wedding) gift; see

Taubenschlag[2], 126 n41 with bibl. Furthermore, the ▽ פרע פרנין is probably based on Heb פרע, to pay and פרנין (= פרנון ↓), marriage gift from bride to groom.

(2) On the two meanings of this word see Jastrow 1213b and in detail ITamar, Alei Tamar, Nashim, 1981, 136a, 354a. See further our discussion of פרנה, with specific ref to Bickerman, RIDA 3/III, 1956, 86–96; and see BCohen, Jewish and Roman Law, New York 1966, 363, Gulak, Das Urkundwesen im Talmud, Jerusalem 1935, 93.
The first meaning is the equivalent of תוספת כתובה, *Tosefet Ketubah.*
παράφερνα, τά (pl), is more usually attested (LSJ[9] 1329a: POxy 905. 7, II CE, JustNov 97. 5, etc). (It is a post-classical word.) However, the sing, *~ον*, appears in Hesych, edLatte 2, 29_{98}.
On this institution in Gk and Roman Law, see Berger 67b, "Things which belong to wife beyond the dowry (*extra dotem*) (C 5. 14. 8)" etc, with bibl; Taubenschlag[2] 126, especially n91 with bibl; GHage, Ehegüterrechtliche Verhältnisse in den griechischen Papyri Ägypten bis Diokletian, Cologne & Gratz 1968, 211–49, and reviews and additional notes on this work listed by Modrzejewski, AfP 26, 1978, 215–16, idem, Scritti in onore di Orsolina Montevecchi, Bologna 1981, 261.
For med Lat *paraphernalia, ~fernalia,* see Maigne D'Arnis 1642, 1610, (from which our modern word derives).

Cf ↓ פרנון, and פרנה

פרגל ↓ פרגל

פרגל (477–78) scourge, whip, lash: *φραγέλ<λιον>* ← *flagellum*

MechYitroBa-Ḥodesh 6, 227_9: מה לך לוקה מאפרגל, Why are you being lashed with the whip. ▽ מאה פרגול, a hundred lashes, מספרגל, read: מ׳ פרגל. // LevR 32. 1, 735_7: בפרגל. ▽ בפרגול, בפראגין, and emended: בטיטראון (↑ טיטראון) MsMunich 117; Ve-Hizhir 1. 50: מכף רגל, read: מאה פרגל; MidPs 12. 5, 109: בפרוגין ▽ בפיראגון, לידקר בטהגון, לידקר בפור אגון; LTEx 20. 6, 1. 136: מאה פרגול; YalkEx 292, likewise; IbidZach 581: בפרגל, ibidPs 659: ברגול; MachPs 12. 24, 1. 76: לידקר בפואגין, etc.
TKelBM 4. 4, 582_{22}: ... פרגל שעשה בראשו מסמר להיות מכה בו, טמא, A scourge, at the head of which he fixed a stud, to lash with it, it is unclean ...

Verbal form: מפרגל, chastens, scourges.
MidPs 94. 2, 417: "כי כאשר ייסר איש את בנו, ה׳ אלקיך מיסרך", כמו דמפרגל ברנש ית בריה, ה׳ אלקיך מפרגל לך, "As a man chasteneth his son, so the Lord thy God chasteneth thee," (Deut 8:5) — As a man scourges his son, so the Lord thy God will scourge you.

φραγέλλιον is a loanword from Lat *flagellum*, (see Lampe 1489ab, MM675a, ArndtGingrich 873a), which passed into Syr (פרגל, PnS 3235, Schulthess 161b) and Arab (Fraenkel 113; Geiger, ZDMG

17, 1863, 421 n2; Vollers, ZDMG 51, 1897, 315; see also Löw apud LW 2, 478a). See also Fleischer, apud Levy 1, 282a. ACameron, AJP 52, 1931, suggests that *flagella* was the popular word for the classical *uirgae* of the Roman *lictor*; hence, it entered Gk in this sense of whip for which there was a perfectly good Gk word.
For טיטראון in LevR 32. 1, 735$_7$ cf ↑ **טיטראון**.
The form מאפרגל may represent a prosthetic *aleph* (as Krauss, LW 2, 477b), as we find this form too: אפרגל, (see Löw apud LW 2, 478a, referring to Vollers, ZDMG 51, 1897, 315). If so, then the reading מאה פרג(ו)ל, would seem to have arisen out of a misunderstanding of מאפרגל, understood as מא׳ פרגל. Concerning ε > υ change (in פרגול) see LW 1, 87, and cf Thumb, BZ 9, 1900, 399—400.
As to the other text-tradition **פראגין, פיראגון, פרוגין, פוראגון** etc, since it is linked to the verb לידקר ב~ it appears to be some kind of spear, eg *φουρκίον, furcilla* (DuCange), a pickfork or perhaps trident? So AC 6, 407b, ibid 1, 236b.(Contra Buber, MidPs 109 n47 who suggests reading: **פרגולין** throughout.)
Note further that טרגול in YBer 1, 15a 30 has nothing to do with our word (contra Jastrow 1214a). So too פרקדל (LW 2, 495b) and פרכיל (ibid 489b) are quite unrelated. (See on פרקדל LCohn MGWJ 44, 1900, 568; JPerles, JQR 16, 1904, 355; Löw, ZDMG 45, 705.) So too this word is not to be confused with פרגל in MKelim 295; see LW 2, 478a sv **פרגל** II.

Cf ↑ **טיטראון**

פראדימוס ↑ פרדימס

פרודום [פרודוס] interrogation, or courtroom as place of interrogation: *πρόοδος*

Sefer ha-Maasim, edLewin, Tarbiẓ 1/1, 1929, 93: **... ועמד בקינדינון (↓), ונדון בפרודום והודה** (sic), ... and stood trial, and was tried with interrogation, (or in the place of interrogation), and pleaded guilty. Read: **פרודוס**.

Lieberman, JQRNS 35/1, 1944, 39—44; idem, Eshkolot 3, 1959, 87—89, ref to DuCange 1247 sv *πρόοδος:* tribunal iudicium, and CGL 2, 90$_{30}$: interrogatio *ἐξέτασις, ἐπερώτησις, πρόοδος*. (Contra Epstein, Tarbiẓ ad loc n3, who suggested emending to: פרורוס: *φρουρά:* prison?)
The term is not found in classical Rabbinic sources, and probably belongs to the later Byzantine linguistic stratum, hence in the Sefer ha-Maasim lit (cf ↓ **קינדינון**)

Syr: פרודון, פרודק, Brockelm[2] 593b.

פרוזבול (פרוסבול) (482) declaration made in court to the effect that the law of limitation, by the entrance of the Sabbatical year, shall not apply to the loan to be transacted: *προσβολ<ή>*

MShev 10. 3–4: **פרוזבול אינו משמט. זה אחד מן הדברים שהתקין הלל הזקן כשראה שנמנעו העם מלהלוות זה את זה ... התקין הלל פרוזבול. זהו גופו של פרוזבול: מוסר אני לך**

איש פלוני הדיינים ... שכל חוב שיש לי שאגבנו כל זמן שארצה, והדיינים חותמין למטה או העדים, A [loan secured by] a *prozbol* is not cancelled [by the Sabbatical year]. This is one of the things that Hillel the Elder ordained. When he saw that people refrained from giving loans to one another ... Hillel ordained the *prozbol*. This is the formula of the *prozbol:* "I affirm to you, such-a-one and such-a-one, the judges in such-a-place, that, concerning any debt due to me, I will collect it whenever I wish." And the judges sign [it], or the witnesses. ▽ פרוסבול. // SifDeut 113, $173_{14\ 15}$, 174_1: פרוסבול, ▽ ~פרוז; BGit 34b, 36a.

MShev 10. 5: פרוזבול המוקדם כשר, והמאוחר פסול, An antedated *prozbol* is valid, but a post-dated one is not valid.

MShev 10. 6, 7 // MUkẓ 3. 10. MPea 3. 6.

TShev 8. 7, 201_{24}, 273_4: ... פרוזבול המקושר, הדיינין חותמין מבפנים והעדים מבחוץ, A tied-up *prozbol,* the judges sign inside, and the witnesses on the outside. ▽ ~פרוס.

TShev 8. 9, 10, 202, 273. YSanh 12. 7, 23a 18, 19.

TBM 1. 9, 372_4: גזרי דינין ופרוסבולין, הרי זה יחזיר למי שכתובין על שמו, Court decisions and *prozbols* (pl), one should return [them] (if they were found in the street) to him on whose name they are written.

TBB 11. 7, 413_{27}: פרוסבולין; ibid 128: פרוזבלין.

THul 1. 25, 501_{32}: פרוסבל (contrasted with גט).

MKet 9. 9. // YKet 9. 11, 33c 12: פרוזבולא; ibid 115; BKet 89a. (~א, Aram sing term.)

BGit 36b: מאי פרוסבול? אמר רב חסדאי: פרוס בולי [sic MsVat 140: ופרוס] בוטי, What is a *prozbol?* Said Rav Ḥisda (Babylonian late II CE authority): *pros boulé* [*u-pros*] *bouté* (a popular etym, perhaps: *πρὸς βουλὴ πρεσβευτῶν*?).

BGit 37a: מאי פרוסבול? ... פורסא דמילתא, What is a *prozbol? Pursa de-milta.* (Again apparently a popular etymology, whose meaning is not clear.)

BMeg 15a: דאמר רב חסדא: זה בא בפרוזבולי וזה בא בפרוזבוטי, As Rav Ḥisda said: This one came with his *prozbolé,* and this one came with his *prozbeuté.* ▽ VL 77: בפרוס בולי, בפרוס בוטי.

In Gaon lit, see Shetarot, Al-Barceloni, edHalberstam, no48, 69–71: פרוזב(ו)ל, פרוסבל, (ibid also citing BGit 36b); Miller, MizMaarav, no230, 63: Gulak, Oẓar ha-Shetarot, nos228–29, 215–16. Schürer (Eng ed[1]) 2/2, 362–63; Blau, Budapest SemJubil vol, 1927, 113; Löw, apud ACSup 338b; TK 2, 569 n30. (Contra Krauss, LW 1, 272–73, 2, 428ab: *προβολή* = *παράβαλον;* AC 6, 417b: *πρὸς βουλῇ, προβουλή,* and so too Levy 4, 106a; Jastrow 1218b, abbrev of *πρὸς βουλῇ βουλευτῶν.*) On BGit 37a, see Jastrow 1147b sv פורסא (I); AC 6, 436a sv פרס; Levy 4, 106b. None satisfactory. Can פורסא דמילתא = פרסישמנג, in BGit 28b, Pehl *pursisn nāmak* (~y), where מילתא translates *nāmak*? This would mean a court-document showing the case had been investigated by judges, and would fit the nature of the *prozbol.* See PerlesES 35–36, and FPerles, OLZ, 1903, 340, ACSup

343a, (contra Levy 4, 127ab). See also Telegdi, JA 226, 1935, 252 no117. Cf BYoma 9a: מאי פורסי ?פרהדרין (LW 2, 480b, where Löw rejects Krauss, LW 2, 435a: [ἔ]φορος). This may well be unrelated to the word in our text.
On BGit 36b, see LW 2, 482a: πρὸς βουλευταῖς; Sachs, Beiträge 2, 70; LLöw, Graphische Requisit 2, 88; Jastrow 1218b: πρὸς βουλῇ βουλευτῶν.
On BMeg 15a, see LW 2, 482b–483a, Levy 4, 105b, and Fleischer ibid 228b. (Fleischer suggests προσβολή, rejecting Levy's πρόσβλησις.)
On the s > z change (in spelling ~פרוז), see Gignac 1, 121–23; eg ἀμφιζβητήσεως (for ἀμφισβητήσεως, ibid121). See further, Mayser 1/1², 171. Very common in Rabbinic Graecitas, see LW 1, 105.
Pl ~ין, as above.

προσβολή in the papyri, see Taubenschlag², 276 n23, where it means transference of surity by court order (by auction).
On the institution of the *prozbol*, see NRakover, Oẓar ha-Mishpat 152–53; KKahana, Sefer Shanat ha-Sheva⁴, Tel-Aviv 1965, 93–122; and, most recently, Gilat, Sefer Baruch Kurzweil, 1975, 93–113.

פרוזבול ↑ פרוזבלין, פרוזבולא

פרוזדוגמא ↓ פרוזדגמא

פרוזדוגייאה, (pl פרסטיגיות) command, decree: *προσταγια (= προσταγή)

TanḥDeutEkev 11: לדואר שהיה מהלך ופרחדוגייאה בידו להכנס, ועבר בתוך הנהר ונפלו הכתבים לתוך המים ונמוחו האותיות ..., Like a *cursor* who was travelling with documents in his hand to place inside [the city] (?), and he crossed through the river and the documents fell into the water and the writing was erased. (Sic edMantua 1563. Not in edprinc.)
GenRabbati 32. 8, 167_{18}: פרישטוגיאה שלו פרושה מיום אל יום ומחדש לחדש והיו מתבהלים בכל יום, His decree was promulgated from one day to the next and from one month to the next, and they were terrified daily. (But // PR 33, 151b: פרוסטומא, read: פרוסטגמא; YalkIs 336: פרוזדוגמא. Cf ↓ פרוזדוגמא.)

Pl: פרסטיגיות
YShev 6. 1, 36c 44: שלש פרסטיגיות שילח יהושע לארץ ישראל, Joshua sent off three decrees to the Land of Israel. ▽ פרחדיגמאות, פרווטגמאות, פרוסטגמאיות etc, (Ratner ad loc 52). // in LevR 17. 6, 386_2: פרחדיגמאות, cf ↓ פרוזדוגמא.

On TanhDeutEkev, see LW 2, 483, suggesting corrupt from פרוזדגמא.
On GenRabbati 32. 8, 18 editor ad loc suggests *prestigiae*. However, the verb פרושה does not fit this term, but does fit the προσταγή.

προσταγή in LXXDaniel 3:28 (95), etc.
On ~*ια* term, see Psaltes 260–62; or perhaps ~*εια*, ibid 262–63.
For ~פריש – *προς*, with the *ο* > *ι* interchange, cf LW 1, 88–89.
On pl form see AC 6, 437a. (Contra LW 2, 483b, and Jastrow 1221a, suggesting corrupt of פרוזדגמא.)

Cf ↑ **דיאטגמא**, ↓ **פרוזדוגמא**

פרוזדוגמא (483) decree, edict: *πρόσταγμα* → *prostagma*

YelamdEx 31:18, apud Ar (AC 6, 418a): מלך בשר ודם פורס פרוזדיגמאות במדינה ואומר: פלן קומוס ..., A king of flesh and blood promulgates edicts in the city, saying: So and so [will be the] *comes* ... // TanḥExKiTissa 15: **פרודיגמאות**; read ~פרוז (or ~פרז).
GenR 41 (42) 3, 402₉: למלך ששלח פרוסטיגמא שלו למדינה. מה עשו בני המדינה? נטלוה וקראוה ושרפוה באש, Like a king who sent his edict to the city. What did the citizens do? They took it and read it and burned it up with fire. ▽ **פרוסטוגמא**, **פרוסטיגמא**, **פריסטיגמא**, **פרסטיגמא**, **פרוסטגמא**, **פרוסטגמין** (pl), **פרוזטגמא** etc. // YalkRuth 596: **פרוזדגמא** (Cf // LevR 11. 7, 231; EstR Proem 11, TanḥLevShemini 9: **כתביו**, **כתבים** = *γραφαί*.)
LevR 17. 6, 386₂: שלש פרוזדיגמאות שלח יהושע בן נון אצלם ..., Joshua the son of Nun sent them three decrees. ▽ **פרוסטגמיות**, **פרסטיגמאות**, **פרגדגמאות**, **פרוגמאות** (with correction: **פרסת גמאות**, **פרגדל**, **פאות פרדגד**!) (with gloss: **פי׳ גמאות אגרות**). // YShev 6. 1, 36c 44: **פרסטיגיות** (↑ **פרוזדוגייאה**), ▽ **פרוזטגמאות**, **פרוסטגמאיות** etc, (Ratner ad loc 52). (Partial // in EstR Proem 11; DeutR 5. 14: **דאטגמא**, but edLieberman 101: **פרוסטיגמא**, cf ↑ **דיאטגמא**.)
PRK 77a, 155₉ ₁₀ ₁₂: למלך ששילח פרוז דוגמה שלו למדינה. מה עשו כל בני המדינה? נטלו אותה ועמדו על רגליהם ופרעו את ראשיהם וקראו אותה באימה וביראה ברתת ובזיע ... קרית שמע פרוז דוגמה שלי הוא, Like a king who sent off his edict to the city. What did all the citizens do? They took it and stood up on their feet and beared the heads (out of respect) and read it with awe and fear and trembling and fright ... The recitation of the Shema is my edict. ▽ **פרוזדיגמא**, **פרוחדוגמא** (with marg gloss: **אגרת**), **פרוזדוגמא**, **פרזגמא** read: **פרז[ד]גמא**. // LevR 27. 6, 637₁: ▽ **פרוסדוגמא** **פרותיגמא**, **תוגמא**~, **פרוסטוגמא**, **פרסטגמא**, **פרסטיגמא**, **פרוסטיגמא**, **פריז**~, **פרוז**~, **דיוטגמא** MsParis 149 (cf ↑ **דיאטגמא**); TanḥLevEmor 10: **פרוזדוגמא**; Bibid 13, 92; YalkLev 642; ibidMich 554; MGLev 1. 2, 14₈: **פרוזדגמא**; ibid 22. 7, 625₂₄: **פרוזדוגמא** ▽ **פרוזדוגא**, read **דוגמא**~; MachMich 6. 3, 40: **פרוסטוגמוס**. (Partial // in EstR Proem 11, LevR 11. 7, 231₁₁ and TanḥLevShemini 9 have: **כתביו**, **כתבים**.)
This text is cited frequently in mediaeval authorities, eg Seder Rav Amram Gaon sect 27, edGoldschmidt 19: **פרחטגמא**; Sefer ha-Manhig sect 39, edRaphael 75:

פרוז דוגמא; MV 12; Siddur Rashi sect 17, 14—15; Abudarhim, Shaharit shel Ḥol, ed Jerusalem 1959, 79; Tur Oraḥ Ḥayyim 61.

PRK 102a, 207_1: שלא יהיו דברי תורה בעיניך כפרוזדיגמא ישנה, אלא יהיו בעיניך כפרוזדיגמא חדשה שהכל רצים לקרותה, that the words of the Torah be not in your eyes like an old edict, but let them be in your eyes like a new edicts which all run to read. // YalkEx 271: פרוזדוגמא; ibid Prov 960; MachProv 22. 2, 31a: כפרוזדיכמא; MGEx 19. 1, 373_{14}: פרוזדגמא. (But SifDeut 33, 59: דיוטגמא, cf ↑ **דיאטגמא**.) Note that MV 322 cites this text as coming from GenR; but it is not in our edd. See editor's note ad loc.

PRK 105a, $213_{6,7,9,10}$: ... לא כפרוס דוגמא שיש לה שנים או שלשה ימים, אלא כפרוס ... דוגמא בן יומא ..., ... not like an edict two or three days old, but like an edict of the same day ... (This is a partial // to PRK 207 above. And cf DeutR, edLieberman 117, where our word is absent.)

PR 33, 151b: פרוסטומא שלו פרושה מיום ליום ומחודש לחודש; read: **פרוסטגמא**, His edict is promulgated from day to day and from month to month. (Cf ↑ **דיאטגמא** on the use of **פרש** in this context.) // GenRabbati 32. 8, 167_{18}: פרישטוגיאה (↑ **פרוזדוגייאה**).

TanḥBGenNoah 17, 42, according to MsVat 34 (Buber ibid n160): פרותי ומיא שתשמור שנים עשר חודש; read: פרוסטגמיא, a decree that you should keep for twelve months. ▽ printed text: גזירה היא לפני. // AgBer 7, 18: פרוזדמיא; MGDeut 9. 11, 178_9: פריזדגמיאות. (But TanḥGenNoah 11: גזירה.)

TanḥBGen Mi-Keẓ 17, 202: עשה יוסף בערמה שלש פרוסטגמיות, Joseph issued with guile three decrees. (With gloss: פי' כתבים.) (But in YelamdGen Mi-Keẓ, apud Ar, AC 3, 37a: דיטגמאות, cf ↑ **דיאטגמא**; GenR 91. 4, 1126_3: גזירות, and so too in EcclesR 9. 15, and EcclesZ 150.)

The great number of different spellings of this word (over twenty) are mainly varying combinations of well-known consonantal interchanges such as S > Z (LW 1, 105—06, Mayser 1/1², 176—78) and T > D (LW 1, 101, Gignac 1, 82—83, Mayser ibid 146) etc. As a result of the (related) S > Z and T > D interchange, the second element became דגמא~, or דוגמא~, this latter through the common A > O interchange. (Cf Gignac 1, 287, citing *πρόστογμα* (for *~ταγμα*) from PLips 64 = WChr 281. 34, corr 43 (368/9 CE), and cf ↑ **דיאטגמא**.) This form was also formed under the influence of the well-known word דוגמא: *δεῖγμα* (LW 2, 187b—188b), also spelled דיגמא, and hence form: פרסדיגמא. (Incidentally, this spelling misled Buxt to identify the word was *παράδειγμα*, 1808, but cf ibid 1829.) In another case the *~γμ~* was assimilated to *μ*; hence, פרוזדמיא in AgBer 7, 18. Cf Gignac 1, 177, eg, *προστάματος* (for *~τάγματος*) Archiv 5, 383, 73. 1 (early II CE?), and cf my remarks in Bar-Ilan 16/17, 1979, 29. Note also the (artificial) attempt to make the word more "Greek-like" by adding an *~ος* term in MachMich 6. 3, 40. As to MachProv 22. 2, 31: דיכמא~, cf LW 1, 211.

פרודתיקין in AgEst 6. 10, 62, and פרודתקיון in Trg2Est 6. 10 has nothing to do with our word (contra LW 2, 481b), nor with *πρόσταξις* (Jastrow 1217b), nor with *praedictum* (AC 6, 414a), nor with

προσθήκη (Levy, TrgWb 2, 288a), but is from the Pehl *fravartak*, meaning: letter, epistle, and should be written פררתקין. (Geiger apud ACSup 336b and 337a and cf Fleischer apud Levy, TrgWb 2, 573b–574a). See further Noeldeke, ZDMG 46, 1892, 139; Hübschmann, ibid 326; Fraenkel, ibid 55, 1901, 355.
On *πρόσταγμα* see Modrzejewski, JJP 5, 1951, 186–206; MM 551a sv *προστάσσω;* ArndtGingrich 725b; Mason 81a. See Lieberman's discussion in JQR 35, 1944, 7–10.

Lat: *prostagma*, Maigne D'Arnis 1812.
Syr: פרסטגמא, פרוסטגמא, PnS 3281, 3248.
Cf ↑ **דיאטגמא, פרוזדוגייאה**

פרחדוגמא ↑ פרוזדימיא, פרוזדיכמא, פרוזדיגמא, פרוז דוגמה

פרוטוגמיא ↓ פרוטגמייא

פרוטוגמיא (484–85) marriage of a batchelor and a virgin (lit: first marriage): *πρωτογάμια* → *protogamia*

YDem 4. 2, 24ab: בשבת של פרוטגמייא התירו ... בשבת של פרוטגמייא, On the Sabbath of the *protogamia* they permitted it ... etc.
LevR 11. 2, 221$_3$: ואותן שבע שנים הן הן פרוטוגמיא של צדיקים לעתיד לבוא, And those same seven years (before the advent of the Messiah), they are the *protogamia* of the righteous in the days to come. // YalkProv 944: פרוטיגמא, read: פרוטוגמיא.
Ibid line 4: וסימנא, דאכיל פרוטוגמיא אכיל משתותא, and the mnemonic sign is: he who partakes in the *protogomia* will have a share in the [wedding] feast. // YShev 4. 10, 35c 27: פרוטגמייא.
MidPs 14. 6, 114–15: משל לבן מלך שאירס לבת מלך וקבעו פרוסטגמיא ביום פלוני. בנו של מלך מצפה לשמחתו ... ומי מעקב? ... פרוסטגמיא מעקב, Like unto a prince who betrothed a princess and they fixed the *protogamia* for a certain day. The prince awaits his happiness ... And what is delaying [it]? ... The *protogamia* delays [it].
▽ פריגמיטיא. Read: פרוטוגמיא.

Lieberman, Annuaire 9, 1949, 411 (= Texts and Studies 275); idem, GH 9. He accepts the interpretation of Rivmaẓ (= R. Isaac b. Melchiẓedek of Siponto, S Italy, mid XII cent, who knew Gk well), comment to MDemai 4. 2, edNSachs, Jerusalem 1975, 58. Lieberman adds (orally) that it is not certain that this was always the meaning or the only meaning. On LevR, see Perles, MGWJ 9, 1860, 342 n9; idem, ibid 16, 1867, 302. (See further, Krauss, BZ 2, 1893, 530–31; Geiger, JZ 5, 161; Maarich 66–67; SachsBeiträge 1, 152: *πρὸ τοῦ γάμου*; Buber in MidPs ibid n32: *προθεσμία*; Jastrow 1219b.)

פרוסטגמיא in MidPs, with (common) intervocatic *sigma* (Pantelidos, BNJ 10, 1927–28, 373–81, cf ↑ גמיקון), perhaps influenced by *πρόσταγμα*.

The word appears in CIL 8/4, 25045_8 (Carthage), EDiel, ILG 1, 1003: *app|e|llatur protogamia,* (see ibid 191 for bibl). Lieberman (above) claims that Rivmaẓ' interpretation suits context of inscr. See on this inscr ESeckel, Sitzungsberichte Berlin Akad 1921, 989; PMaas, BNJ 3, 1922, 134. (In some of the texts the word may have a different meaning. See, eg, JTabory, SCI 5, 1979–80, 16–22).

Cf ↑ גממסות

פרוכימטוס (485) *pro forma,* for external appearance: *πρὸ<σ>χήματος*

YelamdNum 23. 7, apud Ar (AC 6, 426b), GrünhutLikkutim 6, 66a: למלך שהוציא כרוז: למחר יוצא אני ודן בני פרוכימטוס Like a king who gave out a notice: Tomorrow I shall go out and judge my children *pro forma* [alone] ...

Lieberman, (private communication 4 Dec 1981). The loss of the *sigma* is like the loss of a medial *sigma,* common in papyri; see Gignac 1, 130. (Contra Ar ibid, who explained: פי' כן קורין לאבוקט בל"י, וי"א הנכנס בראש המלחמה (advocate). The advocate is, of course, פרקליטוס (↓ פרקליט), while he who enters the battle first is the פרוטומכוס: *πρώτομαχος* (cf Fürst 185b). Jastrow 1220b and 1221b emends to פרופוסיטוס: *praepositus*. But none of these meanings make any real sense in our passage.)

פרוזבול ↑ פרוסבל, פרוסבולין, פרוסבול

פרוזדוגמא ↑ פרוסטוגמוס, פרוסטגמיות, פרוסדוגמא

פרוטוגמיא ↑ פרוסטגמיא

פרוסטיא patronage: *προσ<τα>τεία*

DeutR 5. 8: כל מי שנשען בבשר ודם עובר, אף פרוסטיא שלו עוברת, Anyone who relies upon flesh and blood passes away; so too his patronage passes away. ▽ edprinc: פרוסטיה, edLieberman 99: פרוסטמיא. // MachPs 146. 1, 2. 280: פרוסטיא. Perhaps read פרוסט[ט]יא(~ה)

Fürst 182b; Lieberman, Tarbiẓ 3, 1932, 455 n5; idem, DeutR 99 n1; idem, GH 49–50. (Contra SachsBeiträge 1, 169; AC 6, 437a.) Note that haplological syllabic ellipsis is not unusual (see Mayser $1/1^2$, 218), and especially after *σ* (see Gignac 1, 66).

Cf Cowley, JEA 2, 1915, 212 publishing POxyBodl MsHeb d 83 (P)b, a papyrus from c 400 CE: ולפרוסטטין, explained by ed as "a new word, no doubt equivalent to פרנסין." Meaning: president or presiding officer, LSJ[9] 1526b sv *προστάτης* II 3, and LSJSupple 128a.

פרן (491) (1) give marriage gifts (on part of bridegroom), (2) endow with dowry (on part of bride's family); deriv verb formed from פרנה, פרן: *φερνή*

(1) Aram form
Trg YIEx 22: 15: מפרנא יפרין, he shall surely give her a marriage gift, (transl: מהר ימהרנה, "he shall surely endow her"). // Y2 and FragmTrgKlein ibid: מפרנה יפרן. Cf Samaritan Trg: פרן יפרננה, and LXX: *φερνῇ φερνιεῖ* [infin abs + finite verb]. TrgYIDeut 21:13: ותפרין יתה, and he should give her marriage gifts.

(2) Heb form
GenR 60. 13, 653_7 = ibid 74:16, 875_4: ולא היו מפרינין אלא בפה, and they (Rebekah's family) did not give her marriage gifts, but merely [words] of mouth. // YalkProv 947.

(1) For מפרוני in TrgIEx 22:16, cf ↓ **פרנה**.

(2) See apparat in GenR ibid, citing ▽ מפריעים, מפריצין, מפסין, מפצין, which should all be corr, and מברכים, ~ין, which is an editorial corr (?) based on Gen 24:60, "And they blessed Rebekah," whereas main reading is based on verse 59 ibid, "And they sent Rebekah away". See further Minḥat Yehuda, apud GenR ad loc, and Sokoloff Geniza 148 n12.
מפרין (▽ מפריז), in MBM 5. 6, is from a (different) Heb root: פרה. So too in TBM 5. 13, 382_{11}, YBM 5. 6, 10c 3–6. (Contra BenIehuda 10, 5191b, and n3.)
This verb corresponds to the Gk *φερνίζω* (?).

Syr: פרן, אפרן, PnS 3268.
Cf ↓ **פרנה**

פרנא ↓ פרנה

פרנה (also **~א**, **~פור, פורן, פרן**) (490–91) (1) marriage gift, or settlement, from groom to bride, (2) deed attesting to such gift, (3) transf, good luck, or profit: *φερνή*

(1) YKet 6. 1, 30a 57: ולא ממרק לה פורנה, and he does not pay off [the entire] marriage settlement.
Ibid 7. 6, 31c 20, 21: תיפוק בלא פרן, let her be divorced without [receiving] the marriage settlement.
Ibid line 21: תיסב פרן שלים, let her take her marriage settlement in full.
Ibid line 23: תהוי נסבות פלגון פרן, let her take half her marriage settlement.
Ibid line 25: פלגון פרן, half the marriage settlement.
YBB 9. 6, 17a 17: מן פרניך, from your marriage gift.

CantR to Cant 1: 5: לא מן פרניך אלא מן פרנין דידך; sic edprinc, corr in modern edd: מן פרנין דידי, not from your marriage settlement but from mine. (Perhaps belongs with פרנון ↓)
YBB 10. 15, 17d 11: חמוי דברתיה דר' חגיי הוה ערבא בפורנה דברתיה דר' חגיי, והוה מבזבזה בנכסייא ..., The father-in-law of R. Ḥaggai's daughter was a bondsman for (his son's) marriage gift to R. Ḥaggai's daughter, and he wasted his properties ...
Ibid 9. 1, 16d 45: פרנא.
YPes 4 ad fin, 31c 7: אנא מחשבנא גולדנה (צ"ל גדלוניה) מן פרני, I will reckon the additional amount from my marriage gift.
BKet 67a: פרנא.
TrgYIEx 22:16: כמפרוני בתולתא, read: כפרני, like the endowing of virgins (transl: כמהר הבתלות, "according to the dowry of virgins"). // TrgNeofiti: כנימוסי פרני בתולתא (נימוס ↑). (Cf LXX ibid: *φερνή*.)
GenR 40 (41) 7, 394[7]: כאינש דבחר פרנה דאימיה, like a man who choses his mother's marriage settlement (?). ▽ א~, פורנה, א~. // YalkGen 70, 267[45]. (See discussion below.)

(2) YKet 7. 6, 31c 22: ... אייתון פרנא ניקריניה. אייתון פרנה ואשכחון כתוב בגווה: אין ... תהוי נסבה פלגון פרן, Bring the deed of the marriage settlement [and] let us read it. They brought the deed of the marriage settlement and found written in it: If ... let her receive half of the marriage settlement.
Ibid 9. 13, 33c 22: אורחא דאיתתא מימר: אבד פורנה, עביד חורן, It is the way of a woman to say: The deed of the marriage settlement is lost. Make [me] another.

(3) BKet 54a: פורנא ליתמי, It is the heir's good luck, or profit.

(1) For the correct reading in YPes ibid, see LiebermanYK 446.
As the passage in GenR 40 (41) 7, the commentary to GenR explains: Like a man who choses his mother's *ketuba*, obviously interpreting פרנה as *φερνή*. But Ar, AC 6, 431b, explains as "harlotry", understanding פרנה, פורנה etc. as *πόρνη*. The first explanation is accepted in ACSup 341a. However, we should note another homily on the same verse in Gen 13:10, "And Lot chose him all the plain (*kikar*) of Jordan", in GenR ibid 394[2], Yalk ibid 267[40], MGEx 13:10, 229[14] (where further // are listed): "the plain (*kikar*) of Jordan" (Gen ibid) – "For by means of a whorish woman a man is brought to a piece (*kikar*) of bread" (Prov 6:26). This supports the Aruch's interpretation.
On TrgYIEx 22:16, see Löw, apud LW 2, 348a sv מפרונא. (Contra Krauss ibid.) See LevyTrgWb 2, 60b, and cf Samaritan Trg: כפרן; ZBen-Ḥayyim, Ivrit ve-Aramit Nusaḥ Shommron 2, 512[305].

(3) For this meaning see Jastrow 1230b sv פרן, and in greater detail in MAFriedman, Jewish Marriage in Palestine 1, 78 who prefers the meaning trousseau (meaning 1), ibid n128.

The different forms of the word may be explained as follows: פור~ for *φερ~*, ε > υ, see LW 1, 87, Gignac 1, 274, Mayser 1/1², 46, and cf Psaltes 20. Cf ↓ פרנון. פור~ may further be influenced by פורנא I and/or II (LW 2, 434ab): *furnus, πόρνη*.

As to the term, א~ and ה~ interchange regularly, see LW 1, 15.
For the change from η in the Gk term to A in the Rabb term, see LW 1, 15.

On the institution of the φερνή and its relationship to the Biblical *mohar* and Rabbic *Ketubah*, see BCohen, Jewish and Roman Law, 350–52, and in greater detail MAFriedman, Jewish Marriage in Palestine 1, Tel-Aviv New York 1980, 76–79. (Cf LW 1, 213.)
The primary meaning of the word in Gk is the wife's property or dowry. There is a transfer in the connotation of the word from the dowry brought by the wife to "bride-money" paid by the husband, (see EJBickerman's study in RIDA 3/III, 1956, 86–96, idem, Studies in Jewish and Christian History, Leiden 1976, 1, 201–15). Thus in the LXX φερνή transl מהר (Gen 34:12, Ex 22:15, 16). In Palestinian Rabb sources the word comes to be more or less identical as the *ketubah*, and, indeed, Maimonides (Hilchot ha-Yerushalmi, edLieberman, New York 1947, 61), defines: כתובה שמה פורנא, the *ketubah* is called φερνή. And just as the *ketubah* meant either the actual marriage settlement or the marriage contract, so too with פרנה, (1) and (2) above. The designation of the mediaeval Italian *ketubah* was: הדין שטר פרנה, this *pherne* document. The word continues to be used in the post-Talmudic period, eg responsum attributed to Natronai Gaon, OhGKet 203, no505: ופורנא זו כתובה. See MAFriedman, Jewish Marriage in Palestine ibid.

On the φερνή in Gk and Roman law, see GHage, Ehegüterrechtliche Verhältnisse in den griechischen Papyri Ägypten bis Diokletian, Cologne & Gratz 1968, 19–210; additional notes, reviews and comments on this work listed by Modrzejewski, AfP 26, 1978, 215–16, and see idem, Scritti in onere di Orsolina Montevecchi Bologna 1981, 261.

Cf Syr: פרניתא, PnS 3268, and Bruns-Sachau pass.
Cf ↑ פראפרנון, פרן, ↓ פרנון

פראפרנון ↑ פרה פרנון

פרוזדוגמא ↑ פריז דגמיאות, פרותיומייא, פרוסטיגמא

פרקולה ↓ פריקולא

פרוזדוגייאה ↑ פרישטוגיאה

◇**פרנון** (490) marriage gift from bride to groom: *φέρνον (= φερνή)

GenR 80. 7, 960₃: "הרבו עלי מאד מהר ומתן" — "מהר", פרנון; "ומתן", פראפרנון(↑), "Ask me never so much dowry and gift" (Gen 34:12) – "Dowry" (*mohar*), *phernon*; "and gift" (*u-matan*), *paraphernon*. ▽ Ar (AC 6, 431b): פורנין, (pl of פורנא, cf ↑ **פרנה**, or corr פורנון = פרנון?); פורטו, read פורניך? ון~?, פראנון, פראינון, פאראנון, corr accordingly, (influenced by פראפרנון). // YalkGen 134, 685₁₄: פורנון; TrgY2Gen 34:12: פורן וכתובתו, dowry and marriage settlement, cf ↑ **פרנה**.

The form פורנון shows the not uncommon ε > υ change; see LW 1, 87, Gignac 1, 274, Mayser 1/1², 46, and cf Psaltes 20. Cf ↑ **פרנה**.

Though *φέρνον is not attested, παράφερνον (in sing, more usually παράφερνα in pl) is attested in Hesych, edLatte 2, 29_{98} (and so too we find the cognate φερνόφορος), demonstrating that *φέρνον must have existed. See ↑ **פראפרנון**.
פורנין may be pl of **פורנא**, or corr to **פורנון**, as suggested above. Alternatively, it may be a dim [*]φέρνιον, from *φέρνον. Such a form is found with a different meaning, see LSJ[9] 1922a.
See also פרנין in CantR to Cant 1. 5 (↑ **פרנה**).

Cf ↑ **פרנה**, and **פראפרנון**

פרנה ↑ פרניך ,פרני

פרוזבול ↑ פרסבל

פרוזדוגמא ↑ פרסטומא

פרוזדוגייאה ↑ פרסטיגיות

פרקולה ↓ פרקולא

פרקולה (written draft of) sentence, read by judge to the guilty party: *per<i>cul<um>* (+ fem term)

PRK 159a, 356_2: ללסטים (↑ **ליסטים**) שהוא נידון לפני הקוסטינר (↓). כל זמן שהוא מתריס הוא לוקה. הודה הוא נוטל פרקולה ..., It is like a robber who is being tried before the *quaestionarius*. As long as he opposes [him], he is flogged. [As soon as] he admits [his guilt], he receives the sentence ... ▽ א~. // YalkPs 854: **פרקילא**, ibidProv 961 ad fin, MachProv 28. 12, 76a: **פיקולא**, read: **פרקולא**. But partial // in MidPs 100. 2, 425 and // read: **ספיקולא** (↑).
PRK 159b, 357_9, 358_2: ללסטים (↑ **ליסטים**) שהוא נידון לפני הקוסטינר (↓). בתחילה הוא קורא אילוגין (↑) שלו, ואחר כך הוא מכה אותו, ואחר כך הוא נותן לו כמס (↑), ואחר כך נותן לו פרקולה ואחר כך יוצא ליהרג ... ואחר כך נותן להם פרקולה — "תאשם ישורון כי מרתה וגו'", Like a robber who was tried before a *quaestionarius*. At first he reads his *elogium*, then he flogs him, then he gives him the bridle-hook, then he gives him the sentence, and then he is led to execution ... And then He gives them the sentence — "Samaria shall become desolate for she hath rebelled ..." (Hos 14:1). ▽ א~, **פרגולא**. // YalkHos 532; MachHos 14. 2, JQRNS 15, 1924–25, 212: **פריקולא**, **פירקולא**.
MGEx 8. 11 (65_{19}) 123_3: (↑) **בשעת עקתיה עביד פרקולה, בשעת רווחיה עביד דימוס**, In time of distress he sentences [himself] (i e sees himself as guilty); in time of relief he pardons himself (sees himself as innocent).

Lieberman, JQRNS 35, 1944, 33–34. (Contra Buber, PRK 159a n47, emending to ספיקולא (↑) on basis of parallels etc; likewise Hoffmann, MGEx 65 n3, Fürst 159a, Krauss, LW 2, 407b–408a. On the other hand, SachsBeiträge 2, 181 n152, followed by PerlesES 89, suggests *proloquium*; AC 6, 448ab: *φραγέλλιον* (cf ↑ פרגל); Levy 4, 138b: *πρόκλησις*; Jastrow 1240b: *furcilla, furcula*.)
For *periculum* (*periclum*), see CodTheod 4. 17; Berger 627a.
The term ה~, א~, (fem or neut pl) may possibly be influenced by the similar sounding word ספיקולא (↑), *specula*. The form פרגולא (PRK 357_9, MsOxfNeubauer 2234–11) reflects the $\kappa > \gamma$ interchange; see Gignac 1, 77–80. Cf ↓ קטאדיקי.

Cf ↑ ספיקולא

פרקולה ↑ פרקילא

פרקטולין, פרקטילין, פרקלט ↓ פרקליט

פרקליט (496) (1) mediator, intercessor (2) advocate, attorney: *παράκλητ<ος>*

(1) MAvot 4. 11: העושה מצוה אחת קונה לו פרקליט אחד, He that performs one precept gets for himself one intercessor.
SifraTazri'a Perek 3. 14, 72b: חטאת דומה לפרקליט שנכנס לרצות, A sin-offering is like an intercessor who comes to appease. // BZev 7b.
TPea 4. 21, 61_{76}, 24_{31}: שהצדקה וגמילות חסדים שלום גדול ופרקליט גדול בין ישראל לאביהם שבשמים, For charity and righteousness are [cause of] great peace and a great mediator on behalf of Israel before their father in heaven. // BBB 10a.
ExR 18. 3: פרקליט טוב — זה משה, A good mediator – This is Moses.
YBer 4. 1, 7b 26: שני פרקליטין ליום, two intercessors a day. // PRK 61b, 120_7, PR 16, 84a.
PRK 191b, 427_8: שאין פרקליט טוב לירידת גשמים יותר מן הקרבנות, For there is no better intercessor for rain than the sacrifices. ▽ פרקלין, read: פרקליט. // PR 201a; EcclesR 7. 14.
YTaan 1. 1, 63c 42: הן באין פרקליטין למים, They come [as] intercessors for water.
(Gaon comment to) Mid to Cant, edMann, HUCA 14, 1929, 334_4: שאין לך פרקלט לפני המקום גדול הימנה, For there is no greater mediator before the Lord than her.
Ibid 335_{13}: שהיא היתה פרקלט של האומה בראש גלותן, For she was their mediator during their exile. Ibid line 15: תהוי להון פ[רק]ליט בראש גאולתן, He will be their mediator during their redemption.
Gaon Comment to Mid to Cant, edLerner, Koveẓ al Yad 8 (18), 1975, 160_{23}: כנגד שני פרקלטין [של ישראל] ..., like the two mediators [on behalf of Israel] ... (Perhaps under the influence of BShab 32a.)

(2) BShab 32a: שכל העולה לגרדום (↑ גרדון) לדון, אם יש לו פרקליטין גדולים, ניצול, For anyone who goes up to the *gradus* to be judged, if he has powerful advocates, he [may] be saved. ▽ MsOxf: פרקטילין. // Sheiltot, edEpstein, Tarbiz 7, 1935, $14_{48\ 49}$: פרקטולין (metath).

TrgJob 33:23: חד פרקליטא, advocate (Aram term), contrasted with קטיגורייא (↓ **קטיגוריא**); ibid 16:20: פרקליטיי (pl Aram form).

The two fragm of the Gaon comment to MidCant are from the same work (see Lerner ibid 143). See MM 485ab; ArndtGingrich 623b–624a; DeissmannLAE 336; EHatch, Essays in Biblical Greek, Oxford 1889, 82–83.

See also Worrel, ZfA 24, 1910, 94, where *Parāqlīṭōs* appears as a name of power in an Abyssinian magical text.

Syr: פרקליטא, פרקלוטא, פרקלטא, PnS 3299, 3251.
Lat: *paraclēta*, Souter 285a.

ק

קטאדיקי ↓ קאטריקוס, קאטיריקון, קאטריקום

קאלוריסין ↓ קאלוחסין

◇**קאלוריסין** (498) good buy: *καλὴ αἵρεσιν* (i e ~ις)

ExodR 43. 8: העבד הזה שאתה מוכר קאקגריסין הוא או קאלוחסין הוא? ... האיך לקחת אותי, בעבד טוב או בעבד רע?, This slave that you are selling is he a bad buy or a good buy? ... Did you buy me as a good slave or as a bad slave. Read with MsParis 187/15: קאלוריסין, (and **קאקיריסין** ↓). Perhaps we should read ... כעבד.

Krauss, LW 2, 498b, and LW 1, 273–74, however, his emendation to קאלוגריסין is to be rejected. *καλὴ αἵρεσις* appears in a papyrus from Ashkelon from 359 CE, discussing the sale of a slave (Wilcken, Hermes 19, 1884, 423), and there the phrase means *bona fide*, (LW 1 ibid). It further appears in Syr, in Land, Anecdot, leges saeculares 223 (Bruns-Sachau 31_7): אן נזבן גברא עבדא קאלא ארסיס, It is not infrequent in papyri; see Preisigke 1, 225 sv *αἵρεσις* 3: *καλῇ* (*και πιστῇ*) *αἱρέσει* etc. Thus *—αἵρεσις*, and not *—ἄρσις*, (contra Land ibid, PnS 395, cf Brockelm[2] 51a). Bruns-Sachau's emendation (ibid) to: קאלאפרסיס (followed by PnS and Brockelm) is unnecessary. Indeed, this emendation misled Perles, ZDMG 35, 1881, 140, to emend likewise in our text, and he was followed by Löw (LW 2, 498b), Fürst 188ab, AC 7, 53b–54a. Likewise one may reject the suggestions of Brüll, Jahrb 4, 1879, 117: *καλῆς σχέσεως*; Buxt 1847, followed by Levy 4, 232a: *καλοκἀγαθος*; Levy 1, 362b: *καλὸς ὅσιος*; and Jastrow 1306b, who reads: קאלואיתיסין: *καλοήθης*. As to the grammatical confusion — *καλη* (nom) *αἵρεσιν* (acc) —, this is probably because the two words were seen as one, as indeed the spelling attests, and given the common acc term. (Cf ↓ **קלסטרא** for a slightly different example of such grammatical confusion.) See Sperber, Sinai 93, 1983, 150—52.

Cf ↓ קאקיריסין

קאקיריסין ↓ קאקגריסין

◊**קאקיריסין** (499) bad sale: *κακὴ αἵρεσιν* (i e ∼*ις*)

ExodR 43. 8: העבד הזה שאתה מוכר קאקגריסין הוא או קאלוחסין הוא? ... האיך לקחת אותי, בעבד טוב או בעבד רע?, This slave that you are selling, is he a bad sale or a good sale? ... Did you buy me as a good slave or as a bad slave? Read with MsParis 187/15: קאקיריסין ▽ MsMunich 197. 1: קאקאריסין, (and **קאלוריסין** ↑).

Krauss, LW 2, 499a and LW 1, 273, referring to Syr: קקא ארסיס (PnS 3709, explained there as *κακὴ ἄρσις: pactum malum* = Bruns-Sachau 31_{13}, there unnecessarily emended to: קקא פרסיס). Also Bar-Bahlul 1829_{17}: קקי ארסי (read: ארסיס, PnS ibid). See ↑ **קאלוריסין** for full discussion. (Contra Perles, ZDMG 35, 1881, 140: קקי פרסין, following Bruns-Sachau; Buxt 1947, followed by Levy 4, 232a, Fleischer, apud Levy 1, 438a; Jastrow 1306b: קאקריסין: *κακοῦργος*; Brüll, Jahrb 4, 1879, 117: *κακοεργέτης* as alternative; Levy 1, 362b: *κακὸς χείριος*.)
For *κακὴ αἵρεσις*, cf Georgius Monachus, ed CdeBoor, Leipzig 1892, 802, 8: *ἐφ' ὧν ἡ κάκιστος αἵρεσις* (cited in Psaltes 188). As to the grammatical confusion of *κακὴ* (nom) and *αἵρεσιν* (acc), cf ↑ **קאלוריסין**. See Sperber, Sinai 92, 1983, 150—52.

Cf ↑ קאלוריסין and ↓ קקריסין

קומפרומיסין ↓ קוזמוטמוריסין

קרטיס ↓ קוטרס, קוטריס

קונטרוסון ↓ קויראנטריסין

קולר ↓ קולאר

קילה ↓ קולין

קולר (508) (1) neck-iron or collar (for slaves, prisoners of war and criminals) (2) figurative: (burden of) responsibility (3) transf: chain of men, gang, band: *κολλάρ<ιον>* ← *collar<e>*

(1) MGit 6. 5: בראשונה היו אומרין: היוצא בקולר ואמר: כתבו גט לאשתי, הרי אלו

... יכתבו, At first they use to say: He who went forth in a neck-iron and said, "Write a bill of divorce for my wife," they should write it. // MTevulYom 4. 5; BGit 13b; BBB 126b; BMen 30b; BḤul 75b.

Explained thus in YGit 12. 1, 41b 45: סוף דבר: בקולר של סכנה? אלא אפילו בקולר של ממון. שכל קולר בחזקת של סכנה, [Is the Mishna talking only] ultimately about a neck-iron of danger (i e imprisonment and punishment during the periods of persecution)? [No,] even a neck-iron for money [matters], (i e imprisonment for debt etc). For every neck-iron may be assumed to be dangerous (i e, for imprisonment in either count may be assumed to carry the danger of capital punishment).

BGit 65b: גניבא יוצא בקולר הוה, Geniva was one who went forth in a neck-iron, (i e had the status of one assumed to be subject to capital punishment).

BGit 7a: ונתנוה לגניבא בקולר, and Geniva was put in a neck-iron.

MKelim 12. 1: הקולר טמא, a neck-iron is [susceptible to] impurity.

TAZ 2. 4, 463_{19}: אין מוכרין להן ... ולא קולרין ולא שלשלאות של ברזל, One may not sell them ... nor neck-irons, nor fetters of iron. // BAZ 15b (pl).

SifNum 96, 96_{16}: אוסרם בזיקים ובקולרות, chain them in manacles and neck-irons (pl).

YMeg 3. 8, 74c 15: בניו מסורין בקולרין. איכן היא גבורתו?, His children are placed in neck-irons. Where is his power?! // YBer 7. 4, 11c 31; MidPs 19. 2, 164.

YNed 10 (9) 1, 41b 45: ... שהנודר כאילו נותן קולר על צוארו, For he who vows, it is as though he places a neck-iron on his [own] neck.

Ibid 146: לקוסטורי' (↓ קוסטריא) שהיתה עוברת, וראה קולר פנוי, והכניסה את ראשה לתוכה, Like a prison guard who was passing by saw a free prisoner's neck-iron, and placed his head in it.

PRK 113a, $231_{10\ 11}$: ... כת של בחורים שלולין בקולרין, a band of youths fettered in neck-irons ... // LamentRProem 34, 37, YalkJer 327. Partial // PR 29, 137a: היה נותן את הקולר על צוארו, he would put the neck-iron round his [own] neck.

TanḥGenVa-Yeshev 3: ... והיו חייבין לירד מכופתין בקולרין, and they were [actually] obliged to go down (to Egypt) chained in neck-irons ... // B ibid 18, 188: ... ראוין היו ישראל לירד למצרים בשלשלאות ובקולרין, The Israelites should have gone down to Egypt in chains and neck-irons; GenR 86. 2, 1052_3 in apparat: שלול בקולרין ▽ ובקולרין; AgBer 62 (61) 3, 122: שלולין בקולרין ▽ ibid 123 n11: בקולרין שלולין; YalkHos 5. 28: שלול בקולרין. (In the reading שלול בקולרין, קולרין is sing corresponding to κολλάρι<ο>ν.) (Cf // BShab 89b; MidPs 105. 5, 450; LTGen 39. 1, 196; YalkGen 145, 745_{70}, without our word.)

TanḥNumKedoshim 15: ... למי שנתון בקולר, Like one who is placed in a neck-iron.

TanhDeutShoftim 9: והקב״ה יושב ושולח עליהם מלאכים בקולרין ובשלשלאות, ומשליחן לתוך האור, and the Holy One blessed be He sits and sends upon them angels with neck-irons and chains and throws them into the furnace.
ExR 31. 10: הוציאו אותם השונאים בקולרין, The enemies led them forth in neck-irons.
ExR 36. 1: וכופתין אותן בקולרין, and they chain them in neck-irons. (Cf YalkJer 289.)
DeutR 6. 13: לגיבור שהיה הקולר בצוארו. נפנה מאותו קולר. לאחר ימים ראה הקולר נתון בצוארו של אחר. התחיל צווח ... אמר להן: ... אני יודע באיזה צער הוא נתון, Like a hero who had the neck-iron on his neck. He was released from that neck-iron. [A few] days later he saw the neck-iron placed on someone else's neck. He cried out ... He said to them: I know how muchpain he is suffering, // edLieberman 107.
EstR 3. 5 (to Est 1:9): ומשלשלן לקולרין, and chain them in neck-irons. // MidPs 10. 6, 95.
AgEst 3. 14, 37: ומהם השליח בקלורין, ומהם השליח בשלשלאות של ברזל, some of them he threw into neck-irons, and other of them he threw into fetters of iron. // AbbaGurion 3. 12, 31: בקולרין. (Not in // in EstR 7. 13; MidMegillatEst, in Horowitz, Aggudat Aggadot, Berlin 1881, 69, = BHM 6, 54.)
HechR (BatMid 1, 124): מיד נוטל הקב״ה שני קולרין של ברזל ומניחן על כתפו של משיח, Forthwith the Holy One blessed be He takes two metal neck-irons and places them on the shoulder of the Messiah. // PR 3b, 162a: מביאים קורות של ברזל ונותנים לו על צוארו, They bring beams of iron and place them on his neck. (Surely we should read: קולרות, instead of קורות; cf ibid 161b: עתידין להכניסך בעול של ברזל. Cf below on TBeza 3. 11 where we find קולר ▽ קורות.)
TrgY2Num 21:29: כפותין בקולרייא, chained in neck-irons (Aram pl term).
TrgEzek 19:9: ויהבוהי בקולרין (transl: בסוגר).
AgBer 64 (63) 1, 128: שהיו שלולין בקולרין, for they were chained in neck-irons.

(2) LamentR Proem 33, 36: ... על שהעביר קולר מצוארו ונתנו בצואר הרבים, because he removed the burden of responsibility from himself (lit: the neck-iron from his neck) and placed it upon the (lit: neck of the) masses ... // YTaan 4. 10, 69c 28: ושמט הקולר מצוארו ותלייו בצואר הרבים; EZ 9, 188; YalkKings 234.
BSanh 7b: עשרה שיושבין בדין, קולר תלוי בצואר כולן, Ten who sit in judgement, the burden of responsibility rests upon them all. // BHor 3b.
BSanh 44b: יהרג, ויהא קולר תלוי בצואר העדים, Let him be killed, and the responsibility will rest upon the witnesses.
B hevu 31a: מניין לדיין שיודע בדין שהוא מרומה, שלא יאמר: הואיל והעדים מעידין אחתכנו, ויהא קולר בצואר עדים? ..., Whence [do we know] that a judge who knows

that a case is fraudulent should not say [to himself]: I shall sentence, and the burden of responsibility will rest upon the witnesses ...

(3) TYev 14. 7, 53_{53}, 259_{20}: בקולאר של בני אדם, a band of people ▽ קולר. // BYev 122a (with addition).
BKid 72b: הוה אתי אליהו מפיק מינן צוורני צוורני, קולרין [קולרין], [Elijah] would come and send entire gangs and groups away from us. (See Rashi's reading ad loc for additional קולרין.)

On meaning (3) see PerlesBeiträge 13, suggesting: *καβαλλάριος* (= MGWJ 1892, 65). Rejected by Löw in LW 2, 508b. Krauss, TA 2, 666 n15, suggests *corolla*, which is equally unlikely. We have followed Jastrow 1329b, and Schlatter 69.
The word appears in two sing forms: קולר, the most usual form, and קולרין corresponding to *κολλάρι<ο>ν*. It has a masc and a fem pl form, in common with many words in Rabbinic Graecitas, see LW 1, 181–82 (and cf ↑ **סנהדרין**).
TBeza 3. 11, 296_{42}, 206_{11} *should be read:* **סואר של קורות**, and not קולר (cf TK 5, 979–80), and cf above PR 36, 162a where we suggest reading קולרות (?) instead of קורות.
DuCange 683: *κολλάριον collarium* (GlossGrLat). Cf Hesych, edLatte 2, 490_{24}.
Collarium, Maigne D'Arnis 536a; *colarium*, ibid 535a.

Syr: קולרא, PnS 3644.

קומפרומיסין ↓ קומטומוריסין, קומטומורוסין

קומנטריסים, קונטרוסון [קונטריסין] (509–10) officials in charge of public records, especially registrars in public prisons: *κο<μμε>νταρήσ<ιος>*, *κο<με>νταρίσ<ιος>* ← *commentariensis* (+ pl term)

The term appears in a number of different forms which have here been set out as follows: (1) קומנטריסים, (2) קונטרוסון.

(1) קומנטריסים
YYev 16. 4, 15d 22: מקמנטריסי המלך שמע: מת פלוני, נהרג פלוני, אין משיאין את אשתו, If he heared from the record-officials of the king that so-and-so had died, so-and-so had been killed, one does not permit the marriage of his wife. // BGit 28b, 29a: מקומנטריסים של גוים; TYev 14. 7: קונטרוסון (see below).

(2) קונטרוסון
TYev 14. 7, 53_{46}, 259_{15}: שמע בקונטרוסון של מלכים שהיו או[מרים]: פלוני בן פלוני מת או נהרג, לא תנשא אשתו ;read: בקונטריסין (or מ־), He heared at (or: from) the record-officials that they said: So-and-so the son of so-and-so died, or was killed, his wife may not (re)marry. ▽ MsErf: מקויראנטריסין (sic, not ~קור as in 259_{15}),

read: מקומנטריסין (see above). // BGit 28b, 29a: מקומנטריסים; YYev 16. 4, 15d 22: קמנטריסי (see above).

Lieberman, TK 6, 176; idem, Annuaire 7, 1939–44, 397 n12, explaining that these were officials in the *officium* of the proconsul in Caesarea, and at times served as executioners too, or superintended them. Cf PerlesES 133, LW 2, 510a. Berger 398b.
The "abbreviated" form קונטריסין finds its parallel in **קונטרסים** ↓: *co*<mme>*ntarius* (+ pl term). For such (partial) loss of syllable (partial haplography), see Mayser 1/1², 217–20; Gignac 1, 313. Note also that *commentarius* = *commentariensis* (Cypr Epist 81).

Cf ↓ **קונטרסים**

קומפרומיסין (510–11) (1) agreements of disputing parties to submit the controversy to arbitration (2) agreement, covenant, mutual promise: *κομπρόμισ*<*ο*>*ν* ← *compromiss*<*um*>

(1) YMK 3. 3, 82 a42: ושטרי בירורין — ר' יוחנן אמר: קומפרומיסין, Or deeds of arbitration (cf MBM 1. 8) – R. Yoḥanan said: agreements to submit to arbitration. ▽ edConst: קונפרומוסין.

(2) LevR 6. 5, 137_5: אמר ר' יוחנן: קופראמסאות נתנו ביניהן, שאינו כופר בהן והן אינן כופרין בו, Said R. Yoḥanan: They made a covenant between them, that he would not deny them and they would not deny him. ▽ קופרא מסאות, קופר אמסאות, קופרמסאות, או' דקמסיות (↑ **אורקמסיא**). // MGDeut 9. 16, 179_7: אורקמסיות (↑ **אורקמסיא**).
MGGen 30. 25, $540_{6\ 8}$: בעת שהקב"ה אומר לאומות העולם: בואו ודינו עם בני ועשו קופרומיסין, וכן הוא אומר "קרבו ריבכם יאמר ה', הגישו עצמותיכם יאמר מלך ישראל (יעקב — במקרא)". והן אומרין לפני הקב"ה: רבון העולמים, מי עושה קופרומיסין על ישראל? והקב"ה אומר להן: אני. וכן הוא אומר "נורא אלקים ממקדשיך, [קל ישראל הוא נותן עז ותעצמות לעם ...]", At the time when the Holy One blessed be He says to the nations of the world: Come and dispute your cause with My children, and make a mutual agreement. And so it says, "Produce your cause, saith the Lord; bring forth your strong reasons, saith the king of Israel (Jacob, in MT)" (Is 41:21). And they say before the Holy One blessed be He: Who forces the agreement on Israel? And the Holy One blessed be He replies to them: I. And so it says, "O God, Thou art terrible out of Thy holy places. [The God of Israel is He that gives strength and power to his people]" (Ps 68:36). ▽ קפרומיסין, קופדומיסין. // MidPs 20. 3, 174: מי יבוא בדין עם ישראל קוזמוטמוריסין; perhaps supply: [ויעשו] קוזמוטמוריסין, Who will come and dispute with Israel and make an agreement; YalkPs 680: "הגישו עצמותיכם", קומטומורוסין של בני עשו. והם אומרים:

מי עושה קומטומוריסין של ישראל?, "Bring forth your strong reasons," the agreement on the part of the sons of Esau. And they reply: Who will make the agreement on the part of Israel? And they reply: Who will make the agreement on the part of Israel? In both cases read: קומפרומיסין (?).

On MidPs 20. 3 and YalkPs 680, see LW 2, 510a; SachsBeiträge 2, 179; Levy 4, 265a; AC 7, 122a, all emending to קומנטריסין; *commentarius*, here "pleas". (cf ↓ **קונטריסים**): Jastrow 1332b, on the other hand, suggests emending to: קומנטרובוסין: *controversiae*, controversies, arguments. However, in view of the clear readings in the // MGGen 30. 25, perhaps we should read: קומפרומיסין, or possibly: קומפרומיסירין: *κομπρομισι<ά>ρι<ο>ν*, DuCange 701 = *κομπρόμισον*. I have transl: עושה ק׳ על ... in MG ibid "to force", in which case the verse cited from Ps 68:36 "O Lord, thou art terrible" etc, is apposite, in that it describes the power with which God forces His will on Israel. Or perhaps לעשות ק׳ על means "to guarantee the agreement", in which case the second half of the verse, "is He that gives strength etc.," was in the homilist's mind. (First suggestion more likely.) The issue remains somewhat problematic.

We note a variety of forms of this word: ~ין (masc pl term), ~יות, ~אות (fem pl term). קומ~, קונ~ (see LW 1, 112 for M > N interchange, and CGL 2, 111_{97}: *compromissum*), קופ~ (LW ibid 127 for omission of M).
On LevR 6. 5, see LiebermanGH 6. For first meaning (1), see Berger 401b. For meaning (2) see DuCange 701 sv *κομπρομισιάριον*: *eadem notione*, in GlossBasil. *συνταγὴ* ... *συνταγή* (in pl) is a covenant or agreement, eg Iamb (IV CE) VP 31. 185. This is clearly a secondary and derivative meaning. See also Souter 66: *compromissum*, "that which is the subject of a mutual promise". The Gk is, of course, derived from the Lat.
See further Taubenschlag[2] 402–03, and Modrzejewski, JJP 6, 1952, 239–56.

Cf ↑ **אורקומסיא**

קונטרסים ↑ קונאטירסין

קומנטריסים ↑ קומטרוסון

קונטרס document, memorandum, or sheet of paper: *co<mme>ntari<u>s* (?)

YalkPs 749: משל למי שמבקש לעלות לבימה (↑). נטל קונטרס חלק ונתן לדיין, It is like unto a person who wished to go before the tribunal. He took a blank document (or sheet of paper) and gave it to the judge. // (More correctly, source): MidPs 45. 5, 271: קרטס: *χάρτης* (*charta*), sheet of paper.

Or perhaps from mediaeval: קונטרס, (possibly substituted by editor of Yalkut), from Lat *quinternus*, meaning a quire of five sheets (ten leaves). See MBeit-Arié, Hebrew codicology, Paris 1976, 44–45 n77, (citing Ben Ḥayyim, Ivrit ve-Aramit Nusaḥ Shomron I, 1957. Heb sect 99 n36; already in

ANeubauer, Les écrivains juifs français du XIVe siècle, 1893, 95). (Contra Krauss, LW 2, 510a.)

Cf ↓ קרטיס, קונטרסים

קונטרסים (510) public register, records kept in offices of higher magistrates about their official activities: *co<mme>ntari<u>s* (+ pl term)

SifNum 134, 180_{21}: אדם שנתון בקונטרסים של מלכות, אפילו נותן ממון הרבה, אי אפשר ליעקר, A man who is registered in the imperial records, even if he pays out much money (in bribes), it is impossible [for him] to have himself removed [from the records]. ▽ בקונאטירסין, בקונאטרסין. // MachIs 44. 22, 1. 148_{18}: בקונטראסין; MGExod 30. 12, 649_{1}: קפגטרסין, ▽ קפטריסין, read: ק[ו]מנטריסין.

KraussMT 5/1, 160 no380. See Berger 398b.

Cf ↑ קומנטריסים, ↑ קונטרס

קייסטור, קוסטינר ↓ קוסטור

קוסטינר ↓ קוסטינור, קוסטינוס

קוסטינר (514) (1) torturer in court for extracting admission from the accused (2) executioner: *κυ<αι>στι<ω>νάρ<ιος>* ← *quaestionarius*

(1) PRK 159a, 356_{1}: ללסטים (↑ **ליסטים**) שהיה נידון לפני הקוסטינר, Like a bandit who was being judged before a *quaestionarius*. ▽ קוסטינאר. // YalkPs 854; ibidProv 961 ad fin; MachProv 28. 12, 76a: קוסטינור, read: ~נר.
PRK 159b, 357_{8}: same phrase. // YalkHos 532; MachHos 14. 2, JQRNS 15, 1924–25, 212.
PRK 164a, 371_{5}: ללסטים (↑ **ליסטים**) שברח מפני הקיסטינר, Like a bandit who ran away from the *quaestionarius*. ▽ קוסטינר // EcclesR 11. 9; YalkEccles 989.
MidPs 10. 5, 94 according to MsParis 142 and edVenice: הקוסט(י)נר שהיה מכה ומסיר צלע וחוליה בבת אחת, The *quaestionarius*, who would flog and dislocate a rib and a vertebra at the same time. ▽ קיסטור (= *quaestor* ↓ **קייסטור**). // MachPs 10. 16, 1. 62: הקיסטינר; YalkPs 650: הקיסטור, corrected in late edd to הקוסטינר.
Yelamd to Deut 1:1, apud Ar (AC 7, 145a), GrünhutLikkutim 5, 87b: ולקיסטינרין, *quaestionarii* (pl).

(2) NumR 1. 11: כאדם האומר לקוסטינר: סב רישיה דפלן, Like a man who says to the executioner: Take so and so's head [off].
PR 10. 38a: שמעו הקוסטינרי׳ ונטלוהו לחתוך את ראשו, The executioners heared, and

took him away to cut off his head. ▽ הקוסטברי, קוסטנרין, קוסטנרוס, read ~רים (?) (pl).

DeutR 2. 29: בא הקוסטנר ליתן את החרב על צוארו ... אלא שקהת החרב מצוארו ונהפכת על הקוסטנר, The executioner came to put the sword on his neck ... but the sword rebounded off his neck onto the executioner. // YalkEx 167 (165) $30_{32\ 34\ 35}$: קוסטנר, קסטינרו, ▽ קסטיגור, קוסטיגור (influenced by *castigo?*); MidPs 4. 3, 40; MachPs 4. 6, 1. 28; CantR 7. 5; YBer 9. 1, 12 (13)a 34–35: קוסנתירו, קוסנתר (metath) (sic edprinc), ▽ MsVat: קוינטנר, MsSirilio: קיוסנטרו, קוסטינר; TanḥDeut, apud GinzbergGS $115_{5\ 8}$. (Our word not in // in ExR 1. 31.)

MidPs 6. 3, 59: משל למלך שהיה לו שני קוסטנדין רעים ... פעם אחת סרחה עליו מדינה, והיה קורא לקוסטנדין; read: ~רין, It is like unto a king who had two evil executioners ... Once a city rebelled against him, and he appointed the executioners [as governors over the city]. ▽ קוסטנרין. // YalkPs 635; MachPs 6. 6, 1. 38: קוסטנרין.

LTCant 1. 3, 14: ... שבא הקוסנטור בימי מלכות הרשעה ... להרוג את רשב״ג, For the executioner came in the days of the evil Empire (= Rome) ... to kill R Simeon b Gamaliel ... Read: קוסטונר. ▽ קוסטנוס, Schechter, JQR 8, 1895, 315 = Aggadat Shir ha-Shirim 99, = MidCant, edGrünhut 49b; read: קוסטנור. (Cf partial // Grünhut ibid 3b: קוסטור: *quaestor*. See below.)

MidCant, edGrünhut 6b, edWertheimer 21: הקוסטניר, והקוסטינר. // BHM 6, 29–30 (from MidAsseret Harugei Malchut); Massechet Kalla edHigger $161–62_{72}$ in apparat: קסטינר, וקסטינרו. (This is actually a continuation of the preceding text.)

LamentR 2. 1, 98: שלשה דברים משמש אותו המלאך: ספקלטור (↑) וכהן גדול וקייסטור (קייסטור ↓) ... וקייסטור, כד״א ״וקסת הסופר במתניו״, That angel served in three capacities: as an executioner, and as a high priest, and as a *quaestor* ... As a *quaestor*, as it is written, "with the writer's inkhorn by his side" (Ezek 9:2). ▽ edprinc etc: קסנטור; Ar (AC 7, 89b): קייסטור. // YalkEzek 349 modern edd: קסנטור, but edprinc: קריסטור, read: קויסטור. But reading: קסנטור perhaps to be read: קסטונר (metath). (See below.)

Cf MV 325: מלמד שמסרו לקוסטינר שלו, פי׳ לממונה על חייבי הריגה ותרין מלאכי חבלה קיימין לקבלי. בקוסטנירי וגוזלי.

On LamentR 2. 1, see LiebermanGH 142, who reads: קייסטור (↓) or: קויסטור in all cases, explaining: *quaestor*, executioner, or more exactly the judge who condemns to death (since it cannot be identical to the ↑ ספקלטור), ref to Mart 7. 32. 7, where the *quaestor* is found in this capacity. Nonetheless, perhaps קסנטור should be emended to קוסטונר (as in LTCant 1. 3,14, above), *quaestionarius* (?). See Schlatter 68–69. Sophocles 694b, executioner (Lyd 140. 13); Souter 337b, torturer etc, (CIL 2, 4156, 3. 12401, 8. 20251, IV CE onwards); DuCange 674:

On *qu~* in Gk transliteration see Gignac 1, 225–26. (Note that LW 2, 543b sv קלוסנטרין, 545b sv

קליסנטרי, and 549ab sv קלסטרא, seem to have nothing to do with our word, despite AC 7, 106ab). So Fürst 199a.

Syr: קסטונרא, PnS 3543 sv קונעא, ibid 3675; BB 1815.
Cf ↓ קלצטונירי, קלסטרא, קייסטור

קוסטינר ↑ קוסטנר, קוסטניר, קוסטנוס, קוסטנדין

קוסטריא [קוסטדיא] (515) prison guard: *κουστωδιά* ← *custodia*

AgBer 23, 48: משל למלך שנכנס למדינה ... וקוסטריא נכנס אחריו ... המלך נכנס לפלטין שלו ... וקוסטריא בפילקי (↑ פילקי), It is like unto a king who entered the city ... and the prison guard entered after him ... The king goes into his palace ... and the prison guard into the prison. Read: קוסטדיא.
YNed 10 (9) 1, 41b 45: לקסטורי' שהיתה עוברת וראה קולר (↑) פנוי והכניסה את ראשה לתוכה, Like a prison guard who was passing by and saw a free prisoner's neck-iron (i e chain round the neck) and placed his head into it. Read: קסטודייה.

The use of the fem in YNed 9. 1 suggests the more primary meaning of (the fem) *custodia*, a guard composed of a group of soldiers. However, the context of the passage demands that an individual is being spoken of.
The Gk is, of course, a Lat loanword. See OLD 478c sv *custodia* 5. See further MM356b; ArndtGingrich 448a; Lampe 773b; DuCange 744.
Further Gk forms: *κοστωδία*, PO 94. 20 (22 CE); *κωστωδία* PPar 68A. 8, BG 11 1. 341. 3 (II CE).

Syr: קוסטודיא, PnS 3549.

קוסטינר ↑ קוסנתר, קוסנתיר, קוסנטור

קומפרומיסין ↑ קופרוסימא, קופרומיסין, קופראמסאות

קרטיס ↓ קורטא

קוריוסיס ↓ קוריוסי

◇**קוריוסיס [קוריוסוס]** (519–20) spying informant of an official nature: *κουριῶσος* ← *curiosus*

YelamdLev 16 (apud BatMid 1. 168): קוריוסיס אמר: אם יהיה אדם עשיר יהא הקוריוסיס עושה דינו. ואם לאו, הרי ההגמון ..., The *curiosus* (?) said: If a man be rich, let the *curiosus* judge him. If not, let the *hēgemon* ... Read: (ה)קוריוסוס.

Pl: קורסיות, קיריוסים, קוריוסי

PR 3, 10b: קוריוסי הושיב בפלטרין. כיון שהרגישו ביעקב שחולה, באו והודיעו ליוסף, He placed spies (*curiosi*) in the palace. When they became aware that Jacob was sick, they came and informed Joseph.
Ibid 8, 29: כשם שלמלכי בשר ודם יש קיריוסים הם מודיעים למלך כל דבר ודבר, כך יש לפני הקב"ה קיריוסים ומגידים כל דבר ודבר שאדם עושה במטמוניות בחשך בגלוי. ואלו הן הקיריוסי של הקב"ה — זו הנפש שמגדת ..., Just as kings of flesh and blood have informants who inform the king of every single thing, so too there are such informants before the Holy One blessed be He, and they tell Him everything that a man does in secret places, in the dark [as] in the open. And these are the informants of the Holy One blessed be He — it is the soul which informs ...
MidSam 25. 2, 122: ... שהיה דוד משלח קורסיות לאחריו לידע, For David was wont to send spies after him to find out ... Perhaps read קוריסיות. // YalkPs 765: קוסדריות = *quaestores* (LW 2, 515a, sv קוסטר, ↓ **קייסטור**).

YelamdLev 16 is a problematic text, since the *curiosus* does not usually act in a judicial capacity. Perhaps this text should be emended to read: הקוריליס, the *curiales*, or דיקוריונים, *decuriones*, members of a municipal council in the later Empire. (On the scribal habit of putting the *yod* in the *dalet*, so that *dalet yod* became *heh*, see LiebermanGH 115 n30, ↑ **סנסן**.)
Other ref cited in LW 2, 519b–520a do not belong under this heading. Thus בקורסין in AbbaGurion 1. 12, 16 and //) is to be read בקורסרין, *cursores* (see Zuntz, JSS 1, 1956, 138), and LevR 32. 2, 739 in Mss: יש קול קריאסות (and //) should be explained by the word *καιρός*, see editor's remarks ad loc.

SachsBeiträge 1, 10; Fürst 195b–196ab; Böhmer, Keẓad Maarichin 55; Krauss MT 5/1, 161 no382; AC 7, 200a.
See also Berger 422a sv *curiosi*, and 356b sv *agentes in rebus*. They were a class of police officers, attested from the IV CE onwards, charged with control of the *cursus publicus* (state post), and were called *curiosi*, in allusion to their inquisitive activities.
See further JTriantaphyllopoulos, *Κουρίωσος*, Atti dell' XI Congr Intern di Papir, Milan 1966, 249–59, ref to PVindob Sijpesteijn n22 (cited by Modrzejewski, APF 26, 1978, 180).
κουριῶσος, Lampe 773b, Sophocles; *κουριοσσὸς*, (*κυριοσσὸς*), DuCange 738.

קוריוסים ↑ קורסיות

קטאדיקי ↓ קטאדיקוס

קטאדיקי (524) (1) sentence (2) fine of individual (3) public fine, ie kind of extraordinary tax: *καταδίκη*

(1) YelamdLev 24:10, apud Ar (AC 7, 78b): נתתי קטדיקי על מצרים, I brought sentence (i e punishment) on Egypt. // YalkJer 285: קרטקי, read: קטדקי.

(2) YelamdEx 7:8, apud MannBible 1, 98_{13}: הרי הוא ניתן בבית האסורים, הרי נותנים עליו קטאדיקי, Behold he is placed in prison, behold they place upon him a fine.

ExR 11. 2: לא יטול פלוני בטאריקי זו, שפלוני פטרונו (‡ פטרון) עומד עליהן, So and so will not receive this fine, for such and such, his *patronus*, looks after them. Read: כטאדיקי (?) or קטאדקי.

YelamdEx 7:8—9, apud Mann 1, 98_{13}: נותנין עליו קטאדיקי, they punish him.

ExR 30. 11: קטאדיקי ... (‡) נתן קטדיקי לקרטיס, He gave the fine to the judge ... ▽ (AC 7, 79a): קטריקי, read: קטדיקי.

DeutR 3. 14: לתת עליך קטריקי, ... to fine you ... Read: קטדיקי.

PRK 39a, 72_3: קאטריקו. ▽ קאטריקי, קטריקי; read: ~דיקי. // PR 14, 64a: קטריקי, read: ~דיקי.

PR 10, 41a: מהו קטריקי שלו? "כסף ישקול כמהר הבתולות", What is his fine? "He shall pay money according to the dowry of virgins" (Ex 22:16).

LevR 18. 5, 411_5: בשר ודם גובה קטאדיקי, והק[ב"ה] גובה קטאדיקי — "וענשו אותו מאה כסף", Flesh and blood claim [their] fine, and the Holy One [blessed be He] claims [His] fine — "And they shall amerce him in a hundred *shekels* of silver" (Deut 22:19). ▽ קטדיקי, קטאריקי, קטריקי, קטירקי, קטאריקין (= *καταδίκην*, acc?). MsMunich 117 adds to following gloss: פי' עונש. // YalkLev 567 (571): קטריקי, read: ~דיקי; NumR 7. 3: יש לו קטריקס, read: קטדיקס (= *καταδίκης*, gen? contra LW 2, 573a).

(3) MidPs 17. 3, 126: ... המלך ... אם יתן קטיריקי במדינה, The king ..., if he places a tax on a city ... ▽ קטרגין, קטריגין, קטריניו, read: קטדיקי(ן) (= *καταδίκη(ν)*, acc; cf LW 2,527a).

NumR 9. 1: משל לארכיקיטין (לארכיטקטין) קטאדיקוס על אותה מדינה. התחילו בני המדינה מטמינים כספם וזהבם לתוך המטמונים, It is like unto an architect, [and a] tax [was] placed on the city. The citizens of the city began hiding their silver and gold in hiding places. Read: ... יצא קטדיקוס על // TanḥNumNaso 5 edprinc: ... לארפיטקטון קאטריקום ; later edd (Mantua 1563 onwards) added: שהיה קאטריקוס; TanḥBibid 8, 20: יצא קטריקון על אותה מדינה, ▽ קאטריקוס, קטאדיקוס, קאשי קס; YalkJer 305: יצא קאטריקון ... (~ס); Yelamd, apud Ar (AC 7, 78b), GrünhutLikkutim 4, 8b: קטדיקי.

קטאדיקי of the Yelamd seems to be the most easily acceptable reading. Possibly קטדיקוס, with its different variations should be read ~קיס, gen (see LW 1, 69—70). Or perhaps a form קטדיקס (acc pl, see LW 1, 71—72) developed mistakenly into ~קוס, (ibid n2). However, at some stage קטדיקוס was thought to be a person who deals with the קטדיקי, so that the reading שהיה קאטריקוס evolved. This also by comparison with the partial // in GenR 24:1, 229_4: היה גביי (טימיון) (// YalkIs 426; MidPs 14. 1, 112).

PRK 72_3 is not to be emended to קרטגני (as Buber would have it 39a n168; LW 2, 524a). The meaning is that the red heiffer is a form of fine (homily on Num 19:2).
On קטדיקוס in NumR 9. 1 and //, see LW 2, 573a, suggesting we read קאטוליקוס; *καθολικός*, here "supervisor of accounts" = *procurator a rationibus*; reject.
On ExR 11. 2, we suggested the form כטאריקי as possibility; this in view of the frequent ק > כ interchange in Rabbinic transliteration, (LW 1, 5, 31–32). See also PerlesBeiträge 34, (contra de LaraKK, and Levy 2, 132a: *ταραχή*).
The form קטריגין reflects the κ > γ interchange (cf ↑ **אגדיקוס, אגבה בסטס, אגבאסטס**, cf LW 1, 5, 33). See, eg, *δίγης* (for *δίκης*) in PVindobWorp 10. 8 (143/4 CE), etc; Gignac 1, 79–80.
We note a variety of forms, some legitimate and some merely the result of scribal error. Legitimate forms are: קטדיקי, קטדיקין (~*κην* acc), קטדיקס (~*κας*, acc pl), ~קוס and ~קון (~*κος* and ~*κον*)? Mistaken forms: קטריקי, בטאריקי. (We have not noted here the various positions of the *aleph*.) This קטאדיקי is to be distinguished from קטדיקי: *κατάδικοι*.
See also MM326a

Syr: קטדיקא, קאטאדיקא, קטידיקא, קטאדיקי, PnS 3573; קטדיקס, Brockelm[2] 657b; and cf קטדיקו, BB 1760.
Cf ↓ קטידיקון

קטפורס ↓ קטאפורס

◇קטבלטון (524) payment of debt (to make up for deficiency in revenues): **καταβλητόν*

NumR 4. 8: ... נמצא אותו שולחני חייב קטבלטון. אמר המלך: מי שיורש מקומו יפרע מה שהוא חייב, That money-changer was found owing "revenue debts". Said the king: He who inherits his position will [have to] pay up what he owes.

Levy 4, 279a; AC 7, 78a; LW 2 524a, to which Löw agrees in his index 665b. (Contra Jastrow 1346a, emending to: קטבלימטין: *καταβλήματα*, with Aram pl term, transl "proceeds of taxes". Note *προσκαταβλήματα* in D 24. 97. 98, meaning: sums paid in addition to make up deficiency in revenue.) **καταβλητόν* is a form unattested in Gk sources, and the meaning found here is similarly unattested (cf LSJ[9] 885a; LSJSupple 79b).
On the whole passage, see Ziegler 152.

קטיגוריא ↓ קטגוריא

קטיגור (524) accuser, prosecutor: *κατήγωρ*

Frequently coupled with **סניגור** ↑: attorney for the defence.

MAvot 4:11: העובר עבירה אחת, קונה לו קטיגור אחת, He that commits one transgression, gets for himself one prosecutor. ▽ קטגור.

BRH 26a: (↑) אין קטיגור נעשה סניגור, A prosecutor cannot serve as an attorney for the defence // BBer 49a; YYoma 7. 3, 44b 43; PRK Buber 177b; YRH 3. 6, 58d 21; MGLev 16. 4,, 466_2 (not clear whether // with independent formulation, or from independent but similar source).

LevR 21. 10, 490_3: שלא יעשה סניגור קטיגור, Let not the prosecutor become the attorney for the defence, (partial // to YYoma 7. 3, 44b 43 above).

BḤag 13b: קטיגור יעשה סניגור?, Will the prosecutor serve for the defence? // BKid 5a; Mann, HUCA 14, 1939, 342_{17}: קתיגור.

YSuk 3. 1, 53c 16: אי לזה שנעשה סניגורו קטיגורו, Woe is he whose defence becomes his prosecutor. // LevR 30. 6, 704_2; PRK 182b, 412_2; MidPs 26. 5, 218; TanḥLevEmor 18, B ibid 26, 98; Yalk ibid 651; MGLev 23. 40, 656_{20}.

PRE 46, 111b: והקב"ה שמע עתירתן של ישראל מקטיגור שלהם, And the Holy One blessed be He heared the entreaties of Israel from their accuser. // MV 382.

YalkCant 990: ... עלה קטיגורו, his prosecutor arose ... (And so too in late edd of LevR 19. 2, 420_4 and CantR 5. 11, on basis of Yalk and Matnot Kehunah. But in Mss and CantR edprinc: עלה וקיטרגו cf ↓ **קטרג**.)

ExR 18. 5: מיכאל וסמאל דומין לסניגור (↑ **סניגור**) וקטיגור עומדין בדין. זה מדבר וזה מדבר. גמר זה דבריו, ידע הסניגור שנצח, והתחיל משבח את הדיין שיוציא איפופסין (**אפופסיס** ↑). ביקש אותו קטיגור להוסיף דבר אמר לו הסניגור: החרש, ונשמע מן הדייך, Michael and Samael are like an attorney for the defence and a prosecutor [that] stand in court. The one speaks and the other speaks. The one concludes his case and the other one likewise. [Then] the defence attorney knew he had won, and began praising the judge so that he should give the verdict. The prosecutor wished to add a point. Said the defence attorney to him: Be silent, and let us listen to the judge.

Ibid 43. 1: למלך שהיה דן את בנו, והיה הקטיגור עומד ומקטרג (↓ **קטרג**). מה עשה הפדגוג שלבן? כיון שראה אותו מחייב, דחף את הקטיגור ועמד לו במקומו, מלמד על הבן סניגוריא (↑), Like a king who was judging his son, and the prosecutor was standing and accusing. What did the son's tutor do? As soon as he saw that he was [about to] declare [him] guilty, he pushed away the prosecutor and stood in his place to plead the son's defence.

Pl:

PRK 53b–54a, $102_{10\ 12}$: ... העמידו בימה (↑), ויעמדו סניגורין, Set up a tribunal, and let the defence attorneys stand forth ... // PR 15, 77a; MidPs 81. 6, 367; YalkEx 190, $123_{46\ 48}$; ibidPs 831; MGEx 12. 1, $169_{6\ 8}$. But // MachPs 81. 18, 2. 50 reads: והעמידו סניגורון (↑ **סניגרון**) וקטיגרון, where קטיגרון: *κατήγορον* (acc), just as סניגורון: *συνήγορον*.

PR 40, 168b: אתה יושב בדין ודן וקטיגורים עומדים לפניך, You sit in judgement and judge, and the prosecutors stand before you. Ibid 167b: קטיגורים.
MidPs 8. 2, 75: הייתם קטיגורין ביני לבין ישראל, You were accusers between Myself and Israel. ▽ קטיגטין, קטיגורתין; read: קטיגורין.
TrgJob 33:23: מלאכא חדא פרקליטא (↑ פרקליט) מן בני אלף קטיגורייא, one single angel is an advocate out of one thousand accusers, (Aram pl term), (transl: מלאך אחד מיני אלף).

Concerning MachPs 81. 18, 2. 50, the hapax קטיגרון, though undoubtedly a secondary reading compared to the primary קטיגורין found in the (mainly earlier) //, is not a corrupt, but surely denotes *κατήγορον*, parallelling in that text the סניג(ו)רון (↑): *συνήγορον*.
Common in early and later Rabbinic literature, eg MV 325 etc. From it is formed the verb קטרג ↓.
κατήγωρ in Rev 12:10 (and PMagLond 124. 25, IV/V CE) is not a Heb adaptation of *κατήγορος*, but a Gk "vulgarism", formed in the same way as *ῥήτωρ*, (starting from the fact that the gen pl is *κατηγόρων*, whether the word belongs to the second or third declension). See DeissmannLAE, 93–94; MM 337b; Psaltes 175; ArndtGingrich 424b with bibl. See also NLewis, JJP 9/10, 1956, 118–225.

Syr: קטגרנא, PnS 3595.
Cf ↑ סניגור, ↓ קטיגוריא, קטרג

קטיגוריא (יה~) (524–25) (1) charge, accusation (2) Accusation (personified): *κατηγορία*

(1) BKet 112b: דור שבן דוד בא, קטיגוריא בתלמידי חכמים, [In] the generation when the Son of David comes (i e the Messianic era), there will be accusation [levelled] at the scholars (ie ill will and hatred). // YalkIs 409; MachIs 6. 13, 59_4: קטגוריא; (THG 269, 137 = OhGKet 374: קרטיגיניא, קרטיגיא!; Response of Ri Megash 40: קטגריא).
GenR 31. 5, 279_6: הגיע קץ קטיגוריה שלהם, the end of their charge has arrived. ▽ יא~, קטיגורי׳, (whence mistakenly) קטיגורים, read: יה~. // YalkGen 51, 175_{11}: הגיע קטיגוריא שלהם, their charge has arrived; LTGen 6. 13, 38.
ExR 15. 29: שנים עומדים בפני המלך. אחד מלמד קטיגוריא שלו, ואחד סניגוריא (↑) שלו לא כל המלמד קטיגוריא מלמד סניגוריא ..., Two men standing before the king. One prosecutes and one pleads his defence. Not all who prosecute plead defence ...
TanḥLevMeẓora 2: קטיגוריא של נוב, the charge of Nov.
Ibid Kedoshim 12: לשון קטיגור (sic edprinc), read: קטיגור׳ = קטיגוריא, a formula of accusation.
ARN I 2, 10: באותה שעה היו מלאכי השרת קושרין קטיגור על משה ..., read: קטיגור[יה], At that hour the angels conspired to [level] charges against (or speak ill of) Moses.

PR 40, 168b: אילו אומרים זכות, ואילו אומרים קטיגורים, read קטיגוריה, These speak well, and these speak ill (lit: a charge). (The reading ~ים is influenced by קטיגורים, pl of קטיגור (↑) above in same line.)
PRK 164a, 370_{10}: דלא יתעביד סניגוריא (↑) קטיגוריא, that the defence should not turn into prosecution.
LevR 19. 2, 422_3 in apparat.: היה אלף קורא קטיגור לפני הקב"ה, read: קטיגור[יה], And [the letter] *aleph* raised accusation before the Holy One blessed be He.

(2) LamentR 1. 13: באותה שעה קפצה קטיגוריא לפני כסא הכבוד, At that hour Accusation jumped up before the seat of holiness. (Note edBuber 76 has: מדת הדין, the aspect of stern judgement.)
TanḥLevTazria 9: נכנסה קטיגוריא לפני הקב"ה, Accusation entered before the Holy One blessed be He.

MM 337ab; ArndtGingrich 424b. (For a slightly different meaning and strangely rare usage in patristic Gk, see Lampe 732a.)

Syr: קטגוריא etc, PnS 3594; (קטרוגין, Schulthess 178b).
Cf ↑ **קטיגור, סניגוריא**

קטיגרון ↑ קטיגור

קטידיקון [קטדיקין] (524) those having judgement given against them, condemned persons: *κατάδικ*<*οι*> (+ pl term)

Abba Gurion 1. 12, 16: קטידיקון של אבא לא נדונו ערומים, Those condemned by my father were not executed naked. Read: קטדיקין. ▽ (Buber ad loc n229): קטדיקי, קטריקי read: קטדיקי: *κατάδικοι* (pl). MsCant 33: אנדידיקי: *ἀντίδικοι* (cf ↑ **אנטידיקוס**). // LTEst 1. 12, 92: המחוייבים לו; EstR 1. 12: אנדיתיקוס, read: אנטידיקי, cf ↑ **אנטידיקוס.**

This hapax is a derivative from קטאדיקי.
For *oi* as *yod*, see LW 1, 22, and cf Gignac 1, 265–66 (on *oi* > *η*).

Cf ↑ **קטאדיקי, אנטידיקוס**

קטיריקי ↑ קטאדיקי

◇**קטפורס** (526) lashes, flogging (as punishment): *καταφοράς* (acc pl)

ExR 30. 7: לשנים שעלו לבימה (↑) לידון ... אותו שזרק אבן באיקונין של שר לקח ה'

קטפורס (read: לקה), Two who came up before the tribunal for judgement ... The one who had thrown a stone at the prince's image was flogged with five lashes.
LevR 18. 5, 411_4: בשר ודם נותן קטאפורס והק[ב"ה] נותן קטפורס, "ארבעים יכנו", Flesh and blood give lashes, and the Holy [One blessed be He] gives lashes – "forty stripes he may give him" (Deut 25:3). // NumR 7. 3: קטפירס; read: קטפורס; YalkLev 567: קטפרס.
PRK 81b, $179_{3\ 4}$: עשר קטפרס אתה לוקה, you will be flogged with ten lashes.
▽ קטאפראה: καταφορά (+ Aram pl term). // YalkEx 225 ad fin. (// in MechBe-Shallaḥ 1, 86: מכות, TanḥBExBeshallaḥ 8, 57: מגלבין, cf above p 20.)

καταφοράς is literally translated "downward strokes of the whip." The specific meaning "lashes, as a punishment," seems to be peculiar to Rabbinic Graecitas. I have not found it in Gk lexicon. See LSJ[9] 919b sv καταφορά 2. For Lat *cataphora, catafora*, with slightly different meanings, see Souter 42b.
מטרופס in LW 2, 333ab has nothing to do with our word, contra Fraenkel ibid). See Epstein, Tarbiz 1/2, 1930, 124–25, ACSup 252b–253a, from Pehlevi, (contra all explanations cited in LW ibid, and add: F. Perles, MGWJ 76, 1932, 291: μετάπορος, punisher).

Syr: קאטאפורס, Brockelm[2] 661b.

קטפורס ↑ קטפרס, קטפירס

[0]קטרג (526–27) denounce, prosecute; deriv verb formed by metath from קטיגור corresponding to: *κατηγόρεω*

YShab 2. 6, 5b 8: מכאן שאין השטן מקטרג אלא בשעת סכנה, From here [we know] that the Satan does not denounce but in times of danger. // ibid lines 13, 16, 18, 20.
YSheb 2. 6, 5b 23: ... בשלש מקומות השטן מצוי לקטרג, In three places the Satan is wont to denounce ... // EcclesR 3. 2.
YSanh 17 (10) 1, 27d 22: ... בשעה שהיה הנביא בא לקטרגו, when the prophet came to denounce him ...
YSanh 9 (2) 6, 20c 39: ומי קטרגו? אמר ריב"ל: יו"ד שב"ירבה", And who denounced him. Said R Joshua ben Levi, the *yod* in "yarbeh" (= "[neither] shall he multiply", Deut 17:17). // LevR 19. 2, 420_4; CantR 5. 11. (Cf partial // without our word in ExR 6. 1; TanḥExVa-Era 5; B ibid 2, 18; AgBer 76 (75) 2, 146.)
GenR 49. 14, 515_9: והקטיגור (↑ קטיגור). ▽ והמקטרג, and he that brought foreward charges, i e the prosecutor.
TanḥGenVa-Yigash 1: שהיוצא לדרך השטן מקטרגו, for he who goes off on a

journey the Satan [seeks to] denounce him (i e he is prone to danger, to the Satan's denunciation).
TanḥLevKedoshim 5: ... בשעה שאדם מבקש לקטרג את חבירו, when a person wishes to denounce his fellow ...
TanḥLevKedoshim 12: ... אני הייתי מלמד עליכם סניגוריא (↑). האיך עשיתם אותי לקטרג עליכם?, I used to defend you. How did you force me to denounce you?
PRK 108b, 221_{12}: שיהא לי פתחון פה לקטרג לשרי אומות העולם, so that I have an excuse to prosecute against the princes of the nations of the world. ▽ לקטרוג (noun), an excuse for prosecution against ...
PRK 180a, 406_{8}: לפי שישראל ושרי אומות העולם ניכנסין ומקטרגין לפני הקב"ה בראש השנה ..., For Israel and the princes of the nations of the world enter and denounce [one another] before the Holy One blessed be He on Rosh ha-Shanah (New Year's day). // EstR 7. 12 (to 3:8); YalkEst 1055.
MidPs 55. 1, 290: ... לא היה לדוד אוהב יותר מאחיתופל, והיה בעל מקטרגין שלו, David had no greater friend than Aḥitophel, and he was his denunciator ... ▽ מקטרותיו, later edd: בעל מחלוקתו [emend].
MidPs 57. 4, 298: והיה יצרו מקטרגו, and his inclination would denounce (or perhaps in the sense of: rebuke) him.
MidPs 81. 5, 367: ... כל המקטריגים, מקטרגים ... , ... All the prosecutors, prosecuting ...
PR 10, 38b: מלאכי חבלה באים ומקטריגים אותו, injurious angels come and prosecute him.
ExR 31. 11: ... כשהיה השטן מקטרג, when the Satan denounced ...
ExR 43. 1: והיה הקטיגור (↑ קטיגור) עומד ומקטרג, and the prosecutor stood up and prosecuted.
TrgPsJNum 29: 1: ... למערבבא סטנא אתי למקטרגא לכון, to confuse the Satan who comes to denounce you ...
TrgJob 37:20: ארום יקטרג ... (transl: יבולע).

Very common in all periods of Rabbinic Hebrew.
בעל מקטרגין in MidPs 57. 4 seems to be some kind of specialized, or idiomatic, term.
See Lieberman, Sefer ... Alon 233 n26 (ref to Yalon, Mavo le-Nikkud ha-Mishna 176 et seq) on מיקטרג, called to court, prosecuted. Cf Hesych, edLatte 1, 467_{45}: *διωκόμενον· κατηγορούμενον.*
The form לקטרוג (noun) in PRK (108b) 221_{12}, in MsOxf Neub 151 (1) seems to be secondary to לקטרג (verb), since the noun is not found till the mediaeval period, (see e g BenIehuda 12, 5900). The Oxf Ms was completed 1291.

Syr: קטגר, PnS 3596, Schulthess 178b.
Cf ↑ קטיגוריא, קטיגור

קטאדיקי ↑ קטריקס

קרטיס ↓ קטריס

לו קיבוסת ↑ קיבוסת

◇**קייסטור** (515) judge, in a criminal case (with the right to condemn to death): *κυαισίτωρ* ← *quaesitor*, or: *κυαίστωρ* ← *quaestor*

LamentR 2. 1, 98: שלש דברים היה משמש אותו מלאך: ספקלטור (↑) וכהן גדול וקייסטור ..., וקייסטור, כד"א "וקסת הסופר במתניו", That angel served in three capacities: as an executioner, and as a high priest, and as a judge ... As a judge, as it is written, "with the inkhorn by his side" (Ezek 9:2) (i e as the judicial official who writes the verdict, death sentence). ▽ edprinc etc: קסנטור (cf ↑ **קוסטינר**); Ar (AC 7, 89b): קייסטור. // YalkEzek 349 modern edd: קסנטור, but edprinc: קריסטור, read: קויסטור.

AC 7, 89b, and Levy 4, 299a, sv קייסטור: *quaesitor*, who distinguishes this word from קסדור, ibid 143b and 344b, sv קסדור, which he explains as *quaestor*.
For *quaesitor* see OLD 1533c–1534a sv *quaesitor* 1; Berger 662b, sv *quaesitor*; Sophocles 694b: *κυαισίτωρ*; DuCange 674: *κοιαισίτωρ*. The *quaesitor* is equated with the *quaestionarius* in CGL 5, 140_{29}, 238_5. Perhaps, hence variant readings קייסטור — קסנטור = קסטונר (metath).
However, LiebermanGH 142 n9 reads: קייסטור (~קוי) = *quaestor* throughout. He finds in Mart 7. 37. 2 evidence of the *quaestor* dealing the death sentence: Nostri mortiferum quaestoris ... signum? See ibid 142–47 for a detailed discussion. Perhaps this is the *quaestor sacri palati*; see Berger 664a, and cf OLD 1534c sv *quaestor* 1 & 2. The **ספר** in Ezek ibid is seen as a *γραμματεύς*, being a high official (see Deismann Bible Studies, Edinburgh 1901, 110–112).
According to the above this is just a specialized meaning of קוסטר: *quaestor*, see LW 2, 515a sv, (which, however, needs much correction). The *quaestor* is equated with the *inquisitor* in CGL 4, 383_9. However, there two very similar terms are often difficult to separate. See, eg, CGL 5, $238_{7,9}$.
Jastrow 1327 sv קויסטור explains as *quaestor* in sense of chancellor (a non judicial position); cf ibid 1336a sv קוסדור.

Syr: קוסטרא: *quaestor*, PnS 3676; קואסטור, Brockelm[2] 655b.
Cf ↑ **קוסטינר**

קילה ↓ קיל

◇**קילה** (503, 529) (1) chamber, cubicle (2) prostitute's cubicle (3) cell, in a prison: *κέλλα* ← *cella*

(1) GenR 31. 9, 281_9: קילין ומדורין, chambers and compartments (pl, transl: **קינים** in Gen 6:14, meaning "rooms"). // Trg1Gen 6:14: קולין.

Ibid 31. 11, 283_7: ש"ל קילים היו בה, Three hundred and thirty chambers (or cubicles) were in it (the ark). ▽ ק~ין, קולין, קילוס (the latter an obvious corrupt under influence of קילוס, see LW 2, 547—48 sv קלס III).
Ibid 284_1 (continues preceding text): הקילה עשר אמות על עשר, each chamber was ten cubits by ten. ▽ הקיל, קיל, קול, כל קיל וקיל. // Yalk 53, 178_{26}—179_{30}: קיל, קילין; MGGen 6. 14, 159_{10}: קילין; ibid (considerably developed) 160_1—161_9 (from Ar, AC 7, 93b—94a): קילה, קיל, קילין.

(2) SifNum 131, 170_{21}: ... ובנו להם קילין ... והושיבו שם נשים מוכרות ..., and they built them cubicles (for prostitution), ... and placed women in them to sell ... ▽ קולין, מקולין (corrupt, under influence of *macellum*, LW 2, 349, slaughter-house or meat market). // TrgYNum 24:25: ... ואקים ית בנתהון דמדיינאי בקולין, and he (Balaam) set up the daughters of the Midianites in cubicles; MGNum 25. 25, 435_{17}: קילין; but ibid 436_6: קלעים, tents (in market), following BSanh 106a: קלעים; so too NumR 20. 23; YalkNum 77: קעילין, curtained enclosures; YSanh 11 (17), 28d 6: קנקלין (LW 2, 555b, cf ↓ קנקנים).
Trg1YNum 25:8 (apud Ar, AC 7, 101a sv קליינון): לגו קלא, into the (prostitute's) cubicle, (transl: הקובה, tent).

(3) CantR to Cant 8:13 (according to edprinc): למלך שכעס על עבדיו וחבשן בבית קילין, Like a king who was angered with his servants, and imprisoned them in the jail-house (lit: house of cells). ▽ modern edd: קולין.

(1) See LW 2, 503b sv קולא III, and ibid 529b sv קיל, and 555b sv קנקלין (which Löw ad loc sees as *cella* too, but cf ↓ קנקנים). So too LevyTrgWb 2, 350a sv קולא II, where the etym (*καλία*) is rejected by Fleischer (575b, and again apud Levy 4, 480ab). He (following Buxt 2025) sees קילא as deriving directly from *κέλλα, κελλίον*. (He refers further to Dozy, Supplement au dictionnaires arabes 2, 401b, and Sitzungsberichte der KSächsGesdWissJ, 1885, 47. Further comments by Löw, LW 2, 503b—504a, and again 529b.)

(2) Krauss, LW 2, 503b sv קולא III. Note the variety of // traditions (and corrupt) on the Balaam story.
For the specific meaning of prostitute's cubicle, see OLD 295c sv cella 3c. See further Schlatter 66—67 (which, however, needs correcting).
On TrgNum 25:8, see AC 7, 101a sv קליינון and cf LW 2, 505b—505a sv קוליין, with Löw's (correct) note ad loc. See further PnS 3634: קליתא.
See RHillel to Sifre Balak, edKoleditzky, Jerusalem 1948, 120: קילין, לשון יון הוא שקורין ללשכה קילון.
(3) See Krauss LW 2, 503ab sv קולא II, and Levy 4, 260a sv קולא, who suggested *κλοιός*, neck-iron. But this was rightly rejected by Löw (ad loc), who refers one to קולא III ibid, *κέλλα*, cella. See further AC 7, 95a sv קלא, ibid 90 n4.
קילין here may also be sing, *κελλι<ό>ν* (eg *κελὶν*, IGLS 2072), the compound with בית being: the house of the [prison] cell, like בית הסהר, prison, in Gen 39:20. (Cf compounds with in BenIehuda 1, 535—37.)

The specific meaning of prison-cell is perhaps (?) unattested in class lit. *κέλλα, ~ίον, cella,* frequently means monastic cell in Patristic lit (see Lampe 741a; DuCange 629–30; Souter 45a), from which, via Aram to Arab (Löw, apud LW 2, 529b; Vollers, ZDMG 51, 1897, 315).
The above gives some indication as to how much confusion there is in the lexica about this word and some others closely homonymic. (Note LW 2, 503–04 lists four entries under **קולא**, and in 521–30 קיל and קילא.)

Some general remarks: The form: **קולא** shows the *ε* > *υ* interchange; see LW 1, 87 (and cf ↑ **פרנה**), Gignac 1, 274. Eg, *δύσμας* (for *δέσμας*), PRyl 135. 11 (34 CE), *ὐλέου* (for *ἐλαίου*) OOslo 16. 1 (III cent CE). (Cf Mayser 1/1[2], 46 and 80.)
Lat *cella* perhaps related to Gk *καλία*, hut (Skt: *śāla*); see OLD 295b.

Syr: קילא, PnS 3602; קלא, 3622; קליתא, 3634.
Cf ↓ **קנקנים**

◇קילוון (542) I ordered, I decreed: <*ἐ*>*κέλευον*

GenR 63. 8, 688$_8$: **אנא קילוון**, I ordered. ▽ קליין, קילון, קלוון, קיליוון. // YalkGen 110. 519$_6$: קלוון; Ar (AC 7, 98a): קלוון. But // in LevR 22. 5, 578$_2$: קלוונין, קלוואנין. ▽ קלונין; EcclesR 2. 20: קל וונין, sic edprinc. Perhaps to be emended: קלוואון. ▽ ed Hirshman line 270: **אנא** קילוואן, קילוונין. (Not in later reworkings of this text in TanḥLevKedoshim 8, B ibid 8, 76; MGLev 14. 20, 240 = GasterMaasiyot XXVI, 19; YalkLev 615.)

LiebermanGH 6. (Contra LW 2, 542b, suggesting *κελεύων*.) However, the form קלוונין with its variations remains problematic. See also ↓ **קילווסים**, where a form קילווני' is cited from PR 10, 38a. It should further be noted that a group of Mss (MsAdler, commentary to GenR, edprinc) has: **אנא** יהיב קילוון, showing that קילוון is (or was thought to be) a noun. I have not suggested **אנא** קילוון to be read as one word, *ἐνεκέλευον*, from *ἐγκελεύω*, since the meaning "to order" is apparently unattested for this word in later Gk. On the other hand, *ἐγκέλευσις*, meaning "command", is found in Patristic and Byz sources.
As to קיל~ — *κελ~*, see LW 1, 16–17, (Gignac 1, 249–51), that *epsilon* is frequently interchanged with *iota-yod*. Cf ↑ **קילה**.

Cf ↓ **קילווסים**

קילוון ↑, קילווני' ↓ קילווסים

קילווסין ↓ קילווסים

◇קילווסים (usually written ~ים), (~ין) (542) (royal) command, order decree: *κέλευσις*, *~ιν* (acc sing term)

YNed 12. 4, 41c 34: נפקת קלווסים מן מלכא, an order went forth from the king. Read: ~סים.

GenR 5. 3: נלך ונעשה קיליפסין של הקב"ה, Let us go and carry out the commands of the Holy One blessed be He. ▽ קלוסין, קלווסין (acc sing term), קילוסי', קלפסים, read: ~סים (nom). // YalkPs 848: נעשה קלוסים להקב"ה, read: קלוסים של הקב"ה. (Partial // in PR add 1, 182b: היו רוצים לעשות גזירת קונם, They wished to carry out the decree of their Creator.)

LevR 7. 6, 161_1: ... נומוס (↑ נימוס) הוא וקילוסין הוא, It is the law and the decree ... ▽ וקילוסים, וקלוסים, וקלוסין, read: ~סים, וקילוסך, read: ~סין. // YalkLev 480: קילוסין; MachZach 2. 9, 21; ibidPs 73. 21, 2. 5: קלוגין, read: קלוסין.

LevR 37. 2, 860_2 according to MsMunich 117: קילווסים. (Printed ed has: כרוזא.)

LamentR Proem 5, 6: ... בשעה שהפלתי קלסים על אומות העולם להגלותם, When I cast down upon the nations of the world a decree to exile them ... Read ~יס. ▽ MsBM 27089: קלבסים. // YalkEzek 363: קלווסין; Ar (AC 7, 97a): קלבסים, read: ~יס.

Ibid 1. 5, 69: בגין דעברת על קילווסים דידי, because you transgressed my command. ▽ printed ed: קלוונין, read: ~סין. (Cf ↑ **קילון**.)

Ibid 5. 5, 155: אפיק קלווסין, issued a decree. ▽ Ar (AC 7, 98a): קילופסין. (Printed ed: פקיד ואמר.)

TanḥBGenVa-Yera 14, 93: מיד ירדו ועשו קילווסין של בוראן, Forthwith they descended and carried out the orders of their Creator. (Tanḥ ibid 9: ועשו שליחות בוראן, sic edprinc.)

Ibid Mi-Keẓ 4, 191: קלווסים אחת אני מוציא עליכם ואתם נהרגים, I issue one command against you, and you are killed. Read: ~יס.

PanimAḥerim (to Est) II. 3, 66: מה ראית שאתה מבטל קילוותו של מלך?, read: קילווסין, For what reason do you transgress the order of the king? // YalkEst 1054: קלבסים, read: ~יס.

Ibid 69: קלווסין שנכתבו (read: שנכתבה) הסיעו אותה לכל האיגרות בשביל שיפרשו אותה בכל המדינות, The decree which was written, they transferred it to all the documents, so that they should be promulgated (lit displayed) in all the cities. (Note how the acc sing term ~ין, which looks like a Sem pl, has been confused with the pl. Hence, שנכתבו [pl] despite אותה [sing].)

PR 10. 38a: א"ל המלך: והאיך אני עושה, שכבר הוצאתי קילווני' עליו שישאו את ראשו, ויתלו אותו, Said the king to him: How shall I act. For I have already issued an order that they should raise his head and hang him. Read: קילווסי'. ▽ edprinc (Prague 1656): קילווסי'. (However see ↑ **קילון**.)

Ibid: ונמצא קלווסים שלך קיימת, and thus will your order be carried out. Read: ~יס.

PR 10, 38a: יכולה קילוילוסיו שלך קיימת, ובנך במקומו ואינו ניזוק, Your order can be kept, and your son may [still] remain safe in his place. Read: קילוילוסין.

The reading in PR 10, 38a is not to be further emended (contra ed ad loc, and lexica), but is an example of dittography. See Mayser 1/1², 219–20, eg: CairZen 59323. 13 (249a): ἐπικαλ[αλ]ούμενον, and cf LW 1, 196–71 (which however requires some correction). For further discussion of this phenomenon cf ↑ **אילוגין**. On ~קיל = κελ~ see below.
On LamentR Proem 5, 6, reject Eisler's suggestion (apud Buber ad loc n7): λοκος? (λόχος?). However, the suggestion that we emend to: קלירסים: κλῆρος (+ pl term), i e lots, should be considered despite the evidence of the readings, since the root נפל (in Hiph. cast) is connected with "lots" (Est 3:7), but not with "commands". (Suggestion of Buxt 2033, followed by SachsBeiträge 1, 162; Fürst 203b; Levy 4, 305b–306a; AC 7, 97a; LW 2, 545b, and again in ACSup 362b. On "casting" lots, see CTKraemer, Excavations at Nessana 3, New Jersey 1958, 68–69.)
On PanimAḥerim II. 3, 69: בשביל שיפרשו אותה בכל המדינות, see Lieberman, JQRNS 35, 1944, 7 n40, that פרס, פרש is a technical term for the promulgation of an edict. Cf ↑ **דיאטגמא**.

The word is frequently found with ~ים, ~ין term, because it was thought to be a pl. Thus ~יס was mistakenly read ~ים, and the alternative ~ין term was sometimes substituted. For a similar such case, cf ↓ **קרטיסים**, usually written קרטיסים, or ~ן, and ↑ **ליסטים**.
Note the many variations in the transcription of ευ: ו, וו, יו, ב, פ, פי; LW 1, 23–24. The alternating forms ~קל, ~קיל, represent the differing ways of transcribing the *epsilon*, often transcribed with a *yod*; see LW 1, 16–17, and cf Gignac 1, 249–51. For the alternative acc sing term, ~ין, cf ↑ **אפופסיס, גרדון, סניגרון, קטיגרון**, ↓ **קרטיסים**. [Note that the root קלס, to praise (LW 2, 547a–548b sv קלס III), is not formed out of κελεῦσαι, as Krauss suggested, but probably from κάλος, καλῶς. See Löw apud Krauss, LW 2, 548a, citing Brockelm² 323; but cf Brockelm² 669a; ACSup 363b, with bibl. Cf Bacher, Terminologie 2, 190: καλῶς; Bevan, Noeldeke Festschr 581 Sem root; DeSolaPool, The Kaddish, Leipzig 1909, 59. And, most recently, Lieberman, Alei Ayin, 75–81, κάλος.] The form קלוסין noted above may be under the influence of the root קלס.

Cf ↑ קילוון

קילווסיס ↑ קיליוסיס, קילופסין, קילוסין, קילוילוסין, קילוותו

קילה ↑ קילין, קילים

קילווסיס ↑ קיליפסין

קמוניא ↓ קימוניא

קינדינון, as in עמד בקינדינון, stood trial, (idiomatic; lit: stood in danger): *κίνδυνον* (acc sing term)

Sefer ha-Maasim, edLewin, Tarbiẓ 1/1, 1929, 93: ... ועשה דברים רעים, ונתפש

(sic) ‏לרשות השלטון, ועמד בקינדינון, ונדון בפרודום (↑פרודום) והודה‏, ... and he committed evil crimes, and was arrested before the governor, and stood trial (literally: in danger), and was tried with interrogation, and pleaded guilty.

Epstein, ad loc n2; Lieberman, Eshkolot 3, 1959, 88 n79, that this is the equivalent of the Lat *periculum*: trial, or judgement, (cf ↑ **פריקולא**). (On the reading: והודה, and not: יהודה, see SHKook, Tarbiẓ 2, 1930, 119.)
Cf GenRabbati 116$_7$: קינדוקוס; read with ḤofesMatmonim 42 (apparat): קינדונוס: *κίνδυνος*, danger (Fürst 215b).
The term is not found in classical Rabbinic sources, and probably belongs to the later Byzantine linguistic stratum, hence found in the Sefer ha-Maasim lit (cf ↑ **פרודום**).

קוסטינר ↑ קיסטינר

קוריוסים ↑ קיריוסים, קיריוסי

קילה ↑ קלא

קילווסים ↑ קלוקין, ~ין, קלבסים

קילון, קילווסים ↑ קלווניך, קלוון

קילווסים ↑ קלווסן, קלווסין, קלווסים

קלסטרא ↓ קלוסטר

קלסטרא ↓ קלוסנטרין

קילווסים ↑ קלוסים

קולרין ↑ קלורין

קילוון ↑ קליון

קלסטרא ↓ קלסטא

קלצטונירי ↓ קלסטנירו

קלסטרא (549) tormentor, executioner: *κολαστήρ*

BSanh 104b, according to Ar (AC 7, 106a): כמדומין אנו שאדונינו בן קלסתרא של מלך, It appears to us that our master is the son of the king's executioner. ▽ Ar ibid catchword: קלסטרא, MsMunich קלסטא (see RabbinoviczVL 319). Not in printed edd.

MGGen 27. 3, 468_1: אמרו שהיה קלוסטר אחד נידון לפני הגמון באותה שעה, They said that an executioner was being sentenced by the governor at the same time. ▽ קלסטר, קלצטר. (Cf partial // in SifDeut 307, 346: פילוסופוס; so too YalkDeut 942.)

The form קלסטא in MsMunich perhaps corresponds to *καλεστ<ής>* = *κλητήρ* (= *κῆρυξ*), envoy, herald (cf LSJ[9] 866a). The *aleph* at the end, טרא~, may be an Aram term.

LW 2, 549ab; Levy, REJ 11, 1885, 207.

קלוסנתרין in Trg1Est 2:21: תרין קלוסנתרין (ref to: סריסי המלך); AbbaGurion 2. 21, 20: קלוסנטרון ▽ קלוספטרון, קלונסנטרין; YalkEst 1053: קלוסטרין; EstR 6. 13: קלסריקין (קון~ in edprinc) (cf AC 8 Add 73: *κλεισουράρχης*?); RabbinowitzGM 167_{15}: קלסריקין, has been related to our word and explained as pl of *κολαστήρ*. Thus Levy, TrgWb 2, 365a; idem 4, 315a; AC 7, 106b. Krauss, however, in LW 2, 543b explains as *καλάσιρις*, (on the etym of which see now Czerný, Coptic Etymological Dictionary 329, cf Crum 813b, from Egyptian *kri-sri, g'l'syr*, warrior, kind of soldier, see bibl ibid). Brüll, Jahrb 5, 1883, 122: *quaesitor*; Löw, apud Krauss LW 2 ibid, follows Fleischer apud LevyTrgWb 2, 576a: Syr: קסטונרא: *quaestionarius*. However, Buber, AbbaGurion ad loc n53: *καλος* (!) *σενατωρες* (*senatores*), which makes good sense in the context. First suggested by DeLaraID 81. (On *σενάτωρ* see Sophocles 984a; DuCange 1352; TDrew-Bear, Glotta 50, 1972, 219–20.) Note reading קלוספטרון in ▽ to AbbaGurion: *καλὸς πάτρων* (*patronus*, cf ↑ **פטרון**). קלינסנטרין ibid would correspond to *καλον* (acc) *σενάτωρ* + pl term, where the grammar is not so strictly adhered to. (Cf ↑ **קאלוחסך, קאקגריסין**: *καλὴ* and *κακὴ αἵρεσιν*!) Cf MV 314 (in name of LevR, but not in our edd): פנטיר הוגנים, read: סנטיר הוגנים: *σενάτωρ εὐγενής* (contra LW 2, 600b sv אפנטי). *καλοι σενατωρες* makes a suitable contrast to: הברברי הזה "this barbarian", in the continuation of the text.

As to: קלסריקין שהן שומרי הסף, in EstR 6. 13, this seems to be another word (**καλασιρικ<ος>* + pl term?). At any rate, all this seems to have nothing to do with *κολαστήρ*.

Cf ↓ **קלצטונירי**

קילווסיס ↑ קלסים

◇**קלצטונירי** (545) tormentor, executioner: **κολαστ<ι>οναρ<ιος>*?

BAZ 18a: ר' חנינא בן תרדיון וקלצטונירי מזומנין לחיי עולם הבא, R Ḥanina ben Taradion and his torturer are summoned to the World to Come. ▽ MsJTS: **קלסטונירי**, in marg: קלסטינר (explained as: [שר] הטבחים, [chief] executioner], קליסטנרי, קלסטינריה, קלסטינר (see RabbinoviczVL 44). // MGGen 27. 3, 468_6: קלסטנירו. ▽ קלסטרינך.

See Krauss LW 1, 142: *κολαστήρ*; and cf ibid 109 for σ > צ (in στ); AC 7, 106ab; Levy 4, 315a.

(Contra Krauss LW 2, 545b: *quaestionarius*, and so too Jastrow 1381b, following PerlesES 135, who also cites DeLara's suggestion: *καλός + senator! Cf* ↑ קלסטרא. But DeLaraID 81 ref to קלוסנתורין, cf LW 2, 543b.) This form may be influenced by *quaestionar<ius>*: cf ↑ **קוסטינר**. The ~*arius* term was very popular in the later Roman period; see the remarks of ACameron, AJP 52, 1931, 234.

Cf ↑ קלסטרא

קלסריקין, קלסתרא ↑ קלסטרא

קמומיא (531–32) Gemoniae, steps on the Aventine hill in Rome down which bodies of criminals were dragged to the Tiber after execution: *Gemoniae* (sc *scalae*)

BAZ 10b: כל דזכי למלכא שדו ליה לקמוניא חלילא, Anyone who bests the Emperor (in an argument), they pitch him down to the Geminae (steps). ▽ Ar (AC 7, 121b): קימוניא; MsJTS 10a 4 corrects: לקמונינותא to לקמוניא (see Abramson ibid 149a).

LW ibid; AC 7, 121b. (Contra Jastrow 1384: *καμίνιον*, furnace.) Not to be confused with קמוניא = קמוליא; *κιμωλία*, cimolian soil, (LW 2, 531b sv קימוליא).
On g > k, see LW 1, 100, and cf Gignac 1, 77–80; eg, *καμβροῦ* (for *γαμβροῦ*) PApoll 41.5 (708–9 CE), *πρᾶκμα* (for *πρᾶγμα*) PMichael 126. 15 (538 CE).
For ref in Lat lit, see OLD 757b sv.

קמיסמסין ↑ גמיקון

קמנטריסי ↑ קומנטרטיסים

קנטיאון punisher, executioner: **κεντεων* (from *κεντέω*) (?)

MachPs 50. 22, l. 275: אמר הקב"ה: אם יבא מלאך המות ויאמר לי, למה נבראתי? אני אומר לו: קנטיאון בראתיך לאומות העולם, Said the Holy One blessed be He: If the Angel of Death comes and says to Me: Why did you create me? I [will] tell him: I created you [to serve as] an-instrument-of-punishment for the nations of the world. // ExR 51. 18: סטטיונר (↑).

// in ExR 51. 18: סטטיונר (↑), for which reason Buber (MachPs ad loc) emended our word accordingly. However, the emendation seems unnecessary, as Hesych, edLatte 2, 460$_{27}$, has: *κεντήματα ζημιώματα*. Hence **κεντεων*: punisher, executioner, (literally: stabber). Cf *ζημιωτής*: executioner, Eust. 1833. 53.

◇קנקנים [= קנקלים] latticed screens, barriers (in law court): *καγκέλλ<ον>* ← *cancelli* (+ pl term)

GenR 73. 8, 926_4: הוי רואה עצמך כאילו אתה נתון לפנים משבעה קנקנים ויושב ודן, ואני נדון לפניך, Consider yourself as though you are sitting in judgement behind seven *cancelli,* and I am being tried before you. ▽ קנקלים, קנקילים, קנקינוס, קינקלין. // YalkGen 133, 669_{54}: קלקלין; (partial //) STovGer 33. 17, 186: קנקולין.

LamentR 1. 31, 67: ... נסבוניה ויהבוניה לנו מן שבעה קנקלין, והוון שאילין ליה, They (the Roman soldiers) took him (R. Yoḥanan b. Zakhai) and placed him within seven *cancelli,* and interrogated him ... ▽ edBuber 67: לפנים מז׳ בתים clearly an emend.

Lieberman, JQR 35, 1944, 19, explains that in the first text the defendant has been tried within the *cancelli* and *vela.* (The number seven is typological, and partly determined by the context. Cf LamentR 1. 9, 72: שצלם גדול היה שם נתון לפנים משבעה קנקנים, a large idol was there, placed within seven *cancelli,* etc.) This corresponds to the regular procedure of the IV CE (Mommsen, Römisches Strafrecht, 1899, 359, 362; Berger 693ab sv *secretarium*). The second text also reflects IV CE procedure, where the questioning takes place within the *secretarium.*

קנקן = קנקל, the L > N interchange being extremely common; LW 1, 99, Gignac 1, 109 etc. קנקל derives from *κάγκελον* ← *cancellus,* (as does the Arm *kankeln*) and not from Gk *κιγκλίς* (LW 2, 534a, following Brockelmann, ZDMG 47, 1893, 30; Hübschm 173). However, the terms *κάγκελον* and *κιγκλίς* are so close in form and meaning that they were frequently confused with one another. Thus LSJ[9] 950b, Lampe 753a explain *κιγκλίς* as latticed partition in *δικαστήριον,* law court. Whereas LSJ[9] 848a sv *κάγκελος* = *cancelli, κάγκελον τοῦ δικαστηρίου,* bar. (See also LSJSupple 76a: *καγκέλλιον, ~λιν,* VI CE; Lampe 681a; DuCange 530, etc.) Because of these similarities they were confused in Rabb parlance (LW 2, 534a, Löw's remark). Hence ▽ קינקלין, obviously: *κιγκλί<ς>* (+ pl term), etc. They were also confused in the lexica, (LW 2, 533b; AC 7, 138b; Jatrow 1394a; Levy 4, 341b). On the relationship between these two words, see J & LRobert, REG 79, 1966, 363, and ibid 77, 1964, 200, for the exact meaning of *κιγκλίς.* ACameron, AJP 52, 1931, 235, remarks that *cancelli* had a remarkable popularity in Gk, for which there is no obvious explanation (and cf ibid 240).
As to the ▽ קנקינוס = קנקילוס, in the OxfMs, perhaps this should be simply emended to ~נים, or is it an acc pl, reflecting the Lat phrase *intra cancellos* (?).
The word is very common in Rabb lit (LW 2, 533b), where it appears in a variety of forms (some influenced by *κιγκλίς,* see above), meaning any type of (latticed) barrier. (Note: קנקלין in YShev 2. 8, 34a is *κάλυκιν,* dim of *καλύξ,* LiebermanTK 2, 502, and has nothing to do with our word.) This, then, is a specialized meaning of the word.

Arm: *kankeln,* Brockelmann, ZDMG 47, 1893, 30; Thumb, BZ 9, 1900, 435.
Syr: קנקלא (קינקלא), PnS 3671, BB 1812; קונקלא, Brockelm[2] 679a.
Cf ↑ וילון, פסליון

קוסטריא ↑ קסטור[י]יה]

קנטרסים ↑ קפגטרסין

ספקלטור ↑ קפיקליטור

קקריסין according to court ruling: *κὰ κρίσιν*, partial haplography for *κα[τὰ] κρίσιν*

DeutR 3. 2, edLieberman 84, and MsMunich apud Buber, Likkutim VII: לא תהא סבורין שאני עושה אתכם כעבד שאדונו מבקש למכור אותו קקריסין, בכל מה שמוצא, Do not think that I am treating you as does a master who wishes to sell his slave according to court ruling, for whatever he finds. ▽ in printed edd: קוריסין, read: קקריסין, or perhaps ק[ק]יריסין, where **κιρισιν* is an example of anaptyxis. // MachAmos 4. 12, 35: קקריסין.

Lieberman ad loc nא, (ref to Dig 21. 1. 17. 12). According to him, this word has nothing to do with Syr: קקא ארסיס, perhaps found in ExodR 43. 8: קאקיריסין (↑), despite similarity of form, (hence, contra LW 2, 520b sv קוריסין, and ibid 449a sv קאקגריסין). On *κὰ* for *κατὰ*, see Gignac 1, 313; eg: *κὰ* (for *κατὰ*) *καιρόν*, PMichael 41. 47 (539–54 CE). Note also CGL 3, 538_7: kadike (= *καταδικη*) *condamnatio*.
On anaptyxis, Gignac see ibid 311–12; eg: *χαριτίνων* (for *χαρτίνων*) BL iii, 29 (240–41), *πυριγισκῳ* (for *πυργίσγῳ*) PO 912. 24 (III CE). The disappearance of one *qof* in the readings in printed edd may be an example of haplography, see ibid, 313.

קרטיס ↓ קרדום

קרטוס [קרטיס] (568) judge: *κριτής*

ExR 30. 11: טרד אפרכוס, סימא לדוקוס, נתן קטריקי (קטאיקי ↑) לקרטוס, He drove out the *eparchus* (prefect), blinded the *dux* (captain), [and] punished the judge. ▽ MsParis 187/15: קרטוס, MsSassoon 920/1: קכטוס, read: קרטיס throughout.

LW 2, 568a; Levy 4, 377a; AC 7, 196a; Dalman[2] 390a. (Contra Jastrow 1354b sv קטאדיקי, who reads: קומיס: *comes;* ExR, edMirkin 2, 44: *κράτος*, the authority.) Cf LW 2, 271b–272a sv טרטין III (add: MGNum 11. 4, 165_{12}) and reject (with Löw ibid) emendation to קרטין (see ACSup 207b). See MM 361a; ArndtGingrich 454b. The ~וס term perhaps influenced by other terms in passage.

Syr: קריטיס, PnS 3744.
Cf ↑ **ארכיקריטיס**

קרטיס ↓ קרטים

כרטיס, קרטיס (567, 297) (1) document of endebtedness, iou, (2) sheet of paper (papyrus), (3) record: *χάρτης*

(1) YKid 3. 4, 64a 24—55: חד בר נש הוה חייב לחבריה מאה דינדין בקרטיס. שלח חמישין גבי שליחא. א"ל: אין לא יהב לך קרטיסה, לא תתן ליה כלום, A man owed his neighbour a hundred *denarii* against an iou. He sent him fifty by an agent. He told him (the agent): If he does not hand the iou over to you, give him nothing.
YKet 9. 13, 33c 21, 23: ... ההן דיזיף מן חבריה, וחזר ויזיף מיניה, צריך מימר: לבד מן כרטוסה קדמייא דאית לי גבך ... אלא כי אורחא דבר נשא מימר; אבד כריסטו עבד חורן ..., He who borrowed from his friend, and borrowed from him again, he (the debtor) must say (in the iou), "apart from the previous iou of mine which may be in your possession ... But so too it is usual for a person to say [to his debtor]: His (read: Our) iou is lost; make me out another one, (Pnei Moshe). ▽ MsLeiden has כריסטן, which was corrected in the margin by the ed: כרטיסו; read: כרטיסן. (or ~סי, my iou).
YKet 9. 11, 33c 6: כהן דמר: אבד ברטיסן עבד חורן, Just as one says: My iou is lost; make [me] out another one. ברטיסן, sic MsLeiden! Read: כרטיסי.

(2) MidPs 45. 5, 271: משל למי שמבקש לעלות לבימה (↑). נטל קרטס ונתן לו לדיין. א"ל: ולא כתבתו! אמר ליה: לא היה לי פנאי ..., It is like unto someone who wished to come before the tribunal. He took a sheet of paper (i e a document) and gave it to the judge. "You have not written [anything] on it," said [the judge] to him. "I had no time," he replied ▽ קרטס חלק (a clear sheet of paper), printed ed: קרדום, read: קרטס. // MachPs 45. 4, 1. 252: קרדום, read: קרטס; YalkPs 749: קונטרס חלק, see ↑ **קונטרס.** The meaning seems to be that the judge thought he was receiving a written plee for clemency presented before the tribunal, but actually all he got was a plain sheet of paper.
BGit 69a: קורטא, sheet of paper. ▽ קורטיסא, קורטמא; read: קורטסא.
Sefer ha-Razim, edMargulies 71_{95}: קח כרתיס ירטיקון, Take a sheet of Hieratic (priestly) papyrus. Partial (derivative) // Ḥarba de-Moshe, edGaster XXII_{10}: כרטיס; ibid line 18: קרטים, read: קרטיס. (Not strictly Rabbinic texts but closely related.)
Assaph the Physician 649_{41}: קרטיס או כרטיס הוא קלף, i e the *cartes*, with a *qof* or a *kaf* which is parchment, (SMuntner, Introduction to the Book of Assaph the Physician, Jerusalem 1957, 135 [= Leshonenu 17/4, 1951, 220]).

(3) LevR 34. 12, 797_3 apparat (according to MsMunich 117): אמר להון: כמה אפקתון? אמר ליה: הא קרטימיא קומך, סב קרי, He asked them: How much have you spent? They answered him: Here are the records (accounts); take [them and] read

[them]. Read: קרטיסיא. ▽ printed ed: כתבא; Ar, AC 7, 196b: קרטסיא (edVenice: קרטמיא).
LevR 21. 2, 477_3 (according to Mss Oxf Neub 147 and 2335, Jerusalem 245): בקוטריס שכתב (▽ שהכתיב) משה בספר תורה, in the sheet of paper (or perhaps document) which Moses wrote (dictated) in the Torah scroll.
Ibid 478_6: ... בקוטריס שהכתיב (▽ כתב) משה, in the sheet of paper (document) which Moses dictated (wrote) ... ▽ printed ed and Mss: **איסקיפטורין ↑**, סווקטירים, קטרים. Probably קוטרים corresponds with קרטים (metath), under the influence of the mediaeval word קונטס, or קוטרס, a word derived from Lat *quinternus*, a quire of five sheets (= ten leaves).

(2) In MidPs 45. 5, 271 the meaning may not be simply "a sheet of paper" (2), but some kind of legal document. See LSJSupple 150a, Lampe 1519b.
Note that LXX Jer 36:23 translates מגלה by *χάρτης*, scroll.
On Sefer ha-Razim etc, see Margulies introduction 1—2.
(3) For ▽ סווקטירים cf ↑ **סקבטרין.**
The word appears in two main forms with a ~ק and a ~כ, and so too in Syriac (below). The form with the *qof* seems somewhat more frequent; hence, we have chosen it as the main heading. This may be under the influence of similar sounding words **קרטום ↑ [קרטים], קרטיסים ↓**. On *χ* > *κ* see LW 1, 100; Gignac 1, 93—95, eg *χιτών* / *κιθών*, *χύτρα* / *κύθρα*.
The reading קרדום we have corrected to קרטס, seeing the *dalet vav* as a *tet* which was split up into two. Alternatively, it may be that we should emend קרדים, since the t > d interchange is not uncommon; see LW 1, 101, 107, Gignac 1, 80—83.
On the ~יא term, see LW 1, 172.
כרטוסה should probably be read כרטיסה, but may also be an example of *η* > *υ*, see Gignac 1, 264.
The primary meaning of *χάρτης* refers to the material on which the document was written, and in the later Empire *χάρτης* indicated the document itself. See Berger 388a.
On *χάρτης* see NLewis, Papyrus in Classical Antiquity, Oxford 1974, 70—78.
Bacher, ZDMG 47, 1893, 510; Fraenkel 245; LLöw, Graphische Requisiten, Leipzig 1870, 1, 97.

Lat: *c(h)arta*
Syr: כרטיסא, קרטיס, קרטיסא, PnS 1820, 3743.
Arm: *k'art, 'k'artez, k'artean*, Brockelmann, ZDMG 47, 1893, 11; Thumb, BZ 9, 1900, 422.
Arab: *qrṭas*.
Cf ↑ **קונטרס**

קרטיס ↑ קרטיסה

◇**קרטיסיס** (frequent corrupt: ~ים) (568) (1) royal prohibition (2) Roman festival, commemorating conquest of eastern countries: *κρατήσις*

(1) PRK 104b, $212_{12\ 14}$: **למלך שהיה משיא את בתו וקבע קרטיסין בים, ואמר: בני רומי לא יחתון לסוריא ... התיר קרטיסים**, Like a king who was marrying off his daughter, and he fixed a decree concerning sea [travel], saying: The people of Rome may not go to Syria ... he cancelled the decree. ▽ קראטיסים, read: קר(א)טיסים. // YalkEx 273 (415_{30-32}); MidProv 21. 22, 90: התיר גזירתא קרטיסים, where גזירתא is, of course, an inserted gloss. (// in ExR 12. 3, TanḥExVa-Era 15, YalkPs 873, גזר, גזירה. So also Yiẓḥak Aramaa, Akedat Yiẓḥak, Yitro 44 ad init.)

(2) MAZ 1. 3: ... ואלו אידיהן של עו"ג: קלנדא, וסטרנורא וקרטיסים, And these are the festivals of the idolatorous gentiles: the Kalendae, the Saturnalia, the commemoration of empire ... Read ~ים ▽ MsKaufmann: וּקְרָטֵיסִים (with *samech?*).

TAZ 1. 4, 460_{27} = YAZ 1. 2, 39c 32: וקרטיסים, יום שתפסה בו רומי מלכות*Kratēsis*, the day the Roman empire seized dominion.

BAZ 8b: קרטיסים ▽ MsJTS: קרטיסים. DeutR 7. 7: וקרטיסים.

Most sources have ~ים, ~ין, since the word was thought to be a pl. For a similar example of this phenomenon, cf ליסטים, ~ין, which is, of course, ליסטיס(↑): λῃστής. Cf also ↑ קילווסים.

Jastrow 1417a; Krauss BZ 2, 1893, 536–38; LW 2, 568; LiebermannGH 8–9.

The primary meaning of κρατήσις is power, dominion, etc. Rabb Graec preserves two specialized secondary usages

(1) LiebermanGH 8–9, referring to Joannes Jeiunator, de poenitentia (PG 88, 1932c), cited by Sophocles 689b. The gloss in MidProv is exactly correct (as was noted by Jastrow 1417a). (Contra Levy 4, 376b: *κράτος; AC* 7, 195b: *cordicia;* Perles, MGWJ 1892, 112: *κόρτης*; Fürst 13, idem, MGWJ 1894, 307; Ziegler 350: *χάρτης*, cf ↑ קרטיס.)

(2) LiebermanGH 8 (= Greek 10–12), *κρατήσις* = date of conquest of Alexandria by Augustus 30 BCE (Wilcken, Ostraka 1, 778; BGU 174, PFay 89. 2, I CE), fixed by senatorial edict as festival and beginning of new year (Dio Cassius 51. 19. 6). Cf Graetz, MGWJ 1871, 229; Fürst 209b; Lewy, RheinMuseum 1893, 536; Brüll, Jahrb 1, 1874, 162–63; LevyTrgWb 1, 23b, sv אידא; ACSup 379a, Rosén, JSS 8, 1963, 60. See, most recently, the illuminating remarks of DRosenthal, Mishna Avoda Zara – A Critical Edition with Introduction, Hebrew University doct diss, Jerusalem 1980, 241–42 (Heb).

Note that קותאיוסים, to be read קרתאיוסים, in AgEst 5. 2, 52 (noted by Krauss at end of entry קרטיסים, LW 2, 568a, and ibid 523b, left with question-mark), has nothing to do with our word, and is *κραταίωσις* (LXX Ps 59 (60) 9). See Sperber, Sinai 76, 1976, 55. (Or *καθωσίωσις* = *maiestas*, CGL 2, 335_{36}, according to a private communication of Prof HJacobson, Urbana; now in Illinois Class Stud 5, 1981, 60.)

Cf ↑ קרטיס, קרטוס

קרטיסים ↑ קרטיסין

קרטיס ↑ קרטסיא, קרטס, קרטמיא

קייסטור ↑ קריסטור

כירו מניקייה ↑ קרקומניקיאה

קטאדיקי ↑ קרקטי

קטיגור ↑ קתיגור

ר

רדופין ↓, דיפורין ↑ רידופין

רדופין separation, unilateral dissolution of marriage: *ρεπούδι<ο>ν* ← *repudium* (metath)

CantR 8. 10: אנו דומים לבת מלכים שהלכה לעשות רגל רדופין בבית אביה, סוף שחזרה לביתה בשלום, We are like unto the daughter of a king who went for a period of separation [back] to her father's house. [But] in the end she returned safe to her home.

YPes 8. 1, $35d_{14\ 17}$: אמר ר' יוחנן: ברגל רדופין שנו. אי זהו רגל רדופין? אמר ר' יוסה בי ר' בון: זה רגל ראשון שאביה רודפה לבית בעלה ... רגל השני, מהו שיעשה רגל רדופין? לעולם יש לה רגל רדופין. אלמנה מהו שיהא לה רגל רדופין? ... לעולם יש לה רגל רדופין ..., Said R. Yoḥanan: The Mishna is speaking of the period of *repudium.* What is the period of *repudium?* Said R. Yose b R. Bun: It is the first period when her father has to chase her [back] to her husband's house (i e because she had left his house, and come to her father's; Pnei Moshe) ... etc. // YKet 7. 4, 34b 38 (abbreviated version).

See Tur-Sinai, Sefer Yoḥanan Lewy, Jerusalem 1949, 59–64, and Ha-Lashon ve-ha-Sefer[2], 1955, 279–856, and in BenIehuda 13, 6447 n3, who further suggests that רגל in רגל רדופין is *regale repudium* (cf CantR 8. 10), or רגל = *legale repudium.* We understand רגל in the Heb meaning "period". The text in YPes is difficult (cf BPes 87a), see commentators ad loc. Tur-Sinai himself could not interpret the whole text, (ibid 64). Note that the text is given in the name of R. Yoḥanan, who also used the term דיפורין (↑) in the sense of *repudium.* (Contra Ziegler 361, who interprets רדופין: *repotio,* drinking after wedding, first festival after marriage. See also the most recent discussion by R Kimelman in HTR 73, 1980, 590–91 n101.)

Cf ↑ דיפורין

רהבונא down payment, first installment: *ἀρ(ρ)αβών*

TargEst II 3:11 (according to edLagarde): זבונא יהיב רהבונא ומזבננא שקיל רהבונא, The buyer gives a down payment, and the seller receives a down payment. ▽ in printed edd: דהבונא; read: רהבונא.

SFraenkel, ZA 9, 1984, 4; idem, ZDMG 55, 1901, 355; ACSup 382a. (Contra Jastrow 281a sv דהבונא: price in gold, cash, from דהב; so too Levy, TrgWb 1, 163a, Dalman[2] 92a.) The reading with a *resh* is borne out by the Syr: רהבונא, PnS 3830 (Brockelm[2] 716b).
On *ἀρραβών*, see MM 79a, ArndtGingrich 109a.
On Sem origin of *ἀρραβών*, from ערבון, see Lewy, SemFremdw 120, 130; Lagarde, Mitteil 1, 212; EMason, Recherches sur les plus anciens emprunts sémitiques en grec, 1967, 30–312; and cf ADeissmann, Bible Studies, 1901, 183–84, doubting that the double *rho* is "established by the Hebrew origin of the word." See also CGL 3, 277_{18}: *ἀρραβών arra*.

Arm: *ṛemon, ṛimon*, Brockelmann, ZDMG 40, 1892, 36, 41.
For Coptic, see Czerný 11.

◇[0]**ריטור, לאיטור** (301) advocate: *ῥήτωρ → rhetor*

Attested in two forms: (1) ריטורס (pl), and (2) לאיטור (sing)

(1) YelamdEx 7:8–9, apud MannBible 1, 102_9: ריטורס שעומדים לפני פר[עה] יודעין שבעים לשון, The advocates (or perhaps governmental speakers) that stand before Pharaoh know seventy tongues ... // TanḥBDeut, Add to Devarim 1, 3: **שבעים לשון עומדין בפלטין שלפרעה**; supply the missing: **[ריטורס שיודעים]** at the beginning.

(2) SifDeut 343, 394_5: **משל ללוטייר שהיה עומד על הבימה (בימה †), נשכר לאחד לדבר על ידיו ולא פתח בצרכי אותו האיש תחילה, עד שפתח בשבחו של מלך**, It is like unto an advocate who stood on the platform of the tribunal, [because] he was engaged by someone to defend him. But he did not first open with the requests of that man (i e his client), but only after he had begun with praise for the king. ▽ **ליטאר, לאיטור**. // YalkDeut 951: **לאיטר** (edprinc), MGDeut 33. 2, 749_{24} (= MidTan 208): **ניטור**. YBer 3. 1, 6a 43: **ואפילו ליטור יוצא ועורר עליה** (sic also SY 32_{53} and Hilchot ha-Yerushalmi, edLieberman 27), ... even an advocate goes to contest the legality of the case. // Semachot 4. 14, 121_{53}: **ליטול**, read: **ליטור**. (Absent in // YNaz 6. 1, 56a 24 etc.)

Fleischer, apud Levy 2, 532b; Krauss, LW 2, 301ab; Fürst 129a; Perles, MGWJ, 1893, 359; Ziegler 111 n3; Zlotnick, Mourning 115; Lieberman, JQRNS 35, 1944–45, 27; idem, TK 5, 1242. (Contra Levy 2,462b: *λάτρις, latro*, and so too AC 5, 36b on YBer ibid; Mussaf: *lictor*; Graetz, Geschichte 4[2], 309 *delatores*; Ginzberg, Perushim ve-Ḥiddushim 2, 87 on YBer: ליעור.)

ריטור(ס), though less attested, would seem to be the main form, corresponding closely to the Gk, Lat, Syr and Arm forms (below).
לאיטור, on the other hand, would seem to be the result of dissimilation of the initial *ῥ*, (aspirated) *rho*,

under Sem influence. (But note λαφανίνου, for ῥαφανίνου, in PGen 66 iii 2 = PAbbin 66. 50, c346 CE, Gignac 1, 105.) The interchange of the liquids R > L is common in both Gk and Sem. See, eg, LW 1, 99; Epstein, Mavo le-Nusaḥ ha-Mishna 128; Gignac 1, 102–07, 109 etc. (On R > N, MGDeut: ניטור, see LW 1, 99, and cf Gignac 1, 109–10.)
On YelamdEx ibid, see Mann ad loc, n44, 46, and p97.
On SifDeut, see Blau, REJ 27, 1893, 296.
As to YMeg 3. 2, 74a 41, which reads ליטורין (cited in LW 2, 301a), see Lieberman, Annuaire 7, 1939–44, 397 n12, explaining as *lictores*, members of the *officinium* of Proconsul of Caesarea, (contra Schwab, Tarbiẓ 1/3, 1930, 113 n1, suggesting: ליטור[ג]ין: λ(ε)ιτουργοί).

Syr: רהטרא, רהיטרא, ריטור, PnS 3838.
Arm: *ḫretor*, see Thumb, BZ 9, 1900, 426, 451.

ריטור ↑ ריטורס

דיאטגמא ↑ ריש גמיות

ת

תיטה ↓ תיהי, תיבה, תחי, תורה

[0]תיטה theta, the mark signifying the sentence of eath: θῆτα → *thēta*

LamentR 2. 1, 98–99: "והתוית תו [על מצחות האנשים]" ... חתוכין ופספס; read: כתיטה בפסיפס, "And set a mark [upon the foreheads of the men]" (Ezek 9:4) ... Like the [letter] *theta* (θ) in the vote of condemnation, (*theta* being the first letter of *thanatos*, death, see below). ▽ edBuber: התורה; Ar (AC 6, 383a): התיבה; Mussaf (apud Ar ibid, citing Ms reading). (↑ פסיפס) כתיטה בפסיפס. (Not in // in YalkEzek 349, edprinc etc.)
Ibid: ורב אמר: על שנתנה בכל צד תי"ו תיהי תיהי ותחי תחי; read (with Lieberman's emend, see below): ורב אמר: [התיו היא] אות שנהגית מכל צד: תיו כי ותיו תיטה, And Rav said: The (Hebrew letter) *tav* is a letter that can be pronounced (meaning: read) all ways: *tav* is *chi* (χ), and *tav* is *theta*, (i e, the old Heb letter *tav* looks like a Gk *chi*, χ, which is a sign of the cancellation of a debt, and the *tav* is equivalent of the Gk *theta*, which signifies death). ▽ רבנן אמרו: שהוא נהנה מכל צדדיו; edprinc: עד ... שהוא. (Absent in YalkEzek ibid.)

Mussaf (AC ibid) writes: Or sometimes those who ruled guilty wrote the letter *theta*, because it is the first letter of *thanatos* (θάνατος) which means death ... This trad is also found in R Beḥayye, to Ex

20:17, ed Chavel 205 (quoting Ha-Emunah ve-ha-Bittaḥon, chap 19 ad fin, edChavel 423? editor's note ad loc). It is specifically mentioned in Isid, Orig 1. 3. 8 (PL 82, 76b): Θ, quae mortem significat. Nam iudices eandem litteram *theta* apponebant ad eorum nomina quos supplicio afficiebant etc. Meaning that the letter *theta* signifies death, because the judges put that very letter next to the names of those they condemn to death. Isidor's formulation derives directly from the Scholiast to Pers, Sat 4. 13. And cf Mart 7. 37. 2 (edFriedlander, Leipzig 1886, 493): Nostri mortiferum quaestoris, Castrice, signum? est operae pretium discere theta novum. See also OLD 1938a sv *thēta*: standing for *θανατωτέον* ..., writing on tables voting for sentence of death to be passed on an accused person. On the letter *chi* as a mark of cancellation of bonds, the erasing out of ious, see Deissmann LAE 332–34 and Berger 379a, sv *cancellare*. (On the *chi*, see LW 2, 284b sv כי.)
The whole issue is discussed in considerable detail in LiebermanGH 142–47, which I have drawn upon (with some reservations as to the emend of the second LamentR text). One may add that these meanings for the *theta* and the *chi* are found in later magical lit. See, eg, Macarius & Chiflet, Abraxas seu Apistopistus, Antwerp 1657, 86, where the θ and the χ on the top right and left of amuletic texts represent condemnation and absolution, respectively. Similarly, the *theta* sometimes appears over a tortoise, symbolizing death. Cf Berger 338a sv A, (Krauss PR 117 n46).

Cf ↑ **פסיפס**

ADDENDA ET CORRIGENDA

p. 17 bottom:
The following references may be of more than tangental interest: Johannes Kramer, "L'influence du Grec sur le Latin populaire: Quelques réflexions," Studii Classici 18, 1979, 127–35 (with bibl on Greco-Latin bilingualism); Ad Maidhof, Neugriechische Rückwanderer aus den romanischen Sprachen unter Einfluss des lateinischen, Texte und Forschungen zur Byzantinisch-Neugriechischen Philologie, Athens 1931.

p. 21 Add:
אברא is certainly not from the Lat *vero*. See AC 1, 176, that it may be from Pehl *var*, (*āvar*), *ēvar*, truth (Geiger, apud ACSup 5b, and cf DNMacKenzie, A Concise Pahlevi Dictrionary, London 1971, 85 sv *wābar*). Or it may be from Sem (ברי, according to Levy 1. 16a, or אבר according to Jastrow 44b, cf Geiger ibid). Hence, reject LEisler, Beiträge zur rabbinischen Sprach- und Alterthumskunde [hereafter: Eisler] 3, Vienna 1882, 13.
So too אחריות, surity (Jastrow 41b), has nothing to do with Gk *ὀχυρότης* (Eisler 2, Vienna 1876, 73–74).

p. 21 Add:
איסגנטרין in EstR 7. 8 // Abba Gurion 3. 4, 22; YalkEst 1054 ▽ טורין~, אשוגיניטון, איצטגטיטור, has nothing to do with *signatorius* (Levy 1, 116b; Buber, AbbaGurion 22 n45), nor *συνεκτέον* (Eisler 2, 23), *ἐγγενητὴς* (AC1, 164b), nor *equestris* (Jastrow 89a), nor *εὐγενέστατον* (Sachs 1, 164, Fürst 31b–32a; LW 2, 15a sv אוגניסטטו). Most probably it is **εἰσγενέτωρ* (= ~*τής*), meaning something like "direct descendant" (and אשוגיניטון: **εἰσγεννητόν*). Cf Hesych, edLatte 1, 370_{59}: *γεννήτορες γονεῖς*; and LSJ[9] 494a sv *εἰσγενέσις*.
I may possibly be taken to task for not including טבלא (LW2, 254) and פנקס (ibid 466–67) which both appear in a text of clearly legal connotation: BGit 20a: עבד שיצא בכתב שעל גבי טבלא ופינקס יצא לחירות, A slave who achieves his liberty through writing on a *tabula* or a *πίναξ*, is duly manumitted. ▽ MsVat 140: טבלא

דפנקס, the *tabula* (leaf of the *πίναξ*, for a *πίναξ* could have several leaves, cf MShab 12. 4: דפי פינקס etc). Partial // Avadim 3. 11, edKirchheim 30, edKaniewski 172: **יוצא באנטוקטא**, (↑) ובטבלא ופנקס, he achieves his liberty with a *vindicta,* and with a *tabula* and the *πίναξ*. EEUrbach, Papers of the Institute of Jewish Studies 1, London, 1964, 60, rightly explains that this text is referring to *manumissio per epistulam* (on which see Berger 576b). It is true that טבלא: *τάβλα* ← *tabula* can have a legal meaning (see OLD 1889a sv *tabula* 8), as can *πινακίς* (Lampe 1082a), though I am not so sure about *πίναξ* → *pinax*. Nonetheless, I find no evidence in Rabbinic lit that these words mean anything more than a writing tablet on which anything, including a document (of divorce etc) can be written. (Contra Krauss, LW2, 254b sv טבלא 2 – testament.) See further on this text Brüll, Jahrb 5, 1883, 119, and cf ↑ **אנדוכתרי, אנטוקטא.** Incidentally, in a problematic text in YMaasSheni 4. 9, 55b bottom: חמית בחילמאי לביש חד פינקס דתרי עשר לוחין, I saw in my dream [that I was] dressed in a *pinax* of twelve tablets, there may be an oblique reference to the "twelve tables" (?). But cf // LamentR 1, 52. Note further the use of פנקס referring to the heavenly account book in MAvot 3. 16, and YRH 1. 3, 35a 50 (: שלש פנקסיות; but // BRH 16b: ג' ספרים), and cf DuCange 1170 sv *πίναξ*: *Liber Poenitentialis.*

p. 22 Add:

פוס (= פייס), LW2, 429b–431a from *πεῖσις* etc (and not from Sem פסס, as Jastrow 1166ab suggested), means primarily: appear, conciliate, pacity. I thought that it did not have a legal sense. However, it does. It also means to indemnify, to pay off (BenIehuda 10, 4912b, sv פיס). See YBM 6. 7, 11a 43: רוצה אדם ליתן כמה ולמכור פירותיו למי שיפייסנו על ידי משכון, which must here bear the derivative meaning "to pay off with a pledge". (Cf SifDeut 115, 175_{11}: הבא משכון כדי להגיס להפיס ▽ את דעתו, cf Finkelstein, EpsteinFestschr [= Tarbiẓ 20, 1950], 103n6; Lieberman, TK1, 187.) This meaning is found in Gaon lit as well. See THGHarkavy 310, 177: ... שאפייסנו מן ממוני ... איני מתפייס ואיני נוטל .... See further examples in BenIehuda ibid. For the Syr פיסא, see Brockelm[2] 576a (Levy 4, 40b).

p. 22 Add:

פיונטייא in YSanh adfin, 30e38, is probably not *punitio-poenitio* (LW2, 440b), but it remains uncertain what it is. (// TSanh 14. 13, 437_{26}, does not have this word.)

p. 22-23 Add:

On פניאס see Eisler 2, 63–64: *φυγάς*.

p. 23 Add:
I have not included פרוכסין (490), found in YBM 2. 5, 8c 39, from *πράξις* (LWibid, Jastrow 1230c, AC6, 428a), Buber TanḥBLevEmor 88 n91 (contra AC3, 59a sv דוכסן), despite the fact that the context suggests a legal connotation: אלא מחמי פרוכסין דידכון, היך אתון יהבין. היך אתון דיינין (and cf // in GenR 33. 1, 302_5, LevR 27. 1, 620_4, TanḥLevEmor 6, Bibid 9. 88, etc, which do not have this word). Since I have not found any other evidence for *πράξις* meaning "legal practice" or "legal conduct," I assume that here the meaning is simply "practise, conduct, doing" or something the like.

p. 25:
See now Lieberman's remarks in Hebrew Language Studies presented to Professor Zeev Ben-Ḥayyim, Jerusalem 1983, 329—333 (and cf idem, JQR 35, 1944, 5—6).

p. 25 note 4 end:
See LBlau, Papyri and Talmud in gegenseiter Beleuchtung, Leipzig 1913 [hereafter: Blau] 20, on שטר סלוק *παραχώρησις* etc.

p. 35 sv אגדיקוס:
On *ἄγροικος* — *ἀγρικός*, see discussion in GPShipp, Modern Greek Evidence for the Ancient Greek Vocabulary, Australia 1979, 30.

pp. 38-39 sv **איסקבטיריי:**
Reject Eisler 2, 59: *scriptor.* See further Sergio Daris, Il Lessico Latino nel Greco D'Egitto, Barcelona 1971 [hereafter: Daris], 44—45.

p. 39 sv ⁰איסקריטור:
See Ginzberg, ACSup 430a: *scriptores*; Eisler 2, 39.

pp. 43-44 sv אנדוכתרי:
See Eisler 3, 16—17, and reject.

p. 44 sv אנטוקטא:
See Daris 83—84.

pp. 47-48 sv אנקלווסים:
See now, however, Lieberman, Hebrew Language Studies 333, explaining that

אנקלווסיס = אנקווסיס = *ἐνοικήσις*, right of occupation (LSJ[9] 57b sv *ἐνοικήσις*, BGU 1115, 39, I BCE etc). See Taubenschlag[2], 262 etc. He explains the additional *lamed* as under the influence of other words beginning ~אנקל (eg **אנקלומא** ↑, **אנקליטון** ↑, etc). (This may also be an additional reason for the spelling of **אנקלסיא** ↑.) He cites as a parallel example the case of *οἰκονόμος*, which appears in TBM 3. 5, 392_5 as: והאנקולמוס, and so too in TBB 3. 5, 402_{16}: אינקולמוס, as also in BBB 68b: אנקולמוס (several times), while normally the word is spelled איקונומוס (see LW2, 40b [598c], and Eisler 3, 17. According tothis we should translate: Leave him to stay on until he completes – read: ימלא – his right of occupation.

pp. 48-49 sv אנקליטון and p. 50 אנקריטיריין:
See now DSperber, Researches in Talmudic Literature, Jerusalem 1983 (Hebrew), 193–95. Dr Berachiahu Lifshitz, of Jerusalem, suggests (in a private communication, July 1983) that אנקליטון in some sources may be the document of appeal, the *libelli appellatori* (see my remarks in Bar-Ilan 16–17, 1979, 15). So he understands: ליתן לפני א~. He further suggests that the "hanging" of its appeal is a figurative use to be associatively related to the image of the sword hovering over the neck of the judge (cf BYev 109b, BSanh 7a, BAZ 30a etc).

p. 61 sv אפיקלין:
Cf Daris 84.

p. 62 sv אקוליתוס:
For Syr: **אקלותיא** (sic and not ~קאל, as mistakenly printed above), cf *ἀκλουθῶ* etc + *ἀκολουθῶ*. See Shipp, Modern Greek Evidence etc, 51.

p. 65 sv ארכי:
אריכא in MidPs 1. 5, 6 has nothing to do with *ἀρχή*. See Lieberman, Tarbiẓ 5, 1933, 108. On *aleph* – *'ayin*, see LW1, 14, and note that in Beth She'arim 3, ed NAvigad, Jerusalem 1971, 17: *ΑΕΚΣΟ* ... is transcribed: **עאיק[ס]ו**.

p. 65 sv ארכי יודיקי:
On mongeral (ie hybrid) forms note the following:
Krauss, LW2, 571 sv קרקפל (add to ref: MGGen 57. 41, 485_{11}) suggested: **καρακεφαλή*, but this was called into doubt by Löw adloc, and rejected outright by Zuntz, JSS 1, 1956, 133.
As to אגרדמוס = *ἀγορανόμος* in (usually?) Babylonian sources (LW2, 11), Schorr,

He-Haluẓ 13, 1899, 112 suggested that it was from **agoradominus*, an attractive but doubtful suggestion.
See POxy XLIV no 3192 (307 CE): *ὀνομάγγωνες*, a hybrid of Gk *ὄνος* + Lat *mango* (cited by Modrzejewski, SDHI 47, 1981, 472).

pp. 68-69 sv ביא:
See Eisler 3, 23, rejecting Landau's *βοή*, and suggesting *βία*, with add bibl.

p. 72 sv בנפקין:
See Daris 33.

p. 73 sv בריות:
See Daris 37.

p. 74 sv גייס לוקס:
For a (possible) similar example of cacophemistic distortion, see SKlein, Ereẓ ha-Galil, Jerusalem 1967, 99 n59.

p. 75 sv גמיקון: For the medial *sigma* see GenR76.6, 904^2, MSM.

p. 82 sv דיגטסים
On *κ* > *γ*, see Beth She'arim 2, edMSchwabe & BLifshitz, Jerusalem 1967, 93 no210: *τέγνοις* (= *τέκνοις*).

p. 86 sv דייתיקי:
See SifDeut 334, with comment JRHillel, edKoleditzky 186 n**א**: דייתיקי, which should, of course, read: דייתיקוס: *διάδοχος* (LW2, 198ab sv **דידכא**). See Sif edFinkelstein 383_3 and notes. On what I called a popular etym in BBM 19a and BBB 1353: דא תהא למיקם ולהיות (cf ↑ **אפותיקי**), see LiebermanTK 6, 1567, introduction 18–19, that one should read: למיקם ולחיות. So too in TBB 8. 10, 409_{24} read: לעמוד ולחיות. This corresponds to the Gk formulae: *Εἴη μέν με ζῆν καὶ ὑγιαίνειν*, or *Εἴη μεν μοι ὑγιαίνοντι καὶ ζῶντι*. See RYaron, Gifts in Contemplation of Death in Jewish and Roman Law, Oxford 1960, 24 et seq.

pp. 86-87 sv דימוס I:
See Eisler 3. 34.

p. 97 sv טולמיסן:

Cf PMedinet Madi 2 (III CE), edForaboschi (Testi e Documenti LIII, Milan 1976): *ἐτόλμησεν ... συνκοιμηθῆναι τῇ γυναικί* (cited by Modrzejewski, SDHI 47, 1981. 492).

p. 97 sv טומטייה:

Contra MLattes, Saggio di giunte e correzioni al Lessico Talmudico, Torino 1878, 134: *incetta* (based on reading: טומריא).

p. 104 sv כמס:

On *χάβος – κημός* see Shipp's discussion 563, where he cites Frisk, who denies any etym connection between the two. However, *χάβος* and *χάμος* (Byz) are probably connected. See his comments on *μ* > *β* change, ref to modern *χηβάδα*, clam > ancient *χήμη* (Stephanidis in Andriotis, *Ἐτυμολογικὸ Λεξικὸ τῆς κοινῆς Νεοελληνικῆς*,[2] Salonika 1967 [[1]Athens 1951]).

p. 108 sv ליסטים:

Prof MSokoloff sees ליסטים as a correct pl form (oral communication).

p. 109 sv ליסטים:

On ליסטטרין see Eisler 2, 52, emending to: טליסטרין: *εἴδωκος τηρός*; reject.

pp. 111-112 sv מיסטיוסים:

Eisler 2. 53.

p. 113 sv נוטרין:

Cf Daris 75.

pp. 122 sv סנדטור:

Cf Daris 109.

p. 126 sv סנהדרין:

For a strange vocalization of the fem pl, see Piyyute Yannai, ed MZulay, Berlin 1938, 270. (My thanks to Prof Yahalom, Jerusalem, for calling my attention to this source.)

p. 128 sv סניגור:

See Blau 17, from "Hell. Volksprache ...", etc.

p. 132 sv ספיקולא:
For an example of *epsilon* transcribed by *yod*, see Beth She'arim 3, ed NAvigad, Jerusalem 1971, 17: *ΑΕΚΣΟ ΕΦ* transcribed: עאיק[ס]ו.

p. 135 ss ספקלטור:
Daris 108.

p. 141 sv פטרון:
Daris 90.

p. 143 sv פטרמוניא:
Cf Daris 90.

p. 147 sv פי סניגוריא:
Daris 116.

p. 150 sv פסטמא:
See NLewis, BASP, 13, 1976, no31 on POxy xlviii 3123 (cited by Modrzejewski, SDHI 47, 1981, 520).

p. 153 sv פראפרנון:
See Shipp 553

p. 154 sv פרגל
Daris 116.

p. 159 sv פרוזדוגמא:
See Beth She'arim 3, edNAvigad, Jerusalem 1971, 18.

p. 160 sv פרוסטיא:
Eisler 2, 66, prefers *πίστις* (with added *resh*); reject.

p. 163 sv פרנה:
Shipp 552–53 notes that this word meaning dowry occurs "only in Ionic and perhaps in Doric. In Attic it is common in tragedy, but quoted from prose in LSJ only from Aeschin 2. 31, where it is in a mythological context, perhaps from an orator's source (*λέγεται*). *Προίξ* is the common word in the orators," surviving in the demotic *προῖκα*. Note also the editor's remark on PNessana 18 line 23

(CasparJKraemer, Excavations at Nessana 3, Princeton 1958, 59), that even though *φερνή* does not occur in papyri after the III CE, *παράφερνα* are still spoken of.

p. 167 sv קאלוריסין:
Cf Eisler 3, 86, and reject.

p. 170 sv קולר:
Daris 57.

p. 172 sv קומפרומיסין:
Daris 61.

p. 175 sv קוסטריא:
See Daris 65.

p. 176 Add:

קטא he acquired; Aram form from: *κτάομαι*

YTer 8. 5, 45d 9: אין קטא קטא שיחור, ואין אובד אובד מרגלי, If he acquired he acquired a lump of coal, and if he lost he lost a precious stone. ▽ MsVat: **קניא**, MsSirilio: **זיטא**. // YAZ 2. 41a: קטה; Hagahot Maimoniyyot, Rozeaḥ 12. 4: **קטא**; Derashot ibn Shuaib Ki Teẓe (edCracow 86b): דאי קטא ... מרגלין; ḤIDA, Kikar le-Adan 174a (citing Hagahot, in name of Meiri): קטה, with gloss: פירשו בו לשון ריוח ... (Maasiyyot, apud Lonzano, Shetei Yadot 47b: אף תרויח תרויח ...)

Lieberman, Tarbiẓ5, 1933, 100. (Contra Jastrow 1345b sv קטא = קטע, cut, pluck; so too AC 7, 79b sv קטה 2; cf Levy 4, 280a sv קטה.)
MM 361b–362a; ArndtGingrich 456a. The meaning suggested by the Meiri (above), "to profit", does not seem to be attested for *κτάομαι*.

p. 178 sv קטאדיקי:
On קטריקי see Eisler 2, 73–74.

p. 180 sv קטיגור:
See Blau 17, from "Hell. Volksprache ...", etc.

p. 184 sv קייסטור:
Daris 65.

p. 186 sv קילה:
Daris 53.

p. 192 sv קנקנים:
Cf Daris 48.

p. 193 sv קקריסין:
See LW2, 520b sv קוריסין, ref to ibid 499a.
sv קאקגריסין:
Eisler 2, 73: קוריסין = Lat *carus*. Reject both.

p. 197 sv רדופין:
Daris 99.

ADDITIONAL NOTES
by
Prof. Joseph Meleże-Modrzejewski*

* Where comments were received at an early stage of the printing of this volume, they were incorporated (in translation) in the relevant entries. See above: אומולוגייא (33), אוני (35), איניאומין (38), and אנטיכריסים (46). However, comments received during the final stages of printing have been presented here in the form in which they were received. Note, the numbers in brackets appearing after the entry-heading refers to our pagination above. My own additional remarks appear in brackets at the end of each comments, with the letters DS.

אנדוכתרי (43) et הרנירק טיונוס (92)
Comparer: *οὐιδικτᾶτος* (= *vindicatus*) – *SPP* xx 48 (IIe s. de n.è.) ligne 6: *Καραβίων οὐινδικτᾶτος ἀπελεύθερος* – affranchi d'un Romain; *οὐιδίκτα* (= *οὐι<ν>δίκτα*) – *Gnomon de l'Idiologue* par. 21 (Lois des Romains, 1971, p. 531). La *manumissio vindicta* est possible dans le cadre provincial de la Judée romaine, comme en Egypte; ces textes sont des témoignages importants de mon maintien dans l'Orient (cf. M. Kaser, *PRR* II², 1975, p. 134).

ארכי (65); ארכיון (66)
Ἀρχή au sens "tribunal": dans la réalité judiciaire "autorité civile" et "cour de justice" peuvent être étroitement associées; cf. par exemple *P. Hal.* 1 (IIIe s. au

n.è.) lignes 225–226: *ὁ δὲ κληθεὶς μαρτυρείτω ἐπὶ τῆι ἀρχῆι καὶ ἐπι τῶι δικαστηρίωι*. C'est peut-être par de telles associations que l'on eu vient à *ἀρχή* = cour de justice (des gentiles).
Ἀρχή pour *ἀρχεῖον* – à rapprocher de *ἀρχή* = notariat (papyrus du Haut-Empire), p. ex. *BGU* I 183 = *M.Chr.* 313,10: *παροῦσα ἐπὶ τῆς ἀρχῆς* – dans une homologie matrimoniale rédigée au bureau notarial, *γραφεῖον*, d'un village du Fayoum); – *ἀρχεῖα* juifs: un *ἀρχεῖον τῶν Ἰουδαίων* à Alexandrie: *BGU* IV 1151 = *CPJud.* II 143 (13 av. n. è.), lignes 7–8; un autre à Hiérapolis de Phyrgie: CIJ II 775. Sur les archives dans l'Antiquité: E. Posner, *Archives of the Ancient World,* Cambridge Mass., 1972.

גמיקון (75)
La théorie de Taubenschlag sur le rapport entre *ἄγγραφος* et *ἔγγραφος γάμος* est périmée; mieux vaudrait citer H.J. Wolff, *Written and Unwritten Marriages in Hellenistic and Postclassical Roman Law,* Heverford, Pennsylvania 1939, et ses travaux indiqués dans mon article "La structure juridique du marriage grec," Scritti Montivecchi, Bologna 1981, p. 231 = *Symposion* 1979, Athènes 1981, p. 39. Le *γάμος ἄγγραφος* n'est pas une "union provisoire," mais un vrais marriage, auquel manque seulement une convention écrite; il peut être transformé en *ἔγγραφος* par la rédaction d'un acte (plusieurs exemples dans les papyrus, en dernier lieu, le *P. Oxy* XLIX [1982] 3487 (65 de n.è.), cité dans ma chronique *RHD* 61, 1981, p. 161.

גניסיסים (76)
γνῶσις – sens courant dans les papyrus:
1⁰ judgement, sentence
2⁰ (plus tardif) liste, inventaire
C'est peut-être le sens dans le passage cité (Sefer ha-Maasim): "ils etablissent *des* inventaires"? Je prefère, mois aussie, le mot avec un *vav*. Cf. *διαγνώσεις* = rationes (liste de comptes).

דיאטגמא (81)
Pour l'équivalence *diatagma = edictum,* on peut citer Plutarque, *Marcellus* 24. 10: *τὰ διάγραμματα τῶν ἀρχόντων Ἕλληνες μὲν διατάγματα Ῥωμαῖοι δ'ἔδικτα προσαγορεύουσιν*. Elle se substitue, vers la fin du IIe siècle de l'Empire, à celle de *edictum = διάγραμμα*, plus ancienne (dans le texte de Plutarque, *διάγραμμα* est devenu un terme générique).

דיגטסים (82)

= *δι<ά>ταξις* [דיטגסים]?

Peut-être *δι<α>ζήτησις* [דיזטסים], "inquiry"? Il est plus facile de confondre *gimel* et *zayin* que de faire une inversition doublée d'un échange *κ* > *γ*. Mais je crains que cela n'aille pas pour le sens; il faudrait supposer une *enquête écrite* par ordre du roi (?).

דיוקטא (83)

Je suis reduit par l'hypothèse = *διοικητής*, au sens romain de *procurator*. Cela vas particulièrement bien pour Césarée, siège du gouverneur impérial qui porte le titre de *procurator* (Tacite) conjointement avec celui de *praefectus* (inscription de Pilate, trouvée à Césarée en 1961). Cf. Strabon, 17, 3, 25 (840): *ἐς τὰς Καίσαρος ἐπαρχίας ἡγεμόνας* [= *praefectos*] *καὶ διοικητὰς* [= *procuratores*] *Καῖσαρ πέμπει.* Sur la nomenclature des gouverneurs de Judée: J.-P. Lémonon, *Pilate et le gouvernement de la Judée,* Paris 1981. *Διώκτης* est rare; les dictionnaires ne donnent qu'une seule référence: 1re Epître de Paul à Timothée 1, 13; mais le sens n'est pas judiciaire (!): Paul s'accuse d'avoir été "blasphémateur, persécuteur, violent" (*τὸ πρότερον ὄντα βλάσφημον καὶ διώκτην καὶ ὑβριστήν*); il s'agit d'un comportement humain, et non pas d'une fonction. (Prof. Modrzejewski here bears out my second suggestion in the discussion above 83. DS.)

דייתיקי (86)

διαθήκη, testament:

Il faudrait citer A. Biscardi, "Osservatizioni critiche sulla terminologia *διαθήκη – διάπιθεσθαι*," *Symposion* 1979, Athènes 1981, p. 21–35.

דיפורין (89), רדופין (197)

Dans les papyrus on trouve aussi bien *ῥεπούδιον* qui *ῥιπουδιον*. Je pense que les textes talmudiques transcrivent la deuxième forme, avec *iota*. Le terme ne désigne pas seulement (comme ici) une "unilateral dissolution of marriage" mais est utilisé comme synonyme de divorce en générale, et même avec un sens plus vaste, englobant rupture des fiançialles (D. 50, 16, 191: *repudiam etiam futuram matrimonium potest*). Exemple intéressant: *P. Herm. Rees* 29 (586 de n.è.), divorce par consentement mutual (!) d'un couple des Samaritains en Egypte (!), désigné comme *διαλύσεως ἤτοι ῥεπουδίου ὁμολογίαι.*

Pour la metathèse, un exemple nouveau: *νειλοκαλάμη* pour *λινοκαλάμη*: voir K.A. Worp, in *Miscellanea Papyrologica,* Florence 1980, p. 367–368, à propos du *P. Laur* III 75 (589 de n.è.).

מיסתיוסיס (112)

Le rapprochement du bail et de la vente signalé par le Talmud de Jérusalem est très interessant du point de vue juridique, car il nous rappelle le *caractère "réel"* (*contractus re*) de la *μίσθωσις*; outre Taubenschlag, que vous citez, il faudrait citer aussi la critique de sa théorie (celle d'une *misthôsis* supposée consensuelle) par H.J. Wolf, "Consensual Contracts in the Papyri?," *JJP* 1, 1946, pp. 55–75 = Zur Rechtsnatur der Misthosis", in *Beiträge zur Rechtsgeschichte Altgriechlands und der hellenistisch-römischen Aegypten*, Weimar 1961, p. 129–154.

נימוס (117)

Je constate avec satisfaction que la *Graecitas Rabbinica* connaît toutes les acceptions du terme grec et qu'elle fait une large place à *νόμος* – coutume; cela me paraît confirmer, après coup, mon hypothèse sur le sens de *νόμος* (coutumes hellenistique importées, coutumes locales) dans l'expérience juridique de la monarchie hellénistique, telle qu'il est possible de la reconstituer pour le royaume des Lagides (J. Modrzejewski, *Essays in honour of C.B. Welles*, 1976, pp. 125–174).

ספיקולא (132), פרקולה (165)

Peut-être le mot ספיקולא est-il à transcrire **σπήκουλα* (*yod* = *η*), forme grecque de *spĕcula*, diminutif de *spes* – "faible espoir" – euphémisme pour "sentence capitale"? פרקולה – *per<i>cul<ium>*, dans une acception analogue, procéderait d'un euphémisme semblable. Ensuite serait venue la confusion associant **σπήκουλα* à *σπεκ<ου>λάτωρ*, terme essentialement militaire (plusieurs attestations dans les papyrus du IVe siècle).

Pour "*σπεκλάριον* = mirror", je vous signale que, dans les papyrus, *σπεκλάρια* (et *σπέκλα*), ne s'emploient jamais pour les miroirs, mais désignent les vitres, carveaux de fenêtres; voir G. Husson, "Carveaux de fenêtres dans les papyrus grecs", *Chron. d'Eg.* 257, 1972, pp. 278–82. – *Σπεκούλιον* est à exclure; c'est un "ghost-word" (*ibid.*, pp. 281–82). (In an earlier draft which I sent Prof. Modrzejewski I included the word, which I myself removed at a later stage. DS.)

פטרמוניא (143)

La forme grecque *παρτιμούνιον* ou *παριμώνιον* est attestée par les papyrus: *P. Vindob-Sijpestein* 2 (Ve s. de n.è.) col. I ligne 12 et col. II ligne 15. Il s'agit du *patrimonium Caesaris*.

פיסטון (145)

Hérodote me paraît bien lointain. Je penserai plutôt à la *stipulatio* romaine sous la forme *πίστει ἐπερώτησεν – πίστει ὡμολόγησεν*, reproduisant la schéma latin *fide rogavit – fide promisit*. Voir P. Mich. inv. 257 (213 de n.è.), ed. F.T. Gignac, *Bull. Amer. Soc. Pap.* 13, 1976, pp. 93–97 = *SB* XIV 11705, ligne 18, et mes remarques sur cette clause *RHW* 55, 1977, p. 142 (= *SDHI* 47, 1981, p. 494). Mais je ne conteste pas le correspondance עשה פיסטון = *τὸ πιστόν* ou *τὰ πιστὰ ποιεῖσθαι*.

פיסטים (146)

Sur la notion, voir la dissertation de W. Schmitz, *Ἡ πίστις in den Papyri*, Cologne 1964.

פרוזדגמא (159)

Sur la notion de *πρόσταγμα*: M.-Th. Lenger, *Corpus des ordonnances des Lagides*, rééd. avec complément, Bruxelles 1980; [idem, Chron. d'Egypte 56, 1981, 311–13; see JModrzejewski, RIDA 61, 1983 170; DS].

קאלוריסן (167) et קאקיריסין (168)

Sur la notion d'*ἄηεσις* en matière de vente (*καλή*, *κακή*), voir Fr. Pringheim, *The Greek Law of Sale*, Weimar 1950, p. 484–486 (papyrus, coutumier syro-romain, sources juridiques byzantines). Le "papyrus from Ashkelon" doit être cité comme *BGU* I 316 (= V. Arangio-Ruiz, *Negotia* no. 135). Le sens de *καλῇ αἱρέσει* dans ce papyrus est: *(emit) bonis condicionibus*, comme le montrent les traductions byzantines du Digeste (cf. Pringsheim, l.c., p. 485), et non pas *bona fide*, comme le pensait Krauss. (This makes even better sense of our passage, DS.)

קומפרומיסין (172)

Outre Taubenschlag, Law[2], p. 402, et mon article, *JJP* 6, 1952, qu'il cité en note, voir aussi K.-H. Ziegler, *Das private Schiedsgericht im antiken römischen Recht*, Munich 1971 (pp. 263–270: documents de l'Egypte byzantine); parmi les textes publiés plus récemment, voir les *pacta compromissi: PUG* I 23 (IVe s. de n.è.), première éd. avec commentaire L. Migliardi et K.-H. Ziegler, *RIDA*[3] 18, 1971, pp. 553–560, et *P. Vindob-Gr.* éd. P.J. Sijpestein et K.A. Worp, *ZPE* 31, 1978, pp. 127–133 (VIIe s. de n.è.); cf. *RHD* 57, 1979, p. 142 (= *SDHI* 47, 1981 pp. 504–505). Il faudrait rappeler que du point de vue romain les jurisdictions rabbiniques ne représentent qu'une sorte d'arbitrage privé; d'où sans doubt l'importance de la notion de *compromissum, κομπρόμισσον*.

Cf. Boaz Cohen *Jewish and Roman Law*, II, 1966, pp. 651–709 (1908).

קוריוסים (176)

Sur les *agentes inrebus,* voir aussi A. Gardina, *Aspetti della burocrazia nel Basso Impero,* Rome 1977, avec une liste prosopographique pp 97–148. (See further JTriantaphyllopoulos, Actes du congrès de Papyrologie de Milan, 1966, identifying *curiosus* appearing twice in Gk in the pl in PVindobSijpesteijn 22v⁰, cited by Modrzejewski, SDHI 47, 1981, 562. DS.)

קומטריסים (171) et ריטור (199)

Je ne comprends pas la mention d'un "proconsul of Caesarea". Césarée est la residence des gouverneurs de Judée qui sont des *préfets-procurateurs,* dépendant du *légat* de Syrie; celui-ci à son siège à Antioche et il est, gouverneur d'une province impériale, *légat d'Auguste pro praetore* (*vir consularis,* certes, mais cela ne veut pas dire "proconsul"!) Je vois mal des licteurs auprès d'un légat d'Auguste, qui n'est pas un promagistrat. Je m'etonne de ce que S. Lieberman ait pu écrire tout cela ...

קטבלטון (178)

LSJ[9] 885a, que vous citez, ne connaît effectivement pas **καταβλητόν*, mais signale chez Plutarque *καταβλητέον* avec le sens "il faut payer". Ce ne serait pas cela?

Je penserais,pour ma parte, à une forme derivée de *καταβλάπτω* (et non pas de *καταβάλλω*), pour exprimer l'idée de réparation d'un dommage.

INDICES

These indices (mainly the Greek and Latin ones) give a certain amount of information (in the form of abbreviations). However, they cannot take the place of the main entry and a careful literary analysis of the material referred to therein.

Usually, when no reference to Tn (= Tannaitic sources) is given, the word is Amoraic (i.e. post c. 220 CE). However, occasionally the Y (= Yerushalmi) and B (= Bavli) quote Tn sources (Beraithot etc.). Likewise Md (= Midrash) is usually Amoraic; however, there is much Tn material embedded in Md sources.

A word appearing in Tn, Y, B and Md sources may come from one (Tn) text and subsequently be cited inB, Y and Md. Hence, the index is no certain indication as to frequency of use. Furthermore, these indices are based on the material incorporated in the dictionary. A word may appear in B and not be cited in the dictionary – though this is an unlikely occurance –, in which case it will not be indicated in the index.

When one word is followed by no abbreviation, it is probably not a main entry, but is to be found in the discussion section.

Key to Abbreviations*

Tn = Tannaitic (Mishna, Tosefta, Mechilta, Sifra, etc.)
Y = Yerushalmi
B = Bavli
Md = Midrash (Aggada)
Trg = Targum
L = Late (Byzantine, Sefer ha Maasim, etc.)
H = Hapax legomenon
S = Syriac (sometimes includes Palestinian Syriac)
Arm = Armenian
Ar = Arabic
Plm = Palmyrene
Lt = Latin (only sometimes indicated in Greek index)

* In the order in which they appear by the entry

GREEK INDEX

Normally only the main Greek form is given in this index. However, in some cases significant Greek variant forms, discussed in the dictionary, are also listed.

LATIN INDEX

PEHLEVI INDEX

GENERAL INDEX

ADDITIONAL WORDS DISCUSSED

מסת"ב 9־050־226־965

נדפס בישראל, תשמ"ה 1984
סידור: רם־אות בע"מ
לוחות: כפיר בע"מ
הדפסה: דפוס אחוה ירושלים

מילון למונחים משפטיים שבספרות חז"ל
השאולות מיוונית ולטינית

מאת
דניאל שפרבר

הוצאת אוניברסיטת בר-אילן
תשמ"ד

אוניברסיטת בר-אילן
המכון למילונאות

מילונים לתלמוד, מדרש ותרגום

א

מילון למונחים משפטיים שבספרות חז"ל
השאולות מיוונית ולטינית

Made in the USA
Lexington, KY
06 February 2015